Prototype Politics

Oxford Studies in Digital Politics

Series Editor: Andrew Chadwick, Royal Holloway, University of London

Prototype Politics

TECHNOLOGY-INTENSIVE CAMPAIGNING
AND THE DATA OF DEMOCRACY

DANIEL KREISS

OXFORD
UNIVERSITY PRESS

OXFORD
UNIVERSITY PRESS

Oxford University Press is a department of the University of Oxford. It furthers
the University's objective of excellence in research, scholarship, and education
by publishing worldwide. Oxford is a registered trade mark of Oxford University
Press in the UK and certain other countries.

Published in the United States of America by Oxford University Press
198 Madison Avenue, New York, NY 10016, United States of America.

Library of Congress Cataloging-in-Publication Data
Names: Kreiss, Daniel, author.
Title: Prototype politics : technology-intensive campaigning and the data of democracy/Daniel Kreiss.
Description: New York, NY : Oxford University Press, 2016. | Series: Oxford studies in digital politics |
Includes bibliographical references and index.
Identifiers: LCCN 2015046237| ISBN 978-0-19-935024-7 (hardcover : alk. paper) |
ISBN 978-0-19-935025-4 (pbk. : alk. paper) | ISBN 978-0-19-935026-1 (Updf) |
ISBN 978-0-19-935027-8 (Epub)
Subjects: LCSH: Political campaigns—Technological innovations—United States. |
Campaign management—Technological innovations—United States. |
Communication in politics—Technological innovations—United States. |
Digital media—Political aspects—United States. | Presidents—United States—Election—2012. |
Democratic Party (U.S.) | Republican Party (U.S. : 1854–)
Classification: LCC JK2281 .K739 2016 | DDC 324.70973/09051—dc23 LC record available at
http://lccn.loc.gov/2015046237

9 8 7 6 5 4 3 2 1
Printed by Webcom, Inc., Canada

Contents

Contents

Acknowledgments

This book has its origins in an early conversation with the late Cliff Nass, a man who was a tremendously generous scholar. In September 2012, I visited Cliff at the Center for Advanced Study in the Social and Behavioral Sciences at Stanford. In a rich, meandering conversation with the spectacular beauty of the Valley below, we talked about the challenge of starting new projects and his new work on multitasking and attentiveness. We also talked about a potential follow-up book to *Taking Our Country Back*. It was an early conversation, but I remember it well because Cliff helped me talk through some of the initial ideas that grew into this book. Cliff had a big influence on me. I learned to teach from Cliff and, though his work was very different from mine, he was on my dissertation committee. I learned much from Cliff. I am grateful that I had the chance to know him.

My initial ideas started to become a real book three months later during a conversation at Yale Law School with another mentor, Jack Balkin. After hearing my inchoate and rambling ideas about the role that data was playing in contemporary campaigning, Jack succinctly and insightfully said, "It sounds as if parties are databases." With that idea in hand, I was off and running with a book proposal less than a month later.

Books are fundamentally collaborative enterprises, although they are only realized through many lonely days and nights. Many institutions and individuals shaped this book in the course of the four years it took to research and write it. First of all, I am grateful that the School of Media and Journalism at the University of North Carolina at Chapel Hill offers such a rich and supportive environment for scholarship. I thank Dean Susan King and the school's faculty, especially Rhonda Gibson, Seth Noar, Dan Riffe, Francesca Dillman Carpentier, Joe Bob Hester, Cathy Packer, JoAnn Sciarrino, Allison Lazard, Tori Ekstrand, Paul Cuadros, Heidi Hennink-Kaminski, Anne Johnston, Paul Jones, Chris Roush, and Ryan Thornburg for the conversation, drinks, and laughs along the way. I would particularly like to thank Adam Saffer not only for his friendship and intellectual companionship, but also for the wonderful network maps he created for this project. I am deeply indebted to my UNC sociology colleagues Andy Perrin, Andy Andrews, and Neal Caren, Frank Baumgartner in political science, and Zeynep Tufekci in the School of Information and Library Science for the intellectual homes they provided across the university. I have also been privileged to work with exceptional graduate students who shaped this project, especially Kylah Hedding, who helped this book along to publication, and Scott Brennen and Christopher Jasinski, who did a lot of the heavy lifting compiling and helping me analyze the staffer data set. I also thank my first two PhD students who are now successful scholars in their own right, Laura Meadows and David Bockino, for the many seminar conversations over the years. And, finally, I thank all the students in my undergraduate Talk Politics classes who discussed many of the ideas in this book with me, and many of whom are now doing the work of digital politics.

I was exceptionally privileged to have had the opportunity to present parts of the in-progress book at a number of forums over the past three years, where I tested ideas, received feedback, and had rich discussions about contemporary politics. I thank the Facultad de Comunicaciones, Pontificia Universidad Católica de Chile, and especially Eduardo Arriagada, for the opportunity to give a series of talks about theory and methods. Thierry Giasson was kind enough to invite me to the incomparable International Workshop on Political Communication at Université Laval, where I had the wonderful opportunity to give an early stage extended book talk. I am indebted to Nancy Baym, Mary Gray, and Tarleton Gillespie for the opportunity to visit and present to the Social Media Collective at Microsoft Research New England. I visited the Civic Paths Working Group at the Annenberg School at the University of Southern California, and thank Mike Ananny for that, as well as his friendship and scholarship over the past decade. I presented at the Department of Communication at the University of Illinois, Chicago thanks to Zizi Papacharissi, who has been generous in supporting my work over the years. I thank Pablo Boczkowski and Woody Powell for the opportunity to present at the Innovation, Organization, and Society Conference, hosted by the Tuck School of Business at Dartmouth, where I also had lengthy conversations about this book with Trevor Pinch, David Stark, and Paul DiMaggio.

Over the years I have been privileged to grow a network of supportive and critical interlocutors who have shaped my scholarship. These people include my Oxford team of Andy Chadwick and Angela Chnapko, Chris Bail, Matt Powers, Michael Delli Carpini, Regina Lawrence, Jeffrey Alexander, Michael Schudson, Francesca Polletta, Deen Freelon, Cristian Vaccari, Nate Persily, Eitan Hersh, Laura DeNardis, Jim Katz, Jesse Baldwin-Philippi, Chris Wells, Edward Walker, Jessa Lingel, Caroline Lee, Alfred Hermida, Phil Howard, Gina Neff, Russ Neuman, Lance Bennett, Young Mie Kim, Joe Turow, Rod Hart, Matthew Weber, and Megan Finn.

It's impossible to overestimate the importance of the ongoing counsel and friendship of my PhD advisor Fred Turner, who remains my most important sounding board for all things academic. I also am very, very fortunate to have had long-standing intellectual arguments and deep friendships with Chris Anderson, Dave Karpf, and Rasmus Nielsen. All four of these individuals were also generous enough to read a draft of this manuscript and provided detailed comments that made it what it is today.

I also thank all the practitioners who dedicated the time, sometimes many hours, to helping me understand their work and experiences, as well as the many others with whom I had formal and informal conversations about politics and technology with over the last four years. In particular, I thank Michael Slaby, Teddy Goff, Ethan Roeder, Alex Lundry, Michael Turk, Rich Beeson, Katie Harbath, Andrew Brown, Josh Hendler, Matt Compton (a Tarheel), Betsy Hoover, Michael Duncan, Morgan Burke, Peter Pasi, Azarias Reda, Matthew Oczkowski, Steve Adler, Bob Blaemire, Matt Lira, Aaron Ginn, Max Fose, and Chuck DeFeo (in addition to all those who sat for interviews but are not named here). I would especially like to thank those who went above and beyond and read a draft version of an initial 500-page manuscript and provided critical feedback on it. In no particular order, those individuals were Patrick Ruffini, Brent McGoldrick, Bryan Whitaker, Caitlin Checkett, Carol Davidsen, Cyrus Krohn, Todd Herman, and the Targeted Victory team of Zac Moffatt, Michael Beach, Abe Adams, Ryan Meerstein, and Rebecca Heisler. My aim was to provide the most rigorous, accurate, and fair study of how the two parties have differentially taken up technology in contemporary campaigning. Any shortcomings in that attempt are my own.

It has been more than a decade since I first followed the hope-filled volunteers on the Dean campaign around the snowy banks of Sioux City, Iowa as a student journalist. Little did I know at the time the long and (generally) happy years of research and writing that lay ahead. It has been a privilege to pursue this work. Throughout that time, my infrastructure was my wife, Destiny Lopez, and daughter, Carmen Stella Kreiss—I would not have made it without their love, laughter, and support. And, I owe much to my parents, Alexandria and Ken Kreiss, who got me to the place where I could even imagine writing a book.

Prototype Politics

1

Party Networks and Political Innovation

On November 6, 2012, Election Day, the Mitt Romney campaign's much heralded Project ORCA quickly crashed. ORCA was to entail thousands of volunteers across the country updating a central database as voters went to the polls so campaign staffers could monitor returns and direct field resources efficiently toward identified Romney supporters who had not yet voted. Ultimately, ORCA was undone by a hurried technical development process that lacked field testing, a lack of collaboration between technically skilled and political staffers on the campaign, a failure to plan for how volunteers would be organized and coordinated on Election Day, and little thought about how the project would effectively scale.[1] Meanwhile, the very public ways in which staffers hailed ORCA as a sophisticated Election Day tool—in part to reassure supporters and those working on the campaign about a candidate that consistently trailed in the polls—meant that when Romney lost there was a ready-made explanation at hand.[2] Even though ORCA's perfect functioning would not have changed the outcome of the election, its failure served as a powerful catalyst for people in the Republican Party to call loudly for a new embrace of technology in the wake of Romney's defeat, and to look to the Obama 2012 campaign's seeming technological prowess as a model.[3]

ORCA's failure and the aftermath of the 2012 election cycle illustrate central themes in this book regarding the new technical basis of contemporary campaigning. ORCA reveals the importance of infrastructure, the new technical advantage of incumbency, and the expertise now required by campaigns. The 2012 Obama campaign achieved what Romney's campaign could not, using its mobile application Pollwatcher, largely because a similar system to ORCA had failed in 2008. Practitioners working for a network of Democratic Party organizations and firms had learned from this experience and had invested in, developed, and field tested new technologies and practices during the 2010 midterm elections and the uncontested primary season throughout 2011 and early 2012.[4] The Democratic Party had this network of organizations and firms in place because since 2004 it had been routinely investing massive amounts of resources to produce the knowledge, skills, practices, and technologies that digital media, data, and analytics, the defining areas of contemporary electioneering, require.

The differences between the Obama and Romney campaigns, including decisions that staffers made about their structure and how to manage technological development, the individuals available to staff them, their comparative valuation of technology, digital media, data, and analytics, and the infrastructures they had available to them, were nearly a decade in the making.[5] The 2012 cycle did not happen in isolation, nor were the differences between the Obama and Romney campaigns solely the product of the idiosyncrasies of their campaign managers or candidates. The Romney campaign was in part the outcome of the history of the Republican Party from 2004 through 2012, which was marked by the comparative lack of investment in the uptake of technology, digital media, data, and analytics in the service of electoral goals. This history came to a point, meanwhile, in a 2012 electoral context that offered the incumbent Obama campaign a host of structural advantages in terms of time and monetary resources for technical development.

This book offers a history and an analysis of the two parties and their affiliated organizations from 2000 through 2014 that documents and explains their differential uptake of technology. In the pages that follow in this first chapter, I provide an analytical framework for understanding why and how campaigns are newly technology-intensive and digital, data, and analytics are at the forefront of contemporary electoral politics. I discuss infrastructure, innovation, and inertia, and the collective making of prototypes that shape parties and their technological futures. I then lay out the historical argument for the differences in the uptake of technology, digital media, data, and analytics by the two parties from 2000 to 2012, and suggest the new directions the Republican Party went in after Romney's loss when it came to see Obama's run as a prototype of a new kind of electoral campaign. Finally, I offer an abbreviated section on method (see the Appendix for a detailed accounting of the evidence that underlies this book) and provide an outline of the book.

Technology-Intensive Campaigning

> I was like, what is the plan, because at that point I knew he [Obama] was going to run and you know he asked me to help come up with a plan, right. Like what should we be doing, how should we be thinking about it, what is different, should we just stand up '08 and do it all over again? The answer is clearly no—there were things about the campaign that weren't perfect the first time and the world moves on us and so we need to sort of be thoughtful about setting up a campaign to win 2012.
>
> —Michael Slaby, chief integration and innovation officer Obama 2012, chief technology officer, Obama 2008[6]

Michael Slaby's quote captures how Obama's re-election team approached the 2012 campaign. In the years after Barack Obama's successful bid for the presidency, veterans of that effort who reconvened around the re-election bid saw themselves operating in an entirely different technological context. To take but one example of these changes, the 2008 Obama campaign's tweet announcing victory was re-tweeted (or shared) 157 times in the days immediately after the election. In 2012, by contrast, the Obama campaign's tweeted photograph the evening of the election of the president embracing the First Lady received more than 800,000 retweets in less than three days. Meanwhile, entirely new sites such as Pinterest, as well as social media platforms with growing user bases and ever changing affordances, such as Facebook, have changed the context within which campaigns seek to commune with voters.

Continual changes in communication technologies and how people use them make for a highly dynamic environment that campaign staffers and consultants have to navigate and innovative in for competitive electoral advantage. While campaigns have long had to adapt to changing media environments, the pace, scale, and social consequences of change are qualitatively different in an era of rapid shifts in the application layer of the Internet.[7] As political scientist Dave Karpf has compellingly argued, "The Internet is unique among Information and Communications Technologies (ICTs) *specifically because* the Internet of 2002 has important differences from the Internet of 2005, or 2009, or 2012. . . ."[8] In this context, bringing a campaign's digital platforms and communication strategies and genres in line with ongoing changes in media, social structures, and cultural practices and creating and adopting new technologies enable practitioners to more efficiently and effectively reach citizens in the media contexts that shape their daily lives.[9]

This book identifies a broad contemporary shift toward *technology-intensive* campaigning, and charts the ways this shift has sweeping implications for the people who practice politics, the work of campaigns and parties, and the ways that citizens engage in democracy.[10] The political scientist Pippa Norris has charted the development since the 1950s from "labor-intensive" campaigns premised on the contributions of party officials and amateurs to "capital-intensive" campaigns waged by paid professionals and predicated on large-scale investments in broadcast advertising and public opinion polling that turned citizens from active participants into passive spectators.[11] Norris argued that we are now in a "postmodern" campaign era, characterized by "politicians as essentially lagging behind technological and economic changes, and running hard to stay in place by adopting the techniques of political marketing in the struggle to cope with a more complex communication environment, rather than driving these developments."[12]

This book, by contrast, argues that contemporary campaigning has entered a new technology-intensive era where parties and campaigns have invested considerable resources in technology, digital media, data, and analytics to not only keep pace with these changes, but also actively shape technological contexts and define what twenty-first-century citizenship looks like. While there are exogenous pressures on candidates to adapt to the new dynamics of hybrid media environments, campaigns and parties have also adopted strategies to both navigate and shape the technological contexts within which they act.[13] The move to technology-intensive campaigns has significant implications for what constitutes political work in the twenty-first century, as well as the people who perform it. In contrast to the widespread assumption of the increasing "professionalization" of campaign staff and practice across much of the political communication literature, this book reveals the at times deliberate deprofessionalization of campaign staff in the attempt to spur knowledge transfer into politics from the technology and commercial sectors and technological innovation.[14] The book also reveals the increasing and rapid specialization of technological work within parties and campaigns, and the fluid careers of staffers who engage in this work.

At the same time, technology-intensive campaigning looks far different from the idea of parties being locked into permanent campaigns. Technology-intensive means parties devoting significant resources and attention to the comparatively mundane, behind-the-scenes work of infrastructure building—the production of technologies, organizations, trained staffers, knowledge, and practices in between elections that affects the technology, digital media, data, and analytics resources that future campaigns can draw on.[15] Many of the technologies that populate this book, such as the parties' database and interface systems, are not simply available "off the shelf" from commercial providers, and they cannot be assembled quickly. Even more, they are inextricably intertwined with the broader infrastructures of the parties as well as the expertise the parties have for maintaining them, and they must be institutionalized and cared for over time or they break down or disappear.

Indeed, parties have struggled with this infrastructure-building work given precarious resource flows and leadership changes. Parties struggle to find the resources to keep staffers with expertise employed and to improve the technological infrastructure that will provide a competitive electoral advantage. As case after case in this book demonstrates, the scholarly emphasis on the most visible aspects of contemporary campaigning—such as social media, email, online advertising, and websites—generally overlooks the ways that technology-intensive campaigning has reoriented parties and campaigns to the backstage infrastructural technology, data, and analytics work that shapes all of electoral strategy and political communication from field campaigning and social media use to fundraising and media buying. This infrastructure-building work also shapes the future media and technological contexts that campaigns and parties will act within.

Technology-intensive campaigning has not only meant changes in the types of people who work in politics and what they do. There have been shifts in how practitioners conceptualize citizens through various sources of data and call upon them to engage in electoral processes. Organizations give rise to and structure political engagement. With technology-intensive campaigning there has been a broad shift toward personalized and socially embedded forms of electioneering that blend data, technological platforms, and what communication scholar Rasmus Nielsen has identified as practices of using "people as media."[16] Practitioners seek to be able to represent "whole citizens" through data as a way of relating to and leveraging their media use, psychological dispositions, and social relationships for electoral ends. Campaigns work to cultivate their supporters and mobilize them to engage their social networks in strategic and even targeted political communication. This work has increasingly defined what electoral participation means, in the process turning those spectators of the capital-intensive broadcast era back into participants, albeit in ways that are highly instrumental.

While we are in an era of technology-intensive campaigning, this does not mean that the two parties and their campaigns have equal capacities to leverage technology, digital media, data, and analytics for electoral purposes. Parties and campaigns in the United States encounter the same exogenous media and technological environments, but as a number of journalistic accounts—as well as research produced by the political consulting industry and the parties themselves—have documented, President Obama's re-election bid was far more sophisticated in its use of technology, digital media, data, and analytics to communicate with voters and mobilize supporters than its Republican rival.[17] Even more, the Republican Party's own internal Growth and Opportunity Project report, a comprehensive assessment of the party's technological systems and comparison with its rival, notes not only Obama's advantages over Romney, but differences between the two parties as a whole in their uptake of new technologies. With respect to the 2012 election, which prompted much Republican soul searching, the report stated:

> Democrats had the clear edge on new media and ground game, in terms of both reach and effectiveness.... The president's campaign significantly changed the makeup of the national electorate and identified, persuaded, and turned out low-propensity voters by unleashing a barrage of human and technological resources previously unseen in a presidential contest. Marrying grassroots politics with technology and analytics, they successfully contacted, persuaded and turned out their margin of victory. There are many lessons to be learned from their efforts, particularly with respect to voter contact.[18]

That these differences exist poses a puzzle for much of the existing political communication literature. For example, rational choice perspectives on campaign strategy suggest that any differences between the two parties and their campaigns, especially at the presidential level, would be both minimal and short-lived. As political scientist Larry Bartels has argued, "In a world where most campaigners make reasonably effective use of reasonably similar resources and technologies most of the time, much of their effort will necessarily be without visible impact, simply because every campaigner's efforts are balanced against more or less equally effective efforts to produce the opposite effect."[19] Meanwhile, political communication scholar Bruce Bimber argued that "[a]t the presidential level, where the resources dedicated to campaigning are enormous, innovations in any one electoral cycle are typically matched soon in subsequent cycles, as happened with radio, television, and direct mail."[20]

And yet, the fact that the GOP Growth and Opportunity Project report found significant differences between the Obama and Romney campaigns reveals that the parties have diverged in their uptake of technology, digital media, data, and analytics, and this has persisted over the course of two presidential election cycles. Instead of conceptualizing individual campaigns as rational actors that operate in discrete electoral cycles, scholars need to look at the ways the histories of parties as institutions affect the differing ways in which they, and their campaigns, contest elections.[21] For example, through analysis of primary historical data, political scientist Daniel Galvin demonstrates that there were significant differences between the two major US political parties with respect to presidential "party-building" from the administrations of Eisenhower to G. W. Bush (with Republicans engaging in comparatively more of it).[22] Galvin explains this by demonstrating that presidents who perceive their party's competitive standing to be weak build institutions to change the political environment so that they are able to grasp a future advantage. As Republican presidents engaged in party-building in an attempt to create political majorities in Congress, future presidents inherited the fruits of this labor and built on what came before. In the long run, Galvin argues, what Republican presidents inherited (and Democratic presidents failed to) shaped their capacities to act electorally and legislatively. Other recent work has similarly identified the importance of institutions and time in the context of the evolution and diffusion of campaign strategies. Political scientists Brendan Nyhan and Jacob Montgomery argued that consultants diffuse campaign strategies through party networks over time, "playing a key role in the process of 'organized trial and error' by which ideas and approaches are developed and spread within parties."[23] The "party networks" these scholars detail encompass many different party actors, including candidates, campaigns, party organizations, and party-aligned consultants (who generally work on only one side of the aisle).

While these scholars do not specifically address the technological basis of campaigning, their ideas of looking at institutional and network processes over time hold clues for how we might explain differences between the two parties and their campaigns, specifically in the highly technical areas of technology, digital media, data, and analytics. In the pages that follow, first I turn to the question of how technological innovations occur before looking at how they transform parties over time.

TECHNOLOGICAL INNOVATION, ORGANIZATIONAL ENVIRONMENTS, AND PARTY NETWORKS

Campaigns need new forms of knowledge and expertise to adapt to changes in media environments and create innovative new technologies and practices that provide competitive advantage. For example, during the question and answer session after the keynote panel of the 2014 political communication pre-conference of the American Political Science Association, an aspiring undergraduate asked Zac Moffatt (the digital director of Romney 2012) and Michael Slaby what she should do career-wise to attain a similar job to theirs, and specifically if she should consider working on Capitol Hill. Moffatt and Slaby both responded with a resounding "no!" Despite their different partisan affiliations, the two embraced the idea of leaving politics to work in industry for a while, or joining an innovative campaign outside of the settled ways and consultant culture of D.C., as a path to career success at the cutting edge of digital and technology on campaigns.

Moffatt and Slaby's response captures a key dynamic that organizational sociologists argue creates the conditions for innovation. While innovation is under-analyzed in the political communication literature, there is a vibrant interdisciplinary research tradition that has sought to explain how innovations arise and organizations emerge in domains ranging from the biotechnology industry to state formation. Sociologists John Padgett and Woody Powell, in their edited volume *The Emergence of Organizations and Markets*, defined "innovation" as "somethings neither present nor anticipated by anyone in the population. . . . *Innovations* improve on existing ways (i.e., activities, conceptions, and purposes) of doing things, whereas *inventions* change the ways things are done."[24] In Padgett and Powell's account, network folding (or recombination) describes the processes through which innovations, inventions, and new organizations emerge. Network folding "involves transposing social relations from one domain into another" through biographies that cross domains or through strategically placed people who reconfigure networks across domains and thus create the possibilities for innovative and new technologies and practices.[25] As Padgett and Powell detailed:

> [W]e often observe organizational innovation triggered by unanticipated transpositions of people from one domain to another, who carry with them production skills and relational protocols that mix with and transform skills and protocols already there. Organizational invention, following such innovation, is usually the slower process of the new innovation percolating around the networks in which it is embedded, tipping them into new topologies and interactional forms along the way. More radical episodes of this process lead to "innovation

cascade." Restructured biographies are the medium through which network spillover is transmitted.[26]

There are a number of examples of such transpositions of staffers across domains and the subsequent mixing of knowledge, skills, and practice to create political innovations. As I documented in *Taking Our Country Back*, the programmers, open source idealists, dot.commers, and technically skilled college students who migrated to the Howard Dean and Wesley Clark campaigns in 2004 helped forge a new set of innovative technologies and digital organizing practices, and after the election founded new organizations that diffused them across the Democratic Party network. A former Facebook cofounder, Chris Hughes, helped fashion the 2008 Obama campaign's My.BarackObama.com platform into a potent organizing force, while a former Google staffer, Dan Siroker, devised many of its analytics practices.[27] On the 2012 Obama campaign it was Carol Davidsen who drew on her data analysis skills gained from years spent in the telecommunications and cable industry to devise an innovative and efficient cable set-top box advertising targeting system called the Optimizer, a set of technologies and practices completely new to the political field. Slaby's work in Silicon Valley venture capital and at the global public affairs firm Edelman between election cycles shaped his approach to the 2012 campaign and his decision to recruit and hire technology industry staffers such as former Threadless chief technology officer Harper Reed.

At the same time, organizational sociologists have also found that successful innovation is premised on hybridity with respect to new inter-field knowledge (such as from the technology industry) mixing with established field knowledge (such as from electoral politics). In their study of innovation in the video game industry, Mathijs de Vaan, David Stark, and Balazs Vedres argue that what is important are the sites of intersection between different groups of people and the cognitive distance between these groups (in terms of their expectations, understandings, skills, etc.). The teams that achieve critical success (defined in terms of winning the acclaim of the field) are made up of cohesive groups that have both overlapping ties ("structural folds") and are diverse in their ideas and insights ("cognitive diversity").[28] As de Vaan, Stark, and Vedres argued:

> The analyses indicate that creative success was facilitated when cognitively distant groups were socially folded. Yes, something must be shared. But it is not necessarily mutual understanding. In the dynamics that we suggest are at play, social intersections between groups do not immediately resolve a tension or create an instant comprehension. It creates a workable space where some misunderstanding is tolerated in the interest of creating a new creole that can escape the limitations of the mutually untranslatable.[29]

As such, what is important with respect to successful political innovation are the points of intersection between and among people who cross fields to enter politics and groups of comparatively more experienced campaign veterans. Indeed, Obama 2012 campaign manager Jim Messina's citation of advice from Google Chairman Eric Schmidt that "[y]ou do not want political people, you want smart people who you are going to draw what you want and they're going to go build it," simultaneously vastly understates the importance of seasoned political practitioners on the campaign and overstates what those coming from industry were able to achieve on their own.[30] For example, a group of 11 individuals who worked together on the 2008 campaign in technology, digital, data, and analytics subsequently went to the Democratic Party or its Organizing for America during the midterm cycle in 2010 and then carried their experiences and shared set of cultural-cognitive understandings and skills to the re-election bid (an additional 22 people who did not work on the 2008 campaign went from the Democratic Party and Organizing for America in 2010 to the 2012 campaign). It was there that members of these groups met with 2008 alumni returning to the re-election bid after pursuing political consulting and commercial ventures during the off election years, as well as people entering electoral politics for the first time from different fields such as the commercial and technology sectors. The gathering of these disparate groups created the "cognitive diversity" that de Vaan, Stark, and Vedres cite, while the intersections between them generally resulted in the productive clash of multiple political and technology industry knowledges on the campaign.[31] All of this was also held together by individuals such as Michael Slaby who had multiple ties across these diverse groups, experiences in different sectors, the ability to speak the languages of different fields and broker relations between them, and, importantly, the organizational authority to manage this cognitive diversity.

Given the well-documented differences between the two parties in their uptake of technology, based on these theories of innovation, there should be differences in their hiring patterns and numbers of field crossers joining their campaigns over the past decade. Democratic Party campaigns should both hire more staffers in the areas of technology, digital media, data, and analytics, and more should come from the technology and commercial industries. This is precisely the case. University of North Carolina graduate students Scott Brennen and Christopher Jasinski and I built an innovative data set on the hiring patterns of every Democratic and Republican primary and general election presidential campaign from 2004 through 2012 as well as the firms and organizations founded after these bids (for the methodology, see the Appendix).[32] We paired Federal Election Commission and other data, including from the nonprofit Democracy in Action site, with LinkedIn data to trace the hiring patterns of campaigns and professional careers of every technology, digital media, data, and analytics staffer we could identify

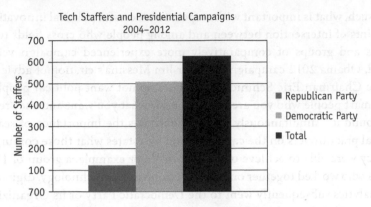

Figure 1.1 TECH STAFFERS AND PRESIDENTIAL CAMPAIGNS, 2004–2012.

during these cycles (N = 629). We found that Democratic Party campaigns hired 507 individual staffers in the areas of technology, digital media, data, and analytics, compared with 123 Republican staffers during this time period (one staffer worked on both sides of the aisle; see Figure 1.1). The total number of staffers hired by presidential campaigns is higher given that a number of staffers worked on multiple presidential bids. Democrats also had considerably greater numbers of staffers in these areas with their primary employment experience in the technology and commercial industries, precisely the hires that would likely enable campaigns to navigate and be innovative in a changing media environment (see Table 1.1).

Democrats also had much higher rates of firm and organizational founding after presidential elections by these technology, digital, data, and analytics staffers, which is also what we would expect from Padgett and Powell's theoretical account of innovation.[33] From 2004 through May 2014, 65 Democratic staffers in these domains founded 67 firms and organizations, compared with 14 staffers founding 15 firms and organizations on the Republican side of the aisle (see Figure 1.2a and b).[34] To take but one example of these firms and the role they play in the diffusion of campaign strategies and technologies, the Obama 2012 chief analytics officer Dan Wagner founded the data and analytics firm Civis Analytics after the election, and was joined by over one-third of the 54-person analytics team on the campaign. Civis Analytics offers a host of applied data science services, including market research, predictive modeling, and an analytics platform, for a range of Democratic Party–affiliated political clients and commercial firms.[35] This matters because parties have limits on what they organizationally and legally are set up to do. As Bryan Whitaker, the former chief operating officer of NGP VAN (the party's premier financial reporting and voter database and interface firm) and director of technology at the DNC during the 2012 cycle,

Table 1.1 Employment Backgrounds of and Organizational Founding by Technology Staffers on Select Primary and General Election Campaigns, 2004–2012

	Obama 2012 (D)	Romney 2012 (R)	Romney 2012* (Primary)	Obama 2008 (D)	McCain 2008 (R)	Obama 2008* (Primary)	Clinton 2008* (Primary)	Kerry 2004 (D)	Bush 2004 (R)
Campaign, Political, or DNC/RNC	73	17	4	26	5	15	7	9	1
Commercial	58	34	8	11	1	4	0	5	1
Journalism or Entertainment	34	1	0	13	2	5	0	0	0
Technology or Data/Analytics	48	7	0	11	0	4	1	1	0
Education or Legal	17	4	1	5	0	2	0	0	0
Government	16	8	0	10	2	4	0	2	2
Mixed or N/A	96	16	10	55	5	20	1	17	2
Total Staffers	*N* = 342	*N* = 87	*N* = 23	*N* = 131	*N* = 15	*N* = 54	*N* = 9	*N* = 34	*N* = 6
Total Staffers with Previous Campaign Work	72	22	10	14	5	11	4	5	0
Organizational Founders	24	3		15	2		1	7	2
Unique Organizations	19	3		16	3		3	6	2

* For the primary campaigns of eventual nominees, people were listed only when it was clear that they worked during the primary season. This meant that they listed the primary campaign on their LinkedIn profile, the timeline they provided matched the primary season, or they were listed as working during the primary in the Democracy in Action data.

Note: Coding is for the *primary* field of employment of these staffers prior to each campaign. For presentation purposes, we combined categories here.

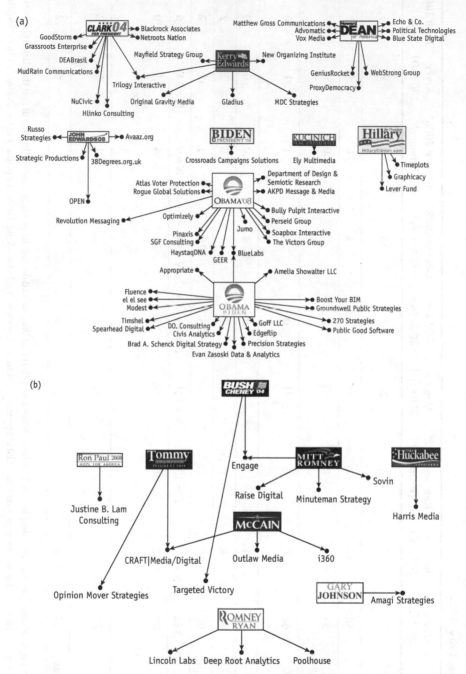

Figure 1.2a and b ORGANIZATIONAL FOUNDING BY DEMOCRATIC AND
REPUBLICAN TECHNOLOGY STAFFERS ON PRESIDENTIAL CAMPAIGNS FROM
2004–2012.* Images created by Adam J. Saffer, Ph.D., using NodeXL Pro.

*Presidential campaigns are connected to organizations when at least one staffer founded the
organization. We coded a presidential campaign as having a connection to an organization based
on the founder's most recent presidential campaign work prior to the founding of the organization.

explained, "Whenever possible, it's wise to develop tools through a software as a service [SaaS] firm. . . . It democratizes the tools so that they can then be applied to, sold to, or licensed to down-ballot campaigns to be able to benefit from innovations as well. My understanding is the DNC isn't able to license these tools, charge for them, and use that money to reinvest in those tools, even though everything that OFA [Obama for America] and the DNC built lives at the DNC."[36]

The circulation of staffers to other sites in party politics after elections and the founding of political consultancies and other organizations are the mechanisms through which the knowledge, practices, and technologies forged on campaigns diffuse to other sites and in turn give rise to future campaigns. Over time, these dynamics transform parties in ways that shape their relationships to technology. As Padgett and Powell argued, adopting a fundamentally biological and evolutionary perspective on social science, to analyze innovation and invention scholars need to chart contingent change over time, as opposed to seeking to uncover universal laws of social life akin to those of physics:

> In the short run, actors create relations; in the long run, relations create actors. The difference between methodological individualism and social constructivism is not for us a matter of religion, it is a matter of time scale. . . . To understand the genesis of objects, we argue, requires a relational and historical turn of mind. On longer time frames, transformational relations come first, and actors congeal out of iterations of such constitutive relations. If actors—organizations, people, or states—are not to be assumed as given, then one must search for some deeper transformational dynamic out of which they emerge.[37]

For example, on a longer time scale, we can see campaigns as the *outcome* of historical party network processes. Over the past decade, a number of political scientists have re-conceptualized political parties as networks of ideologically aligned, yet autonomous, actors that pursue power. Parties are "decentralized, nonhierarchical, fluid systems with porous boundaries among a wide array of actors" that "include interest groups, social movements, media, political consultants, and advocacy organizations, in addition to the usual suspects of elected

---

We opted to include all organizations founded after a founder's presidential campaign work, regardless of the timing or subsequent non-presidential work. As a general approach, organizations founded closer to the electoral cycle appear to the left or right of the campaign logo. Organizations positioned below the campaign's logo were generally founded later after the cycle. Due to layout limitations, firms and organizations could not be positioned spatially according to the years they were founded. Organizational founding data is current through May 2014. For a full list of organizations and years they were founded, see http://danielkreiss.com. Lines from two campaigns to one organization (e.g., Engage or BlueLabs) indicate two founders on different campaigns.

officials, party officials, and citizen-activists."[38] Meanwhile, following a broad "material turn" across much scholarship that explicitly seeks to take account of the role of technical artifacts in shaping social practices, organizations, and forms of communication, technologies such as the party-maintained databases that candidates use and the suite of tools built around them are also a part of party networks.[39]

Party networks form a large part of the infrastructure, or the background context of available resources, that candidates have at their disposal as they organize campaigns for office. Campaigns must assemble and coordinate particular configurations of component parts effectively in order to maximize their chances for success. In the context of political technologies, this means that campaigns seek to assemble tools such as canvassing applications and databases that are largely built within the political field and are provided by parties and party-aligned consultancies, as well as take up commercially available platforms such as Facebook and Twitter. As importantly, campaigns must gather together staffers who know how to wield these tools, or must hire outside consultants to do it for them. There are a number of different assembly options for campaigns as they draw resources from their party network, such as hiring staffers internally versus outsourcing operations to consultants, all of which have implications for political communication.

Over the last three presidential cycles, the Democrats have created a much more robust extended network of staffers, technologies, firms, and other organizations that institutionalized the innovations of their presidential campaigns and carried them across electoral cycles and to down-ballot races. Democratic campaigns at all levels of office have emerged from this robust party network, as they take up party-provided technologies and assemble party-network resources, including the hiring of staffers and consultants with specialized technical expertise who value technology, digital, data, and analytics in the context of electoral strategy. To return to the example that began this book, the Obama campaign in 2012 was in part the *outcome* of the work of the extended Democratic Party network in between cycles as actors crafted a new data architecture, new analytics practices, and technologies such as Pollwatcher, all of which staffers deployed on the re-election bid.

POLITICAL PROTOTYPES AND PATH DEPENDENCE

The question is what set off this historical dynamic so that it was the Democratic Party that invested comparatively more resources in technology since 2004? This question is even more perplexing given that, despite the trends in the Republican Party through 2012, political practitioners widely acknowledge that it was the re-election campaign of George W. Bush that had more sophisticated field efforts, far better voter data and more robust systems for analyzing, managing, and storing data, and more advanced Internet operations than John Kerry's campaign. Even more, the Republican Party was even the "out-party" from 2008 through 2012, which a number of scholars have argued creates incentives to innovate.[40]

The answer to this question lies in the parties' respective paths of development, and specifically the ways that Democrats experienced a critical event in John Kerry's loss that produced new actors within the party and changed the symbolic valuation of technology, digital media, data, and analytics within it. Scholars use the idea of path dependence to conceptualize how organizations become locked into routines and lose flexibility and adaptability over time, until some event triggers a new direction. For example, organizational scholars Jörg Sydow, Georg Schreyögg, and Jochen Koch sketch a process-oriented model of path dependence:

> Starting (Phase 1) with contingency, a critical event (decision, accident, etc.) favors a solution leading unpredictably to a critical juncture. If it triggers a regime of positive, self-reinforcing feedback, this solution progressively gains dominance (Phase II). This pattern is likely to become persistently reproduced and to crowd out alternative solutions to an extent that it gets locked in (Phase III) and is accompanied by immediate or future inefficiency. In short, organizational path dependence can be defined as a rigidified, potentially inefficient action pattern built up by the unintended consequences of former decisions and positive feedback processes.[41]

As these scholars argue, stasis or inertia will occur over time until a triggering event spurs subsequent organizational processes along a new path. These scholars draw on a number of studies of technological development and organizational decision-making to illustrate that random and small things can prove transformational over time. In addition, critical events can be the products of intentional and strategically motivated action: "since organizations are social systems and not markets or natural entities, triggering events in organizations are likely to prove to be not so innocent, random, or 'small.' "[42]

This book demonstrates that critical events in politics occur when a party loses an election that actors within it believed they should have won (or, in the case of Bush 2000, when a candidate *almost* loses and practitioners come to believe that their party underperformed). Election postmortems are a collective process of meaning-making in which party actors and journalists work through, debate, deliberate, and strategically vie to define the reasons for victories and losses (quite apart from the empirical causes that political scientists seek to understand;

social science accounts, while grounded in rigorous evidence, are often not useful to practitioners precisely because they provide little room for action given their structural determinants of election outcomes.) At times, such as after John McCain's 2008 bid, party actors collectively conclude (often in line with political science) that there was little that would have changed the outcome of an election given the dynamics of the economy, incumbency, and the makeup of the electorate. At others, however, parties lose elections they believe they should have won, and craft reasons why. The will to believe that the outcome could have been affected by a different campaign is great because it provides space to act for the future. Perceptions of what one *can* and even *must* do necessarily come prior to action.[43]

During and after elections, particular campaigns are transformed through meaning-making processes into "prototypes" for some actors, a model for future campaign practice, and a set of claims about the world that are actionable for practitioners.[44] I define "prototype" here in the colloquial sense captured in the *Oxford English Dictionary* as "[t]he first or primary type of a person or thing; an original on which something is modeled or from which it is derived; an exemplar, an archetype."[45] Cultural historian Fred Turner argued that prototypes are both artifacts and stories that "make a possible future visible."[46] Party actors and others engaged in interpreting electoral politics, such as journalists, symbolically transform campaigns into prototypes when they appear to disclose an entirely new way of electioneering.

Campaigns can become prototypes during cycles themselves, drawing new actors to politics and giving rise to innovations in electoral practice. For example, once staffers and journalists narrated and performed the Dean campaign as a prototype of a new, radically democratic, digitally enabled campaign, it was able to convene a host of young, technically skilled staffers and field crossers coming from the technology industry who were enthralled by the image of a possible future and brought their expertise and skills to bear on politics for the first time.[47] The Obama campaigns in 2008 and 2012 were prototypes for many who worked on them (and those inspired by these campaigns) in similar ways, bringing newcomers to the political field through their disclosure of a seemingly new way of practicing politics. The idea of prototypes helps explain why individuals cross fields or get involved in politics in the first place. While ideology and working to elect the first African American president was obviously a draw in 2008, for many staffers it was also the possibility of working on new technological projects in politics that could potentially transform democracy.[48] As Chris Hughes told me about his decision to take a leave from Facebook to bring his skills to the Obama campaign, "Something about Obama in particular just really, really resonated with me. . . . And my question was, well there are some obvious things that you can do on Facebook but it is really a larger question of how you are using the participatory web or networking technology for the campaign. . . . That spiraled into conversations [with the campaign] of 'OK what would that look like' and one thing led to another and I was like 'I am really excited about this.'"[49]

While they may attract newcomers to politics, prototypes only become transformative of party networks after elections when actors collectively decide that they need to take a new approach to electoral campaiging, seek out models for a new way of doing things, and determine that a prototype discloses an innovative and efficacious way of practicing electoral politics. The power of prototypes lies in their potential ability to reshape party actors' definitions and understandings of the world and what constitutes competitive electoral advantage. While Dean opened the field to outsiders, it was only after Kerry lost that the wider party network saw the campaign as a prototype in ways that spurred new investments around a shared vision of a new technological future for the party and oriented it in new ways toward technology, digital, data, and analytics. For example, after the election Dean's former staffers (as well as those of the other innovative technological efforts of the cycle, the Draft Clark movement and Wesley Clark campaign) had extraordinary market opportunities to launch new firms and organizations specializing in digital campaigning given their cultural validation as the arbiters of a new form of politics. Thirteen former staffers launched an incredible 18 different firms and organizations after these bids, many of which are now prominent in Democratic politics.

In sum, critical events are often cultural phenomena. When parties lose campaigns they believe they should have won, or actors perceive that they underperformed vis-à-vis their rivals, they seek out reasons why and look to both the winning campaign and the other campaigns of the cycle for clues to understanding the outcome as well as to find models for future action. In essence, this is a dynamic of learning and strategic action to gain competitive parity and advantage, but one that is fundamentally driven by cultural processes as opposed to the structural positions of parties, such as which is the "out-party" or has the power of the presidency.[50] If actors come to collectively recognize a campaign as a prototype and seek to take up its elements in whole or in part in response to an election, it changes their understandings as to what is electorally advantageous, spurs investment across the party network in new technologies, and creates market opportunities for new types of organizations and staffers. The prototype campaign then becomes the catalyst for the diffusion of its innovations in tools and practice through the political field as its former staffers pursue subsequent work and found new firms and other political organizations. While campaigns mimetically borrow innovative elements from one another during cycles all the time, such as the adoption of particular technologies, by the idea of a "prototype" I mean an entire cluster of innovations on the order of Dean's organizational, cultural, and technological uptake of the Internet in 2004 and Obama's melding of digital, data, analytics, and technology in 2012.[51]

Taken together, the theoretical model of political innovation and party networks is as follows. Party networks and campaigns that are able to generate field crossing from the technology and other industries into politics give rise to innovations and new organizations. Organizational innovations and inventions trigger significant transformations in the technological capacity of party networks over time. Campaigns are, in part, the outcomes of party networks that change, or fail to, over time and produce particular types of staffers and organizations, shape the knowledge, skills, and strategies that are valued in electoral politics, and influence the structure and workings of campaigns.[52] Extraordinary events, such as when a party loses an election people believe they should have won, can change the path of a party network and tip it in a new direction by changing perceptions as to what offers competitive electoral advantage.

I now turn to the historical argument of the book. While there are many complicating and contingent factors that I outline throughout this book, generally I show how on the Democratic side of the aisle the Dean campaign became a prototype that spurred party actors to invest in new technologies, setting into motion the historical party dynamics that helped produce the comparative technological, digital, data, and analytics sophistication of Obama's 2012 bid. Conversely, I show how after Bush's re-election victory in 2004 the Republican Party slipped into comparative stasis that only began to change when Romney lost an election that party actors believed he should have won and saw Obama's re-election bid as a prototype for a new type of politics. Drawing on this historical data, I show how the infrastructural workings of party networks shape the organizational dynamics of campaigns and their ability to raise money though things such as small-dollar online fundraising, and demonstrate how these factors interact with specific features of the cycle, such as the electoral context and incumbency, to shape the ability of campaigns to be technologically innovative.

The Democratic and Republican Parties, 2000–2014

While it has received comparatively little attention in the literature, the re-election bid of George W. Bush was the most advanced technical effort of the time.[53] The campaign had online precinct captain programs complementing the work of a massive field effort ("political" in Republican Party parlance), integrated databases, an expansive voter file, and cutting-edge micro-targeting models.[54] Party staffers and consultants on both sides of the aisle roundly acknowledge the Republican Party's competitive edge in innovatively coupling field and new media campaigning during Bush's re-election bid and the campaign's development of many new technological and organizational practices.[55] Meanwhile, John Kerry's data infrastructure collapsed in key swing states, and the Bush campaign far exceeded what Democrats and their allied 527 organizations both executed and expected.[56]

Ironically, the victor's development and uptake of technology during the 2004 campaign cycle was, and is, often an afterthought to the digital and participatory innovations of Howard Dean's losing campaign. During the cycle, practitioners and journalists fashioned Dean's run into a prototype of a new form of Internet-enabled and grassroots politics. Bush's victory during an election that many Democrats thought they should have won, along with evident infrastructural field and data failures, provided the impetus for the party and party-aligned organizations to take up the Dean campaign's innovations in technology and digital fundraising and organizing practices, as well as its participatory emphases. Meanwhile, the symbolic valuation of the campaign, and the candidate's subsequent promising of a new grassroots style of politics with an emphasis on the state parties and organizing, catapulted Dean to become party chair in February 2005. The new chair invested millions of dollars in massive infrastructural projects involving digital platforms and voter data, in part inspired by the Bush campaign's innovations in field campaigning and micotargeting, including commissioning work from firms that then carried these technologies to other sites in Democratic politics. It was during Dean's tenure as chair that the core data infrastructure of the party was created, including the DNC's national and standardized voter file and the Voter Activation Network [VAN] developed database and interface system VoteBuilder that provides access to it. This was a core piece of the infrastructure behind Obama's two runs, and it endures to this day with the buy-in of actors across the Democratic Party.[57]

Meanwhile, even though Dean ultimately failed to become the nominee, the campaign's spectacular fundraising success and seeming promise of a future of Internet-supported political organizing symbolically validated the experiences, knowledge, skills, technologies, and approach of a new generation of staffers.[58] According to the data set, of the twenty-nine technology, digital, data, and analytics staffers on the Dean and Clark bids, none had worked for a previous campaign and 86% had their primary professional backgrounds outside of the political field. Many also had skills forged in the technology and data/analytics industry (17%), various commercial sectors (24%), and were active in open source communities (and for 34% of these staffers, it was likely their first job). In addition, as detailed above, out of the ashes of the Dean and Clark campaigns arose 18 firms and organizations that have since come to play starring roles in the extended Democratic Party network, including the digital political consultancies Blue State Digital (BSD) and Trilogy Interactive and the progressive training organization the New Organizing Institute, all of which carried the technological innovations of these campaigns to other sites.[59] The staffers behind these organizations, as well as others who went to work for other groups in the party network and the national Democratic Party itself, had their success, in large part, due to the market opportunities that awaited them as keepers of the magic of Dean's technologically enabled presidential run, and visionaries of a new Internet-enabled politics, as well as the relationships they forged during this time.[60]

On the other side of the aisle, actors in the extended Republican Party network after 2004 felt little need to rethink their models of campaigning after successfully electing Bush to a second term in such a dominant fashion with respect to micro-targeting, political organizing, and Internet operations. As such, Republicans did not have a critical event on the order of what took shape within the Democratic Party network after 2004 and that gave rise to new organizations and technologies, changed the valuations and patterns of investments in new types of ventures and sets of skills, and transformed the knowledge and understandings of political actors in terms of the ways that campaigns should be organized and conducted. As Alex Lundry, the director of data science on the 2012 Romney campaign, cofounder of the media analytics firm Deep Root Analytics after that cycle, and analytics staffer for Jeb Bush's 2016 campaign, detailed:

> So we win '04. I think a sense of complacency frankly sets in across the right. Whereas you have the Democrats who are facing a situation not unlike what we are facing right now [2013], which is how did we just lose an election where we really should have won or at least we feel we should have won? What did they do that we didn't that we should be investing in? And, they went out and invested aggressively in various institutions and planted a number of seeds which I think have come to fruition like the Analyst Institute, the New Organizing Institute, and Catalist. I point to those three institutions as kind of the pillars of this liberal data analytics ecosystem that were really the key drivers behind the success of 2012, if not directly then at least indirectly in the buildup to 2012.[61]

Even more, while Bush's bid in 2004 was technologically innovative on a number of levels, former campaign and party staffers argue that it was never quite recognized within the party for these things. Patrick Ruffini, founder and president of the Republican digital political consultancy Engage, former Webmaster for Bush-Cheney 2004, and eCampaign director for the Republican National Committee (RNC) from 2005–2007, argued that the Bush re-election campaign was not *narrated* as a technology and digital-intensive effort in the same way that the Dean and the Obama campaigns were, ironically given its extensive innovations in Internet use for field operations:

> I felt like number one there was never really necessarily the credit attached to the Bush campaign. . . . There should have been more of an effort to kind of go out and just talk about the integration between digital and the field operations playing a very big contributing factor in the win. . . . A lot of the history that gets written is driven by the public marketing of these efforts, and by the marketing of what the results mean.[62]

Ruffini is suggesting that "public marketing" matters on a cultural level in terms of providing party actors with the impetus and desire to invest in digital and data technologies. After the Bush campaign, Ruffini argued, the Republican Party network had little motivation to invest in new capacities or launch new firms, in part because technologies were not narrated as an essential part of the re-election bid. Meanwhile, many in the Republican Party saw Dean's bid not as a harbinger of a new world of Internet campaigning, but as a colossal failure (which, of course, on the level of electoral success, it was).

As a result, in a world of rapidly changing technology and increasing need for the knowledge and skills required for the new technical and analytic basis of campaigning, the Republican Party's digital, data, human, and organizational infrastructure experienced comparatively less change after the 2004 cycle than that of the Democrats.[63] This was important given the changing technological context in 2004 and the years after, marked by the rapid emergence and widespread uptake of new social media platforms such as Facebook and YouTube, the growing ubiquity of smartphones that were altering the ways that citizens lived with media, and advances in database technologies and analytic practices. For example, while there was talk about the success of micro-targeting during and after the 2004 election, Bush's highly successful turnout efforts meant that there were few incentives and little urgency to rethink systems such as the party's database and browser tool Voter Vault used for accessing the voter file, even as the Democratic Party was developing a more dynamic system that took advantage of new technologies.

Meanwhile, the Republican Party network of staffers and organizations was not transformed as dramatically as the Democratic Party network after the 2004 cycle. Democratic presidential campaign staffers on the primary and general election bids of the cycle created 23 new organizations to add increasing specialization in the areas of technology, digital, data, and analytics, compared with *two* new ventures launched by Bush veterans (both of which were founded years after the re-election bid). While the Democrats launched a host of new organizations and grew existing ones specializing in digital (Blue State Digital), data (Voter Activation Network [VAN] and Catalist), and analytics services (the Analyst Institute), as well as organizations devoted to building a knowledge base at the intersection of these things and producing staffers with these skills (the New Organizing Institute), the Republican side of the aisle generally remained the same during this period.

Indeed, after Bush's re-election, incoming party chair and Bush re-election bid manager Ken Mehlman kept much of the innovative data and digital media work of the campaign inside the party apparatus, where it was subject to the whims of future chairmen, uneven resource flows, and restrictions on how it could be transferred to other organizations. As one former party staffer argued, "The Republican Party was doing all the technology [after 2004]. New businesses couldn't compete with free offered by the party. They had no access to voter data, and party business generally went to one vendor."[64] The key staffers from the re-elect campaign went to work for the party or into commercial industry instead of starting their own client-oriented consultancies and organizations that could institutionalize and carry the innovations of the campaign to other sites in the party network while providing steady jobs to technically skilled staffers and specialized services around new data and digital technologies. Ultimately, centering technology in the party led to a less diversified network, fewer resources to employ developers, and less subsequent innovation. As Azarias Reda, who became the Republican Party's chief data officer in December 2013 and subsequently its chief technology officer in January 2015, argued regarding the importance of party-affiliated organizations:

> Campaigns are short-lived. . . . So the permanent entity that you have are things like the RNC and the DNC that can do this [technological development] as they stay around, but even then people come in and out of this organization a lot ... and people have different priorities. What this means [is] that even when progress is made, it is really hard to sustain, which is why you end up having a lot of it and outside entities that are actually more permanent then the internal infrastructure. . . .[65]

The 2008 presidential cycle also provided little impetus for change in the Republican Party network. An increasingly unpopular president, a disaster in New Orleans, the failure of signature policy efforts around immigration and social security, a 2006 midterm election that resulted in a Democratic sweep of Congress, and a tanking economy led to a fractured party, diminished energy, and an easily explained away defeat in the presidential election. The cycle featured a wide candidate field that pitted a small number of digital staffers from the Bush re-election team against one another. One incumbent firm, Campaign Solutions, dominated the market for technology consulting services during this period, and had few competitors. As Katie Harbath, a former party staffer and digital strategist on the Giuliani 2008 campaign, described, "you could count the Republican digital strategists on two hands and most of us had all worked together" on the Bush re-election or at the RNC. [66] Meanwhile, John McCain's come-from-behind bid had little to do with technology, unlike his 2000 run, and the candidate had few resources for technological development during the primaries or general election. As a result, those familiar with the campaign's tools, built primarily by Campaign Solutions, cite that they looked much like what the Bush team used on the re-election bid. Chuck DeFeo, the former chief digital officer for the RNC who became CEO of Campaign Solutions in 2009 and at the time this went to press was the vice president (products) at the independent Republican data firm i360, argued that:

> By the time they walk[ed] into 2008 they were literally sitting on not the exact same code base—but not a much more mature product then what we had in '04. They walked into '08 with an '04 product and . . . in my opinion the heart of why we lost our advantage was clearly the political environment. . . . Why we looked so flat footed from a technology perspective is because we stopped investing, we stopped innovating and we stopped fixing. . . . By '08, which was kind of ironic to me, there was not the risk-taking culture in place anymore where from a business perspective the vendors weren't investing anymore, they were reaping, and from a RNC party apparatus you know the leaders that . . . drove that risk-taking, innovate mindset were not necessarily the drivers of '08 and they weren't driving the party any longer. . . . [67]

The dynamic DeFeo described stems not just from the complacency that marked the party after Bush's dominant victory in 2004, but also from McCain's lack of resources throughout much of the primary season and well into 2008. With the candidate nearly broke until his big primary victory in New Hampshire, McCain's campaign had little in the way of resources to invest in technology and skilled staffers (hiring just 15, none with a primary employment background in technology or data/analytics). In addition, during the general election the Republican had comparatively less money to devote to technology, digital, data, and analytics than Obama, who eschewed federal financing. Meanwhile, the Obama campaign poured an enormous amount of resources into the extended Democratic Party network throughout the race, which helped these organizations improve their technologies, build their capacities, and hire staffers, most notably Blue State Digital and Voter Activation Network. As a result of this, Obama's run in 2008 built significant assets for the Democratic Party that later campaigns (including the re-election bid) drew on. In addition to building the capacity of these firms in ways that benefitted their future campaign and party network organization clients, the Obama campaign also provided the Democratic Party with an approximately 13 million person email list, an extraordinary pool of small-dollar donors, and millions of canvass contacts from an expansive field operation. When coupled with the campaign's own ability to engage in significant hiring in the areas of technology, digital, data, and analytics (hiring 131 staffers, 11 with primary backgrounds in technology and data/analytics), Obama's run in 2008 was a massive investment in the capacity of the Democratic Party network as a whole to contest elections that paid dividends for campaigns *in the future*.

Meanwhile, with McCain's loss, the configuration of consultancies, organizations, campaign operatives, and technologies in the Republican Party network also did not radically change, save for the founding of a few firms that grew to prominence during and after the 2012 cycle, including Targeted Victory, which handled the digital for Romney's bid, and the data firm i360.[68] Staffers connected to 2008 bids launched only ten new ventures during and after the cycle (Targeted Victory's founders cited that the lack of new organizations on the Republican side of the aisle during this time was one of the key reasons behind the launch of the firm). In large part, this lack of organizational founding was because the results of the election were easily explained away given the state of the economy, an unpopular incumbent, and the broader political context. Of course, these are likely the reasons for McCain's loss. But it also meant that many actors across the party's extended network did not make a commitment to investing in technology, digital, data, and analytics, or even perceive a significant and consequential gap between the two parties, despite the enormous crush of media around Obama's so-called social media campaign. This explains why some efforts to remake the Republican Party's infrastructure failed. Ruffini, for instance, helped launch a "Rebuild the Party" effort in the wake of the 2008 campaign, focused on closing what he perceived to be the yawning digital gap between Democrats and Republicans. It was an effort that made little headway, even as Democrats were founding a host of new firms and organizations focused on technology, digital, data, and analytics after the successful election—21 staffers on various campaigns founded 26 new organizations after the cycle.[69] Even more, the Democratic Party was investing in technology, digital media, data, and analytics, and its field infrastructure more broadly, through the vehicle of Organizing for America after 2008, where a core group of staffers were involved in creating tools, analytic practices, and organizing models during the midterm cycle in 2010 that powered many aspects of Obama's re-election bid.[70]

As a result, the Republican Party network fell even further behind its rival, and missed key transformations in technology, digital media, data, and analytics that have come to define contemporary Democratic campaigning, such as the movement from micro-targeting based on segments of voters to predictive analytics that score individuals based on their likelihood to support candidates, turn out to vote, and be persuaded.[71] Even more, the Republican Party never developed an extensive small-dollar donor culture and infrastructure to match what the Democrats built beginning in 2004 primarily through email, expanded through Obama's 2008 run, and continued to cultivate at the party between cycles.[72] At the same time, there were accidents of history that erased work intended to address this gap that was done within the Republican Party between 2008 and 2012. Former party staffers argued that chairman Michael Steele invested considerable amounts internally to revamp the party's technical infrastructure, but his troubled tenure was marked by significant debts that ultimately led to projects that were unfinished, financially unsustainable, and abandoned.[73] Meanwhile, the Republican Party's sweeping victories in congressional and statehouse races across the country in 2010 failed to set the party on a different path, given that it seemed that so many of Obama's technologies appeared to have little effect on voter dissatisfaction and disillusionment or the election more generally.

This history helps explain the differences between the two parties during the 2012 cycle that the GOP Growth and Opportunity Project report pointed to. The decisions the Republican Party network collectively made after Bush was re-elected, and the way party actors explained away McCain's defeat, shaped the ways the party's candidates subsequently organized their campaigns, chose their campaign managers, contested elections, and comparatively de-valued technology, digital, data, and analytics as central aspects of electioneering.[74] As sociologist Paul DiMaggio argued, culture is, in part, embedded in networks, infrastructures, and practices.[75] At the level of the party network, what is of analytical interest are the ways that knowledge and skills relating to technology, digital media, data, and analytics become valued, taught, learned, and institutionalized across campaigns, organizations, and electoral cycles, or fail to. The differences that practitioners pointed to between the two parties and their extended networks are the result of a history wherein certain campaign staffers on the Democratic side of the aisle with technology, digital media, data, and analytics skills were not only supported by market opportunities and produced by an extended network of organizations, they became comparatively culturally valued, were provided with resources, and were given autonomy on campaigns. As such, these practitioners became the carriers of skills and practice across organizational contexts and election cycles. The work of actors within party networks shapes the ways technical skills are perceived and valued within campaign organizations over time, the types of staffers that are available for campaigns to draw on, and the recruiting and hiring campaigns engage in. As one former Republican Party staffer summed up the differences in the two parties and their differential reservoirs of expertise with respect to data and analytics during the 2012 election, "where they maybe could have 500 or 1,000 people that could manipulate state-level voter data, and we had 50, maybe. . . ."[76]

For example, the 2012 Obama campaign's efforts to identify technical needs and recruit talent reveal key differences between the two parties at that moment in time. Of the Obama re-election bid's 342 staffers in technology, digital, data, and analytics, 73 had primary employment backgrounds in the political field, and as detailed above 33 worked at the party or Organizing for America in the years between the elections. At the same time, the leadership of the Obama campaign actively strove to attract top talent from outside its party network and even the political field in order to leverage their specialized skills for the campaign. Alex Lundry noted how far ahead his rivals in 2012 were after he saw a job posting for the Obama campaign:

> I was, I think, the first person to notice the job posting that Obama had put up for predictive modelers and they were speaking my lan-guage—like I could have applied for that job that they listed because it described exactly what I did and it was on an industry website and you know in my mind they were doing the right things and I started becom-ing very concerned because it did seem like they were putting together a team unlike anything we'd ever seen before and from all accounts they did. Yeah, I mean I haven't been doing this forever but I have been doing it long enough to say I have never ever seen any sort of political help wanted ad that used the language they did. That they listed the skills they did or listed the software that they did and that was what had me concerned. . . . [77]

Part of the advantage heading into 2012 that Lundry is noting is that the Obama campaign had staffers in positions of authority such as Dan Wagner. Wagner was a former consulting analyst who left the commercial sector to work on analytics for the 2008 bid and subsequently became the targeting director of the party dur-ing the 2010 cycle and chief analytics officer for the re-election campaign (and after the election he founded Civis Analytics to carry this analytics work across the party network). Wagner knew the value of predictive modelers and how to find them.[78] Predictive modeling, or using data to predict an individual voter's attitudes and behavior, is important because campaigns have nowhere near the time or resources to contact every member of the electorate and it affords gains in efficiency over segment-based micro-targeting. It was precisely this blend of a comparatively deep bench of staffers with specialized skills in data and analyt-ics within the party network, the prominent roles, organizational autonomy, and resources they enjoyed on the campaign, and their initiative to look outside the field to find talent—48 staffers with primary employment backgrounds in tech-nology or data/analytics and 58 with their primary work in commercial indus-tries—that was behind much of the Obama re-election bid's success.

By contrast, the Republican Party network had fewer practitioners with tech-nology, digital, data, and analytics skills in 2012, its presidential campaigns hired considerably fewer staffers in these areas, and they were comparatively undervalued on the Romney campaign, among others of the cycle. All of these things were shaped by the party's history since 2004. It is striking, for instance, that the Democratic primary campaigns of Howard Dean and Wesley Clark each hired more staffers in the areas of technology, digital, data, and analytics (11 and 18, respectively) than any of the Republican campaigns of the 2004, 2008, and even the 2012 cycle, except for Romney's 2012 primary bid (23) and McCain and Romney's general election bids (15 and 87, respectively). Practitioners on both sides of the aisle argue that these things were the result of a cultural orientation within the Republican Party network where candidates and campaign managers did not see technology, digital, data, and analytics as essential assets for contemporary campaigning. As a result, there was less talent for 2012 Republican campaigns to draw on and, even more, an incumbent group of consultants oriented toward traditional media-buying and communications were well ensconced on the Republican side of the aisle through the 2012 cycle and often were the drivers of campaign strategy.[79]

For example, in separate interviews, a number of former staffers on the Obama and Romney campaigns cited cultural differences between the two parties that shaped the organizational structures and work of the two general election bids in 2012. As one former Obama campaign staffer, speaking of a private post-election Google-sponsored event that brought together practitioners from both parties who worked in technology, digital, data, and analytics, argued:

> What seemed to be sort of a consensus in the room and one that I absolutely agree with is that the bigger challenge for the Republicans is culture, not technology. Republicans have enough money to invest in the same type of technology that we invest in. They have enough money to pay talented young people to come into the party and execute and create models but they don't have a culture of making decisions based on data-driven analytics. They have a culture of working with consultants and outsourcing those kinds of decisions to their mail consultants, their TV consultants, and they [the consultants] have their own specific interests. It's just harder because the leadership hasn't embraced the idea of kind of strong arming all of that stuff to the side and allowing data to really determine strategy, which again I do think it is one of the things that the 2012 [Obama] campaign did the best because there really was buy-in among the leadership.[80]

As this staffer argues, the comparatively greater use of data and analytics on the Obama campaign, and in the Democratic Party more broadly during this time period, was not simply a question of resources. It was the product of a cultural shift toward seeing these things as organizationally important and electorally advantageous that was brought about by work in the party network post-2004 (this difference between the two parties is not inherent, as Bush's demonstrable advantage in 2004 reveals; it is the product of the historical cultural work of party networks since that moment in time). As echoed throughout this book, practitioners on both sides of the aisle used markedly similar language in citing that the Obama re-election bid moved away from practices grounded in "gut instinct," "experience," and "seniority" and toward more identifiable and transparent metrics in electoral decision-making.[81] Although data remained poorly integrated across the campaign's many applications and primarily served to orient staffers and generate efficiencies (not unproblematically reveal the empirical world), beginning with the computational management practiced on the 2008 Obama campaign and carrying through to the re-election bid, staffers wielding data had legitimate internal organizational authority to track and evaluate expenditures, fundraising, messaging, design, and electoral strategy more broadly. The Obama campaign's hierarchy not only saw data as a valid guide to organizational decision-making, it often elevated its status over other knowledge claims, such as experience, while also recognizing its limitations.

By contrast, a number of former Romney staffers repeatedly stated how they were frustrated and blocked by campaign hierarchies that at times put little faith in data and looked much more skeptically at many aspects of digital. As a Romney senior staffer described the role of data on the campaign:

> We had plenty of meetings where this data was discussed and shared. Then when decisions were actually made, sometimes decisions were made in those rooms and sometimes decisions were made at some other point by other people. And, you know, I think the role of data in those decisions is, I think, who knows, sometimes decisions were made in that room that I think were not executed on because of people who felt differently about how they should go. They were in a position to not act on it—and so the thing is, you have to have leadership and people who are in the decision-making, in a directive position on the campaign, who say "I am going to trust the data and I am going to stick with it or I am only going to override it when I feel exceptionally strong about it in a particular way." And, I don't think that everybody on the campaign had that commitment. I think a lot of people on the campaign did, but I don't think everybody did.[82]

While the demands of electoral cycles and the structural positions of the candidates as detailed in the following pages prevent direct comparisons, the differences in the hiring, status, and organizational valuations of technology, digital media, data, and analytics staffers within the two presidential campaigns are clear. Romney had about 30 staffers working in an analytical capacity across all the departments of the campaign.[83] By contrast, the Obama campaign had nearly double that number working in a stand-alone analytics department, which the campaign made a pillar of its organization. The Obama campaign also provided staffers in technology, digital, data, and analytics with comparatively greater autonomy. The Obama campaign's digital director in Chicago had a seat at the senior staff table, and was at the same level as the heads of departments such as communications, field, political, policy, operations, and finance. Romney's digital team, by contrast, had to go through an extensive vetting process for all of its public communications. As Caitlin Checkett, the campaign's digital integration director, described:

> So whether it was a tweet, Facebook post, blog post, photo—anything you could imagine—it had to be sent around to everyone for approval. Towards the end of the campaign that was 22 individuals who had to approve it. . . . Not everyone had to give a thumbs up [but they had the opportunity]. The digital team unfortunately did not have the opportunity to think of things on their own and post them. Obviously that was us protecting ourselves. . . . The downfall of that of course is as fast as we are moving it can take a little bit of time to get that approval to happen.[84]

Zac Moffatt, Romney's digital director, went so far as to describe the campaign as having "the best tweets ever written by 17 people. . . . It was the best they all could agree on every single time."[85] These and other staffers stated that in practice not all of these people signed off on or even reviewed digital content (the people from legal, research, and strategy were the most important on the email list). That said, these digital staffers cited that there were enough hands that touched the digital content that over time staffers self-regulated to produce content they knew would get approved.

Again, the argument of this book is that this was not simply the result of the whims of one campaign, campaign manager, or electoral cycle. The Romney campaign was largely the *outcome* of the Republican Party network's history since 2004. This history shaped what candidates and actors in the extended party network perceived and valued as electorally advantageous. These cultural orientations shaped the practitioners whom candidates selected as their campaign managers, and whom they in turn hired as staff, the resources they devoted to different aspects of campaigning, the decisions they made as to organizational structure, and the roles they determined staffers would play on campaigns.

All that said, there is also a new development in electoral campaigning: a technical advantage of incumbency. In addition to the historically conditioned cultural differences between the two parties, staffers on both sides of the aisle explain the Romney campaign's shortcomings vis-à-vis the 2012 Obama campaign with regard to technology, digital, data, and analytics in terms of *time* and *resources*. Given that Obama did not face a primary opponent, the campaign had a year and a half and comparably greater resources to start putting together its team and infrastructure and developing its technology "products." The idea of technology "products" is new in politics and reflects the contemporary reality that campaigns at the highest levels are now often active developers of new technologies. Staffers on both presidential campaigns conceived of their technological development in terms of producing "products" and used the language of "product managers" when discussing the staffers in charge of projects ranging from mobile canvass applications to data integration. Given this work, campaign staffers argued that they needed time to plan and strategize around technical needs and recruit talent to meet them, as well as resources and opportunities for field testing.

While scholars have noted the lengthier primary season and even have suggested that there are now permanent campaigns (a claim that does not apply in the context of technology), the changing *temporal* aspects of campaigning in the context of technological development have gone almost entirely unanalyzed in political communication research.[86] With digital convergence and technological change, all political communication practices, from advertising and field canvassing to direct mail, have taken on new technological dimensions and are now premised in some way on digital media, data, and analytics, where longer periods of technological development and ongoing infrastructural work offer competitive advantage.

This means that the traditional advantages of incumbency, such as name recognition and resources, now have a new technical dimension. As the 2012 Obama campaign's innovations in purchasing cable advertisements and set-top box targeting detailed in this book reveal, even ad buying and delivery are now increasingly driven by digital convergence, extensive stores of data accrued across electoral cycles and modeling practices, and a much more fine-grained ability to gain real-time data on the electorate. There are also massive new content challenges given the proliferation of platforms for messaging and advertising, and the possibility of both narrower ad targeting and digital social influence.[87] At the same time, the gathering of useful data from multiple platforms and the development of analytics around it are now extended across time, as historical stores of data facilitate predictive modeling, which reveals the importance of infrastructure. The upshot of all of this is that it takes considerable time to determine goals and assess needs, recruit staffers with the necessary expertise, train new hires, develop and test new technologies and messages, create metrics, clean and integrate data, and craft practices around new platforms such as Instagram and Twitter, as well as navigate ongoing changes in the algorithms of platforms such as Facebook.

This book reveals numerous examples of the new technical advantage of incumbency on George W. Bush and Obama's re-election bids, and details what the process of developing electoral technologies and practices more generally looks like on contemporary campaigns. Large-scale data projects such as the Obama campaign's Narwhal and the construction of its new organizing platform,

Dashboard, took months of planning, investment, and dedicated (and costly) staff resources. Technical development on the campaign was challenging from an organizational and technical perspective. Staffers had to secure the buy-in of multiple stakeholders across many different organizational departments both in Chicago and in the states and engage in extensive field testing. In this context, it is easy to see the advantage the Obama campaign enjoyed with the comparative luxury of dedicating resources to these projects during an uncontested primary. Even then, in practice these projects did not always prove as useful as staffers intended.

Romney's digital and political teams, by contrast, were hamstrung by a long Republican primary that was draining in terms of resources and morale. While many political scientists saw the primary race as a foregone conclusion, that was not the perspective or experience of staffers inside the campaign. The fact that staffers perceived that their candidate could lose the nominating contest led to decisions about resource allocation and strategy that were consequential in terms of the staffing patterns and development projects of the campaign.[88] The long primary meant that the Romney campaign had less time to develop and field test technologies and comparatively fewer resources to do so, especially given that the campaign's leadership, drawn mostly from the ranks of communications professionals, pursued a broadcast advertising strategy to overwhelm its comparatively underfunded opponents. With a long primary and large proportions of budgets devoted to traditional advertising instead of field or digital, Romney staffers cite having a much narrower window to not only develop and test new tools such as ORCA, but more broadly limited time to integrate the voter contact aspects of the campaign in all its forms, from digital outreach to door knocking. Speaking of the 2012 campaign, Aaron Ginn, a self-described Silicon Valley "growth hacker" whom the Romney campaign hired to expand the user base of its in-house social network, argued:

> So this was the first time ever for an incumbent to have this level of competitive advantage that is time based. That people are expecting all of these digital tools to help them now—get out to vote, donate remotely, donate through your phone—and it was very challenging for the team to keep pace with that. So much so that whenever we would beat Obama to the punch on a Facebook feature such as "Commit to Mitt," Obama released his literally three hours after we did because he already had it made, you know, or his team already had it made, and they just did not release it yet and they released it in response to that. So, that is a huge luring point as someone who works in Silicon Valley—it is a very logical thing but to many people in politics it is not. They think that they can continue to be transactional in every 2 or 4 year election cycle.[89]

Ginn, who cofounded the Republican technological effort Lincoln Labs after the election in response to what he perceived as the party's failures in 2012, argued that time matters not just for technical development, but as importantly for the efforts of campaigns to recruit staffers with specialized expertise.[90] In sum, with a long primary campaign that was draining in terms of resources, Romney's staffers had little in the way of time or money to make strategic planning and staffing decisions and to recruit people with specialized expertise, all of which the Obama campaign did throughout 2011.[91]

Again, however, there were also significant differences in the technology, digital, data, and analytics infrastructures available to the two candidates in their extended party networks that were nearly a decade in the making and that compounded Romney's structural disadvantage in terms of the electoral context. The 2012 Obama campaign was successful precisely because its technically skilled staffers innovated *around the infrastructure that pre-dated the electoral cycle and existed in the extended party network.* In 2008, the Obama campaign developed some tools in-house, but relied much more extensively on resources already developed by the DNC and firms such as VAN and Blue State Digital. In 2012, with more resources and a longer time frame, and the luxury of not having to build tools while contesting primaries, the campaign sought to improve upon this infrastructure. This meant large data integration projects such as Narwhal and work with the party on the implementation of HP's Vertica for the purposes of analytics and modeling, all of which was premised on the data infrastructure put in place by Dean while party chair. The Obama campaign also benefited from the organizational learning of firms such as NGP VAN, which as noted earlier had its own version of Project ORCA fail during the 2008 Obama campaign (called Project Houdini), but which had the time to develop and field test a robust vote-monitoring tool called Pollwatcher for the 2012 cycle based on the lessons it learned. And, the campaign built on the voter modeling and analytics work that staffers such as Dan Wagner conducted for the party in 2010, even though that election entailed sweeping losses for Democrats.[92]

The extended Republican Party network failed to develop comparable infrastructural resources for the 2012 Romney campaign. As detailed earlier, Michael Steele's investments in technology after the 2008 cycle proved fleeting given the need to retire the party's debts. As a result, former staffers argue, there was little technological development after 2008, and many legacy systems were still in place when Romney ran in 2012. One former party staffer with close knowledge of its systems actually used the word "entropy" to describe what happened to the Republican Party's infrastructure from 2004 through 2012.[93] Meanwhile, with comparatively lower rates of hiring and firm founding in the areas of technology, digital, data, and analytics during two previous presidential election cycles, the Romney campaign had fewer resources to draw on for its own staffing and technical needs.

One example of a Republican technology that practitioners widely argued did not keep pace with Democratic innovations was the GOP Data Center, the party-provided database and field tool built and maintained by the consultancy FLS Connect that was in essence a relaunched version of Voter Vault for the 2012 elections.[94] Numerous Republican Party practitioners across an array of campaigns and organizations stated that GOP Data Center was significantly behind the Democratic Party's VoteBuilder system and lacked both usability and functionality during the 2012 cycle.[95] Even more, practitioners cite that this was still the case in 2014, and as a result Republican campaigns often used field tools and even voter data provided by third-party vendors such as the NationBuilder and the Koch brothers-backed i360. This means that data does not flow as seamlessly back into the RNC's data ecosystem as on the Democratic side of the aisle, where all candidates use the same standardized system for canvassing and accessing voter data.

Methodology

As I explore in greater detail in the Methodological Appendix, this study takes a historical and relational view of political campaigns, showing how they are not just the product of any one electoral cycle and the individual decisions of candidates and campaign managers. This book argues that campaigns are in large part the *outcomes* of party network processes that unfold over time, including the work of people and organizations that build infrastructure, staffers who cross fields, and organizations that emerge after campaigns. Accordingly, this book adopts a historical approach to the study of technology in electoral politics to explain differences in the two parties' respective capacities to wield technology, digital media, data, and analytics in electoral contests.

The evidence for this book is drawn from a number of primary and secondary sources. First, I conducted formal interviews with 55 party and campaign staffers and consultants active in politics over the last two decades (and in some cases, even longer) for this specific project, and spoke with dozens more both formally and informally at political events around technology and politics over the past four years. I also drew on more than a dozen of the interviews I conducted for *Taking Our Country Back*. I conducted the majority of my interviews for that book between 2009 and 2011, and conversations routinely extended into the post-campaign work of Obama staffers. Interviews generally lasted between 1 and 4 hours, with the average interview being 1.5 hours. I selected interviewees on the basis of organizational records, Federal Election Commission filings, quotes and profiles in journalistic articles and trade magazines, LinkedIn profiles, and snowball sampling. Given the historical nature of this work, I conducted all interviews on the record, although interviewees could declare any statement to be off the record or not for attribution.

The second key source of data for this book is primary and secondary documents, such as a 400-page internal postmortem on the 2008 Obama campaign and public reports such as the 2012 Obama campaign's Legacy Report and the Republican National Committee's Growth and Opportunity Project report. The Internet Archive's WayBack Machine was also an essential resource for recovering the public web properties of campaigns and parties from the 2000 cycle on.[96] I also kept a data set of political and trade journalism articles relating to technology, digital, data, and analytics on campaigns and in parties, which grew to encompass hundreds of articles. These articles were often the starting points for my own inquiries, and also served as a way to identify interviewees. The third key source of evidence was the data set that my research assistants, Scott Brennen and Christopher Jasinski, put together on the professional careers of 629 staffers working in technology, digital, data, and analytics from 2004 to 2012 and rates of firm and organizational founding. This data set served as the backbone of the entire study, as it provided the broad empirical contours of the differences in the two parties in terms of their hiring patterns, field crossing, and organizational founding that the historical and interview data could explain. This data set also provided an expansive record that I drew upon to locate interviewees and inform discussions of their work. This data set also provided important evidence of the organization and structure of parties and campaigns. Finally, my fieldwork at the 2012 Democratic National Convention and trips to consultancies and practitioner forums provided invaluable firsthand experiences of technology use in electoral politics.

Outline of the Book

I have structured the book chronologically, focusing on tracing the history of the Republican Party from 2000 through 2014 and the Democratic Party from Obama's re-election bid through 2014. In addition to detailing this history, I analyze broader shifts in technology, culture, and social structures over the last two decades as seen through the lens of electoral politics and the perspectives of those who practice it.

CHAPTER 2

Chapter 2 charts the work of the 2000 McCain campaign and 2004 Bush re-election bid in detailing the history of the Republican Party from 2000 through 2004. Despite the candidate's defeat, John McCain's primary campaign is rightly lauded by practitioners for its innovations in Internet fundraising and mobilization. I show how these innovations were premised on the creative recombination of new and old media logics. Staffers had to pursue what I call "demonstration projects" to convince campaign stakeholders of the Internet's utility for securing volunteers and monetary resources. Internet staffers secured organizational legitimacy, autonomy, and resources through successful demonstration projects—a practice that has not changed much for digital staffers over subsequent electoral cycles. The chapter then turns to the infrastructure-building projects of the RNC in the years after Bush's election in 2000. Those working at the party learned not only from the McCain campaign, but from the ground efforts of the extended Democratic Party network on display in Al Gore's general election campaign. Republican Party staffers worked to build capacity for ground campaigning, revamp the party's data infrastructure, and refashion Internet operations to complement the political program. In tracing this history, this chapter provides an extensive empirical look at Republican Party dynamics from 2000 to 2004, as well as the re-election bid, primarily through the lens of Bush's eCampaign operation as it intersected with the larger political operations of the campaign.

CHAPTER 3

This chapter charts the history of the Republican Party network from President Bush's re-election to John McCain's defeat in 2008. In the wake of Hurricane Katrina and the party's failures to enact legislative changes on immigration and social security, Republican political fortunes suffered, and the Democrats took control of the House and Senate in 2006. Meanwhile, in the middle of an extraordinary financial crisis, Obama handily won the presidency in 2008. Although better campaign technologies, more sophisticated modeling, and a better data infrastructure would hardly have stemmed the electoral tide (as Democrats learned in 2010 and 2014), this chapter argues that behind the scenes the Republican Party's extended network and its electoral infrastructure failed to keep pace with Democratic innovations from 2004 through 2008.

This chapter explains the different fortunes of the two parties during this period, arguing that after the 2004 election the Republican Party brought much of the talent and technology of Bush's re-election bid inside the party organization. In a theme that runs throughout this book, I argue that the party was ultimately ill-suited to develop innovative new technologies given its organizational structure, continual turnover in chairmen, deference to the candidate during presidential elections, uneven resource flows, and inability to license tools to campaigns and third parties (which generates revenues to invest in their continual development). I argue that the technologies, knowledge, and practices at the background of politics are particularly "fragile infrastructures" that require constant maintenance, care, and concern, or they fall apart and even disappear. Meanwhile, few of Bush's staffers went on to found firms and organizations to institutionalize and extend the innovations of the 2004 campaign and diffuse them to other sites in the party network, even as the Democrats were building their own "hybrid network ecosystem" of technology, digital, data, and analytics consultancies and knowledge-producing organizations around the party's data infrastructure. The chapter concludes by looking at some of the differences between the McCain and Obama campaigns in 2008, and shows how the Republican's difficult path to the nomination, unfavorable electoral context, and acceptance of campaign finance limits meant comparatively fewer resources for technological development and the hiring of staffers and consultants, which in turn limited the party's technology, digital, data, and analytics capacities in subsequent electoral cycles.

CHAPTER 4

This chapter traces developments in the Democratic and Republican parties in the aftermath of the 2008 election and follows the Romney campaign through the primaries of the 2012 cycle. It argues that John McCain's defeat in 2008 was easily explained away by actors in the extended Republican Party network as the product of an unfavorable electoral context. As a result, there was comparatively less impetus to rethink the party's approach to electoral politics than for the Democrats after 2004 or Republicans after 2012, and the party also failed to keep pace with technological and organizational developments in the Democratic Party after 2008 as well. Meanwhile, the work that was done within the party, aimed at improving its technological and data infrastructures, suffered from the effects of Michael Steele's troubled tenure, which left the party in significant debt. Going forward, the new chairman Reince Priebus was faced with the need to pay off the debt, which subsequently impacted the infrastructure available to the Republican nominee in 2012. The chapter also follows the Romney campaign as it took shape during the 2012 cycle, and offers some points of comparison with the Obama re-election campaign, analyzing how the bid was in part the product of historical party network processes that comparatively undervalued technology, digital, data, and analytics in electoral campaigning and the structural challenges of a long and resource-draining primary. The chapter also argues that Romney faced a different "digital opportunity structure" than the challengers attempting to defeat the establishment Republican. These aspects of the political environment and staffers' perceptions of them provided the possibilities for and limits on specifically digital mobilization that subsequently shaped the campaign's uptake of technology.

CHAPTER 5

This chapter chronicles the history of the two parties and their presidential campaigns through the 2012 cycle. I show how the Obama re-election campaign was, in significant ways, the outcome of a set of historical processes that took shape during the period of 2008–2012. A number of staffers who worked on the 2008 campaign further honed and created new specialized knowledge and skills during the 2010 midterm cycle in ways that benefited the re-election bid. It was during the disastrous 2010 midterm cycle that much of the groundwork was laid for the 2012 re-election campaign with respect to the technologies and expertise for wielding digital media, data, and analytics in the service of electoral politics. The chapter also argues that the Obama campaign enjoyed a significant new technical advantage of incumbency over its rival, which provided greater resources and time for planning, development, and the recruitment of staffers. In doing so, the chapter provides a detailed look at each campaign for president. Despite many successes, I show that the Obama 2012 campaign's vaunted technological sophistication was not recognizable to staffers in the moment as they struggled with the development of new electoral tools and data integration. I also show how the long primary cycle and rapid scaling of the Romney campaign affected its organization and technical development.

CHAPTER 6

This chapter shows how in the months after a 2012 election Republicans believed they should have won the party took an extraordinary inward look at itself, documented its many failings vis-à-vis the Democrats, and launched new initiatives to correct for them. Meanwhile, in the extended party network, former Romney staffers launched new digital consultancies and existing firms re-evaluated their work and made new investments in technology, digital, data, and analytics. The chapter reveals the work of these actors during the 2014 midterm elections, and analyzes the state of the party network with respect to technology, digital, data, and analytics through the lens of two high-profile campaigns of the cycle: Mitch McConnell's Senate re-election bid and Scott Walker's gubernatorial re-election campaign. I argue that while the party clearly sought to make progress post-2012, issues with the GOP's field tools in part have led to a much more fragmented data ecosystem in the party network, with more rival data sources and competing campaign management platforms than on the Democratic side of aisle. The upshot in 2014 was that data was not captured as seamlessly within the Republican Party network as on the Democratic side of the aisle.

At the same time, with respect to the Democrats, this chapter again reveals how fragile political infrastructures are. While the Obama 2012 campaign built an extraordinary number of technologies in-house, practitioners cite that the party had little money in the months after the election to maintain them and keep developers on staff. In part as a result, people wandered off to other pursuits. Meanwhile, developing these tools within the campaign (instead of through an outside firm) meant that the party assumed control over these assets after the election, and these tools could not be easily legally transferred or licensed to other entities. That said, this chapter shows how an extraordinary 19 different firms and organizations emerged from the campaign, which served to institutionalize and extend many of its innovations in technology and digital, data, and analytics practice and carry them to down-ballot races. In addition, firms such as NGP VAN learned from the cycle and embarked on new projects around things such as data integration, as did the party itself. Meanwhile, 18 of Obama's former technology staffers went to work on 2014 bids, carrying with them a particular approach to digital campaigning. This chapter concludes with an analysis of the political economy of campaign consulting and the barriers to the diffusion of innovations in campaign practice through an analysis of five Democratic state-level bids in 2014 and interviews with party staffers and digital consultants who worked on multiple bids during the cycle. In the end, I show how, despite its advantages over its rival, the Democratic Party network is uneven with respect to how candidates and campaign managers approach, value, and see the efficacy of technology, digital media, data, and analytics for electoral politics.

CHAPTER 7

In the concluding chapter, I tie the history presented in this book together by returning to a discussion of the implications of a move toward technology-intensive campaigning and developing three interrelated concepts that will likely characterize the future of technology, digital, data, and analytics in electoral politics. First, I argue that increasingly campaigns and other political actors value parties for their role *as databases*. Through their databases, parties bind together extended party networks and help to coordinate the work of disparate organizations. Second, I argue that much of the history detailed in this book can be captured in the idea that a central dynamic of contemporary campaigning lies in practitioners' attempts to reveal "whole citizens" in data. To date, doing so has proven elusive to practitioners on both sides of the aisle given that it is premised on integrating data across many of the diverse applications and data sets that campaigns use and that are often siloed and therefore reveal only fragmented individuals. Third, I argue that contemporary electioneering can be conceptualized as a form of "networked ward politics," a data-driven, personalized, and socially embedded form of campaigning that parties and campaigns, especially on the Democratic side of the aisle, developed through prototypes as they have contested elections and have responded to changes in American culture, social structures, and communication technologies.

2

Electoral Innovation at the Grand Old Party

On the night of February 1, 2000, a triumphant John McCain stood on stage at the Crowne Plaza Hotel in Nashua, New Hampshire, and declared that his campaign "didn't have the machine. We had the insurgent campaign, and we had the grassroots and the volunteers from all over this state which made this possible."[1] On the podium in front of the candidate was a placard with an American flag and the URL www.mccain2000.com on top. The placement of the URL was a novel move for a presidential campaign at the time.[2] Staffers on McCain's bid noted that the networks left the web address in the shot during the entire speech. As a result, there was a huge spike in traffic and, subsequently, online fundraising, which was widely reported in the political press. McCain raised over $1 million in the two days after his NH victory, and recruited 26,000 volunteers and raised another $3 million in the 10 days after, with approximately $6.4 million total coming in online for the campaign during the primaries.[3] This public display of fundraising success proved vastly influential as a demonstration of the power of the Internet for electoral campaigning. Internet staffers on both sides of the aisle pointed to McCain's online success during subsequent elections in order to legitimate their work for campaign management and staffers working in other domains of electoral practice.

This story of successful online fundraising reveals the underlying dynamics of what political scientist Andrew Chadwick called the "hybrid media system."[4] New media do not independently exist on their own, or replace old media; comparatively newer and older media interact in complicated ways. McCain's staffers rather adeptly recognized that they needed the power of the televisual gaze to drive traffic to the campaign's website. Only then could the interactive affordances of digital media enable the campaign to translate the energy and enthusiasm of the candidate's far-flung supporters across the nation into volunteers and, more important, money. In a hybrid media system, actors can be innovative by creatively combining established media practices and logics in new ways.[5]

In many ways, the 2000 presidential cycle was the starting point for subsequent shifts in electoral campaigning.[6] The McCain campaign used digital media in a number of innovative ways, especially small-dollar fundraising, providing a model for future practice. At the same time, an electoral innovation that featured people—an old technology—coupled to new organizational processes and digital databases also debuted during the cycle. As communication scholar Rasmus Nielsen has extensively documented, the union efforts around Al Gore's candidacy to use "people as media" drove the candidate's high turnout in key states, exceeding both polling forecasts and the Bush campaign's expectations.[7] The 2000 electoral cycle gave rise to a new era of field campaigning given this high profile demonstration of its efficacy, social science findings that in-person contacts are effective, and the increasing realization among practitioners that audiences were both newly fragmented across media and saturated with political messages. And, as Nielsen and political scientist Eitan Hersh have documented, field campaigning is premised on extensive voter databases and specialized analytic practices that help campaigns identify their supporters and those voters that can be persuaded, as well as get them to the polls.[8] Even more, these databases and the modeling practices around them have subsequently become the backbone of all voter contact efforts, whether at their doorsteps, in their email inboxes, or on their social media accounts.

Ironically, it was the Electoral College victor who was in many ways behind his rivals in harnessing the power of online and in-person voter contact. However, with President Bush in office, the Republican Party embarked on an extensive effort to invest in on-the-ground political canvassing and meld it to Internet operations, all underpinned by a common data infrastructure. As a result of this infrastructural work by the party between presidential elections, four years later the Bush re-election campaign became the most sophisticated electoral effort of the time, with an extensive micro-targeting, voter contact, and turnout operation, an online precinct captain program, and linked databases that facilitated the entire effort.

On the other side of the aisle, John Kerry's voter databases crashed in key battleground states, sign-ups to volunteer online went unanswered, and the campaign's allied 527 organizations failed to match either the data or turnout operations of the Bush team.[9] It was the Democrats who were left picking up the pieces after a presidential election they expected to win. They turned to the Bush campaign as one model, which became a prototype for the Democratic Party's own work to revamp its field operations, data infrastructure, and voter modeling expertise post-2004. Meanwhile, Dean's failed bid elevated the candidate to party chair on the back of his promises to rebuild the party's technological operations, invest in state parties, and implement a new Internet-enabled "people-powered politics" at the party.[10]

Empirically, this chapter takes an in-depth look at the 1999–2000 presidential election cycle and details the subsequent attempts by Republican staffers to institutionalize the innovative approaches to the Internet and field by the McCain and Gore campaigns within the party, which culminated in the president's re-election bid in 2004. I discuss the development of Voter Vault, the party's national voter database, in 1995, and its online user interface built in advance of the 2002 midterm cycle (and, again revealing the technical advantage of incumbency, field tested during that cycle).[11] Through firsthand accounts provided by staffers, the chapter discusses the innovative John McCain primary campaign in 1999 and details Karl Rove's and party chairman Ken Mehlman's substantial investments in party infrastructure following the 2000 elections that provided the background context for the re-election bid in 2004. In the years between the 2000 and 2004 elections, the party built the databases and organization, hosted the trainings, commissioned the online platforms and manuals, created a culture of experimentation, and conducted the trials that paved the way for Bush's re-election victory. In the process, party staffers created a new mindset, as well as a set of practices and technologies, and generated talent for the party.

Analytically, this chapter argues that stakeholders only accept new media practices and technologies after "demonstration projects" offer evidence that an innovation furthers progress toward the existing goals of an organization. Staffers need the autonomy and resources to experiment with new media practices, even as actors in the wider campaign structure need to recognize and value these practices in order to leverage the resources they potentially can bring. Extending Chadwick's analysis, this chapter shows how creative recombination of the workings and logics of different media can produce innovations in media practice, from leveraging mass media to drive traffic to digital properties to coordinating people through digital databases for more effective canvassing operations. This chapter also analyzes how innovations can occur at the edges of a field, among challengers, and then can be brought to the center of and institutionalized within a political party. Finally, this chapter reveals the emergence of a mediated form of personalized and socially embedded campaigning that blends data, technological platforms, and using people as media. As Chuck DeFeo, the former chief digital officer of the RNC from September 2013 to February 2015 as well as eCampaign manager for the RNC in 2002–2003 and Bush-Cheney 2004, described, "Both the sound bite and the actual strategy of the Bush-Cheney '04 campaign was empowering the president's grassroots supporters to spread the president's positive message. . . . Every tool that we rolled out . . . every Bush volunteer center tool, it was just about you signing up and you talking to somebody else. That word of mouth strategy was the strategy of the entire field operation of the Bush-Cheney campaign. . . ."[12]

Innovation at the Edge: The 1999–2000 Presidential Cycle

Staffers on both sides of the aisle hold John McCain's 2000 presidential bid in high regard and laud it for its innovation. That said, McCain's run itself was an amalgam of the practices of a number of different campaigns that staffers looked to as potential models for the Arizona senator, revealing one mechanism for the diffusion of digital campaign strategies. One of these campaigns was Jesse Ventura's insurgent run for governor on the Reform Party ticket in Minnesota in 1998. Shortly after the election, Wes Gullett, a longtime McCain aide who served as the senator's campaign manager in 1992, traveled to Minnesota to talk with Ventura's staffers. Ventura had adopted a number of innovative practices, including holding rolling press conferences with journalists on his campaign bus and using email for things such as contacting people two hours before the candidate arrived in town to invite them to show up for rallies. Soon after arriving back in Arizona, Gullett hired Max Fose as the nascent presidential campaign's Internet manager.[13] At the time, Fose was a 27-year-old who started his political career interning with McCain in 1993 and worked on and off for the senator in the years after. Fose subsequently became a key administrative linchpin of the presidential run who found the offices, bought the computers, and performed the other necessary grunt work on the campaign.

Fose and Gullett, who became a senior advisor to the campaign, saw Ventura and McCain in similar terms as challengers to establishment candidates who had public images as outsider, insurgent political figures who engaged in "straight talk." As such, McCain's staffers sought to develop a national model of Ventura's communications and Internet strategy. Staffers believed that engaging in sit-downs with the press and adopting the Internet as a tool to speak directly to people would symbolically help construct, just as much as it reflected, McCain's image as a straight-talking, outsider candidate. In addition to using Ventura as a model, Fose cited looking at what Democratic presidential candidate Bill Bradley was doing early in the cycle, as well as actively experimenting with the comparatively new medium, of the Internet, attempting to figure out what might work as the campaign went along by seeing what supporters were reacting to using data from their web properties.[14]

In a theme that is apparent throughout this book, the McCain bid reveals how organizational structure shapes the adoption of digital campaign strategies. At the beginning of the cycle, the McCain bid was small for a presidential campaign, and Fose and Gullet had a close relationship with the candidate given the years they had worked for him. When they needed to run things by McCain, they had both access and credibility, which Fose cited was "very significant in not only getting him to understand what we were doing online but getting his buy-in, getting the rest of his finance team to buy in, getting him to talk about it."[15] That said, even with an influential organizational role and candidate buy-in, Fose and Gullett needed to demonstrate the Internet's utility for the campaign on the terms that were most valuable to an organization challenging a candidate with strong institutional backing: recruiting supporters and fundraising. One reason is that the Internet was such a new medium for campaign practice at the time, and therefore staffers needed to legitimate themselves and their work in ways that were not expected of their counterparts working in areas such as broadcast advertising (although different assessments of the strategic value of the Internet persist until this day, as I detail throughout this book).

For example, former staffers connected with the bid recounted that they needed to convince the campaign hierarchy early on to invest in the Internet because the campaign had limited resources, essentially the $2 million transferred from McCain's Senate race in 1998. In this context, Fose looked for "wins," or successful actions such as victories in online polls, well-attended events and town halls, and lucrative fundraising emails, such as the first one the campaign sent out, which raised approximately $20,000 from an email list of approximately 10,000 people. These demonstration projects were crucial at securing organizational legitimacy for the Internet operations on the campaign. As Fose related:

> So there was a fight always for money. What we had shown early on was wins. . . . Once we showed that we could raise money online everyone was buying in because it became a very great tool to raise money. And then the grassroots people saw it when we would do events in New Hampshire, we would drive turnout at events and the grassroots people started buying in. So the little victories and the anecdotal information on the ground was definitely a key factor in getting more buy-in from staff.[16]

Staffers needed to demonstrate the power of the Internet to further the ends of the campaign before the leadership would invest scarce resources in the medium and integrate it organizationally with the rest of the campaign.[17] This dynamic is well known to scholars who have written about innovation in other fields. As the sociologist David Stark has argued:

> Whether in science, politics, civic associations, or business, it is not enough just to embark on a search for an unknown breakthrough . . . you must present the category-breaking solutions in forms that are recognizable to other scientists, citizens, activists, investors, or users. . . . Innovation, as Joseph Schumpeter observed, is recombination; but, as Schumpeter argued as well, it is also deeply disruptive of cultural taken-for-granteds and routines of organizational cognition.[18]

When "wins" occurred, there were spillover transformations in the wider campaign organization. In demonstrating the Internet's usefulness to the campaign in terms of fundraising and volunteer recruitment, these staffers gained greater ability to make claims on organizational resources, status, and authority. Even more, the demonstrative success of the Internet on the campaign changed the "cultural taken-for-granteds" that Schumpeter noted. As online fundraising dollars and volunteerism increased, it furthered a new empirical understanding of the world within the campaign, revealing to staffers that the electorate was now increasingly online and willing to become involved in electoral politics through the Internet. McCain's increasing online fundraising and volunteer recruitment success also taught staffers that the campaign could leverage the Internet for purposes beyond the narrowly informational, then the dominant use of the medium.[19] These understandings then shaped subsequent decisions the campaign made about things such as resource allocation. Meanwhile, practitioners in both parties active during future presidential cycles stated that McCain's run influenced their understanding of the role of, and possibilities for, the Internet in politics.

The McCain campaign developed a number of innovations in digital political practice. The campaign used the political technology firm Virtual Sprockets's version of a content management system (CMS) to launch the first state-level campaign webpages in politics, which featured a mix of national and state content.[20] The campaign turned parts of these websites over to staffers in the states and even volunteers (anticipating the approach of the Dean campaign four years later), through a password permission system that enabled individuals to update these pages.[21] Staffers argued that this decentralized approach, in turn, resulted in more money and volunteers for the campaign. The campaign also built an online phone-banking tool with Virtual Sprockets that was an innovation in how campaigns conducted canvass phone calls. This was the first use of a phone from home tool in the context of electoral politics, and it was a technology that subsequent campaigns, parties, and consultancies developed and deployed during future cycles. Volunteers signed up by providing their names and email addresses online, and then downloaded the names and phone numbers of 10 voters in three early primary states, New Hampshire, South Carolina, and Michigan. Volunteers called people whom the political program was not going to be able to reach because of a lack of resources, and read a script or talking points provided online.[22] They could then enter directly into the system whether these voters were supporting McCain, Forbes, or Bush. From the McCain campaign's perspective, the system generated efficiencies in enabling volunteers to engage in distributed campaign activities at their convenience, which political scientists Bruce Bimber, Andrew Flanagan, and Cynthia Stohl note more broadly accords with the desire among citizens to have greater flexibility in their civic participation.[23]

Internet fundraising, state websites, and online calling tools are all standard campaign technologies now, but were innovations during the 1999–2000 cycle. And, to implement them required what practitioners argued was a "different mindset" than that of staffers working in more established areas of campaign practice. In addition to organizational structure (particularly whether Internet staffers enjoy autonomy), staffers' conceptions of the public and how they perceive the electoral context and what is advantageous in terms of strategy shape how campaigns take up digital media and the ends to which they put tools to use.[24] As Fose described the McCain campaign's approach and conceptions of the public:

> Most campaigns, they think everything inside of the building is top secret. We operated the exact opposite. We opened the doors; it's no secret we have to win New Hampshire, right? In order to do so we have to raise money and we kind of created that whole transparent campaign and it was new to people not only inside the campaign but outside of it to have that kind of information and that kind of ownership—the Internet allowed us to do that. . . . [25]

This mindset led to a distinct set of organizational and technological decisions. Fose made this comment in the context of discussing the McCain campaign's system of volunteer contributions to the state websites, which resulted in very few instances of inappropriate content, and he specifically credits the Obama campaign with making many similar decisions two presidential cycles later.[26] One commonality between these two campaigns, as well as Howard Dean's, is that all these candidates were considered challengers to the establishment frontrunners.[27] Staffers on all these bids argued that in the absence of the institutional resources commanded by the frontrunners, they saw the imperative of going beyond existing practice. McCain's staffers' approach was driven by the deep sense that their candidate was a long shot and they had to try many different things to win (and not just with respect to the Internet, but also McCain's bus tours and extended question-and-answer sessions with journalists). This reading of the electoral context was coupled with a comparatively positive view of volunteerism more generally among staffers working with digital media on the campaign, a very similar dynamic to the Dean and Obama campaigns. Indeed, a number of Internet staffers who worked on subsequent Republican campaigns argued that the McCain campaign was both innovative and bottom-up as a counterpoint to claims that disparities in technology use and organizing strategy are driven by innate ideological differences between the two parties.[28]

Translating supporter enthusiasm into resources is a labor-intensive process premised not only on technical systems, but also organizational structures and work. It is worth considering all the organizational planning and capacity-building that took place during the run-up to the 2000 New Hampshire primaries. McCain's fundraising appears a distinct achievement of the informational affordances of the Internet only if the background organizational and technical work of the campaign drops out of the picture. About a month before the primary, at the candidate's request, McCain's senior staff met on a Saturday in the context of all the polling showing that it looked like the candidate was going to win New Hampshire. The team wanted to do all that it could to prepare for the victory. From a technical perspective, this meant creating more server capacity and implementing redundant servers to ensure that the website would stay up given the anticipated crush of donations. The campaign also debuted a popup on the website to raise money, developed new graphics for the anticipated victory, and planned a fundraising email to send after the returns were in. And, as noted earlier, staffers also made the decision to feature the campaign's URL on all signs and in front of the podium during McCain's victory speech so that mass communication audiences would be directed to the website.

Following McCain's New Hampshire victory, the campaign received an influx of cash online that in the past would have taken weeks to come in through people mailing in checks, which then had to be processed. Despite this influx of resources, McCain went on to lose in South Carolina in a contest that was marred by allegations of dirty tricks by the Bush team.[29] In an ongoing dynamic that digital media work best at translating interest and enthusiasm into resources, with this loss staffers note that there was a drop-off in daily traffic. The campaign spent the remainder of the contest going on to the other primary states and attempting to engage supporters through emails to their list (which stood at approximately 160,000 addresses at the time) that pushed their narrative about the state of the race and what needed to be done moving forward. In the end, despite victories in Arizona and Michigan, George W. Bush locked up the nomination with victories in states such as California.

After the election, having helped raise over $6 million online, nearly 20% of the entire campaign's total, Fose and Gullett launched a consultancy called Integrated Web Strategies (IWS). Reflecting how early it was in the world of digital campaigning, the new firm only had a few competitors, including Becki Donatelli's Campaign Solutions and the digital public affairs firm, Grassroots.com.[30] In a dynamic that was echoed by staffers of the Dean bid post-2004, Fose remembered that:

> We got a ton of earned media off of what we were doing and we saw it as an opportunity to launch a company and to keep doing what we were doing for others. So IWS was, we had a ton of people calling us saying, "I want to do what John McCain did and raise all that money online." Well, what we quickly found out is there weren't many candidates like John McCain as far as the charisma and the willing[ness] to invest not only their resources, but the campaigns' earned media and energy into the online.[31]

Institutionalizing Electoral Innovations

As is well documented, George W. Bush's campaign in 2000 went through an incredibly close general election, with the Supreme Court deciding the outcome after halting the recount in Florida.[32] Interestingly, for what was ultimately a winning campaign, Bush's staffers were jolted by the experience and looked to learn from their rivals. During the primaries, the McCain campaign became a symbolically powerful prototype of using the Internet to garner electoral resources, in part through the legacy media attention the campaign received. Meanwhile, as staffers on both sides of the aisle evaluated the general election, the Gore campaign became a prototype of a field-driven campaign that revealed the effectiveness of volunteer and paid staff voter contact operations, especially given that it drove turnout beyond the expectations of the Bush team.[33]

In numerous interviews, former Bush staffers on the 2000 and 2004 bids and party staffers cited that the Republican's incredibly close margin of victory, the growing sense of the potential of the Internet for electoral campaigning, and the surprising success of McCain's and Gore's efforts during the cycle, provided the impetus for overhauling the Republican Party's electoral apparatus in the years after the 2000 election. The goal, former staffers stated, was to place a cross-medium, voter contact-driven approach at the center of all the party's political operations. As Michael Turk, the eCampaign director for Bush-Cheney 2004 and longtime digital consultant for Republican Party causes and candidates, related:

> I think with institutions, something will sort of prompt or spur innovation and so they will either, a new leader will come in or you will have sort of an election outcome like you did this year [2012] where everybody expects you to win and everything goes completely the opposite direction, and you have got to go figure out why and that prompts people to sort of spend a lot or to do a lot to really sort of invest in catching up. I saw that in 2000, after the 2000 campaign, between 2000 and 2004 because the election was so close. . . . So the GOP in 2000 really put a lot of emphasis in changing their ground game and that included some of the things that we were doing online as well in terms of giving people the ability to organize themselves.[34]

Turk nicely captures how critical events that change the path of a party can have cultural dimensions. The electoral expectations of party actors in 2000 (and 2012) were violated, which led to intra-party assessments and debates about the outcome and new investments to seek to replicate what seemed to be advantageous during the cycle. For example, after Bush's narrow victory, there was a widespread sense among party staffers that the GOP needed to improve on an infrastructural level in terms of the party's voter contact operations and the technical means to support them. To this end, soon after Bush's election, Karl Rove, a senior advisor in the new administration, Ken Mehlman, director of the White House office of political affairs, and the leadership of the RNC, including Jack Oliver, then deputy chairman, thoroughly assessed where the party was in terms of its voter databases, turnout operations, and digital infrastructure, such as its email address list.

The first order of business for the party lay in revamping its data infrastructure and voter turnout efforts with an eye toward the re-election bid. The RNC's voter file went through a number of iterations over the years. In the 1990s, the voter file, called Voter Vault, was basically a national collection of state party databases cobbled together from public information, historical records, direct-mail files, and fundraising and some commercial data. The basic process of building state voter files has not changed much in 20 years. Parties and campaigns rely primarily on public records.[35] While each state is different, typically state parties go to their secretaries of state or county clerks and purchase voter data for counties. This data includes information on citizens that is in the public record, such as voter registration, party affiliation, turnout history, and demographic data (which varies depending on the state). It was, and still is, a highly unstandardized process, with different counties having different capacities to produce and maintain data, and even different categories of data entirely. The state parties then supplement this voter data with other public record data to get a fuller view of the electorate. One example, particularly relevant for Republicans, is data about people who claim veteran status on their property taxes. State parties also supplement these public records with some commercial consumer records and data gathered through surveys, where parties keep track of the phone numbers of voters who responded and their responses. Parties also keep historical data from canvasses that they and their campaigns run.

Throughout much of the 1990s, Republican state parties provided all of this data to the national party, where it was processed, further supplemented, and sent back. The RNC handled the processing of all this data because most states did not have powerful enough computers to handle the data. The RNC also matched these voter files to additional databases, including those that listed changes of address, death records, phone numbers, and additional commercial databases such as magazine subscription lists. The RNC compiled all of this state data into a national voter file and kept a copy of it, while sending back enhanced individual files to the states.

This was the way that the party's data infrastructure worked through the 2000 cycle. In early 2001, as part of the much broader push within the party to overcome the gap in ground operations on display during the 2000 cycle, the party rolled out a new voter database and interface system. This improved Voter Vault further centralized the national party's management and control over state voter files. One impetus behind the more nationally centralized control is that the state parties lacked the capacity that collecting and manipulating data required. This was especially the case given the lack of trained staffers at the state level with the skills to manipulate data. For example, one challenge of the earlier Voter Vault system was that enhanced voter files were returned to the state parties as raw Foxpro.dbf databases. To do anything with them, state parties had to have people on staff who understood Foxpro and knew how to access and manipulate the data in useful ways. Given the lack of staff capacity, the practical result was that a lot of state parties would hand the voter file to their direct mail vendor, who would use it to run labels or queries to generate state party-defined target universes.

The Republican Party redesigned Voter Vault as a technical means of overcoming this limited expertise at the state level. Voter Vault provided state parties with a user interface that enabled staffers to more effectively work with the voter file. This lowered the technical expertise hurdle for the state parties and saved staff resources and time. State staffers found it easier to generate their own walk lists, for instance, without outsourcing the voter file to direct mail vendors. In other words, Voter Vault was premised on the same data that states had been collecting and the national party was appending to these files, but used an interface and architecture that made voter files much more accessible and actionable. The improved Voter Vault also created much more continuity across state files and facilitated queries across the country as a whole, in effect nationalizing the voter file well before the Democrats.[36] This meant that the party had access to a more holistic view of the electorate. It also became easier for the national party to append additional information to the state voter files. Former staffers cite that between 2000 and 2004, the party began more systematically adding consumer data to Voter Vault, including information about what kinds of cars voters drove and the alcohol they drank. This enabled more extensive micro-targeting based on consumer segments, although the foundation of voter modeling was (and still is) based on publicly available data such as party registration and turnout history given their predictive value.

Alongside this revamping of Voter Vault, the party invested heavily in its voter turnout operations. It is worth considering the approach to political on the Republican side of the aisle through the 2000 general election. Rich Beeson, who got his start in politics in the 1980s working for Senator Bill Armstrong of Colorado, served as a regional political director for the West for the party during the 2000 race. Beeson cited New Mexico as an example of how the party approached its political efforts on Election Day in 2000 compared with the Democrats:

> We just stopped. We said 'ok, we have got, all of the missiles were in the air, we have got all of the turnout mail, all of the turnout phones, that is all done.' People had different routines on Election Day. Some would go get a haircut, some would have a dinner or lunch, you would take the staff out to lunch on Election Day. This whole idea of actually going out and campaigning and trying to pull people out to the polls [was foreign.] And we would watch these, we would see these busloads of Democrats.[37]

The highly visible, and by all accounts successful, turnout efforts of the Democrats during the cycle spurred changes within the Republican Party. At the RNC, Rove and Mehlman created the "72-hour program," a reference to Bush's lead in the polls disappearing in the final three days before the election. Rasmus Nielsen has extensively detailed the history of the 72-hour program and the Strategic Task Force to Organize and Mobilize People (STOMP), an effort to redirect resources from safe districts to competitive ones.[38] The 72-hour program was designed to mobilize volunteers for voter registration and turnout operations, and used data and targeting to match volunteers and voters who shared the same cultural and social affiliations and geographic locations.[39]

In addition, the party replicated political scientists Alan Gerber and Donald Green's classic field voting experiments during special elections in 2001 (including state Senate races).[40] The party set up control precincts where nothing happened (i.e., no voter contact through calls or door knocks), others where there was just paid direct mail, others where there were just phone calls, others that only had volunteer door knocks, and others that featured calls, knocks, and mail, and so on. What the party learned is that in-person canvassing works, and more specifically that a volunteer from the voter's neighborhood who said, "I am supporting this candidate for these reasons," worked best at persuasion and turnout. These special election field experiments in turn shaped the party's field efforts during the 2002 midterm elections, where turnout operations were rolled out across the country with an emphasis on competitive Senate races in Minnesota, Georgia, and South Dakota.

More broadly, former party staffers argued that during this time period a new culture within the party took root oriented around the value of canvassing operations, data, and testing. Brent McGoldrick, who served as the RNC Victory executive director of West Virginia during the 2004 cycle, where he coordinated the voter contact operations, argued that the 72-hour program was part of a broader metric-driven mindset that was implemented within the party. From his perspective, the focus on data and analytics during this time period:

> was relentless. You knew there was someone at the top of the pyramid who was driving this. So anything we did on a campaign level was tracked, reported back, went into spreadsheets, went back to Washington. Everything. Every little thing. It was new for the Republican Party. It was like if somebody came by and wanted a bumper sticker you were going to track their name and get it back. If they wanted a yard sign, anything like that. So there was an obsession with metrics. . . .[41]

Technology, Digital Media, Data, and Analytics on the Bush Re-election Bid

All of these investments after the 2000 election cycle came together in the Bush re-election bid, which staffers on both sides of the aisle described as an exceptionally well-conceptualized effort that integrated innovations in digital, data, and analytics with a people-intensive ground effort to an unprecedented extent in electoral politics.

On the digital side, the RNC hired Chuck DeFeo as its eCampaign manager in 2002. This position was set up specifically for the re-election bid and organized within the communications department. With a sitting president, the party could begin planning and building infrastructure for the re-election bid comparatively early in the cycle. DeFeo had been active in Republican Party politics for nearly a decade at the time, including working for Senator John Ashcroft as a technology aide from 1996 to 2000 and serving as a consultant on McCain's bid during his first run for president. DeFeo then followed Ashcroft to the attorney general's office in 2001, where he helped establish the first chief information officer's division at the Justice Department before becoming the eCampaign manager at the RNC.[42] DeFeo would later transition to become the eCampaign manager of Bush-Cheney 2004 in June 2003, a position he held through the president's re-election. This position on the campaign was originally organized in the communications department as well, although as I detail in the following, that changed given the importance of the voter contact operation.[43]

The basic blueprint for the RNC's eCampaign department and key pieces of its infrastructure were in place early on. Bush and his party enjoyed the technical advantage of incumbency. The ability to start planning a re-election bid with party resources two years prior to a presidential election is a significant, and largely new, incumbent advantage given the organizational, time, and field testing requirements for technical development and the importance of building and maintaining a data infrastructure years in advance of a presidential run. As DeFeo put it, "It wasn't just the value of incumbency, it was basically the value of forethought. When you have two years to sit down and work on something and you really plan in an organized manner both from an offline and online perspective it's amazing what you can do."[44]

For example, DeFeo wrote the strategic eCampaign plan for Bush-Cheney 2004 during the summer of 2002 while at the RNC. It was a two-year plan that called for leveraging the energy around the 2002 midterm cycle for the re-election bid and outlined what needed to be in place organizationally and technologically on Election Day in 2004. DeFeo then worked backward from there to specify the timeline necessary to achieve these things. Once DeFeo got the strategic plan approved in 2002, the RNC issued a request for proposals (RFP) and hired a prominent Republican political technology firm, New Media Communications, founded by the consultant Mike Connell, to build GOP.com and GeorgeWBush.com. The party received multiple responses to its RFP, including from a number of commercial firms, but ultimately signed a seven-figure, two-year contract with New Media Communications given its experience in politics. The contract also stipulated that New Media Communications could resell the codebase that the

RNC was paying for to their clients given they were a Republican digital consult-ing firm. Much like Blue State Digital's contract with the DNC four years later, the idea was that the RNC would subsidize the development of a codebase that a num-ber of Republican political campaigns and allied organizations could then take advantage of through the consulting services of New Media Communications.[45]

Throughout the development process, DeFeo communicated daily with Mehlman and personally delivered reports on his progress on a quarterly basis to Rove. These reports to Rove consisted of one- to two-hour-long meetings where DeFeo went over the work of his team, which grew from two people in 2003 to five full-time staff in 2004, with a robust outside developer team of four to five people. The tools New Media Communications was working on with the party during this time (and rolled out for the re-election bid) included a "Walk the Vote" tool, which enabled supporters to register at GeorgeWBush.com, access the online Bush "Volunteer Center," and receive a list of targeted voters geographically close to them and a script to deliver. Volunteer canvassers then used Microsoft Maps to plot these households and recorded the results of canvasses online to send back to the campaign. The Walk the Vote tool, similar in concept to systems on the Obama campaign in 2008, enabled volunteers to more easily contribute to the campaign outside the formal field office program.

The emphasis on tools to support voter contact reflects the broader approach of the eCampaign operation and the campaign more generally. As noted above, DeFeo transitioned to the campaign in June 2003 to serve as the eCampaign man-ager, where his role was to support the work of other departments, especially the political and communications departments. To this end, DeFeo's team included a number of liaisons to other departments who sat in on all of their staff meetings. As DeFeo describes the goals of his department and how his team was evaluated:

> We had political metrics, we had communications metrics, and we had fundraising metrics, but our primary metric was 51% of the vote and so in terms of our obligations to raise money they were not high. Of course we raised money but our primary interface was really with the political division. It was touching voters.... Ken Mehlman had this chart, "the value of a touch point." The pinnacle touch point was a person that the voter knew telling them to vote for George W. Bush and the number of times that conversation had to happen was like two. And then you come down to, of course, email's on there and then that 30 second TV spot and how many times somebody would have to see a 30 second TV spot to potentially be persuaded....[46]

The campaign eventually changed its organizational structure with respect to the eCampaign department to facilitate this work on political operations. Patrick Ruffini, who worked in online communications for the RNC in 2002–2003, was hired as the webmaster and blogger for the re-election bid in June 2003. Unlike contemporary campaigns, where there is much greater specialization, as webmaster Ruffini had a four-part job writing the blog and doing outreach to bloggers while at the same time creating updates and graphics for the homepage and debugging the software tools that the campaign was putting out. Ruffini described the campaign as "experimenting with all of these different ways of engaging and interacting online."[47] Importantly, the emphasis on online organizing was not a separate initiative of the eCampaign team; it was part of the integrated strategy of the campaign more broadly. As Mehlman's chart makes clear, the whole ethos of the Bush 2004 bid was to go further than any campaign had before in terms of on-the-ground organizing, and the eCampaign team was enrolled in that effort. Ruffini related how the eCampaign team was originally organized within the communications department, but staffers realized that even with the orientation toward field and the volunteer tools, this structure was not enabling them to serve the political department and the other departments on the campaign as much as they would have liked in practice. As a result, Ruffini cites that the eCampaign department was reorganized in March 2004 to become its own stand-alone department. Staffers argued that this organizational autonomy provided the department with the opportunity to direct the bulk of its resources toward supporting the political team.

Heading up this new stand-alone department was Michael Turk, a longtime veteran of Republican Party politics. Turk got his start volunteering for the Republican Party of New Mexico in 1994 during the era of Newt Gingrich's "Republican Revolution." Turk drew on his technical and statistics skills and developed a new data-driven system that helped the state party allocate resources toward competitive races. Turk subsequently worked for Dan Quayle's 2000 presidential bid on voter databases and modeling, a position that provided him with the chance to work closely with the data brokerage firm Aristotle, before moving to the national party to work on voter data and the online GOP.com site. Turk subsequently went to Grassroots.com, then a for-profit activism destination site, before becoming the executive director of the party in New Mexico in 2003, which put him in close contact with the Bush re-election bid.[48] Turk said that Bush staffers asked him to come and talk about the Internet and analyze what the campaign was doing on the web at the end of 2003 and the beginning of 2004. According to Turk, the Bush team believed that their site was not doing enough to publicize and facilitate volunteer opportunities such as canvassing, and the fundraising staffers saw a large gap when they compared their efforts with Dean's Internet operation.

After evaluating the Bush site, Turk argued that the operation needed more orientation toward political engagement and recommended that the Internet team become its own department with a senior staff head reporting directly to campaign manager Ken Mehlman, instead of being run out of the communications department. The idea came from Turk's survey of commercial firms, where this structure was commonplace. At the time there was not a defined group of specialized staffers running Internet operations for campaigns. Even more, with some exceptions (such as the 2000 McCain and 2004 Dean campaigns), in 2003–2004 it was uncommon to see the Internet or new media more broadly as a specialized area of campaign practice on the order of fundraising or communications. As such, campaigns tended to use the Internet according to the communication genres and needs of the department that had organizational jurisdiction over the medium, which was often communications (this persisted through the 2014 cycle; staffers connected with the Romney bid in 2012 argued that digital on the campaign was in service to communications). For example, staffers on campaigns at the time cited that communications departments tended to use the Internet to push content out, often in the well-established genre of press releases, instead of capitalizing on the interactive and engagement affordances of the medium.

The re-election bid hired Turk as the eCampaign director, a new position that meant a seat at the senior staff table with access to discussions about the campaign's strategy, messaging, and daily activities (there was another layer of very senior advisors and consultants such as Karl Rove a rung higher up the organizational hierarchy, with direct access to the president). Numerous former staffers argued that this reorganization in spring 2004 resulted in eCampaign staffers being better able to serve multiple departments, especially political, instead of being oriented to communications.

In practice, this meant more extensive engagement in online voter identification and turnout efforts based on the campaign's micro-targeting. The campaign ran its first tests of its micro-targeting models in May and June 2004. This entailed periods of heavy calling and on-the-ground outreach by volunteers and political staff, who then reported back the results to test voter models. This was implemented throughout the swing states (with staffers in the states at times questioning why this had to be done and so early in advance of the election). Staffers argued that the effort proved highly effective. As Rich Beeson described, the 2004 cycle was the first where "you could go in and really start digging down and seeing, you know, where these voters were and what their tendencies were."[49] Michael Turk detailed how in the overall context of the campaign this meant that "[t]he Bush campaign was very driven by—we knew exactly how many people we need to turn out based on these projections, we know exactly where those people are, we are using micro-targeting to figure out exactly who those people are. That sort of data-driven approach was really something that was done very much in 2004."[50]

The campaign's micro-targeting, derived from the party's voter file, oriented the entire campaign, including the eCampaign operations; eCampaign staffers worked with the staffers and consultants doing the campaign's micro-targeting, including those from the Republican consultancy TargetPoint. The eCampaign team developed a number of tools in the attempt to reach priority groups revealed through modeling. Staffers cited that the canvassing program offered through

GeorgeWBush.com targeted voters that the campaign's modeling predicted were 85%–90% likely to be Bush supporters (in other words, the online canvass program was directed toward confirming the vote choices of highly probable Bush supporters). The campaign provided volunteer canvassers joining the re-election effort through the Internet with a yellow PDF with bullet points to print out and read on neighborhood walks or during phone calls. The in-person volunteers coming through the political operation received more extensive training and were tasked with voter registration, persuasion, volunteer acquisition, and turnout depending on the phase of the campaign.

All of this was managed through Voter Vault, which had a complex set of permissions for accessing data built into it that were largely controlled by the national party. DeFeo cites the movie *Glengarry Glen Ross* to illustrate how access to the voter file worked at the time. There were some leads, or voter records, that were really important and others that were less so. The professional political programs run by the RNC and the re-election campaign's political apparatus with its paid staffers and comparatively highly trained volunteers "had access to the real voter file," according to DeFeo.[51] The eCampaign staffers worked with a different universe of comparatively lower priority contacts that they could upload to GeorgeWBush.com (i.e., those likely Bush supporters cited earlier). The role of the Internet in this case was to provide efficiency at the margins. The campaign did not want to spend its scarce professional and trained volunteer resources on voters that were highly likely to vote for Bush and turnout. The online walk and calling tools helped the campaign reach these voters that in the past would have been ignored, purely for efficiency's sake, while providing volunteers coming to the campaign online with positive canvass experiences. Meanwhile, there was a hierarchy of data access, with a state party staffer serving as the data administrator for voter file records in her state. This staffer provided the rights to access the data, primarily on the basis of geography. A field staffer in charge of a particular county, for instance, just had access to data from that county. Later versions of Voter Vault provided staffers with access to more data. More broadly, in 2004 the RNC and the re-election campaign were wary about just letting anybody log in and download the voter file, so Voter Vault was built with tiers of access controlled by the RNC's political department.

Digital media enabled the campaign to design more flexibility into its political program and provide supporters with the opportunity to "personalize" their participation according to their interests and time.[52] The campaign used the Internet to organize voter canvasses outside regular political operations. Campaigns generally organize all their canvasses on set days and times, when they ask their volunteers to convene and contact voters. In contrast, the eCampaign tools expanded the universe of potential volunteers, enabling people to canvass at their own convenience according to their own schedules. The campaign also used the Internet to make targeted voter contacts based not only on the voter modeling information detailed earlier, but also innovatively on the characteristics of the volunteer. The campaign recognized that matching volunteers with targeted voters might make canvasses more persuasive, and therefore sought to match the demographic (such as age and sex) and affinity (occupation, military service, etc.) characteristics of volunteers and voters. The campaign matched volunteers and voters not only through the canvassing of the political operation itself, but also through an online email and letter program that allowed Bush supporters to send messages to voters with similar characteristics in states such as Iowa. The theory was that the letters supporters wrote would discuss issues that resonated with the people receiving them.

All of this added up to a data-driven operation that revolved around voter contacts across many different mediums. Speaking about the campaign's efforts on Election Day, Michael Turk described how the Internet operation complemented what was going on in the field and enabled the campaign to redirect resources to where they were most needed through an online calling tool:

> In 2004, the last 48 hours of the campaign, we knew looking at our data that we were weak in Florida and Ohio—those were the two places that we really needed to focus on. So we pivoted. . . . and actually in the last 48 hours changed the programming in our database and tools so they would more heavily sample the data out of Florida and Ohio. We told them in selecting the data you are going to display for a user of these tools, choose first from Florida and Ohio, don't pick Wisconsin because we knew that that was not as competitive. So you can make decisions like that based on the data that you are seeing.[53]

To support these voter contacts, the party and the campaign devised systems to tie various streams of data together. DeFeo noted that he was able to marshal a number of different vendors to work together in advance of the election given that he worked at the RNC and had an incumbent in office, which provided him with leverage (a dynamic echoed by Obama staffers in 2012). Staffers cited that the Bush campaign had one hosting provider and stored all of its online data in one location. This system offered a way to synch data together, including the voter file and the data that was coming into the campaign online and from Bush-Cheney field offices.

Former staffers at the party and the campaign also noted that the campaign developed an extranet that enabled staffers to more efficiently channel volunteers coming in through the party's and the campaign's web properties into the political effort (which was run by the campaign itself).[54] For example, the Republican Party's massive email acquisition program launched in early 2002 netted over 6 million addresses, which staffers revealed when Bush filed for re-election. This infrastructural effort was prompted by the fact that coming out of the 2000 cycle the Bush-Cheney campaign only had between 200,000 and 300,000 email addresses, and staffers were unsure how many of these were actually current. The campaign sought to move the people on the email list into the volunteer program, up what practitioners call the "ladder of engagement."[55] In addition, anytime someone registered at GeorgeWBush.com, they were automatically geocoded through a postal code, and then their county and precinct information were appended to their supporter record. The new registrant then automatically received an email from GeorgeWBush.com. Meanwhile, if the new registrant lived in a state with an active political operation, the local county coordinators or precinct captains could contact the registrant via an extranet email. As a result of all these efforts, staffers cited that the campaign was able to build a database that contained information on between 1.3 and 1.7 million volunteers. As importantly, the extranet allowed national campaign staffers to monitor the progress of local field offices in contacting potential volunteers. The national, regional, and state leadership could also log in to the extranet and monitor the efforts of local political staffers with respect to different types of voter contacts, including voter registration and volunteer signups. All of this data was color-coded on geographical maps. The colors of these maps changed as progress toward the campaign's political goals took shape, which staffers at all levels of the campaign monitored. This data, in turn, was synched with other data from the political operation.

What is important is that the 2004 Bush campaign integrated its online and offline operations, digital and political, in ways that accorded with the geographic requirements of electoral politics.[56] And Bush's re-election bid was not only the most advanced campaign of the cycle in this regard, it had greater capacity in some respects than Obama's bid four years later. Unlike the Dean campaign, Bush's team believed that it was more important that a new registrant connect with a county coordinator or precinct captain than the national eCampaign team. Meanwhile, the Kerry campaign struggled to bring together its Internet and field operations, and relied on zip-code targeted emails that urged potential volunteers to show up at local field offices. Finally, even the Obama campaign in 2008 did not have the functionality to automatically alert field staffers on the ground to new online volunteer signups and enable them to send an email from a field office (this problem was solved, in part, by the 2012 campaign's Airwolf program).[57]

All that said, the Bush re-election bid was not seamless. The Bush campaign also faced an issue that has plagued campaigns up through the 2014 cycle: data integration. While the extranet provided for some integration, the voter file and interface system that was Voter Vault was still a different platform than the online tools. Practitioners stated that while online data could be pushed into Voter Vault, there were still integration issues with respect to the different streams of data the campaign received and worked with.

In all, however, staffers across the Republican Party network argued that this digital and data infrastructure furthered the campaign's and the party's political efforts to an unprecedented extent. Staffers within the political operations of the campaign, for example, argued that having access to a robust voter file and voter relationship management tool was revelatory. Michael Beach was a 72-hour field coordinator with the Ohio Republican Party/Bush-Cheney campaign during the last three months of the election, and subsequently served as the national victory director of the RNC during the 2008 cycle. Beach describes being able to hit the ground running in the 72-hour program, in contrast to the Bush campaign in 2000, for which he volunteered. Logistically, Voter Vault enabled political staffers to better coordinate their operations on the ground for the thousands of volunteers making tens of thousands of voter contacts. Voter Vault helped political staffers more efficiently target voters, deploy volunteers in geographic space, and shape the targeted messages being delivered on the doorsteps of citizens.

And, contacting voters was the pillar of the Bush operation. Former staffers involved in the political operations of the Bush-Cheney re-election bid stated that the campaign had a rule that organizers were not supposed to be in the office that often. Organizers were expected to travel to multiple cities and attend things such as fish fries, meetings in church basements, and college information days. Indeed, the re-elect's political operations had the hallmarks that journalists and scholars would later come to associate with Obama: an ethos of volunteer engagement and voter contact. This mentality manifested itself through the drive to constantly sign people up to volunteer and the push to recruit team leaders, who would then recruit their neighbors. More broadly, staffers argued that the campaign was defined by the active encouragement and empowerment of citizens to get involved—one of the normative values of partisanship that political theorist Nancy Rosenblum identifies.[58]

Conclusion

At the end of the day, Bush's eCampaign existed on the margins around the far more expansive political and communications operations. As DeFeo summarized, "in the grand scheme of things it wasn't a huge program but it was useful. It was closing some gaps."[59] Unlike the Dean campaign, which was built around online mobilization that stood almost entirely independently from what was taking place on the ground, the Bush re-election team stressed on-the-ground political operations in key states and used the eCampaign to complement these efforts. The campaign used the Internet to supplement work in the field, pulling volunteers into the campaign and letting those who preferred low-cost or personalized engagement, as well as volunteers in states not electorally important, to make phone calls to comparatively lower-value targets. The Bush team leveraged the eCampaign in the service of a broader electoral strategy, of which it was only one, but not insignificant, component. Meanwhile, through the efforts of the RNC from 2000 to 2004, the Bush re-election bid had access to the most extensive voter data, micro-targeting, models, and database and interface systems then in politics, which provided the orientation for the entire campaign and underpinned the political operation.

The end result of all these efforts around technology, digital media, data, and analytics was a Bush re-election campaign that far outpaced the John Kerry campaign and the Democratic Party, as well as its extended network of Super PACs, including America Coming Together.[60] The RNC's competitive advantage during the cycle had a number of dimensions. From a technological perspective, the Bush team had a far more extensive set of online organizing tools, access to more expertise within the party network, a more robust national and accessible voter database that was available up- and down-ballot, and a data infrastructure that achieved at least limited integration across the multiple platforms and databases used by the campaign, compared with their Democratic rivals. From an organizational perspective, what is clear is that the Bush team thought deeply about how technology, digital media, data, and analytics could further the electoral strategy of the campaign, and built the sociotechnical systems to facilitate the "personalized political communication" on the doorsteps and phones of voters that Rasmus Nielsen describes.[61]

All of these things were the result of work between election cycles, and the learning that occurred by looking at Bush's rivals during the 2000 and 2004 cycles. The success of the re-election bid is all the more remarkable given where things in the party stood in 2000. As Michael Beach, echoing other staffers cited above, described: "Until then every campaign that I worked on did not have an active field component on Election Day. Election Day was time to pick up a suit for the election night party and go see a movie. That all started to change in 2002 and 2004 was a complete mind shift."[62]

The question of the next three chapters is, what happened after 2004 so that the parties' respective presidential candidates were in reverse positions during the 2012 cycle, with the Democrats enjoying all of the comparative advantages in technology, digital media, data, and analytics that Bush had in 2004? As I turn to in the next chapter, the institutional dynamics within the Republican Party after the re-election bid are central to explaining the differences between the presidential campaigns on display during the 2012 election cycle.

3

Republican Party Inertia in a Changed Political Context

In July 2007, John McCain's second bid for the presidency was on the verge of collapse. Despite starting out with a top tier candidate in a crowded field that included prominent Republicans such as former New York City mayor Rudolf Giuliani and governors Mitt Romney and Mike Huckabee, the McCain campaign found itself trailing in the polls for much of the year, and fundraising slowed to a trickle. McCain's bipartisan leadership on immigration reform did not play well with the conservative Republican primary electorate that viewed the candidate warily, especially given his history of making skeptical comments about social conservatives. With much infighting on the campaign and tight resources, a number of McCain's top staffers left and the campaign downsized significantly, even as many went without pay.[1] Things got so bad that the McCain campaign released a seven-page memo for supporters in July 2007 called "Road to Victory 2008" with a section entitled "Living off the Land: A Plan for Financial Viability."[2] The memo detailed how the candidate could still win by taking advantage of free media opportunities, raising small-dollar donations, and running a lean organization.

Despite a new need to "live off the land," a number of journalism outlets noted the candidate's comparatively large payouts earlier in 2007 to a new technology-oriented political consulting firm called 3eDC.[3] It was a superstar group of sorts, founded by the longtime Republican technology consultant Mike Connell, McCain campaign manager Rick Davis, and Becki Donatelli, founder of Campaign Solutions and consultant on the McCain 2000 campaign.[4] The price tag was as hefty as the experience of these consultants. The *Wall Street Journal* estimated that the campaign sent close to 10% of its second quarter individual donor fundraising to firms with ties to Davis, including approximately $1 million to 3eDC and its subcontractors for technology services.[5] Meanwhile, despite these resources, individuals with knowledge of 3eDC stated that the venture did not end well. There were too many voices in the design of the platform it was developing for the McCain campaign, and the rough financial time for the candidate simply compounded issues. While the group built a number of tools for the campaign, when it imploded during the summer due to the candidate's lack of money and a subsequent lack of staff, a lot of them did not deploy or were delayed until the general election. Meanwhile, according to a number of former party staffers, across the board the campaign was under-organized.

McCain's fortunes turned around after the candidate's New Hampshire victory, of course, but the comparative differences between the two parties' eventual nominees and the infrastructures they were drawing on early in the cycle were readily apparent. While Obama also faced an extended primary, the campaign relied on a robust toolset developed and field-tested between presidential elections by Blue State Digital (BSD) through significant investments from the Democratic Party. This platform, alongside the Democratic Party's database and interface system VoteBuilder, were key pieces of infrastructure behind the campaign's extensive and lauded small-dollar online fundraising and ground effort.[6] For example, when My.BarackObama.com launched in February 2007, thousands of groups around the country formed to support Obama's fledgling candidacy and begin fundraising and organizing for the campaign.

What happened between elections so that the Obama campaign had access to a robust infrastructure of technology, digital media, data, and analytics resources, while the McCain team was embarking on extensive new development in the middle of an election cycle? As I documented in *Taking Our Country Back*, the 2004 cycle kicked off an extraordinarily innovative period on the Democratic side of the aisle. It was the Democratic expectation of victory in 2004 that led to a shift in thinking about how campaigns *should* be run when Kerry lost. As a result of party actors seeking out a new direction, there was an explosion of market opportunities for those practitioners and consultancies that could legitimately claim to have a grasp on the future. And, Democrats increasingly saw this future being defined in terms of technology, digital media, data, and analytics. Democratic Party actors looked to the Dean campaign as a prototype of a new approach to digital campaigning and grassroots participation more broadly, while seeing the Bush re-election bid as a data-driven, ground-intensive effort that outperformed the Kerry campaign and its allies in the wake of their multiple technological and data failures during the cycle. The extended Democratic Party network subsequently collectively invested millions of dollars in the digital platforms, data infrastructures, political consultancies, and organizations to produce expertise and trained staffers that still continue to provide the foundation for the party's campaigns.

On the Republican side of the aisle, there was comparative inertia in terms of technological development after 2004. This inertia was caused by many different institutional factors that I document here, but more broadly politics is composed of fragile infrastructures. As a number of scholars have argued, all infrastructures require maintenance, care, and repair.[7] That said, the technical artifacts, knowledge, practices, skills, and many of the organizations that constitute the infrastructure for politics are especially fragile. Campaigns are highly temporal organizations that have to scale rapidly in the face of often uncertain resource flows. They are quickly assembled, often involve people from many different fields and with limited work experience, and have to draw and fit together many different resources from more enduring organizations such as parties and consultancies. Meanwhile, people walk away from campaigns the day after the vote, and while parties have longevity, they struggle to retain technical talent and maintain technologies after elections. Technical development within parties is often subject to the waxing and waning of resource flows, the competing demands of many different stakeholders, and the decision-making of party chairs. Finally, many consultancies face the same ebb of resources in off-election years, and apart from the investments of comparatively well-resourced presidential campaigns and parties, there are seldom the large institutional clients that will make significant improvements to existing infrastructure, especially, practitioners argued, on the Republican side of the aisle.

In this context, the organizations and people tasked with building, maintaining, and improving the infrastructural components of party networks are highly consequential. Actors in extended party networks such as political consultancies and software as a service firms struggle to build, maintain, and institutionalize technologies, knowledge, practice, and skills after elections and in the face of their own variable resource flows, while also remaining innovative to respond to and help shape shifts in media and culture. The Democratic Party's comparative success over the past decade in the areas of technology, digital media, data, and analytics was due to its hybrid party network ecosystem developed after the 2004 election cycle, which is considerably larger than that of the extended Republican Party network. This ecosystem is made up of many different types of organizations and held together by a shared partisan identity and culture of collaboration. It is anchored by a party apparatus that literally *is* a database for many organizations, which serves as a binding agent for the cognitively, culturally, and financially diverse and hybrid network around it. This network is cognitively diverse because it consists of organizations that house staffers who have many different sets of skills and knowledge, from analytics to digital communications expertise, and culturally diverse given the broad range of causes, interests, and identities represented within the Democratic Party.[8] And the network is financially diverse in that there are many different revenue models for the organizations and firms in the extended Democratic Party network.

While political technologies are fragile and often break down and even disappear, the Democratic Party's hybrid network ecosystem developed in part through the extraordinary and continual launch of new organizations after presidential elections, helped institutionalize the innovations of its campaigns, kept expertise in the field and produced new staffers with specialized knowledge and skills, and engaged in the maintenance, care, and further development of the extended party's technical infrastructure. In contrast, the Republican Party failed to develop a diversified network ecosystem post 2004. After Bush's re-election there was an attempt to institutionalize the innovations of the campaign within the party, a structure that ultimately provided less stability, flexibility, and resources when compared with the Democratic Party's robust, hybrid network ecosystem of party-provided infrastructure, new commercial consultancies, and aligned organizations. In the end, the Republican advantage during the Bush re-election campaign proved fleeting without a robust network of actors to maintain and further develop the extended party's fragile infrastructure. As Michael Turk, who after the Bush re-election campaign went on to become the eCampaign director of the RNC, described, "I saw what I was doing within the RNC as continuing to build the platform, not as a commercial entity, but within the RNC. And, knowing what I know now, I don't think that was ever necessarily going to work because the minute that you change people in the chairman role suddenly you are going to have a whole different set of agendas."[9]

The housing of many of the Bush team's innovations and staffers within the party meant that technological development was subject to the formal apparatus of the party, the decisions of particular party chairmen, and the changeling nature of the party's financial fortunes. The Democrats faced a similar situation after the 2012 re-election bid, when many of the technologies the Obama campaign built ended up within a party organization with little in the way of resources to maintain them. That said, a key difference is that the Republican Party network also had lower rates of new organizational development post-2004 compared to the Democrats, in part because key members of Bush's re-election team went to the party or left electoral politics altogether soon after the campaign. This left a set of entrenched incumbents with established relationships with the party in place, and relatively few vehicles to institutionalize the innovations of the Bush campaign and carry them across election cycles and down-ballot.

In sum, this chapter argues that the fragility of technologies within the Republican Party after 2004 and the small size and less diverse structure of its party network in terms of being dominated by a few incumbent firms, coupled with the resource gaps between the two presidential candidates in 2008, are key to understanding the different fortunes of the two parties with respect to technology, digital media, data, and analytics up through the 2012 cycle.

The Republican Party after 2004

After Bush's re-election, former party staffers argued that Voter Vault underwent a series of changes. Steve Ellis, who had been running the voter file program at the RNC, left, and former party staffers stated that there were a number of debates within the party about how to best manage the data that comprised the voter file and other databases the re-election campaign used. Former Bush eCampaign staffers hoped that the party would achieve data integration by building one integrated platform for Voter Vault, the field tools, and web properties. As detailed in the previous chapter, there was limited integration of the campaign and the party's systems in 2004. The Bush eCampaign team could move data between various platforms, but they were not fully integrated.

Former party staffers stated that the model of Voter Vault changed in 2005. Succeeding Ellis was Chad Barth, who was actively involved in the management of Voter Vault at the application layer. Adrian Grey was in charge of the department of strategy. Bill Steiner oversaw the voter file itself at the data layer. According to former staffers close to the effort, the party began the process of rebuilding Voter Vault, moving it to something PHP (Hypertext Preprocessor) based in an attempt to enable an open community of developers to take root around the party's data.

Former party staffers argued that the rebuild with the firm responsible for maintaining Voter Vault did not go as expected. In part as a result, the Republican political consultancy FLS Connect, founded in 1999, won a contract to maintain and further develop the database and interface system that was Voter Vault at this time (the data continued to be owned by the RNC). FLS was also responsible for hygiene (cleaning the data) and appending additional commercial data to the voter file. The two entities also had a working agreement in which the RNC and its political canvass operations could access all the commercial data in return for FLS using the political data for commercial purposes. In other words, the RNC owned the voter file, while FLS maintained and supplemented the database and provided the platforms to make it accessible to campaigns (through Voter Vault and later the GOP Data Center). As Rich Beeson, a partner at FLS Connect, political director at the RNC in 2008, and Romney's political director in 2012, described:

> They don't sell the data to us. If we are doing work for the committee or we are doing work for a campaign, everybody has access to the files, at least to some base file. And so let's say we are going to go in and do ID work for a candidate—the RNC provides: "here are the voters, here are the registered Republicans, Independents, Democrats." If it's a party registration state we just run it through NCOA [National Change of Address] and we do a phone match and so it's got the latest, the best addresses and the best phone numbers that they can come up with. And then you go in and you do the ID work and the candidate gets to keep the ID work.[10]

The FLS–Republican Party model was similar to that of VAN and the Democratic Party in terms of parties' owning their data, although the Democratic Party coordinates the process for maintaining its data (as detailed in Chapter 5) and the party owns the ID work of campaigns which automatically goes back into the voter file for subsequent candidates to draw on (as detailed in Chapters 5 and 6).

While the Republican Party was crafting a new relationship with FLS Connect around Voter Vault, it also sought to institutionalize much of the Bush eCampaign operation within the party. Soon after the election, the former eCampaign director of the Bush-Cheney re-election bid, Michael Turk, went over to the RNC to take on the same role. It was Turk's expectation that a lot of the best aspects of the campaign would be incorporated within the party, from the organizational work integrating online and political operations to the online platform built by New Media Communications for the campaign. The eCampaign department was not new, and its evolution captures its growing importance within the party. Former party staffers stated that the department was originally launched in the 1990s with one staffer, it grew to two people in the early 2000s, and then after the re-election bid in 2004 the party hired at various points between six and ten people, even more if the staffers running the data back-end are included. Also revealing is the fact that Turk was made a director equal to the other directors, with his own budget and ability to work with (not for) the communications director. The party's new chairman, Ken Mehlman, organized the department based on how it worked in its last incarnation during the Bush re-election campaign.

Turk's primary goal was to bring the technological infrastructure the Bush campaign used to the state parties, including a number of the online field tools that had limited integration with the voter file through Voter Vault. This emphasis grew out of Turk's previous work experience at the New Mexico state party prior to joining the Bush re-election bid. In addition, Mehlman and Turk had a number of conversations about wanting to fashion the RNC's website into an online gathering space for the right of center, in part to convene the distributed independent discourse on sites such as HotAir and Townhall.com (owned by Salem Communications, which Chuck DeFeo decamped to after the election) as well as across the significant network of conservative blogs.

After about a year into these various projects, Turk stepped down, "just burned out having bureaucratic arguments with people."[11] A number of former party staffers who worked in digital cited being frustrated by bureaucratic wrangling over things such as having open commenting on the party's blog, which Turk implemented. Turk stated that the open commenting system began to cause issues as party staffers grew concerned that there was not enough moderation and comments were off the GOP's message in ways the media might pick up on. More broadly, Turk argued that even though he had a senior staff position, the Internet was still not taken seriously when he arrived at the party, and he was not part of the core elite driving decision-making. Indeed, a number of former Republican Party staffers echoed Turk and stated that, across the extended party network, practitioners were still not convinced the Internet was important through much of 2005.[12] It was only in 2006, when journalists and political practitioners widely discussed how the "macaca" video helped unseat Virginia senator George Allen, and video of napping Montana senator Conrad Burns at a federal hearing led to his loss, that perceptions began to change inside the party and across its network (again, quite apart from the empirical reality of whether the Internet caused these candidates' downfalls). As Turk put it, "you know when people started to lose because of the Internet it became much harder to make the argument that nobody had won because of the Internet."[13]

Even with his short tenure at the party, Turk and his team were able to replace all of the content pieces of the RNC's website and implement a more robust content management system that featured an interactive blog and tools that enabled people to share their thoughts about the president's legislative priorities and interact with one another. Turk noted that the one thing they had not finished was the "action center tools," the applications that supported political canvassing. After Turk left, Patrick Ruffini, the former webmaster for Bush-Cheney 2004, left the Energy Department, where he was handling digital operations, and headed back to the RNC to take over the eCampaign department. Ruffini echoed many of the comments made by Turk, stating that the challenges he faced at the party were similar to those of any large political organization, especially the approval process for getting things done. Ruffini also cited working on the party's blogs, and facing the same challenge of how the organization could control its message. Joining Ruffini in 2005 was Matt Lira, a field organizer for the Bush-Cheney re-election campaign, who later went on to work in a number of digital roles for prominent Republican congressmen and served as the digital director for vice presidential nominee Paul Ryan in 2012. Lira turned down a traditional press secretary job because he believed digital was the future, and faced a telling response from many of his colleagues: "at the time I got phone calls from people that were like 'you are throwing your career away, what are you doing, you are stupid.'"[14]

During this period, the eCampaign department worked on a number of projects, including re-engineering the action center tools from 2004 because much of the back-end technology had changed. These included a phone from home tool, canvassing applications, and letters to the editor and absentee ballot registration applications, all of which were tied into a central database. To supplement these tools, staffers also developed flash video players (programmed by the RNC) that had replay buttons and featured content with calls to action. For the eCampaign team, these tools reflected a basic approach of, in Lira's words, "viewing it [the RNC's web platform] as an action center, almost more so than an information source."[15] This reflects the basic realization of practitioners that the individuals engaging with the party through the Internet were already committed supporters, not undecided individuals seeking out more information.[16]

Many of these tools were built in-house by Ruffini and Lira, a process that could take weeks. The party built others in coordination with two or three development firms that the RNC had relationships with and freelancers that the Bush team used in 2004. Still others were modified from what the re-election campaign used. One of the new things the RNC built during this period was a newsfeed that pushed content out to bloggers through an automatically updated widget, essentially providing the party with free ad space on conservative blogs. Lira cites that the RNC had most of the major Republican-aligned bloggers on board with using the widget on their sites.

During the 2006 midterm elections, the eCampaign department was responsible for using these online tools, as well as email, to organize and raise money. In terms of the latter, the RNC used optimization techniques, such as testing the color of donation buttons, to increase contribution rates. More broadly, former staffers argued that there was a data-driven culture in the eCampaign department that ended up producing significant additional revenue for the party around the midterm cycle. In addition to the organizing and fundraising work, the eCampaign team sought to amplify the president's political voice online. This included making sure the president's speeches were available on the Internet and emails were sent out with updates from the administration. While the GOP suffered significant electoral losses during the midterm cycle, according to the accounts of staffers on both sides of the aisle the online work of the RNC was generally on par with Democratic efforts during this time.

There was significant turnover in the party after the midterm elections. A number of former staffers argued that this undermined the continuity of efforts around digital, technology, and data. More broadly, this turnover reveals the challenges of engaging in developmental projects at parties and the fragile nature of political infrastructures more generally. After the midterm cycle, Mehlman stepped down and Mike Duncan took over as chair of the party. Ruffini left to found Engage, a new digital consulting agency, in 2007 with Mindy Finn, a fellow Bush-Cheney veteran and former eCampaign deputy director at the party who was then working for Mitt Romney's fledgling presidential campaign. Chuck DeFeo recruited Cyrus Krohn, the director of content production and election strategy for Yahoo! News & Information, in early 2007 to replace Ruffini. Krohn formally started at the party as the director of the eCampaign department in July 2007. At Yahoo!, Krohn had worked with a number of the campaigns of the 2006 cycle, including Hillary Clinton's, to help them translate candidate interactions on the crowd-sourcing platform Yahoo! Answers into a database of supporters that could be leveraged for political engagement. Krohn also worked with Mitt Romney's primary campaign in early 2007 on a "create your own ad" campaign using Yahoo!'s Jumpcut, an online video-editing platform.[17]

Krohn stated that his first priority was to better enable "data to flow freely both ways through the voter file," particularly Internet data, an aspiration that echoed that of many of his predecessors.[18] Krohn sought to enable vendors to contribute information from digital sources to the voter file, which they could then subsequently extract. Krohn was new to working in politics, having only previously served as an intern to Vice President Dan Quayle, but from a publisher's perspective his idea was standard for commercial ventures. As Krohn put it, the goal was to "take all of the activity that occurs on the website and feed that into the database to append and enhance the file."[19]

To do so, Krohn cited having to figure out a way to get read/write capacity designed into Voter Vault. Krohn estimated that he spent between 20%–25% of his time speaking with Bill Steiner, the Republican Party staffer behind much of the creation and maintenance of the RNC's voter file at the time, who also oversaw many of the micro-targeting efforts of the party.[20] Steiner was in charge of what the RNC calls its strategy department, whose staffers are tasked with maintaining the voter files and architecting the database. While Krohn argued that Steiner was on board with the general vision, one challenge to this effort was a phenomenon that staffers at all levels of the party apparatus during this period described: a set of existing contracts between the party and established, incumbent vendors. As Krohn described:

> I moved to DC, I get started, and there were a couple of things that I recognized real fast. One was that there were existing vendors entrenched inside the party that I was going to have to work with irrespective of the things that I wanted to make.... Basically I had to come in and spend the credits [to existing vendors] before I could go and begin to procure and use new dollars.... So I found out fairly quickly that I wasn't going to be able to create the API [application programming interface] layer to talk to the voter files and that effectively put my prime objective on hold.[21]

In addition, there was a timing issue with respect to opening up access to the voter file through an API (in essence, application programming interfaces are "sets of requirements that govern how one application can talk to another").[22] The party hired Krohn in the middle of the ramp-up to a presidential cycle, and the voter file was in the process of being cleaned and enhanced by the strategy department. Staffers on both sides of the aisle stated that technological development around the voter file is more likely to happen in off or midterm years, when systems can go through a long developmental phase. Strategy was focused on cleaning and maintaining the records, not the interoperability between Internet data and the voter file.

With the vendor credits Krohn did have access to, he worked to redesign the website, content management system, and state party programs. Krohn worked to build out a back-end content management system that helped the state parties expand their online presence. Krohn worked with Mike Connell on the system, which featured templates, graphics, and blogs, as well as a social media layer integrated with the state and national parties' Facebook pages, in addition to other social media accounts. In the end, Krohn stated that he signed up approximately 43 state parties on this CMS, yet the platform was under-utilized, with only several thousand party supporters creating accounts.[23] One challenge was that the older volunteer base at the state level was not technically proficient enough to use the CMS, and this was compounded by a limited marketing budget. In addition, the RNC's system still lacked integration with the national voter file, which meant that what was going on at the state party level in terms of interactions with local members on the Internet was not feeding into the national voter file.

Krohn also worked on building out a cookie pool of the electorate. This was an early attempt (for the political field) at matching the identities of voters to their IP addresses so the party could deliver targeted advertising. While the voter file was off limits to modify, staffers could work with it from a static perspective. What resulted was a system where the party's voter files were overlaid with the registered user IP address databases of publishers such as MSN, AOL, and Yahoo! Following commercial best practices to de-identify data on who was being served with ads and their responses to them, a third-party aggregator appended anonymous cookies (bits of data stored in browsers or on computers that communicate with websites) to the web browsers at the IP addresses of targets. Krohn stated that this resulted in the identification of over 30 million Republicans nationwide to whom the party was able to serve cookie-based advertising.[24]

Heading into the presidential race, the party tested this cookie pool during Bobby Jindal's race for governor of Louisiana. According to former party staffers, Mike Duncan invested in the digital and technology efforts of the party, and identified Jindal's campaign as an opportunity to test targeted online advertising around early voting efforts, with the hope that it could then be expanded nationally for the general election in 2008. The race posed a particularly interesting challenge. Election Day was the same day as the LSU-Auburn college football game, which had important implications for the Southeastern Conference (SEC) championship, and there were concerns that given the sporting culture of the state, there would be low turnout. To promote early voting, the party delivered online advertising to the targeted IP addresses of users identified as Republican and engaged in A/B testing to improve response rates. The ads were the colors of the teams and featured content such as "Are you going tailgating? Don't forget to vote" and "Who wants to vote on game day? Register for early voting." The several thousand people who clicked on the ad saw a PDF that they could populate with their voter registration information. The party logged all this information in a database, and the field team in Louisiana then followed up to make sure these forms were mailed in. After the election, the party evaluated the success of this advertising by going to the secretary of state's office to look at turnout. Staffers involved with this effort stated that 76% of those who clicked on the banner ad and filled out the form actually voted.

Despite this success, Krohn argued that there was a lack of resources to implement this program more widely during the 2008 presidential cycle. Krohn said his team wrote up a report on the cookie advertising program and presented it to Mike Duncan and Karl Rove, both of whom endorsed it. During the months of March and April 2008, after McCain emerged as the presumptive nominee, Krohn's team at the party put together a multimillion-dollar proposal to leverage this cookie pool as part of the campaign's digital outreach efforts (the campaign was in charge of directing most of the party's expenditures on the presidential race). Duncan and Krohn went to McCain headquarters and sat down with Rick Davis, McCain's campaign manager, to present the Jindal pilot study, a proposed budget, and an overall proposed strategy for digital. Duncan and Krohn left without a decision that day, and two days later Krohn said they were told the campaign was not going to fund the project, with the monies of the comparatively cash-strapped bid being devoted to television and direct mail.

The Democratic and Republican Party Networks Between 2004 and 2008

The two parties' extended networks took different paths during and after the 2004 cycle, which have shaped their respective histories in the decade since. It was during this time that the Democratic Party developed a hybrid network ecosystem with a diverse array of consulting and technology firms and knowledge-producing and training organizations oriented around the party's reconfigured core data infrastructure. By contrast, within the Republican Party's network there was considerably less firm and organizational founding, even as its core data infrastructure went through a period of comparative stasis.

As detailed earlier, during the 2004 cycle there was an extraordinary flowering of innovative technologies and practices on the Dean and Clark campaigns. After the election, the former staffers of these bids had a hand in launching 18 organizations and firms that institutionalized and extended these technologies and practices and carried them to other sites in Democratic politics, building on their experiences during the cycle. Meanwhile, seven Kerry staffers had a hand in launching six new ventures after the campaign. Taken together, Democrats founded 23 discrete new ventures after the 2004 cycle. In addition to Blue State Digital, a number of other prominent consultancies emerged after the cycle, including Trilogy Interactive and Blackrock Associates. Meanwhile, the New Organizing Institute, founded by veterans of Dean and Kerry's runs, helped create both a culture of and forums for collaborative practice and knowledge sharing around technology, digital media, data, and analytics for progressives (such as RootsCamp), while training hundreds of staffers in these areas who moved across campaigns and party-allied organizations.

These efforts were only the tip of the iceberg. Dean created the core data infrastructure of the party in the years after the election, including commissioning Voter Activation Network to build the voter database and interface platform, VoteBuilder, that standardized the data and field tools used by Democratic campaigns at every level of office. New funding groups such as the Democracy Alliance emerged during this time period and funded a range of party network ventures, such as the data firm Catalist and the America Votes coalition, made of groups such as the AFL-CIO, Service Employees International Union (SEIU), and Planned Parenthood Federation of America, which among other things coordinates field campaigns for progressive causes in states using VAN field tools. Meanwhile, a number of unions and progressive organizations in the party network founded the Analyst Institute in 2007, a hybrid of a think tank and consulting firm dedicated to bringing social science methods to Democratic campaigns and progressive causes.[25] The infrastructural site ActBlue grew to prominence during the 2004 cycle and has subsequently directed hundreds of millions of small-dollar donations to Democratic campaigns and causes.

These efforts reveal how after 2004 a hybrid network of Democratic Party organizations was collaboratively investing in and building data and technology infrastructure to the extent it was legally permissible.[26] A key motivation for party network actors that drove this work was to ensure that there was a standardized set of tools (provided through VAN) and better data (provided by the party for campaigns and Catalist for allied organizations) for staffers that frequently moved between 501c4s, unions, and campaigns. This hybrid network ecosystem both produced and supported young political operatives through employment opportunities and training. Ironically enough, when it came to technology, digital media, data, and analytics, the old adage about the Democratic Party being a "collection of interest groups" worked to the party's advantage in terms of providing employment and training opportunities for staffers in off-election years, as well as supporting the collective invention of new tools and organizing practices for electoral politics.[27]

Within the Republican Party network, in contrast, there were fewer staffers hired in technology, digital media, data, and analytics during the 2004 cycle and fewer new organizations founded after it. Consequently, there was less innovation between the 2004 and 2008 presidential election cycles on the Republican side of the aisle. On one level, the party did not produce the same number of technology, digital media, data, and analytics staffers during the cycle as the Democrats in part because Bush was a sitting president who did not face a primary challenge. Democratic primary campaigns and Kerry's general election campaign hired 67 staffers in technology, digital media, data, and analytics, compared with six staffers in these areas who worked on the Bush bid. As one former campaign staffer argued, "there was only one game in town in 2004 and it was us [Bush-Cheney]. If you were not a part of our team you really didn't get to work at a level that would give you good experience."[28] This not only meant fewer staffers who had presidential experience in technology, digital media, data, and analytics, it also meant fewer new firms and ventures after Bush was re-elected.

Even then, those individuals who did work in technology, digital media, data, and analytics for the Bush bid subsequently went to work for the party or left politics altogether. Ruffini, for instance, attributed the failure to institutionalize many of the innovations of the Bush re-election campaign to the fact that former staffers did not launch firms and organizations that could house the Bush tools, which would "have been a sort of a vessel for these things to be carried from election cycle to election cycle."[29] Indeed, the Bush campaign produced only two firms in the data set, both of which were founded well after the election cycle (three other Bush 2004 veterans founded firms after working for later presidential bids). Ruffini launched Engage with Mindy Finn in 2007 after a stint at the party.[30] Zac Moffatt, who played a comparatively minor role in 2004, co-founded Targeted Victory in 2009. Meanwhile. As a consequence of this comparative lack of organizational founding and diversity, there were more entrenched incumbent firms on the Republican side of the aisle. As Brent McGoldrick, who after his work with RNC Victory during the 2004 cycle went into commercial consulting, argued, there was a difference in the two parties' approaches to consultancies during the time period covered in this book:

> Republicans for the most part keep their businesses. They almost never sell them . . . a lot of these consultants are entrepreneurs, they want to work their businesses, they are 10–15 person shops, they have been around the block for 20 years, they are very competitive with each other, they are entrenched and I don't see that on the left. They may sell to bigger companies but there isn't this ecosystem of 10–15 [people] Democratic firms. I mean they are out there but they don't drive and influence the party the way that they do on the right.[31]

In contrast to the profusion of new Democratic organizations, there were essentially two dominant Republican firms in the technology space after 2004, New Media Communications and Campaign Solutions. These firms merged in 2005 as Connell Donatelli, Inc.[32] Mike Connell was the founder and head of New Media Communications, the firm that built the Bush 2000 and 2004 sites, and he worked on various projects for the RNC in 2006.[33] Becki Donatelli was the founder and CEO of Campaign Solutions, a prominent Republican consultancy founded in 1998. Donatelli served as president of the merged Connell Donatelli. Meanwhile, Chuck DeFeo became the head of a reconstituted Campaign Solutions and Connell Donatelli after the 2008 cycle after Mike Connell was killed in a plane crash. Republican Party staffers stated that these firms, along with Max Fose's IWS, founded after the 2000 cycle, were the only organizations at the time that had programmers on staff and could actually build out technology infrastructure for a campaign.

At the same time, as the victors during the 2004 cycle, few in the extended party network perceived the need to invest in the areas of technology, digital media, data, and analytics to keep pace with what the Democrats were doing at the time. After all, Dean's digitally innovative effort was an electoral failure, which meant that few Republicans saw it as a prototype, and the party's micro-targeting and ground efforts during the cycle far outstripped what the Democrats were able to put together. As a result, a number of staffers formerly involved in Republican Party politics during this time period argued that the existing vendors to the party rested on their laurels. Chuck DeFeo, for instance, argued that there was a general shift away from an "innovation mindset" within the party network that, in turn, led to the party and its vendors ceasing to invest in its technology to the same extent as during Bush's first term.[34] Meanwhile, a highly unfavorable political environment, especially post-2006, sapped a lot of energy and resources from the Republican Party, which meant fewer investments in technology, digital, data, and analytics and fewer market opportunities for staffers. As a result, quite apart from any new investments, what did exist within the party network was not maintained.

For example, as detailed earlier, GeorgeWBush.com was built by New Media Communications. The RNC-funded codebase during the 2004 cycle was the most sophisticated platform that existed at the time in politics. The challenge, however, is that once you do not continue to invest in technology it gets old very fast, and DeFeo argued that there were not significant investments in technology after 2004. At the same time, echoing Krohn's account detailed earlier, a number of former staffers stated that Voter Vault was essentially the same in 2008 as it was in 2004. While there were some new efficiencies in the platform, and field offices found the interface easier to use, its core functionality was generally the same. Indeed, capturing even broader failures to invest, in an interview in January 2013 Ruffini stated, "I will say that it is probably accurate that in terms of the Voter Vault that I saw in 2006 it was probably roughly the same version as it is today" (as detailed earlier, Voter Vault was relaunched and rebranded as the GOP Data Center in advance of the 2012 cycle).

The collaborative work of the Democratic Party network in the domains of technology, digital media, data, and analytics during this time period takes on added importance in a contemporary environment marked by rapid technological change. Again, as political scientist Dave Karpf has pointed out, the application layer of the Internet has featured continual innovations and inventions in its comparatively short history that have outstripped the pace of development of other mediums. YouTube, for instance, did not exist during the 2004 cycle, but it was during the years between presidential election cycles that a new generation of Democratic digital staffers pioneered its use as an electoral and advocacy tool before the Obama team leveraged it to great effect in 2008.[35] Meanwhile, database technologies were growing more sophisticated, as were best practices around design and usability, which the Democratic Party took advantage of in VAN's

VoteBuilder. These technologies and practices, as well as many new ones, are now central to electoral politics. And, in this environment, the Democratic Party's extended network was able to grasp significant competitive advantage in continually producing the staffers and organizations specializing in the new knowledge and skills that provide the backdrop for contemporary electoral practice.[36]

The 2008 McCain Campaign

This was the context in which the 2008 cycle took shape. In terms of the party's eventual nominee, McCain's bid was rocky from almost the start, even though he was a top tier candidate. The candidate's second quest for the party's nomination began taking shape in 2006. Connell, Donatelli, and Nicco Mele, a Dean campaign veteran and cofounder of the Democratic consultancy EchoDitto who worked with McCain in the 1990s around campaign finance reform while at Common Cause, began talking about the senator's bid in early 2006 (after an outcry among Democrats, Mele left the group in the fall of that year).[37] Max Fose was also involved in discussions about McCain's campaign during the latter part of 2006 and worked with this group through May 2008. The group debated what was going to be the next big thing in terms of the Internet and how they could leverage it for the ends of the campaign, the McCain brand and the color of the logo, and what the website was going to look like, the features it would have, and how prominently it would be featured. The group ended up settling on a site that was going to be video heavy, given that these practitioners anticipated it was going to be the first "YouTube election" and the candidate would have to deliver his message through video.

Fose argued that the group clearly believed the Internet was going to be the centerpiece of the campaign during this initial planning that extended into the early part of 2007, but with some key differences from McCain's earlier run. Contrasting his experiences during the 2000 and 2008 cycles, Fose argued that running as the insurgent candidate made the 2000 campaign cheaper and more experimental when it came to developing and deploying new technologies. By contrast, Fose described how in 2008 the environment was much more of a "let's sit down and plan this out and pull all the pieces together and figure out how we are going to leverage this great tool. It was definitely a planned execution of what was going to happen."[38]

The group decided to build much of the McCain campaign's platform from scratch under the auspices of 3eDC. Individuals involved with the party and on competing campaigns during the cycle, but without financial interests in campaign technology, argued that not having a ready-to-go and field-tested platform was an issue that plagued the McCain campaign throughout 2007, particularly given the waxing and waning of the candidate's fortunes during the primaries.

One former party staffer noted that part of the decision to build McCain's platform from scratch was because the New Media Communications and Campaign Solutions platforms were "not built in a way to be easily portable. . . . We [the Republican Party] needed to do something that was a little more permanent and a little bit more continually developed as opposed to what typically happens, which is a candidate develops a website, they use it for you know 8–10 months or a year and a half and then it goes away."[39] For example, numerous former campaign staffers active during the cycle argued that, in the context of what was on offer from the merged New Media Communications and Campaign Solutions, there was no existing platform that could change exterior designs but keep the same functionality. As one former campaign staffer put it, "the RNC has a lot of different vendors who have a lot of different platforms but I don't think that anybody has really, you know, sort of developed an ongoing platform, at that point certainly."[40]

These staffers are describing Blue State Digital's approach of providing a ready-to-roll out platform for campaigns and other Democratic Party aligned organizations through a software as a service model. The Obama campaign, along with a number of other campaigns during the 2008 cycle, relied on the platform developed by Blue State Digital from the Dean campaign's original toolset.[41] In the years after the 2004 election, BSD worked with a number of clients on the development of the platform, and launched PartyBuilder for the national Democratic Party in 2006, field-testing its systems during the midterm cycle. Through licensing BSD's technology and commissioning modifications in the toolset to build new functionalities and capacities, the Democratic Party made considerable investments in the firm's intellectual property. In essence, the Democratic Party subsidized the development of a platform that a number of campaigns and organizations in the extended party network would go on to use, including Obama in 2008 as My.BarackObama.com.

All of this meant that when Obama formally announced his candidacy in February 2007 the campaign had a technology platform in place that enabled thousands of individuals and groups across the country to organize and raise money for the candidate. In addition, the platform enabled staffers to email these supporters to help generate donations and build a small-dollar donor database. This meant that the Obama campaign had a sophisticated toolset to use at a time when it lacked monetary resources, paying BSD a small up-front license fee and a percentage of its earnings for use of the platform.[42] Once Obama's fortunes turned for the better during the primaries and the general election, the campaign invested significant resources back into the BSD platform to build out the tools and add capacity, which the firm then carried to subsequent campaigns and other organizations in the extended party network through its software as a service model. Indeed, given that Obama opted out of public financing, this meant that the Democrat had approximately $770 million to spend over the course of the election, compared with McCain's $322 million (a number that includes the candidate's public financing).[43] Obama's money was invested, at least in part, in the Democratic Party's ecosystem of firms.

While the Obama campaign was investing in BSD and hiring technology, digital media, data, and analytics staffers throughout 2007 and 2008, McCain's bid faced the challenge of having little in the way of resources in a difficult electoral context. It is highly unlikely that better digital organizing efforts, more developed campaign technologies, or an expansive field operation would have made a difference in terms of McCain's fortunes, of course, but it is worth considering a few of the differences between the two campaigns.

First, former McCain staffers and people at the party during the cycle stated that with resource constraints and little enthusiasm for the candidate, the McCain campaign had to devote much of its Internet operation through the party's convention (when the candidate received federal funding) to forms of transactional and extractive fundraising. At the same time, practitioners noted that the McCain campaign was reliant on the party's email list, which meant many more demands on a comparatively small potential donor base. As Krohn, who was at the party during the cycle heading up its digital efforts, argued:

> Everything seems to revolve around online fundraising but it was more predicated on how quickly to get the dollars in versus building rapport with the electorate to have that relationship-based fundraising apparatus in place. It was the shotgun approach. . . . So it was a fundraising email: "Send it to the whole list." "Well, we just hit the list yesterday." "Hit them again." So I also have three masters at the time. We had the White House who wanted to send out messages from the president. We had the Committee who needed to send out fundraising appeals and then we had the campaign and so there were times where I was being told to hit the entire list for three different groups within hours of each other and those decisions are from people that didn't even recognize it took longer than a couple of hours to just run all the list.[44]

Krohn and others also argued that it was not until comparatively late in the race that the campaign began engaging in more extensive email operations, such as geo-targeting emails and incorporating more non-fundraising requests, such as driving event attendance. That said, the campaign was significantly behind its rival. One challenge was simply that the McCain campaign (and the party) could not compete with Obama's organic approximately 13-million person email list at the time, compiled over many months through candidate events, canvassing, and interest in his candidacy. Obama used this list extensively to not only fundraise, but to increase event attendance and solicit volunteers. Meanwhile, when McCain accepted federal campaign financing after the convention, and in turn its limits, the campaign's fundraising stopped. This meant that the e-Campaign team stopped its email fundraising and things such as online ads that were producing revenue. This also meant comparatively fewer opportunities to build lists of supporters for the Republican Party that could be carried through to subsequent election cycles. Indeed, the differences in the size of the email and donor lists that the two nominees compiled set the stage for differences in the two parties' small-dollar Internet fundraising for cycles to come.[45]

Party and campaign staffers active during the cycle pointed to other differences between the McCain and Obama bids. Some staffers argued that Donatelli and Connell ended up building a robust platform for the general election that had volunteer and online fundraising tools, but given resource constraints and differences in supporter enthusiasm, they simply could not compete with the Obama campaign's large investments in and the outpouring of engagement on My.BarackObama.com—which also paid dividends in future elections for the Democrats. On the social media side, and specifically in terms of Facebook and YouTube, practitioners argued that Obama significantly outpaced McCain in terms of engagement, attributable in part to the comparatively greater interest in and mobilization around the Democrat's candidacy, supporters' production of amateur content, and significantly greater hiring of the new media staffers who produced the regular content these platforms require to sustain interest. Some Republican staffers also argued that this reflects the fact that the Obama campaign skewed younger demographically in terms of the candidate's supporters. That said, this does not wholly explain technological adoption or success by campaigns, especially given the fact that McCain in 2000 and Bush in 2004 ran campaigns that were more technologically advanced and Internet forward than many of their Democratic counterparts. Even more, while social media user demographics skewed younger in 2008, there were core bases of support among young voters for candidates on both sides of the aisle (as Ron Paul demonstrated).[46]

Indeed, when considering differences between the two campaigns, staffers on both sides of the aisle cited the ways the Obama campaign in 2008 helped *create* impassioned supporters through design, messaging, and rhetoric across multiple platforms, from Facebook posts to YouTube videos. Candidates inspire interest and enthusiasm among the electorate (or fail to) through their rhetoric, performances, and charisma, the opportunities to do so bounded by the electoral and cultural context they are situated within.[47] While campaigns often use digital media to translate enthusiasm into electoral resources, practitioners also argued that through their digital media practices they can generate interest and desire among the electorate. For example, Matt Lira, who was serving as the deputy communications director and digital director of congressman Eric Cantor's office for much of the cycle, took a leave to join the McCain e-Campaign team during late summer 2008. Lira joined a department that was then staffed by about eight people, compared with the Obama campaign's well over 60 staffers working in new media during the same period. Lira pointed out that this staffing differential

meant enormous differences in the organizational capacities of the two campaigns to produce content for social media and the Internet more broadly. Many
of the basic operations of the Obama campaign, for instance, such as keeping the
website updated, had dedicated staffers to perform them, which the McCain campaign did not.

On one level, this was a function of resources. On another, other staffers
broadly described the McCain campaign having a "culture that was not friendly
to digital at all."[48] Some former staffers cited pitching the campaign's management about announcing the vice presidential selection via text message and being
denied, which ended up being an innovation of the Obama campaign during the
cycle. Former staffers also argued that the e-Campaign team had little autonomy
on the campaign, was generally undervalued, and was not in a position to win
battles for resources. Even worse, former staffers recounted numerous internal
factions on the campaign that were at war with one another. Of course, the campaign was hamstrung by a lack of funding and enthusiasm throughout the race,
in addition to a very difficult electoral context, and senior staffers made decisions
based on what they believed was going to give them the most electoral value for
their limited money. That said, the broad story of technology, digital media, data,
and analytics on McCain's bid in 2008 could not be more different from that of
the Obama campaign, whose new media team had significant autonomy with
a seat at the senior staff table, an ability to claim organizational resources, and
the capacity to determine its own content according to the genres of social and
digital media, which are distinct from professional communications and finance
practices.[49] This organizational arrangement, meanwhile, was the outcome of Joe
Rospars, a veteran of the Dean bid in 2004, cofounder of BSD, and former new
media director at the party, advocating for this role. Rospars was successful, in no
small part, given his extensive experience and the Democratic Party's collective
fashioning of the insurgent Dean bid into a prototype of a successful new media
campaign.

With respect to ground efforts, former campaign and party staffers on both
sides of the aisle pointed to significant differences between the two presidential
bids and argued that they were attributable in many ways to the extraordinary
mobilization around the Obama campaign. Even more, however, former staffers
in the Republican Party and on McCain's bid also argued that after Bush's re-election bid there was a change in the mindset of the two parties. While Democrats
were investing in new organizing models, data infrastructures, and analytic techniques, there was comparative stasis in the Republican Party. Given that Obama's
expansive field organizing and new media program are well documented, I focus
on the Republican efforts during the cycle here.[50]

Former party staffers argued that between the 2004 and 2008 elections
Republicans continually got better at making volunteer efforts more efficient,

generating more voter contacts, and bringing in more data points.[51] That said, many also pointed out that there was not the same level of innovation as on the Democratic side of the aisle and especially in Obama's run, which placed voter contact through expansive field and digital organizing programs at the center of the campaign and used predictive modeling to generate efficiencies in these operations. Ryan Meerstein, for instance, worked on the Bush-Cheney victory team in 2004 in Central Ohio and served as the political education director of the RNC in 2005. During the 2008 cycle, Meerstein worked in Ohio for McCain. In looking back on his experiences at the party and campaign during this time, Meerstein said that within the Republican Party from 2004 to 2006, and then into the presidential primaries, there was "a little bit of a mindset problem, not necessarily being willing to venture out further then we had and look at new options."[52] The numbers were going up and the party was touching more voters, but staffers such as Meersteen cited that the party's mobilization efforts, analytic ability, and technical development failed to keep pace with what was taking place on the other side of the aisle.

Other former staffers at the party and on McCain's bid cited that there was a move away from ground political organizing in favor of a more targeted model where the approach was to "sit around the office and write press releases about issue X tailored to audience X versus actually going out and developing relationships," in the words of one staffer who worked for a number of Republican presidential campaigns.[53] In the process, this staffer argued, the Republican Party turned away from the very formula that Obama's campaign team emulated on the 2004 Bush bid: a strong political operation, commitment to data-driven voter contacts, broad investments in digital that were in the service of field organizing, and a volunteer-driven effort more broadly. As another former party staffer described, echoing a sentiment that recurred throughout the interviews for this book with respect to the 2008 cycle: "so one side is coasting and the other side is investing in something, it is only a matter of time until that crossover point occurs, and very much that has occurred."[54]

Meanwhile, other practitioners who worked for consultancies that provided data and analytics services for the McCain campaign argued that with respect to voter modeling, the Republican Party failed to keep pace with the Democrats after 2004. Republican consultants cited that while the Democrats in 2008 were performing more individualized predictive modeling, such as generating Obama support, turnout, and persuasion probability scores for members of the electorate, the McCain campaign generally relied on the more static forms of cluster modeling that the Bush re-election campaign in 2004 used.[55] Cluster modeling entails using a micro-targeting survey at a point in time to identify groups to turn out and persuade, as opposed to modeling individuals and tracking them over time in a dynamic and changing campaign environment. As one former data consultant to the Republican Party during this period detailed, contrasting the Obama campaign with the McCain campaign and citing how the Democratic Party also built upon its advantages after the 2008 cycle:

> So they had done quite well in sort of advancing where the ball was between 2004 and 2008 which the Republicans didn't do.... After 2004 the Republicans have this huge micro-targeting edge, they've figured micro-targeting out and the Democrats haven't.... And they kind of, I think, got complacent in thinking of what is the next step for micro-targeting.... I think the Democrats between 2008 and 2012 did what we should have done between 2004 and 2008, and said "ok we have come up with this really great technology but how do we use that to move beyond simply saying, you know this person is or isn't a voter, and start doing predictive analysis of what we can do to make them vote the way we want them to?"[56]

Conclusion

John McCain lost the 2008 general election handily, and he was gracious in defeat. McCain drew on the historical significance of President Obama's election in his concession speech, and pointed to the extraordinary mobilization around Obama as evidence that the candidate inspired millions to believe again in American democracy: "In a contest as long and difficult as this campaign has been, his success alone commands my respect for his ability and perseverance. But that he managed to do so by inspiring the hopes of so many millions of Americans who had once wrongly believed that they had little at stake or little influence in the election of an American president is something I deeply admire and commend him for achieving."[57]

Rhetoric and performance played a large part in Obama's ability to inspire many members of the American public.[58] Digital media and data then translated this collective democratic faith in Obama and hope for the future into electoral resources, from money and volunteers to voter contacts. Digital media also extended the president's performances, while data and analytics underlay the millions of conversations that took place on the doorsteps and the Facebook pages of voters.

Even as many Democrats, and certainly the popular press, saw digital media and field organizing as key factors in Obama's victory, within the Republican Party network there was a prevailing sense that McCain was going to lose the election anyway. This is likely correct, of course, as numerous political scientists have pointed out in their post-election analyses. Regardless of the empirical basis of discussions about electoral outcomes, the stories political actors tell about why candidates win or lose matter. In an election that many

Republicans expected to lose, there was little impetus to rethink the party's approach to technology, digital media, data, and analytics, or even systematically assess where it stood in comparison with its rival. Some practitioners, of course, perceived a yawning, and growing, gap between the two parties in these areas in 2008, and after the election launched new initiatives to close it. However, as I argue in the next chapter, in the absence of party network-wide perceptions of a gap between the two parties, there were not significantly new patterns of investment in technology, digital media, data, and analytics, and these efforts failed to achieve critical mass, which left incumbent vendors and established ways of contesting elections in place. As Chuck DeFeo, who in 2010 became the president and CEO of Campaign Solutions and Connell Donatelli for a short time after an interlude working for a host of conservative websites, described, "Part of the reason I didn't stay in it that long is both the complete level of disappointment and the lack of maturity I saw in the space, meaning in six years the industry had not moved forward. . . . The concept of what a true Facebook and data program was had not penetrated into our field at least on the Republican side. . . . The reality was the budget allocation wasn't there, the desire for true innovation wasn't there, and that is across candidate campaigns, and just overall the right. . . . And so the fact that we ended up in the place that we did by 2012 was also not a surprise to me."[59]

DeFeo's comment shines a retrospective light on the state of the party's technology during the 2008 cycle and the comparative lack of development in the areas of technology, digital media, data, and analytics, even in the years after the election. Even more, and largely unrecognized to practitioners at the time, the massive investments in technology, digital media, data, and analytics that the Obama campaign made reaped dividends in terms of trained staffers, small-dollar donors, voter data, and technical capacity in the years to come. This proved to be an enormous institutional advantage for the Democratic Party. In the next chapter, I follow the Republican and Democratic parties after 2008 through to the primaries in 2012. In doing so, I set the stage for the discussion of the 2012 general election, and explain why the starting points of the two parties' presidential candidates were very different. Throughout, I suggest that the Romney and Obama campaigns were, in large part, the *outcome* of historical party network processes.

4

The Aftermath of McCain's Defeat

With John McCain's resounding defeat, the election postmortems began. Pundits, journalists, and scholars argued variously that Obama was elected on the basis of his charisma, public performances, level-headedness, strong leadership during the financial crisis, comparative youth, and soaring rhetorical skills. Others pointed to fatigue with the Bush administration and the desire among the electorate for a new direction, particularly with respect to the economy and Iraq. In addition to these accounts of the candidate's strengths and the political context, there was wide discussion in the media and the Democratic Party about the Obama campaign itself. Many saw the Obama campaign's field organizing efforts as a new and powerful model for voter persuasion and turnout, even as it was a normatively desirable way of creating citizen participation. Perhaps the most popular theme of post-election coverage and scholarship, however, was that the campaign's adept use of social media platforms such as Facebook and YouTube helped vault Obama into the White House, particularly through the engagement of young voters.

For many Republicans, however, McCain's defeat was easily understood, and campaign tactics hardly mattered. Four years after Bush's successful re-election campaign, the party's nominee fell victim to a disastrous economic context, a deeply unpopular incumbent, and, as a result, an uninspired base and electorate wary of sending another Republican to the highest elected office. In other words, for much of the extended Republican Party network, the 2008 Obama campaign was hardly a prototype adapted to a new empirical reality of a networked electorate with more diffuse and information-bearing social ties, new media consumption habits, and different expectations around electoral engagement. Obama was simply lucky to have the electoral wind at his back. Many political scientists agreed. Less apt to rely on explanations that focus on the idiosyncrasies of candidates or campaigns, or the adept use of media technologies, political scientists largely agree that the outcome of the race was determined by a deeply unpopular incumbent and poor economic conditions.[1] And they are likely right. The structural forces of the electoral context shaped the outcome, far more so than any gaps in the capacities of the two candidates and their parties to take up technology, digital media, data, and analytics.

And yet, the stories that party actors tell themselves and one another about the outcomes of elections matter. The understandings of party network actors regarding the reasons that candidates win and lose elections are consequential for how they develop strategy, allocate resources, and invest to gain competitive advantage in the future. As this chapter details, in contrast to what happened after Bush's near loss in 2000 and Kerry's loss in 2004, comparatively few actors in the extended Republican Party network believed that the party had fallen behind in campaign technology, data, or staffer expertise and knowledge after Obama's sweeping victory. Former party staffers argued that there seemed to be little urgency for the party to reinvest in its technological capacities after the election given that most people expected McCain to lose handily anyway. Accordingly, there were comparatively fewer former party staffers founding new organizations and challenging the incumbent consulting firms around the Republican Party compared with the Democrats after 2004, and those that did asserted that they found limited commercial opportunities. Furthermore, former party staffers argue that the Republican Party's sweeping victories in congressional and state-house races across the country in 2010 reinforced the perception that both parties were evenly matched, especially given that many of Obama's digital resources and data tools, then housed with Organizing for America at the DNC, failed to stem the tide of voter dissatisfaction and Democratic disillusionment.

This chapter charts developments in the two parties and their extended networks and campaigns after the 2008 presidential cycle through the 2012 Republican primaries. This is a period when various theoretical perspectives suggest that there should be significant technological investment and innovation on the Republican side of the aisle to catch up with the Democrats after McCain's loss. Rational choice theories on campaign strategy, suggest that any differences between the two parties and their campaigns, especially at the presidential level, would be both minimal and short-lived. Political scientist Dave Karpf, for example, argued that there are "out-party incentives" to innovate and invest in new technical systems.[2] And yet, as this chapter reveals, it is not so much the structural fact of being out of power that is consequential as the *perception* of the reasons for it.[3] In part because McCain's loss was so easily explained away, the Obama campaign in 2008 did not disclose to Republicans a new empirical world or way of campaigning that would be electorally advantageous. Another way of saying this is that the two parties saw the world in different ways at this moment in time in terms of the need to take up technology, digital media, data, and analytics, even as Republicans likely overestimated their own capacity in these areas vis-à-vis the Democrats.

As a result, the two parties and their extended networks continued along different paths post-2008, with Democrats continuing to invest more in the areas of technology, digital media, data, and analytics compared with Republicans. After the 2008 election, 15 of Obama's former technology, digital media, data, and analytics staffers launched 16 firms, including Revolution Messaging, which handled digital for Bernie Sanders's 2016 bid, and Bully Pulpit Interactive, the industry leader in Democratic online advertising. The firm provided the online advertising services for Obama's re-election bid, and its founder, Andrew Bleeker, later went on to work as an advisor to the Clinton campaign in 2016.[4] Meanwhile, the other Democratic primary bids of the cycle produced ten additional organizations.

By contrast, there were ten Republican organizations launched by technology, digital, data, and analytics staffers who worked on the various campaigns of the 2008 cycle. While there were some attempts to develop a new group of Republican organizations oriented around technology and data on the order of what the Democrats assembled after the 2004 presidential race (23 different ventures, as reported in the previous chapter), they failed to gain much traction in the immediate aftermath of the cycle. The upshot was that while conservatives were making innovative use of Twitter during the 2010 midterm cycle, there were still fewer firms offering specialized technology, digital media, data, and analytics services on the Republican side of the aisle, a comparatively shallower pool of talent for campaigns and party organizations to draw from, and no forums on the order of RootsCamp to institutionalize knowledge sharing across the party network.[5]

Indeed, one indicator of the mindset across the party network with respect to the electoral value of technology, digital media, data, and analytics is the hiring patterns of the 2012 Republican presidential campaigns during the primaries. There were comparatively fewer staffers hired in-house in these areas across these bids than even on the Obama campaign four years prior and, as detailed later in this chapter, they generally had organizational roles with less autonomy.[6] The Romney 2012 primary bid hired 23 staffers in these areas (up from eight in 2008); the next closest Republican primary campaigns were Newt Gingrich and Gary Johnson's, each with four staffers. This is to be compared with 54 staffers on the Obama primary bid in 2008. In other words, whereas across the Democratic Party network there was a mindset that technology, digital media, data, and analytics mattered electorally in new ways after 2004, which then extended through the 2008 and 2012 cycles, there was not a comparable cultural shift on the Republican side of the aisle.

Meanwhile, the Republican Party fell into considerable debt under chairman Michael Steele. While Steele commissioned the building of new data systems and campaign platforms for the party to provide to its candidates, numerous former party staffers and those with knowledge of this time period argued that they were abandoned after Reince Priebus assumed the chairmanship in 2011. Former staffers cited that Priebus immediately sought to retire the party's considerable debt given the impending presidential election, had to engage in the triage of systems to address issues of cost effectiveness and redundancy, and generally relied on working with powerful incumbent vendors responsible for many of the party's existing systems.

In tracing the Republican Party's dynamics from 2008 through the primaries in 2012, this chapter argues that the Romney campaign was, in no small part, the outcome of a set of institutional party network processes.[7] There were fewer and qualitatively different party network resources in technology, digital media, data, and analytics available for Romney to assemble when he launched his bid in early 2011 than those that existed on the Democratic side of the aisle. For one, within the Republican Party network, there was a comparative undervaluing of technology compared with the Democratic Party network. This meant, for instance, campaign managers who prioritized traditional communications operations and elevated the staffers who engaged in them above their digital counterparts, both in terms of access to resources and organizational roles. It also meant that fewer Republican campaign managers and staffers more generally were socialized into the culture of testing that practitioners on both sides of the aisle point to as a defining characteristic of the two Obama runs and Democratic campaigns and organizations post-2004 more broadly, however unevenly it was institutionalized across the party network (as I detail in Chapter 6). Even more, there were comparatively fewer firms on the Republican side of the aisle founded by former presidential campaign staffers providing technology, digital media, data, and analytics services. Finally, compared to Obama's re-election bid, the Romney campaign took shape with a less-developed Republican Party infrastructure with respect to digital fundraising, voter data, technology, and modeling expertise. This had a number of dimensions, including a comparatively small e-mail list for digital fundraising, less canvass data generated in 2008 to provide a basis for a historical look at the attitudes and behavior of individuals, the lack of a robust field tool in standardized use across the party network to capture data in the field and feed it back to the party, and an approach to modeling that had not kept pace with the innovations of the Democratic Party.

These disadvantages were coupled with a long, contested primary that was resource and time intensive for the Romney campaign. While many political scientists saw Romney's emergence as the nominee as a historical inevitability, this was far from the experience of staffers within the campaign, who perceived the race as anything but settled. Indeed, regardless of the extent to which political scientists may have seen the outcome as predetermined based on patterns of elite endorsements, the primaries still had to be contested, and staffers acted according to what they perceived were their best chances for victory.[8] In the end, this meant significant outlays of fundraising dollars for broadcast advertising as the campaign sought to overwhelm its comparatively underfunded opponents, and scarce resources for everything else. Meanwhile, while Romney was fighting off challengers, the Obama campaign spent much of 2011 finding and attracting talent, working out organizational structures and work flows, engaging in technical development, and field-testing tools and voter models. Even more, with the nominee in hand, the Obama campaign could and did have far more extensive coordination with the formal Democratic Party apparatus earlier in the race than the Romney campaign was able to (as detailed in the next chapter).

The Party and Its Network after McCain's Defeat

The differences between the McCain and Obama campaigns in 2008 had significant consequences for the future of the two parties. The amount of spending on a presidential cycle only comes around once every four years. The money that the Obama campaign directed to party-aligned firms such as Blue State Digital and Voter Activation Network supported the development of technologies and capacities that later benefited organizations across the party's extended network. Meanwhile, the campaign's extensive hiring in technology, digital media, data, and analytics produced staffers with expertise and experience that the party and campaigns of future cycles (including the re-election bid) drew extensively on. And, the data that the 2008 Obama campaign produced, including a 13-million member email list, a robust database of small donors, and millions of data points on the electorate gathered from canvasses in primary states and in swing states during the general election, proved to be a significant asset for the party, down-ballot campaigns, and the re-election bid. Even more, the Obama campaign in 2008 produced innovations in technology and practice and a new generation of field and technology staffers and firms that carried them to organizations throughout the extended Democratic Party network.[9]

By contrast, in a tough electoral environment for Republicans with a deeply unpopular incumbent, a failing economy, and a public weary of overseas conflicts, the McCain campaign generated only a fraction of the interest and money that the Obama campaign did.[10] As a result, there was comparatively less hiring, and fewer technologies were built for the bid. For example, political consultant Patrick Ruffini argued that funding woes impacted the technology infrastructure of the campaign: "there is talent that sort of marooned on the McCain campaign and nothing really gets developed."[11] This meant comparatively fewer opportunities to invest in new technologies, the firms and staffers to provide them, and the data infrastructure of the party. It also meant fewer staffers who would gain the experience of working on a presidential campaign and subsequently found their own ventures, and fewer volunteers and donors who could be re-enlisted in future party efforts and campaigns.

Meanwhile, by historical accident, the considerably large investments by the Obama campaign in technology, digital media, data, and analytics came at precisely the moment when there were fundamental shifts in the media ecosystem, and with them the political communication practices of the electorate. Consider the technologies that were comparatively new to the 2008 cycle, and that now shape how citizens routinely consume much political information. It was the first presidential cycle for YouTube and Twitter. While Facebook was founded in 2004, the 2008 presidential cycle was the first in which the social media site was open to the general public. These social media platforms gave rise to fundamental shifts in how campaigns communicate with the electorate and the press, with implications ranging from content production and messaging to organizing and targeting.[12] During this time period, there were also qualitative changes in and a quantitative explosion of data and new means of analyzing and acting upon it, which some commentators have dubbed the rise of "big data." And, while social media captured the imaginations of many journalists and the public during the 2008 cycle, it was also the first cycle in which the Obama campaign pioneered wide-ranging "computational management" practices, or the delegation of managerial, allocative, messaging, and design decisions to the analysis of data.[13]

All of these factors meant that the 2008 cycle was particularly consequential in terms of a shift in media technologies, the rise of data and analytics, and the crafting of new campaign practices to reach and appeal to an electorate that was consuming media more socially and across many more platforms than even during the 2004 cycle.[14] The Obama campaign had the good fortune of being an extraordinarily well-financed run in a highly favorable political context in 2008, and it paid dividends for the larger Democratic Party network that was transformed by it.

Even with these disparities in technology use between the two campaigns during the cycle, McCain's loss did not bring about a shift in the cultural understandings of actors in the extended Republican Party network. While there were some who saw the Obama campaign in 2008 as a prototype of a new, highly participatory and social and technologically sophisticated electoral effort adapted to a changing world, and attributed the Democrat's victory to this, for the most part McCain's loss was expected.[15] As such, numerous former party staffers argue that there was not much impetus for taking stock of the party network's technological capacity or ways of contesting elections more broadly. As Michael Turk argued, echoing the stasis that Chuck DeFeo detailed at the close of the last chapter: "It wasn't 'Oh my god what went wrong with our operation?' . . . McCain wasn't anybody's favorite candidate. He was running against a guy that had a very interesting personal story in a historic context. I mean there was just a lot going against McCain. So unlike in 2000 where you had a very, very, very narrow election where . . . it was much more of a catalyst for that sort of thing than McCain was."[16]

At the same time, practitioners argue that, more broadly, the big incumbent political technology firms that worked with the party during much of the 1990s–2000s had little capacity to invest in technological development during and after the 2008 cycle, and new players did not emerge to compete with them after McCain's loss. In addition, as detailed earlier, Mike Connell, a part of 3eDC and the founder of New Media Campaigns, was killed in a small plane crash in December 2008, about a month after the election. Former staffers argue that Connell's death was a significant loss for the party in eroding the continuity within Republican technological services. Connell's death also meant the loss of a person with considerable experience working on presidential campaigns. More generally, reflecting on the state of Republican consulting at this time, Chuck DeFeo argued that after 2008 there were a number of firms and consultants offering digital services, but nothing on the order of a large firm with the capacity and experience as the Democrats Blue State Digital: "So I think you have some [digital consultancies], but clearly not the stage of a Blue State Digital. . . . I mean it's great when you can do two presidential campaigns. That is six or seven or eight years of work, high level work, to be able to have the staff in place and . . . there hasn't been that on the Republican side clearly for a while . . . the infrastructure has been on the Democratic side and it hasn't on the Republican side."[17]

One of the ways there is technology development between election cycles, given the waxing and waning of party funding and often significant staffing turnover, is through the work of political organizations in extended party networks. The firms and organizations that emerge after presidential election cycles are also the carriers of new technologies and practice honed on comparatively well-financed presidential campaigns to other sites in politics. While Democrats launched a number of new political organizations after the 2004 election and continued to engage in organizational founding after the 2008 cycle as well, there was comparative stasis on the Republican side of the aisle. People in the Democratic Party saw the Dean and Obama campaigns as prototypes of new ways of campaigning and created market opportunities for successive waves of practitioners to found new firms and find work on campaigns and for advocacy organizations. In contrast, Bush's victory in 2004 and McCain's loss in 2008 did not spur the same efforts to create new organizations. Meanwhile, of the Republican firms launched during and after the 2008 cycle, none grew to the prominence of Blue State Digital or disrupted incumbents between 2008 and 2012, like VAN did after 2004 (the closest a firm came to this was Targeted Victory, but it did not play the same infrastructural role as these Democratic firms during these years).[18] For example, former McCain national e-Campaign director and chief technology officer Mike Palmer's i360, launched in the months after the 2008 election to provide data and analytics services to the Republican Party network, only grew increasingly important *after* the 2012 cycle, when *Politico* reported that with backing from the Koch brothers it began investing in campaign software in addition to data after a post-election review.[19] Indeed, it was the Republican Party losing races that actors believed their candidates should have won that, in part, opened the door for i360 to challenge the RNC's hold over data and field tools.

Other efforts to start new ventures failed to gain traction. Shortly after the 2008 election, Bush 2004 veterans Mindy Finn and Patrick Ruffini launched

"Rebuild the Party," a prescient effort directed at making sure the next chairman would, in the words of a *Politico* article at the time, "make bridging the digital divide between the two parties the top priority."[20] The effort largely fell on deaf ears. While a number of senior RNC operatives signed their names to the effort (approximately 15,000 individuals total) and it received a considerable amount of positive press, a number of former party staffers argued that it was not as influential as the founders had hoped, it failed to change minds about the value of new campaign technologies, and there appeared to be few new market opportunities for technology, digital media, data, and analytics staffers as a result.

Even amid the comparative stasis of the Republican Party network, former staffers noted that there was some energy for revamping the party's technological capacity once Michael Steele became chair. On January 30, 2009, Mike Duncan withdrew from the chairman's election in the face of declining ballot support, and Steele subsequently won. Cyrus Krohn left soon after, wanting to head back to Seattle, and Steele's new team asked him to suggest a successor. Krohn recommended Todd Herman, a former colleague at Microsoft who served as the general manager of media strategy and monetization. Herman joined the party in March 2009. Herman stated that his acceptance of the role of chief digital strategist was contingent upon a set of significant organizational changes within the party that he negotiated with the new chairman: Steele provided the digital department of the party with a formal seat at the senior leadership table and marked a clear distinction with the communications department (neither of which was the case during Duncan's tenure).[21]

Herman stated that soon after starting he researched the 2008 Obama campaign, and instructed his staff to do a side-by-side analysis of all the Republican and Democratic social media properties and presence online more generally. Herman visited Seattle and talked to entrepreneurs and venture capitalists who were right-leaning. He also attempted to interview all the individuals he presumed were stakeholders of digital within the Republican National Committee, including the heads of other departments, whom he invited to come to digital's vendor review. The attempt, in Herman's words, was to "crowdsource" the process, bringing a lot of different people at the party to the table whether they saw themselves connected with the digital operations or not.[22] One reason Herman was reaching out, echoed by staffers who served in similar roles on campaigns, was that the digital team's work crossed over into other domains, such as fundraising and communications. Herman stated that these attempts to broaden the circle around digital proved challenging, with people being initially confused as to why he was talking to them. One area of close collaboration, however, was with the political team. For example, Gentry Collins, the political director, handed Herman his strategic plan and Herman did likewise, so there could be better coordination between the two units within the party.

Creating the conditions for effective collaboration between units was not the only challenge. Herman echoed his predecessors in pointing to the RNC's bureaucracy as being a particular hurdle to technological development. Herman stated that the RNC has, in essence, a 168-person Board of Directors given the committee organization of the party. To get things done, Herman stated he had to explain his plans first to the technology committee, and then to the overall board. Numerous former party staffers, including those who have interacted with this board, asserted that technology was often "baffling" to members of this committee and the board, and as a result it was difficult to get things done. This is one reason that a number of former party staffers argued that the technological operations of the party need to be set outside the committee structure, so that the people who understand the technology have the autonomy to shape it.

With continual organizational and staffing changes and the need to convince multiple and diverse stakeholders of digital media's utility for electoral and policy ends, digital staffers at the party at this time also cited the need to engage in demonstration projects to win their autonomy, which is striking considering this echoes dynamics of the 1999–2000 cycle. Herman and other staffers at the party argued that the digital department sought to prove its worth around efforts to oppose Obama's healthcare plan and through its promotion of party candidates in the 2010 midterm elections.

The "Fire Pelosi" effort became the organizing frame for the opposition to the president's healthcare bill and the midterm elections for the party and, as many staffers argued more generally, a galvanizing force for turnout.[23] The digital team got to run the online effort around the messaging "end-to-end." The digital team went to work to prepare for what would happen with the passage of the healthcare bill in March 2010. Herman asked Steele to write blog posts that contained the phrase "Fire Nancy Pelosi" that would be published when the bill passed. In addition, Herman and his team coordinated the launch of the site through an extended network of people they identified through the GOP's social media properties, and that had in the aggregate about 8 million people in their digital reach. These posts linked to a "Fire Nancy Pelosi" website that the RNC built but blocked from Google's search engines until the passage of the bill, which resulted in great search engine optimization. The digital team also built new widgets on the party's new digital platform (detailed below) that bloggers and other content producers could plug into their sites to drive and track fundraising, and that fed information back to the RNC. The party distributed nearly 34,000 of these widgets, which in turn contained links and referred back to the "Fire Nancy Pelosi" site. Coinciding with all of this, Herman's team developed an online advertising program, put $50k in their Google account, and created approximately 2,000 different varieties of online advertisements around the phrase "Fire Nancy Pelosi," which they then tested the performance of. Herman's team then set up ways to track and analyze this effort when it went live, including "taking a snapshot of people's social media footprints when they joined one of our properties."[24]

This preparation work resulted in what many former staffers and journalists argued was a highly successful campaign for the party. As Herman described, when the bill passed and the online operation went live, the party's pages were the first search result for "Nancy Pelosi," and they raised approximately $400,000 overnight and $1.69 million in a week.[25] Also fueling this fundraising was the digital team's testing of email subject lines to find groups of people who would open emails if they said "Fire Nancy Pelosi". Herman argued that this success changed the perception within the party about online donations. On the second or third day of the "Fire Nancy Pelosi" campaign, the party received an upper limit individual donation online, contradicting what former staffers cited was the internal perception that big donors would not give online. Meanwhile, activists and partisans independently took the "Fire Nancy Pelosi" theme and extended it. For example, independent conservative activists created what staffers estimated were hundreds of Twitter accounts, which the digital team at the party then worked to promote. The party's coalition department also created and distributed signs that said "Fire Nancy Pelosi," which subsequently began showing up at Tea Party rallies across the country.

Supporting all this work, some staffers at the party during this period argued that Steele put together a competitive technology infrastructure for the 2010 cycle. The party launched a new GOP.com site in October 2009, with an internal social networking platform, Our.GOP.com.[26] Former staffers stated that the platform attracted several thousand users upon its release. The party also launched an application programming interface (API) in May 2010 that enabled the party and vetted third-party sites to do things such as reward users with "points" for taking party-friendly actions, such as sharing social media content.[27] There was also a GOP Code for America initiative designed to recruit volunteer coders to use this API to create new applications for the party. The digital team also implemented a new email system, the impetus for which came from how impressed staffers were with the email program of the 2008 Obama campaign. The email system enabled the party to test things such as subject lines, body copy, colors, and send times (that said, as detailed later, former party staffers also noted that there were multiple email systems, and even lists, used by the party across different departments).

Herman also set out to achieve what Krohn and others before him tried to do: open the voter file through an API so that web data could integrate with the voter file. Again, this had long been a goal, especially because the party was looking to be able to contact voters across platforms in a more integrated fashion. The API for Voter Vault was a collaborative project involving political director Gentry Collins, strategy director Bill Steiner, and senior technical fellow Bob Ellsworth, as well as the digital team. Former party staffers with knowledge of this effort noted that while it was the right idea, there was still only limited integration between the voter file and data generated across the party's web properties, which Democrats also struggled with through the 2012 cycle. As Herman argued, applications such as the online calling tool "certainly fed data back in to Voter Vault but I would say . . . certainly not as quickly as we liked, not as regularly as we liked."[28]

Meanwhile, Gentry Collins and the political team coordinated the turnout efforts around the 2010 cycle. The digital team played a supporting role in the political department's efforts, engaging in extensive email marketing to party activists in order to recruit volunteers to use the online calling tool and volunteer action center. The online calling tool brought in new people to volunteer and generated data on them for future election cycles. These digital efforts also complemented what was taking place on the ground. Staffers argued that the online calling tool enabled better list segmentation of priority targets than what the McCain campaign could do in 2008, which made these online phone calls more valuable to the party and its candidates. When there were reports that power went out in parts of Nevada on election night in 2010, for instance, the party shifted approximately 25% of its online phone calls to the state.[29] As Herman described, it was "a great moment of teamwork with the political team. I was in the war room that night and that was very meaningful for people to understand, that 'thank god this tool is there.'"[30] Former staffers also describe the action center becoming a Craigslist list for volunteers, with people posting volunteer opportunities across the country.

That said, Herman argued that the party lacked sophisticated tools that could be deployed in the field on canvasses and that the data architecture of Voter Vault was limited. Echoing other practitioners who pointed to similar problems through the 2014 cycle (see Chapters 5 and 6), Herman said that the party did not have the time or budget to develop the field applications that would have enabled voter data to be more seamlessly updated at the doorsteps of voters during canvasses and in field offices, especially compared with what VAN supported for the Democratic Party at the time. Furthermore, Herman argued that at the time Voter Vault was a partitioned system, which made it difficult for users in the states to access data beyond what appeared in narrowly targeted environments, in contrast to the Democrats' VoteBuilder system, which provided field staffers with access to a broader universe of data. As Herman related, "Voter Vault, when it was created, it was rightly considered a massive advance, a huge strategic advance . . . the committee then thought that it was an asset of theirs, that it was so strategically advanced that it needed to be closed and kind of partitioned off. It's when you have a committee full of people, none of whom are really in the technology business, it is easy to not notice technology passing you by."[31]

According to practitioners on both sides of the aisle, the differences in technology and data between the two parties at this point in 2010 were that the Democrats had a more usable and robust suite of tools to guide voter contacts and capture data generated in the field, a data architecture that was more readily and widely accessible to practitioners across the party network, and (near) complete buy-in to using the DNC's data and VoteBuilder. These are not insignificant differences. As Chapter 6 argues, one consequence of the failure of the Republican Party to develop better field tools on the order of VoteBuilder during this period is that during the 2014 cycle some campaigns turned outside the party for their tools and even data, using firms such as NationBuilder and i360 for these purposes. This meant that data did not flow as seamlessly into the Republican Party's voter file from the field as it did for the Democrats, and at times canvass data was taken out of the RNC's data ecosystem entirely with the use of alternative vendors. Meanwhile, during the 2010 midterm cycle the Democratic Party was also honing many of its innovations in predictive modeling based on this data infrastructure that would lie at the foundation of the re-election bid.[32]

These differences between the two parties were exacerbated by Michael Steele's tenure at the Republican Party, which ultimately undid any progress that had been made after the 2008 cycle.[33] Despite Steele becoming chairman with a $23 million surplus, he left the party with mounting debts on the order of approximately $23 million, and a decimated donor base.[34] Meanwhile, even in the context of an extraordinary cycle in 2010, former party staffers argued that Steele's tenure left few assets that could be transferred to the party's presidential nominee in 2012. One former party staffer who was later involved with the Romney campaign argued that when the candidate essentially took over the party as the nominee in 2012, the party only had 500,000 usable email addresses:

> they only raised $7.9 million online in 2010. The single greatest year we have ever had in politics . . . they only had 110,000 donors. . . . That is the real legacy of 2010, the missed opportunity. We should have gone into 2011 with 1 million new donors on the file and the RNC would be able to raise 100 million dollars more. If someone had focused in '10 on activating these people, but it's like this lost story in the history of the way these things are because everyone is focused on technology but by missing the marketing component. . . . It is kind of like a very sad story if you think about it.[35]

This is the context Reince Priebus stepped into when he assumed the chairmanship of the party in January 2011, defeating Steele and others. Despite some progress on the technology front and the party's sweeping victories during the 2010 midterm cycle, numerous former party staffers argued that Steele's tenure as party chair was so fraught financially and culturally, given the chairman's style, that when Priebus was elected chair there was "a throw everything out mentality."[36] Numerous former staffers argued that Priebus's new team scrapped what the digital team had been working on, and there was no money available to invest in building better systems. In this situation, the party went back to relying on vendors that had previously provided it with technology and digital services, which some former staffers argued stifled innovation because these were not cutting-edge firms. Indeed, multiple, independent accounts suggested that entrenched vendors shaped the decision to scrap what Steele's team had put together, with longtime consultants being upset that the party was building its own tools and had opened the voter file up to an API (if only on a limited basis). As one former senior staffer in the Republican Party described:

> When Chairman Priebus came in and they were tens of millions of dollars in debt there was this budget slashing going on. . . . So somebody made the decision during that transition that they decommission all of those servers of all of the great work that has been written, all the code that there is during the Steele period. . . . Somebody was wise enough to pull the code they found on those servers and save that code but then a new team came in . . . they built up their own thing. The party has been successful in fits and starts, but it has been fits and starts and you can't reset every two years and build an operational layer to grow on itself.[37]

While other staffers cited that this practitioner overstated the amount of operable technology that could be run efficiently within the RNC at this point in time, there is broad consensus that the financial situation left by Steele set the party considerably back in terms of its ability to build infrastructure for 2012. Instead of being able to invest in technology, Priebus sought to get the party out of debt, especially given that the party needed resources for the presidential election. As a consequence of all of this, Katie Harbath, a former party staffer and global politics and government outreach manager at Facebook when this book went to press, argued that "we [the Republican Party] basically lost four years."[38]

Furthermore, according to practitioners, there seemed to be little urgency to revamp the party's technology, digital media, data, and analytics operations after the midterm cycle. A number of former staffers asserted that the midterm elections in 2010, when the party's base was excited, mobilized, and highly active online donating money and taking to social media such as Twitter, provided a misleading impression to many in the party. The issue, as Harbath argued, is that "things did seem to be headed in a positive direction after that but I felt like . . . it was by happenstance and luck and not necessarily as institutionalized."[39] Former staffers argued that after the midterm cycle the party did not build a base for the future that would help it weather a change in its fortunes, or even a close presidential race. Instead, the party rode a wave of temporary opposition to Obama's agenda. For example, Michael Beach, who was the national victory director (or "field director") of the RNC during the 2008 cycle and subsequently went on to cofound the firm

Targeted Victory in 2009, saw 2010 as great in terms of electoral success, but awful in terms of political strategy. Beach echoed other staffers in arguing that the 2010 cycle created *complacency* on the Republican side of the aisle. Republican Party figures perceived that any of the disparities that might have existed between the two parties were solved, when in actuality the midterm cycle had an older electorate and an electoral tidal wave behind it. As Beach described it, "'10 was like you had a lot of bad people, had a lot of bad tech vendors, had a lot of bad consultants. . . . They are all of a sudden the toast of the town but all they did was sit on a raft and ride the stream."[40]

As a result, there were few changes in the party with respect to technology, digital media, data, and analytics after the midterm cycle. Even more, numerous staffers with an inside perspective on the party during this time argued that much of the knowledge around A/B testing and list segmentation of emails even regressed in the early months of 2011. Staffers described a party deep in debt, and running a number of different systems that were not cost effective, including four primary email systems given that the communications, finance, political, and digital departments all had separate lists they did not share with one another (which the Romney campaign later had to match). One staffer referred to what happened early in Priebus's tenure as "triage" with respect to the need to pare away systems that were redundant, impractical, and otherwise draining on resources. This is all the more striking given the fact that after the midterm cycle Obama for America began actively coordinating with the DNC to staff up, build systems for the general election, and pursue large-scale data infrastructure projects designed to solve the integration problem for the purposes of voter modeling and analytics more broadly. In contrast, the Republican Party was back on square one and heading into a fractious primary, which significantly impacted the eventual nominee.

The Mitt Romney Campaign Takes Shape

Michael Beach cofounded the Republican digital consultancy Targeted Victory with Zac Moffatt in early 2009. The two previously worked for the RNC during the 2008 cycle. Beach ran the party's political operations through Election Day, and Moffatt directed the party's political education program until the spring of 2007 (which involved coordinating trainings for campaign practitioners), when he joined the Republican Party–allied 501c(4) Freedom's Watch to work on statewide issue advocacy and in the process learned more about television and digital advertising. Beach and Moffatt stated that they were motivated to start their own firm because they perceived a need for year-round product development and keeping Republican talent in the field. They found it frustrating that the party committees often close up shop after elections and lay everyone off. Former staffers are then unemployed for six months, and some leave politics entirely. A political consultancy, Beach and Moffatt thought, could better capitalize on opportunities for year-round product development, actually plan for future markets (unlike the party committees, which were narrowly focused on the upcoming election), and provide a revenue stream to keep talented staffers employed until the next election, a dynamic they saw on the Democratic side of the aisle with firms such as BSD.

Beach and Moffatt stated that the other big firms in this space at the time were Campaign Solutions, Engage (Mindy Finn and Patrick Ruffini's firm), and the David All Group, a start-up digital political consultancy launched in 2007. In evaluating the market, the two also noticed that there were some broadcast advertising firms beginning to move into digital consulting. That said, Beach and Moffatt stated that there were no full-service digital firms offering software as a service (SaaS) on the order of the Democrats' Blue State Digital in the Republican field. Looking to BSD as a model, whose platform served as a partisan club good shared among ideological and partisan allies as detailed in the previous chapter, Beach and Moffatt designed Targeted Victory to offer SaaS.[41] The model was premised on reinvesting profits in the firm during off-election years to build tools that a number of campaigns could later use, instead of moving contract to contract during cycles.[42] The principals then had to determine how to price their platform for multiple clients to recoup their investment money.[43]

The risk for Beach and Moffatt, and political SaaS firms more generally, was that they would develop software for a future market that did not materialize. The potential advantage of this approach, however, is that the firm could be run more like a technology company, with large investments up front in a platform that could provide greater capacity than any one client could afford at a moment in time. One challenge that these practitioners pointed to is that it is tough to start a SaaS business on the right without capital or large clients funding programs year round. Whereas on the left, organizations in the extended Democratic Party network supported market leaders when they emerged (such as VAN and BSD) in the effort to make them better and facilitate technological adoption.[44] Beach and Moffatt argued that on the right this support of market leaders occurs less frequently, and as a result few firms invest capital without having guaranteed work for a client. Indeed, the traditional model for consulting firms entails essentially building to order based on specific client needs during a cycle. This model entails less risk, but also greater variability in resource flows. Campaigns may not have substantial resources until comparatively late in cycles, which means that technological development is often hampered by resource and time constraints.

Moffatt first began talking to members of Romney's Free and Strong America PAC in August 2009. Moffatt went to Boston with Tony Feather, a partner at FLS Connect and longtime Republican operative who was the political director for the Bush 2000 campaign. Moffatt met with Romney and his advisor Beth Myers, as well as a few others, to discuss what PACs and other political organizations were doing to build out lists and infrastructure. Moffatt said that text messaging captured the imaginations of many members of this group, given that the 2008 Obama campaign pioneered the pitch to people to sign up to receive a text message about the vice presidential selection. Moffatt and Beach pitched Romney a text messaging program, 466488 (translating to "GoMitt"), and argued more broadly that the governor should start by focusing on text messaging. Moffatt believed that text messaging had the advantage of being able to cut through competing information by appearing directly in front of voters, making it "a clean touch point."[45]

The Free and Strong America PAC subsequently became one of Targeted Victory's clients. The PAC made a commitment to commission future work from the firm. For the firm, taking on the PAC was not without risk. While many political scientists saw the race as inevitable, staffers within Targeted Victory stated that they believed Romney had a one in four chance of getting through the primaries given their perception that the party's primary electorate had moved far to the right. There was also much at stake because Beach and Moffatt made the decision that they would send their best people up to Boston in the hope that if Romney emerged from the primary, then the campaign would be able to hire them and their resource outlays up front would work out. Beach, who worked on all of the firm's non-Romney business, stated that at the time "we just felt like we had to take a bet on, we wanted our guy to win, I think we were pretty much true believers in the candidate."[46] At the same time, while this bet might cost them time and resources, even if Romney lost there was also the advantage of going to work on the campaign and learning about digital politics at the presidential level.

Their decision meant that Moffatt positioned himself close to Romney as the campaign was setting up its political department and figuring out its data operations. Moffatt moved to Boston with his wife, making the decision that he needed to run his part of Targeted Victory there (with Beach remaining in D.C. to build out other parts of the business) because "if anything happened I wanted to be a part of it."[47] In other words, Moffatt wanted to make sure that Targeted Victory was positioned to run Romney's digital effort. In the interim before the presidential primary really took shape, Moffatt recalls working to get Romney online. Despite running in the primaries in 2008, Targeted Victory staffers stated that at the time Romney only had approximately 1,000 people on his Twitter feed and 60,000 friends on Facebook, in addition to a small email list. More generally, the candidate and his staff were not tweeting regularly or actively using social media, and it appeared that Romney's team did not keep good records after the campaign shut down in 2008. Indeed, it is striking, as Targeted Victory's staffers tell it, how little the 2012 campaign inherited from the 2008 run. Former staffers on the 2012 bid noted that in 2008 Romney essentially self-financed his run, and as a result did not have a large or particularly developed fundraising program. As a result, the digital team started with a pretty raw fundraising database. There were, by Moffatt's estimation, tens of thousands of email addresses (which grew to 6 million by the end of the campaign in 2012).[48] For example, Moffatt recalled that in

2009 the campaign only had 3,000 email addresses tagged to Iowa for a campaign that spent roughly $10 million in the state during the primaries.

After looking at the state of his email and social media, Moffatt proposed that Romney build up his assets for the future and work to help candidates in 2010. The digital team focused on email list building for fundraising purposes and expanding Romney's social media presence (which former staffers said underwent rapid growth during this time). To track these efforts and demonstrate their progress to the campaign, every week Targeted Victory presented the PAC's leadership with a report that stated where the governor stood in digital media against his presumed rivals for 2012, how many people were talking about the candidate online, the amount of social media followers Romney and the PAC were gaining, and the return on investment (ROI) in terms of emails captured and dollars coming in. All of this work for Romney took shape alongside the firm's work for a number of other clients, which grew its staff.

POLITICAL OPERATIONS ON THE PRIMARY BID

In the spring of 2010, while Targeted Victory was building out Romney's digital infrastructure, Matt Rhoades, the director of communications for Romney's 2008 run who would become campaign manager for the 2012 bid, and Rich Beeson, the longtime Republican political operative and partner in FLS Connect, began having conversations about the political (or "field") operations for a presidential run. By fall of that year the governor was going around to various states to promote Republican candidates during the midterm cycle. The Free and Strong America PAC was also making a lot of contributions in those races. By January 2011, Beeson began commuting to Boston on a weekly basis and working out of PAC headquarters, before moving over to the campaign as political director in the spring, when it formally launched. As for the role of the political operations in the campaign, Beeson described having an early meeting with the candidate to talk about the political director position. Beeson stated that in response to a question about what political was going to do for the campaign, he said, "If it's within a field goal . . . we are the ones that will push it across the line. Clearly you [Romney] are the one that this whole thing is built around, but it's our job to make sure that we don't lose by 3 points or less."[49] This is the exact language that 2008 Obama campaign manager David Plouffe used, and it accords with the broad consensus of political scientists as to the potential value of field on a campaign.[50]

That said, throughout 2011 there were significant differences between the Romney and Obama campaigns with respect to investments in political and field operations and the creation of field offices, which persisted during the general election. Obama opened 786 field offices compared to Romney's 284 during the election, and they were oriented toward the candidate, not the party (the Romney

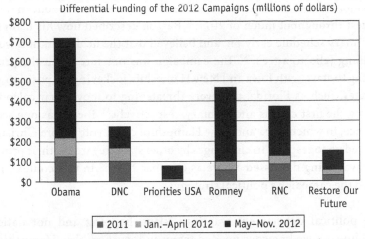

Figure 4.1 DIFFERENTIAL FUNDING OF THE 2012 CAMPAIGNS (MILLIONS OF DOLLARS). The Obama campaign, DNC, and Priorities USA Action Super PAC raised approximately $235.4 million in 2011, $159 million in January–April 2012, and $677.6 million in May–November 2012, for a total of approximately $1.07 billion. The Romney campaign, RNC, and Restore Our Future Super PAC raised approximately $169.9 million in 2011, $113.8 million in January–April 2012, and $708.7 million in May–November 2012, for a total of approximately $992.4 million. Source: "The 2012 Money Race: Compare the Candidates." *New York Times*, http://elections.nytimes.com/2012/campaign-finance.

campaign relied on the party for much of its field operation when he became the nominee).[51] This can be explained in part by the differences in the resources of the two campaigns throughout 2011, when the Obama campaign was building much of its infrastructure.[52] The Romney campaign and the Republican Party raised considerably less money throughout 2011 than the Obama campaign and the Democratic Party, which includes differences between the two candidates' allied Super PACs as well (see Figure 4.1).[53] These differences are important given the resources that needed to be invested up front in technical development and field programs (the former in terms of planning, building, and field testing technologies, the latter in terms of opening offices, mobilizing volunteers, making voter contacts, and engaging in ongoing modeling), while these things reap benefits over time. Indeed, the Romney campaign in 2011 even had comparatively fewer resources than the Obama campaign in 2007, precisely the time in the race when the future president's primary bid was investing in long-term field infrastructure. According to FEC reports, in 2007 the Obama campaign raised $103,787,457 to Romney's $56,884,330 in 2011.[54] While this does not take account of Super PAC funding, it also provides a cleaner comparison of resources for field operations, digital, technology, data, and analytics given that outside groups primarily engage in broadcast advertising.[55]

Even more, there was uncertainty in the timeline of the Republican nominating contest throughout much of 2011.[56] Beeson described how his team looked at the primary schedule early on, and believed that the field operation would be "like nailing Jello to a tree."[57] The campaign was not sure when the primaries were going to start, with Iowa and New Hampshire jockeying for position against other states, such as Florida, that were threatening to move their calendars up to leapfrog the first caucus and primary, respectively.[58] There was one scenario, for instance, in which Iowa and New Hampshire could vote before Christmas as they moved up to respond to challenges by other states regarding their primacy— and this was being discussed as late as October 2011.[59] In this context, Beeson described the campaign's political strategy:

> The political department was into island hopping and not nation building. So we knew we needed teams in Iowa and New Hampshire, although Iowa was just a skeleton structure because we were holding off there until we absolutely had to go in, but New Hampshire, Florida, Michigan, a lot of these early states we put teams in place knowing that as soon as those elections were over and—this ultimately hurt us in the general because we had, it was just a function of resources—but as soon as that primary was over we would leapfrog them to a primary that was three weeks or a month ahead.[60]

As political scientists Hahrie Han and Elizabeth McKenna have extensively documented, Beeson described a significantly different strategy from that which characterized the Obama campaigns in 2008 and 2012. Both campaigns were premised on building more lasting infrastructure on the ground about a year and a half in advance of these elections, all of which was underlaid by an extensive volunteer team leader program.[61] The 2008 campaign also featured long-term investments in field offices that then carried over from the primaries to the general election.

There was also not going to be a large shift in how the Romney campaign used data in support of this political operation. Heading into the 2010 midterm cycle, former campaign staffers stated that the Republican data and analytics firm TargetPoint was able to integrate the many different data sets of campaigns, party organizations, and commercial providers for the first time for the purposes of voter modeling. Data integration had been talked about for a long time on the Republican side of the aisle, but practitioners noted that it was at this point that the technical capacity to achieve it had significantly improved. As a result, firms such as TargetPoint began to talk about and stress the importance of big data for campaigns for the purposes of making voter modeling based on more comprehensive data.

TargetPoint approached the Romney campaign with a multimillion-dollar proposal called the Abacus Project. This proposed project, which was driven by TargetPoint's Alex Gage and Brent Seaborn, would integrate all of the campaign's various systems and databases and make analytics a core part of the infrastructure of the campaign. Alex Lundry, then the chief data scientist for TargetPoint and who would later become the director of data science for the campaign during the general election, noted that the motivation behind the project was not just the improved technical capacity of the firm, but watching what Obama was assembling in 2011. As detailed in the first chapter, Lundry saw a job posting of the Obama campaign during this time looking for "predictive modelers," which became "a motivating factor when we were trying to sell the Abacus Project. . . ."[62]

The campaign ultimately turned TargetPoint down.[63] The reason, according to Lundry, was both a function of price and an under-appreciation of the potential power of analytics. It was not just the Romney campaign, potentially suggesting a broader comparative devaluation of data and analytics within the Republican Party network during this time. Lundry noted that TargetPoint attempted to sell its Abacus Project around D.C. based on the argument that it would create a fully integrated system and ultimately give rise to operational efficiencies, cost savings, the increased ability of different departments on campaigns to coordinate with respect to strategy and tactics, and better targeting across multiple platforms. Lundry stated that no one took TargetPoint up on the offer, in no small part given the cost of building these systems, practitioners' inability to recognize how much time it took, and more broadly the fact that ". . . they could not wrap their heads around the immediate value of doing so."[64]

DIGITAL'S ROLE IN THE PRIMARY CAMPAIGN

In early 2011, Romney formally hired Rhoades as campaign manager and Andrea Saul as communications director as the official campaign organization took shape. Moffatt was well positioned to become the digital director, but his big concern was how the position would be structured on the campaign. Moffatt stated that he would only leave Targeted Victory to join the campaign if the digital director was made a senior staff-level position, he was able to sit in on all the strategy meetings, and there were resources dedicated to digital.

Moffatt became the digital director in June 2011, a senior staff position that was equivalent to the directors of other departments such as communications, political, and finance. Numerous former staffers within the digital department and campaign more generally stated that Moffatt had a seat at the leadership table and voice in the campaign's operations that provided the opportunity for his team to secure resources. That said, in practice, the digital team had narrower jurisdiction and considerably less autonomy in the context of digital communications than its counterpart on the Obama campaign.[65] These organizational dynamics within the Romney campaign were the outcome of a history of party network processes that led to the comparative under-valuing of digital operations on Republican campaigns.

For example, there were a number of jurisdictional issues on the Romney campaign around which department would be responsible for things such as email given that it crossed many organizational domains. One advantage Obama 2012 staffers had is that these jurisdictional issues were largely settled on the campaign in 2008, which carried over to the re-election bid. Moffatt had to push, early on, for the digital department to be responsible for all the email of the campaign, primarily because staffers wanted to control the user experience. Moffatt was concerned that supporters would be receiving upward of 10 emails a day if multiple departments on the campaign were able to independently send email, a similar concern of the new media staffers on the 2008 Obama campaign.[66] Revealing the relative status of departments on the campaign, Moffatt stated that it was Rich Beeson, the influential political director, who ultimately made the internal organizational argument that enabled the digital department to have jurisdiction over email. As a result, Moffatt organized the email operations in line with what he perceived to be the best practices of digital strategic communications, where the list was heavily managed and there were only certain events and requests that could be promoted at particular times. In other words, the list was not freely available for departments to use as they saw fit, which would have undermined the sorts of targeting and requests the digital team wanted to engage in and risked oversaturating the list. Staffers on both sides of the aisle argue that this type of management helps preserve the value of email lists, which ultimately is defined in terms of how many people take actions such as donating and volunteering in response to requests. To facilitate the email program, the Romney campaign hired an email director, a content director, and someone who oversaw the digital fundraising and tied all the different pieces together and created a holistic fundraising plan.

While the digital team won jurisdiction over email, former staffers also said that they lacked autonomy and there was a vetting process for all digital content. Former digital staffers stated that everything they produced for the Internet, including emails, tweets, Facebook and blog posts, and photos, had to be sent around via email for formal approval. This approval chain included the digital leadership, such as Zac Moffatt and deputy digital director Abe Adams, the department directors or deputy directors, as well as a handful of other people. In addition, if the content related to a specific area of the campaign such as policy, than that team needed a say on it. This included upward of 20 people, depending on the point in the campaign and the type of content to be approved, and could also involve the deputy campaign managers and occasionally the campaign manager. Not all of these people needed to sign off on everything, however, but digital staffers argued that the vetting process led to extensive self-regulation where they would only produce content they believed would get approved. More generally, former staffers argued that while the digital team was responsible for the distribution of content across digital platforms, the communications department was responsible for the message itself.

As I have argued, this vetting process was consequential in terms of constraining digital staffers' ability to produce content that met the speed and genre expectations of social media audiences.[67] While the Obama digital team in Chicago had extensive autonomy to produce and distribute content, which was the product of a particular approach to digital honed on the 2008 campaign and within the party more generally (albeit unevenly), the Romney digital team could only work on the design of the website and mobile applications without approval. Former staffers argued that this organizational structure precluded the production of certain types of content. For example, while state-level Obama digital staffers were interviewing volunteers to produce content for various social media platforms, Caitlin Checkett argued that for the Romney team, "So you get into the cycle where a press release is sent to us, it is something that we can add to the site, you can pull a Facebook message from that, some Twitter copy and you don't have to go through the approval process because it was already approved. So I felt like that was a huge problem because of course people don't want to go to your website and read press releases and we knew that."[68]

Former staffers argued that the differences between the two presidential campaigns with respect to content were attributable not just to the lack of autonomy for digital staffers on the Romney bid, but also the favorable financial position of the unopposed incumbent throughout 2011, as detailed above. The Romney campaign had just six staffers working in digital for much of the first eight months, and three off-site developers for the website. As a result, producing original content for multiple platforms on a regular basis was a significant challenge. By necessity, with this small staff, everyone had a hand in everything. This was generally the case until October 2011, when the campaign hired a writer, two designers, and another developer, which brought digital to approximately 13 staffers in total at that point in time. The digital team grew slowly to roughly 17–18 people, including a videographer and content managers, when Romney became the presumptive nominee in April 2012.

Another significant difference between the two campaigns was the degree to which the value of digital staffers was settled on the Obama campaign, whereas Moffatt and other staffers needed to convince relevant actors of the digital team's worth in order to make claims on resources and autonomy. Moffatt, for instance, stated that the digital team needed to "sell people on a vision" for what digital could bring to the campaign.[69] To do so, similar to his work during the early days of the PAC, every Friday Moffatt produced a report on the previous week that detailed what they had accomplished and what the plan was for the coming week. Every month, Moffatt provided metrics for the preceding month about things such as online fundraising, email list growth, YouTube video views, how many people liked the Romney campaign on Facebook, and the number of new followers the candidate and the campaign had on Twitter, as well as projections for the coming month. Moffatt's goal was to establish clear metrics with respect to the attention and engagement the campaign was receiving on social media, even though the relationship between social media metrics and campaign goals such as fundraising and volunteers is actually unclear, which staffers on both sides of the aisle acknowledged. Indeed, these metrics were particularly valuable to Romney's digital staffers as strategic assets they could use to convince relevant actors on the campaign of digital's value and secure resources.

Moffatt also stated that the digital team had a plan to raise $180 million online and needed to do a lot of work to make its case internally for why this was an achievable goal and to secure the resources it needed to reach it.[70] Digital returns were going to be many months out, and required an advance commitment from the campaign to build infrastructure. To help convince relevant stakeholders, Moffatt circulated a fundraising memo to the other directors on the campaign that provided metrics on what success would look like and a road map for how the digital team was going to achieve it. Moffatt also sat down with the other directors to discuss how the digital team would scale donors up the ladder of engagement from contributions of $5 a month, to $10 and later $25, and so on.

While ultimately Romney's digital team stated that they were successful at getting organizational buy-in for their work, the Obama re-election team did not have the same level of scrutiny, nor did it need to convince other actors on the campaign as to its electoral value, given that the 2008 campaign validated digital operations and the Democratic Party more broadly was making significant investments in digital. Indeed, the Republican Party as a whole lacked an online donor pool, infrastructure such as email lists and third-party donation sites like ActBlue to facilitate digital fundraising, and, most important, the valuation of digital small-dollar fundraising efforts as being on a par with large-donor efforts.

ONLINE ADVERTISING, SOCIAL MEDIA, AND THE CAMPAIGN WEBSITE DURING THE PRIMARIES

Targeted Victory conducted a bipartisan study about how voters consume political content, called "Off the Grid," which it released in September 2011 and which shaped much of the strategy for digital during the campaign.[71] The key finding was that people were consuming increased amounts of video, but not live television, although it varied across demographic groups. Even further, the study estimated that approximately one-third of voters were unreachable through traditional television advertising. Moffatt remembers that this finding connected with Rhoades immediately given that he consumed a lot of video, but it was never live. It was the moment when Moffatt asked, "how would our ads get to you?" that the realities of the current media space clicked for the campaign's leadership. And numerous staffers also cited that Democrats are more concentrated in urban areas, whereas Republicans are more geographically dispersed, which makes it harder to find them.

Digital staffers did not know how much they would actually be able to spend on technical development or the staff resources they would have, given an anticipated long and resource-intensive primary. As such, the digital team focused on online advertising early on because it was one of the most scalable parts of the budget. In addition, online advertising furthered list building and fundraising. Data underlay the campaign's online advertising strategy, and staffers recognized the importance and attempted to meet the challenge of integrating data across the many different applications and databases used by the campaign. To do so, Targeted Victory provided access to a "data management platform" (DMP) for the campaign's digital operations. Targeted Victory also created partnerships with a number of companies that are important infrastructural firms in online advertising, such as Yahoo! and AOL. Taken together, digital staffers argued that the Targeted Victory DMP provided one central database that integrated the campaign's voter identification tags across its online databases.

Contemporary digital political advertising reflects larger changes in online advertising that have undermined the business model of the news industry in terms of allowing advertisers to buy audiences in a site-agnostic way.[72] As Moffatt explained, "What we want to do is to buy the audiences that match up to our third party data on your site. So rather than buy 1,000 impressions among people we know nothing about and probably have 50% waste, we are going to go on there and buy 50% of the audience we want, but we will pay you a premium for that because we are able to pay a 10% premium because we are eliminating 40 or 50% of the waste."[73] Staffers began with the same modeling universe that the strategy department provided for other departments to do mail, phone banking, and media buying such as TV and radio. Digital staffers created their messaging based on the audiences they were targeting and used Targeted Victory's DMP to buy audiences through online advertising networks, such as Yahoo! and AOL. In addition, the campaign built out audiences for its online advertising from the traffic it received across the Romney web properties. The campaign also matched individuals in the voter file to cookies and social media profiles for the purposes of targeting groups of people and tailoring content. Sometimes, the campaign matched cookies and profiles to voters of demographic interest to the campaign (i.e., women). At others, the campaign coupled demographics with geography (i.e., women in Virginia) for the purposes of state primaries and, during the general election, the Electoral College. The campaign also matched cookies and profiles based on the voter models created from micro-targeting data, at times supplementing these models with additional online data. All of this meant that the campaign was displaying online advertising to groups of voters of interest according to electoral strategy more broadly.

Online advertising was not infinitely targeted, however, and content was not tailored to the individual. Campaigns can create narrowly defined clusters of thousands or tens of thousands of people as opposed to millions, but the issue lies in creating content that will appeal to these narrowly defined segments. As Moffatt observed, "you can have all this input coming in but I can't do anything special to them" both because of the labor involved in crafting narrowly targeted appeals and the challenge of testing them to actually see if they work and the effort is worth the return.[74] Online advertising is another area where the Obama campaign enjoyed the technical advantage of incumbency. The Obama campaign had more time to supplement its email list through online ads, could engage in more extensive testing, enjoyed longer ROI timelines for online advertising, put together a large team that designed video exclusively for online, and could devote $35 million to persuasion alone.

In the end, staffers cited that the Romney campaign ended up running approximately 20,000 different digital ads, put together by a team that grew to approximately 18–20 people, and even became one of the largest mobile Facebook advertisers in the world in August 2012. In addition to engaging in online advertising early on, the campaign put together a social media operation building on the work of Targeted Victory for Romney's PAC. Rebecca Heisler, a former Targeted Victory staffer, ended up being responsible for the entire social media and digital content program by the end of the campaign. When the campaign began in earnest in April 2011, Heisler noted that she was the catch-all for social media and email marketing, with one other person helping her update the content on the website. Heisler worked closely with Moffatt and Abe Adams, the deputy digital director, on the strategy side for the social media content (Targeted Victory had already been managing the social media accounts for Romney for a year at that point through the PAC). In the transition to formally running a candidate, the campaign made a decision early on to keep Romney's Twitter account in the first-person voice and not tweet when the candidate was on stage at an event such as a debate to make tweets seem as if they were really coming from the candidate. Staffers used Twitter to appeal to strong supporters and try to set the agendas and frames of the professional press. The campaign later changed its approach to the first-person voice (and began tweeting during the debates) during the general election given the opportunity to capitalize on traffic and attention.[75] On Facebook, campaign staffers used both first-person and organizational voices, the latter particularly at the end of the campaign in the push around the early vote and getting out the vote.[76]

In addition to utilizing commercial social media platforms, the campaign built its own website. In October 2010, the campaign chose the open source platform Drupal for its site, rather than WordPress, which a lot of the other Republican primary candidates used. Digital staffers chose Drupal because they believed it was a technology that could make it through the primaries and ultimately have the ability to scale for the general election.[77] Caitlin Checkett, the digital integration director, noted that "it was the most critical decision that we could make and the reason why was that we picked a great technology right out of the gate and we never had to circle back and rebuild our site."[78] Checkett asserted that Drupal was robust enough to support, at the time of the NH primary, 1,000 people at the same time on the campaign's website, while seven months later there could be 35,000 simultaneous users on the site. Checkett stated that the primary thing the campaign needed to add was more servers, going from four to approximately 30 from the primaries to the general election.[79]

The strategy for the main Romney web property was threefold. First, the campaign designed MittRomney.com to introduce people to the candidate. Staffers did this through such things as a standard "about" page, a photo of Romney and his family, and videos, whatever staffers thought would personalize the candidate for voters. Staffers also used the website for email acquisition purposes as well as to drive donations.

One of the things the Romney website was not was a field tool. The reasons entailed issues with organizational structure, time, and resources. Numerous former staffers argued that the political and digital departments on the campaign were quite separate. Former staffers noted that while some digital staffers worked hand in hand with political staffers on a daily basis, there were some technology projects that political staffers pursued completely independently. The political department, for instance, developed the failed ORCA during the general election without any input from digital (as detailed in the next chapter). As one former digital staffer put it, the issue was "not being close enough to the political team or the political team not relying on us," which "is why the political team worked on ORCA when we had almost zero idea about it."[80] Given their separate domains, the digital team mostly focused on digital marketing, while political staffers independently pursued their own projects around digital field tools. Another reason the campaign's website was not designed with field in mind is because of the lack of time and resources during the primaries. Indeed, in the next chapter I demonstrate just how difficult, time consuming, and expensive it was for the Obama campaign to internally develop its web platform for field operations.

Given the time and resource constraints that staffers faced during the primaries, the Romney campaign often turned to commercial vendors for its web development, whereas the Obama campaign brought more of its operation in-house.[81] Each campaign weighed the trade-offs between hiring staffers in the digital and technology domains versus turning to consultancies and outside firms. Hiring staffers provides more accountability over technical development; staffers can manage and direct employees. For example, as detailed in the next chapter, Michael Slaby and others who were responsible for overseeing the infrastructure for the 2012 Obama campaign cited the fact that there is often a lack of ownership and accountability when something is developed outside the direct control of the party or the campaign. Furthermore, relying on multiple external vendors often means systems that rarely interface with one another and the proliferation of data silos at their back-ends. Indeed, these were lessons that grew out of the 2008 campaign, which relied on multiple vendors, and led to decisions to bring more development in-house in 2012.

In sum, outsourcing technical development means that campaigns may give up direct control over the services provided, use tools that are not explicitly designed for politics, and face the problem of multiple loosely integrated systems. That said, staffers on both sides of the aisle argued that this can make sense if resources are scarce or inconsistent, or if a campaign organization has to scale quickly (as the Romney campaign did after the conclusion of the primaries). The trade-off is that while going outside the campaign may provide robust commercial platforms, it also means a lack of control and accountability over the design and functionality of technologies and the need to fit the products and processes of many different vendors together. Romney's staffers cited precisely these issues on the campaign. To meet their development needs, Moffatt hired external developers or specialized firms to work on specific projects. As Moffatt described these arrangements and their fragility: "Every single time something went wrong in the campaign it was just because we had gone through a wave of hiring and somewhere the process broke down. . . . you're really kind of amazed that it didn't happen every day."[82]

These dynamics were apparent on the campaign. The Romney campaign successfully integrated with the commercial firm Eventbrite to offer a tool where attendees to political events could sign up online, receive tickets via email to print, and have them scanned at the event so data went back to the campaign. And yet, Eventbrite was not integrated with the voter file or the other volunteer management systems on the campaign. Meanwhile, the campaign used Salesforce to gather and store all of the web property data, including information from petitions, donations, and registration, and then used this to send emails, but this data was not integrated with the voter file provided through GOP Data Center. As Checkett put it, "It was not the entire campaign that was logging into a centralized CRM [customer relationship management platform]."[83] As a workaround, the digital team would manually flag people in Salesforce based on certain important characteristics they knew from the voter file, such as whether a voter tended to vote absentee.

To use a metaphor, the Romney 2012 bid was a comparatively under-staffed and under-funded digital start-up during 2011 through the primary contests in 2012, as compared with the Obama campaign's Google with its more stable funding, longer-term time horizon, considerably greater staff, and infrastructural resources that came from the party. On the Romney campaign, there were a number of development projects that would have taken considerable time and resources and as a result they did not get built or were until late in the general election. For example, this includes what the campaign called Victory Wallet, a single-click donation system, which was not rolled out until September 2012 (on the Obama campaign an application with similar functionality called Quick Donate was developed by Blue State Digital and launched in March).[84] The Romney campaign first started trying to build Victory Wallet in September 2011, the argument being that the longer it was in use the greater the benefit to the campaign. That said, the campaign had to run through a number of calculations as to its potential return on investment. As Moffatt described, knowing that they had comparatively less resources to spend meant needing to make decisions about how to spend them efficiently:

> Let's say you have a technology you want to build that you believe will cost $150,000 to a quarter of a million dollars [Victory Wallet] . . . you know you probably need to spend $10,000 to $15,000 scoping it out and you are going to be like "OK, this is the ball park of what it is going to cost for the full solution." That was one of the things that someone was like "I could be up on the air for a week with that. We are not doing that." So that was one of the really hard things because, you know I could get where they were coming from because it would have been awesome to have a wallet solution if you were the nominee but if we lost in February when it became live it didn't matter, right?[85]

The Voting Begins

Romney's digital team was small throughout much of 2011 compared with the Obama campaign, with everyone in one room trying to carry out development projects. Romney staffers focused on technical projects they believed they could achieve easily, such as making sure their web and mobile sites loaded quickly. That said, digital was still one of the largest departments on the campaign, with approximately seven people after October and roughly 14 during the active primary season, supplemented by people from Targeted Victory. While Romney's staffers had comparatively fewer resources during this time than their eventual Democratic rival, they had considerably more than their challengers for the Republican nomination. Heading into the active primary season, the Romney campaign had significant resource advantages over the others vying for the nomination.

However, the candidate's staffers faced and perceived a different "digital opportunity structure" than the insurgent candidates challenging the Republican establishment. The social movement scholar Sidney Tarrow defined "political opportunity structure" as the "consistent—but not necessarily formal or permanent—dimensions of the political environment that provide incentives for people to undertake collective action by affecting their expectations for success or failure."[86] Building from this work, digital opportunity structures are features of the political environment and candidates and campaigns' symbolic, material, and relational position in it, which shape the possibilities for using digital media for strategic ends. These opportunities are only realized, however, when a candidate's staffers perceive them, and have the skills to navigate the networked, hybrid media environment. Every candidate faces a different digital opportunity structure. Digital opportunity structures are the hands that campaigns are dealt by the electoral context, the candidate, and the fields of politics and media that shape the possibility for specifically *digital* mobilization. And staffers have to perceive the salient features of their environment and candidate so as to be able to act within this structure more or less well for competitive advantage, even as structures change over time as the result of the actions that campaigns and parties take and the outcomes of electoral contests (such as during primaries).[87] For example, a number of scholars have noted that insurgent candidates have greater incentives to use digital media in the attempt to inspire collective social and symbolic action among their supporters and to secure resources in the absence of institutional party support. In part, this is because challengers to establishment frontrunners can often inspire digital mobilization among passionate subgroups of party activists.[88] There are other features of the political environment that shape the capacity for digital mobilization, if staffers themselves perceive and can take advantage of these opportunities (which is also in part the product of the historical workings of party networks in conditioning the recognition of and skills to act upon digital opportunities). They include the field of candidates, composition of the electorate, the issues favored by the political context, the relative power of groups in the party network, which party holds office, the issues the candidate is running on and the broader political culture, structures and patterns of legacy media coverage, perceptions of viability, the candidate's biography and charisma (a candidate's public persona and the willingness of people to believe and follow her), the media habits of the candidate's supporters and the ideological and party activists she appeals to, and so on.[89]

To illustrate this concept, a common sentiment among Romney's former digital staffers was that digital worked differently for their candidate than for challengers such as Rick Santorum or even Newt Gingrich, who were (ironically) outsider and insurgent candidates. On the Romney campaign, staffers argued that challengers to the frontrunner had advantages in being able to more easily generate and then translate the energy and desire of their supporters into electoral resources, even if it was only from the perspective of these candidates being the anti-Romney candidate. For instance, political scientists John Sides and Lynn Vavreck found spikes in the poll numbers of successive anti-Romney candidates after they received significant press attention.[90] Digital media enabled these challengers to quickly and efficiently capitalize on opportunities in the environment, such as heightened media attention, through things such as online fundraising. Indeed, fundraising totals by month reveal precisely this pattern of large spikes after the heightened media attention toward an insurgent candidate, whether it was caused by an electoral victory, a better than expected showing in a primary, or general journalist interest.[91] As Moffatt described: "I think it is fair to say Rick Santorum out raised us 2 or 3 to 1 online. . . . I think that is a testament to what you can make up for when you don't have some of these other elements in your favor [institutional resources] because you could organize your structure to maximize every opportunity you have. . . ."[92]

During the active primary season, Romney's digital staffers continually worked to support political operations for upcoming contests against the constant drumbeat of online fundraising. As Abe Adams put it, fundraising was "the beat that lives and goes on no matter what else is going on [in] the campaign."[93] To support the campaign's political operations, staffers used digital media to facilitate voter contacts for persuasion and get out the vote (GOTV) purposes. The digital team worked with political staffers to determine what universes of voters to target from the voter file and the messaging to use, and then tried to find these people online. To do so, the digital team used the email addresses they had, as well as other online data, and sought to match them with universes of targeted voters from the voter file.

That said, this was an imperfect process. For example, there are a number of challenges that campaigns face with respect to targeting online advertising for political purposes. As detailed throughout this book, campaigns often store data in different places, and databases are often imperfectly matched together. Staffers on both sides of the aisle cited integration issues with online data, meaning that they could not track the outcomes of online ads all in one place. Even more, political online advertising adheres to industry best practices, and as such is premised upon non-personally identifiable information, which limits the data that campaigns receive back from their efforts. In other words, through things such as cookie and profile matches, campaigns know they are reaching a modeled universe, but cannot track the actions that identifiable people take in response to online advertising (as campaigns can through emails).[94] With respect to online advertising on platforms such as Facebook, there is always a wall between the campaign and the voter. Campaigns do not get data back from the third-party advertisers they use or social media platforms they advertise on in terms of who was actually matched to the voter file, and do not receive data back on what identifiable people did in response to online ads. Campaigns only receive a high-level summary of ad statistics. All of this means that campaigns can only measure the persuasive effects of ads indirectly through things such as tracking polling, including asking people questions such as how often they are online and if they watch television online, and then looking at cross-tabbed data to see if there was attitudinal movement in these groups. Sometimes campaigns will also run online-specific messaging in ads and then ask about this messaging in polling.[95] Staffers do, however, receive things such as names and email addresses if people gift this information to a campaign in response to an ad.

Throughout the active primary season, Romney's digital team engaged in online fundraising and advertising, the latter to further the campaign's political operations. Staffers argued that there was little room for anything else. The unexpectedly long and bruising primary season was draining from both an emotional and resource perspective. This, in turn, impacted technological development. Staffers in digital, political, and analytics stated that internally the campaign's polling suggested that Romney was going to win New Hampshire and Florida (which held its primary on January 31st) and then pull away. In actuality, the primary unfolded in a less clear cut way. Romney narrowly lost Iowa to Rick Santorum, won New Hampshire, but an unexpected Newt Gingrich victory in South Carolina stalled the frontrunner's momentum.[96] While Romney won Florida and Nevada, Santorum hung around with February victories in Colorado, Missouri, and Minnesota. Romney subsequently won Arizona and eked out a very narrow victory in Michigan (a state where the candidate had historic ties through his father). This pushed the race to Super Tuesday on March 6. Santorum won three states outright, which moved the race through the end of March, when a string of Southern victories in Alabama, Mississippi, and Louisiana kept his campaign alive. That said, by early April Santorum was running out of money and losing press coverage, and Romney swept contests in Maryland and Wisconsin, prompting Santorum to suspend his campaign on April 10.

Throughout the entire primary process, Romney had a nearly insurmountable lead in delegates, and was clearly the frontrunner in terms of elite endorsements.[97] That said, the long primary forced the campaign to spend money in unanticipated ways, which undermined the campaign's planning. For example, the digital team initially scheduled its work around the assumption that Romney would quickly emerge as the nominee after Florida. When this scenario did not play out, the leadership directed more of its resources toward television and away from digital, including bidding for spots well in advance of contests in February and March. Staffers cited that this meant that resources for particular, longer-term technological projects were redirected to the primary contests.

Meanwhile, digital staffers had to adapt to the demands of a long protracted primary instead of building infrastructure for the general election. Rebecca Heisler, for instance, who as detailed above was responsible for handling all the social media as well as website content for the campaign, described how her work changed during the active primary season. Heisler was responsible for posting the press releases, videos, microsites, and graphics the campaign was producing. The goal was to get the candidate's message out in a crowded primary field. While Heisler had a deputy during the general election who served as the point person for the communications staffers (which went through digital for its web-based content), during the primaries she was the funnel for the entire communications shop, along with a number of interns. This was demanding, particularly during high-traffic times such as post-debates, when the communications team was generating more than a dozen press releases. Heisler's days during these times would often last from 5 a.m. until midnight.

More generally, staffers had to orient their work around the changing dynamics of the race during the primaries. Digital staffers compared Romney with Hillary

Clinton in 2008 as the more moderate of the two candidates. As a result of being the establishment frontrunner, there was a lot of mobilization against the campaign. Staffers also argued that the press was interested in keeping the race alive. This meant that the digital team was consumed with responding in the moment to the dynamics of the race. For example, staffers cited that when Romney lost Colorado, Minnesota, and Missouri to Rick Santorum on February 7, they had to constantly work to address negative press and online sentiment and pivot to support political operations in upcoming states, all while feeling psychologically drained at the experience of losing multiple primaries. Meanwhile, Moffatt stated that in advance of the Michigan primary on February 28, he knew that if the campaign lost he would have to lay off three of his digital staffers.

Conclusion

In scholarly and popular accounts, the 2012 general election is often looked at in isolation, without considering everything that came before. This approach misses the importance of the history of party networks, the fragility of political infrastructures, and the work that takes place (or fails to) between presidential election cycles in shaping campaigns. The 2012 Romney primary campaign took shape in a context where there was considerably less investment in technology, digital media, data, and analytics across the Republican Party network than on the other side of the aisle after the 2004 cycle. This ultimately meant fewer party and party network technologies, assets, and infrastructure for the Romney digital team to draw on, and fewer staffers and firms with expertise in the areas of technology, digital media, data, and analytics, than what the Obama campaign had available to assemble. It also meant that the Romney campaign's leadership was drawn from the ranks of communications professionals, and as a result there was less autonomy for digital staffers than on the Obama campaign.

At the same time, simple comparisons of the general election campaigns of Obama and Romney also miss what the contested primary cycle looked like and ultimately how the two general election campaigns had different starting lines. While to many political scientists the outcome of the primaries may have seemed inevitable, this was not the experience of the campaign among those who worked on it. The extended primary was financially and emotionally draining in ways that impacted strategic planning and technological development, all of which put the Republican nominee at a distinct disadvantage when compared with the incumbent president's campaign. While the Obama campaign was shooting the moon on technology, digital media, data, and analytics projects during the primary season, the Romney campaign was consumed with actually contesting the primaries.

Even more, running uncontested, during the primary season Obama also out-raised Romney by a considerable margin, which meant more resources for field offices, digital staffers, and technological development projects. According to political scientist David Magleby, throughout the Republican nominating contest Obama raised and spent considerably more than Romney. Magleby notes that Obama had $97.5 million in cash on hand, compared to Romney's $22.5 million, in June 2012, and Obama spent $200 million in June-August compared to $126 million by Romney.[98] Ars Technica analyzed the two campaigns' spending on information technology, and found that the resource-intensive primaries forced the Romney campaign to outsource much of its infrastructure and consulting, while the Obama campaign "insourced" by building internally, as detailed in the next chapter. Ironically, the upshot was that in the long run, Romney's campaign spent more on information technology products and consulting, even as many of these technologies were less reliable and had to be patched together.[99]

Ultimately, the structural position of the Romney campaign and the particular choices its leadership made resulted in products not built and technologies developed and then put on hold. By the time the RNC had a presumptive nominee on April 25, which opened the door to resources flowing to the general election candidate, the Romney campaign was already significantly behind its rival. I turn now to a closer look at how the Obama re-election campaign spent its resources in 2011, before turning to the general election.

5

Re-electing the President

While the Romney campaign was making its way through 2011 and months of contested primaries, the Obama re-election bid was staffing up, developing its organizational structure, planning its long-term technical operations, and building new technologies. The seeds of the re-election campaign were planted back in 2010 during a devastating midterm cycle for the Democrats, which served as the proving ground for new digital, field, data, and analytic practices at the party. Party staffers who worked during the midterm cycle carried these practices to the re-election bid, where they were joined by veteran 2008 staffers and others, including people from outside politics. Without an opponent, these staffers spent 2011 developing the campaign organization and key pieces of its technological infrastructure. All of this means that when Romney became the presumed nominee at the end of April 2012, the Obama general election campaign had essentially already been under development for well over a year.

This chapter reveals how the Obama campaign was the beneficiary of the technical advantage of incumbency, which has taken on new importance given the pace of changes in technology, media, culture, and society. Ongoing changes at the application layer of the Internet and shifts in media and cultural practice have meant fundamental changes in the nature of sociality, cultural life, and collective action, which are increasingly shaped by the affordances of platforms and the economic, technological, and cultural contexts they take shape in.[1] For example, as scholarship over the past 20 years has demonstrated, there are new intermediaries for the distribution of news and political content, new actors involved in the production of political culture, new dynamics of attention and forms of social affiliation and cultural expression, new ways that audiences overlap and move across different websites, new and renewed genres of political communication, and new forms of networked social structures more broadly.[2] The media practices of the electorate, activists, and journalists change, often dramatically, from cycle to cycle as new platforms emerge and comparatively older ones change. In response, campaigns have sought to build new technologies and platforms, and take up and adapt to continual changes in existing commercial ones, to gain strategic advantage over opponents. Accordingly, the technological environments that campaigns act in for competitive advantage, and which they in turn shape, have grown more complex. Voter databases have come online and become more sophisticated, the sources of data have exploded, and the expertise required for everything from managing technical systems to analyzing data has grown more specialized.

These changes mean two important things for contemporary campaigning. First, while many scholars have detailed the electoral advantages that incumbents have, there is a new technical advantage for incumbents that has generally gone unremarked upon in the academic and popular literature. Presidential campaigns often seek to develop new tools and applications in-house or with vendors during electoral cycles, and the opportunity to run unopposed or only face token opposition means longer development timelines. A longer period of time to run an uncontested campaign means more opportunities to strategize around development, recruit staffers, build and test tools, and integrate technology, data, and analytics across organizational departments. This is especially advantageous given that an incumbent campaign can learn what went right, and wrong, from the previous presidential bid, as the Bush re-election campaign did in 2004, and draw on resources such as email lists and supporter databases honed during the earlier run. Even smaller campaigns, such as congressional bids that likely do not have resources to engage in development, likely benefit from incumbency in terms of time to find expertise, learn how to integrate and supplement party and vendor provided tools, and build lists of supporters to digitally engage. With comparatively less time, challengers face the daunting technical tasks of building technologies quickly and with little time for testing and fitting together the databases, tools, and applications provided by the many commercial firms they often must rely on. They also face the organizational challenge of finding and recruiting staffers with expertise. Second, and related, being an incumbent means having more time to draw on party-provided infrastructure in the course of an electoral run. The Obama campaign in 2012 benefited greatly from being able to formally collaborate with the DNC over a year in advance of the election, take advantage of the party's staffing and technological resources, and work with the party to build an important back-end data infrastructure to address the challenges of working with many different technologies and vendors.

This chapter traces the resources, planning, expertise, and infrastructure behind Obama's re-election campaign. To do so, I chart the history of the Democratic Party's extended network from Obama's election in 2008 through the general election in 2012. The re-election bid's success was the result of a number of factors, including a robust extended party network that gave rise to particularly strong valuations of knowledge, skills, and practice in the domains of technology, digital, data, and analytics, and produced staffers with this expertise, as well as many infrastructural technologies for them to use. I argue that the campaign was also the product of the new technical advantages of incumbency, an organizational structure and culture that valued digital, data, and analytics, and the recruitment of staffers from the technology and commercial sectors whose knowledge and skills mixed with those of people on the campaign from the political field.

This chapter also makes the broader argument that presidential campaigns value their party organizations primarily *as databases* during electoral cycles. This is a theme I return to in the conclusion, but here I explore it empirically. While party organizations serve many functions, from providing services to candidates and organizing elections to building tools and attacking rivals, from a presidential campaign's perspective they are first and foremost a voter file and a set of tools for accessing it. This is a shift from previous eras of strong party organizations that campaigns valued primarily for their ability to mobilize the electorate, a capacity they had through the 1950s and 1960s but subsequently lost.[3] Parties are important as databases because they not only receive privileged access to public voter files from states, but also supplement this data with commercial information and house the accumulated records of voter contact forged over a decade (or longer in some cases, although record-keeping was nowhere near as advanced as it is today). Building, maintaining, cleaning, and supplementing databases, as well as making them available to the campaigns (and even the nonprofit and advocacy organizations in their extended networks) that use them to shape electoral strategy and guide the media messages they deploy across platforms and voter contacts by paid staffers and volunteers, are increasingly the most valuable services that parties provide.[4] At the same time, parties are often the producers of and repositories for analytics expertise and the proving grounds for new practices around this data, as demonstrated by the Republican Party's development of STOMP in the years between the 2000 and 2004 election cycles and the Democratic Party's analytics work after Obama's election in 2008.

As this chapter reveals, it was the Democratic Party's voter file, in the making since 2005, that served as the backbone for much of the Obama campaign and provided the technical object that people in the campaign and within the party convened around, drew on to shape all aspects of electoral strategy, and used to coordinate their activities. Meanwhile, the Republican Party lacked a comparable data infrastructure, as well as field and analytics tools and digital assets, for its nominee to draw on. As one former Republican Party staffer who also worked on the Romney campaign put it, echoing the narrative of the last chapter, the party lacked APIs to open its voter file to outside data and had poor field tools:

> You do wonder when the party shows up on day one of when you are the nominee, and you ask the question of, 'OK what assets can you provide us with?'—I think if you can't provide more assets than the last time you [were] asked the question, then I don't necessarily think that something is going right. So whether it's an email database, whether

it's voter contact, whether it's volunteers, whether it's, whatever it is. So I know that we received less than what they [the McCain campaign] theoretically received in '08.[5]

I begin this chapter by detailing and analyzing the history of the Democratic Party's extended network after Obama's election in 2008 through 2011, when the key infrastructure of the re-election bid was put in place. I then turn to the general election, providing a side-by-side look at the Obama and Romney campaigns.

The Democratic Party from 2008 to 2011

The core innovation of the Democratic Party after the 2008 presidential cycle lay in the work of modernizing the analytics of the party and the underlying infrastructure that supported it, including maintaining the voter file and improving the way it was made available across the extended party network. In the pages that follow, I briefly describe the way that data worked on the 2008 campaign before detailing how the party and Organizing for America carried this work forward to the 2010 midterm cycle.

DATA AND ANALYTICS ON THE 2008 OBAMA CAMPAIGN

The biography and experiences of Ethan Roeder, who was involved with both of Obama's runs and served as the executive director of the New Organizing Institute from March 2013 to October 2015, reveal broader changes in the decade before the 2012 cycle with respect to data and analytics in the Democratic Party. Roeder got his start in electoral politics in 2002 as a field organizer and subsequently joined the nonprofit gay civil rights organization Lambda Legal in 2005, where he learned how to work with Excel and online databases. When Obama announced his candidacy in 2007, Roeder had an easy time joining the campaign given how few people had his experience with field campaigning and political databases, and how in demand this skill set was across the numerous campaigns of the cycle.

In early 2007, the Democratic Party network's data infrastructure was still nascent. It was the first presidential cycle to feature the national use of VAN's VoteBuilder, which made the DNC's newly rebuilt voter file, produced under Dean's chairmanship, available in the states (it was also the first presidential cycle for the third-party data firm Catalist). Roeder had never served as a voter file manager on a campaign before, but wielding a set of complementary skills, he stepped into the role for the Obama campaign first in Nevada, and then in a host of other primary states, all while training other people to do the job he first learned in early 2007. At the time of the 2007 primaries, the role of the voter file manager in a state such as Nevada was to implement electoral strategy. The voter file manager worked with the field director and state director to figure out where the campaign was going to conduct door-to-door canvassing based on the numbers they believed they needed to win and the resources available (i.e., the volunteers and staffers the campaign needed to be efficiently deployed for the purposes of knocking on doors, often in neighborhoods with high proportions of Democrats). The voter file manager then defined the voter contact universe and the criteria used to constitute it, as well as the volunteer prospects that needed to be contacted every morning. The position was very tactical, premised on using information in the voter file to craft and implement field strategy.

Initially, targeting was based on voter segments revealed through polling during the run-up to the caucuses in Nevada. The campaign conducted internal polling that staffers used to discover the demographic and psychographic segments of voters that likely were strong supporters of Obama, such as women or college students who had particular characteristics. Other broad segments of interest to the primary campaign were African American and young voters. In some cases, segments could be even more narrowly defined, such as the independent friends of non-registered Democrats. The voter file manager was responsible for identifying individuals within these segments in the voter file so they could be targeted for contact by the campaign.

This segment-based targeting shifted to predictive voter modeling in advance of the Nevada caucuses. Roeder remembers when, two months before the caucuses, former management consultant and analyst Dan Wagner came to Nevada with "Obama support" and "caucus" models for the state campaign. Wagner later became the targeting and analytics director of the DNC from 2009 to 2011 and the chief analytics officer of Obama 2012 before founding Civis Analytics. This was the first time Roeder worked with models, which were different from older micro-targeting practices in not being premised upon preexisting demographic or psychographic segments derived from polls. Predictive modeling involved scoring actual individuals based on the characteristics they shared with other individuals whose preferences the campaign knew through things such as multivariate analysis of long-form surveys.[6] Roeder used these models alongside other targeting universes, which he was still segmenting on the basis of polling.

The decentralized data practices of the Obama campaign during the primaries gradually became standardized in terms of tools, data, and analytic modeling during the general election. With limited resources during the primaries, state staffers relied on whatever they had in hand to identify voters and get them to the polls. By the general election, the modeling work of the campaign had become more standardized and centralized. Roeder went to Chicago to become the national data manager for the campaign during the general election. All of the states had predictive support models (likelihood of supporting Obama), turnout models (likelihood of turning out), and synthetic models that helped the campaign get at particular target universes. Without a defined cadre of specialized staffers to draw from in the Democratic Party network at that point, Roeder said that the campaign hired many field organizers who had worked during the primaries and had an interest in computers and databases. These former field organizers received a week of training, and Roeder's data team grew to 107 by the end of the campaign. The analytics (or targeting) team, meanwhile, remained small in 2008, especially compared with four years later, with approximately five people on staff.

ORGANIZING FOR AMERICA AND THE DEMOCRATIC PARTY DURING THE 2010 MIDTERM CYCLE

After the 2008 election, Roeder stayed on in Chicago to write an extensive internal postmortem of the campaign.[7] Despite the campaign's near universal acclaim in the media and scholarship, the postmortem identified a number of challenges staffers faced, foremost among them the lack of data integration on the campaign. With the proliferation of vendors after the 2004 cycle, including BSD and Catalist, the 2008 campaign struggled to integrate multiple sources of data and make them actionable in order to leverage potential efficiencies. Even with this extensive postmortem, however, and widespread knowledge that the various databases of vendors in the extended party network were poorly integrated with one another and the DNC's voter file, numerous former party staffers argued that there was little done immediately after the election to address the issue. Again revealing how fragile political infrastructures are, one significant challenge was that there was little money or will for continued technical development after the election. Roeder stated that this was the case after the 2012 election cycle as well. Speaking of the party from 2004 through 2012, Roeder argued that:

If you don't have the organization at the very top doing the harder to see, more drudgery kind of infrastructure building, such as matching databases to each other, it does not get done. That kind of an investment has a more hazy ROI, it is not easy to prioritize. So frankly I think that in 2010 and then 2012, and even now after the 2012 election looking at the amount of resources that the DNC has put into sustaining a tech presence, which is next to nothing, I think you see that we have yet to really figure out how to bring the practical considerations of running a party from one cycle to another into agreement with the very clearly stated long-term need of better integrated data.[8]

A number of former party staffers echoed Roeder's comments. The core challenge is that structurally the Democratic Party found it hard to secure resources for technology and retain talent after electoral cycles. As a result, people with expertise and skills in things such as technology, data, and analytics often went off to new ventures, both in politics and outside the field. This was not necessarily a bad thing from the perspective of the Democratic Party, as firms can more easily institutionalize the innovative work of campaigns and carry knowledge, practice, and tools across party networks than the national party can. That said, the founding of new ventures, in addition to the ongoing proliferation of data across the many different applications and platforms used in contemporary politics, makes data integration a massive challenge. And, even though the Democratic Party was in a particularly advantageous position to work on data integration given its ability to bring all the relevant vendor and organizational stakeholders to the table, numerous former staffers argued that the resources simply were not there after 2008 (or 2012).

This is not to say that the party did not do important work on other fronts after the 2008 campaign. In the wake of the president's election, there was a spirited internal debate about where the resources of the campaign should go and what the nature of Organizing for America, the organization being built to house them, should be. The decision, made by people such as Michael Slaby (the 2008 campaign's CTO), President Obama, Michelle Obama, and others, was to make Organizing for America an independent project but organizationally house it inside the DNC. This meant that all the organizing and mobilization that Organizing for America engaged in was ultimately determined by the interests of the party as a whole, and could not be independent of it. While these decisions about how to structure Organizing for America in all likelihood limited some of the potential for supporter mobilization, housing it in the Democratic Party meant saving money on fundraising and organization.[9] It also meant comparatively more resources for the party's field program. Even further, housing Organizing for America at the party enabled volunteers from the first Obama run to be rolled more seamlessly into the re-election campaign than would have been possible with an outside, independent entity.

Most important, while much about Organizing for America's effectiveness has been debated, one overlooked aspect of the organization is that housing it at the DNC helped create continuity between the 2008 and 2012 campaigns. Numerous former staffers noted that the leadership at the DNC and Organizing for America were seamlessly integrated, and that many of these people headed to the re-election campaign together. These people included Dan Wagner, Mitch Stewart (who played a number of important roles in the 2008 field campaign and later served as the national director of Organizing for America and the battleground states director of Obama 2012), and Betsy Hoover (the deputy field director for Obama 2008, regional director of the DNC, and online organizing director of the re-election campaign) as well as her husband Jeremy Bird (a 2008 veteran who served as the deputy national director of Organizing for America and the national field director of the 2012 campaign). As a team, these individuals worked together, built on the lessons they learned in 2008 and during the 2010 midterm cycle, innovated to solve problems, and carried knowledge, skills, and practices to the re-election campaign. (And, after 2012, Stewart, Hoover, and Bird helped cofound 270 Strategies, a Democratic-allied organization specializing in field organizing, technology, digital, data, and analytics.)

The analytics innovations detailed later in this chapter, which received such deserved renown on the Obama 2012 campaign, had their origins in the party's work during the run-up to the 2010 midterm cycle.[10] After working on the Obama campaign in 2008, eventually ending up as the Great Lakes targeting lead, Dan Wagner served as the targeting director of the DNC from 2009 to 2011. It was during the devastating 2010 cycle for the Democrats that Wagner's team did its pathbreaking work around the testing and validating of voter models. In the process, Wagner honed his craft, built a talented team with party resources, and created the basic organizational framework for analytics as a large, stand-alone department that drove the electoral strategy of the party in 2010 and the re-election bid. Members of Wagner's team at the party during the midterm cycle became the core of the re-election bid's analytics department. These people included Andrew Claster, who worked for the DNC as the targeting director; Caroline Grey, who was the targeting operations director for the DNC/Organizing for America; Tim Trautman, who was the targeting operations manager for the DNC; Elan Kriegel, who was the senior modeling analyst at the DNC; and Emily Norman, an elections analyst at the DNC who came to the party from McKinsey & Company.

In the words of Michael Slaby, the work of the party during the midterm cycle "ended up being central building blocks for the kinds of stuff that we did—modeling, targeting, and analytics."[11] All that said, a number of former staffers at the party and on the 2012 bid argued that the data infrastructure remained fragile and largely was built cycle to cycle. Even with the president as the head of the Democratic Party, former staffers argued that it struggled to find direction with respect to technology during the years when there was no presidential nominee on the ballot. The dynamics around the midterm elections illustrate this. As Roeder, who became the director of data, technology, and election administration for the New Organizing Institute between elections argued, "There was a huge investment in Wagner's team and I think that was the right investment to make. But there wasn't enough investment made beneath his team and, frankly, I know for a fact that he had to dedicate some of the resources of his team to shoring up the database architecture and infrastructure issues that underlay the work that he had to do.[12]

Roeder went on to say, "it is all so fragile that the investment from one cycle to another makes a huge difference in the product."[13] In other words, data infrastructure and architecture need to be a continual object of concern, maintenance, repair, and investment, and the Democratic Party struggled with this after the 2008 election. I turn now to the dynamics of the 2012 campaign.

Obama's Re-election Bid

Even though staffers in the party network lamented the fact that more was not done with respect to data integration between 2008 and the effective start of the presidential cycle after the midterm elections, Obama's re-election bid enjoyed a number of advantages over its general election rival. The re-election bid had many of the assets of the 2008 campaign at its disposal, including a massive email list to fuel small-dollar donations, the party's extensive voter file that housed contacts from the president's earlier run and a robust field-tested interface technology for accessing and updating it in the field, and data on volunteers and donors to be tapped for another run. In another important technical advantage of incumbency, the campaign could also formally coordinate with the party, which it began doing early in 2011.

THE DNC AND OBAMA CAMPAIGN'S WORK ON DATA AND ANALYTICS

People who worked on the 2008 run—especially those at the party and those tracking developments within it during the off years—knew that data integration would be a challenging issue for the 2012 campaign. They also knew the many disconnects between the digital and field operations during 2008. These were big areas of concern to Michael Slaby who, as noted earlier, worked in venture capital and for Edelman between elections. Slaby began talking with the new campaign manager Jim Messina in January 2011 and wound up back on the campaign full-time by March as the chief integration and innovation officer, a senior staff position reporting directly to the campaign manager. The position did not exist in 2008. It was a position that was organized with broad purview over all the technology, data, and analytics operations of the campaign, and was designed specifically to create more integration in the data and synergy across these different departments.

Michael Slaby was directly involved in April 2011 in hiring the chief technology officer (CTO) for the DNC, Bryan Whitaker, the former director of field and information services with the Service Employees International Union (SEIU).[14] The goal was for Obama for America and the DNC to be far more coordinated than ever before not only in terms of technology, but also budgeting and staffing. This marks another considerable incumbent advantage: the campaign's ability to formally coordinate with, and draw on the resources of, the party organization over a year in advance of Election Day. Staffers wanted to reduce the resource expenditure redundancies between the two entities as well as the overlaps between different staffers. To this end, the party and campaign created a shared budget and organizational chart that matched staffers at each entity with counterparts in the other organization. Bryan Whitaker, for instance, had counterparts in Chicago that he interacted with on a daily basis: Michael Slaby, chief technology officer

Harper Reed, director of data Ethan Roeder, chief analytics officer Dan Wagner, deputy chief technology officer Mike Conlow, and data manager Ben Fuller.

For the campaign, the DNC was primarily the voter file. In 2012, the DNC was essentially the largest voter file company in the world, and engaged in the constant work of maintaining, cleaning, and appending the party's data with additional information. Whitaker was involved with the contracting for the commercial data appended to the voter file and working with vendors around phone and address hygiene (people die and move, which means these files need to be continually updated). Whitaker also managed all of the development of VoteBuilder on behalf of the Obama re-election bid, state parties, and down-ballot campaigns. In a telling piece of data about the resources that the party provided for Obama's re-election bid, Whitaker gave the campaign approximately 75% of his time, with the other 25% dedicated to down-ballot races (a dynamic that one former party staffer referred to as "the DNC of Barack Obama").[15]

The party and campaign collaborated closely around data and analytics. Whitaker inherited a staff of 12 from his predecessor, which grew into approximately 45 people by the end of the campaign. The party's voter file was a straight MySQL server database that contained all of the party's data dating back to 2004, consisting at the time of this writing of approximately 800 data points on each voting-age individual. The foundation of the Democratic Party's voter file is publicly available data including the names, addresses, party affiliations, dates of birth, and turnout histories (and in some states, demographic information as well) of citizens, as well as cumulative canvass data.[16] This information is not standardized across the states.[17] State parties collect public data from secretaries of state, and there are considerable differences in quality, format, and basic categories. This data is supplemented by information from many different sources, including the browser cookies of people who visit websites, optimization data from A/B testing, signup data from online forms, social network data, email data, and data gleaned from people posting comments on campaign websites and signing petitions. There is also long-form survey data that gets appended to the voter file, in addition to data that is not expressly collected for political purposes, such as consumer information acquired from various vendors, magazine subscription lists, and credit card information.

Obama for America's database was built on top of the party's voter file. Within the Democratic Party, the DNC's voter file is always at the foundation of any candidate-specific additions, which includes data on funders, volunteers, and activists stored on NGP VAN's MyCampaign. These additions are built around the DNC's data in VoteBuilder that accrues across electoral cycles through campaigns sharing updates to the voter file from their voter contacts. The candidate-specific data in MyCampaign that was added was not shared with the party automatically at the time, however, it was only swapped or sold (a senior party staffer stated that campaigns now receive and contribute back information on volunteers and activists, a change made during the 2014 cycle). Obama for America has the largest file in NGP VAN's MyCampaign, which was built from Obama's two runs. Candidates also bring additional sources of data to their campaigns, for example from third-party firms such as Catalist and TargetSmart.

There were a number of changes in the party's data management that took place between 2008 and 2012 to support the party and the campaign's voter modeling, driven in part by the learning that occurred during Obama's first run. During the 2012 cycle, there were weekly voter file updates in half a dozen states of electoral importance on new registrants, people turning 18, deaths, and people who moved, in addition to other information. By contrast, in 2008 there were approximately two updates to the voter file during the last month of the cycle. Another area of improvement came with respect to phone records, a seemingly mundane technology that has vast import for political campaigns given that it is still the most reliable way to reach people if campaigns do not have paid labor or volunteers to knock on doors.[18] Phone records are appended to voter records by vendors, and the party tested their effectiveness in different categories such as landlines and cellphones. Staffers cited that this testing, and the subsequent decision to use multiple vendors, ultimately resulted in a 5%–6% improvement in phone number accuracy that allowed the campaign to reach tens of thousands of additional voters.

The party also significantly improved its data architecture. The party used Hewlett-Packard's Vertica analytics database environment to enable campaign staffers to create voter models, do regression analysis, and generate individual-level predictive modeling scores. Dan Wagner and Bryan Whitaker went through a rigorous RFP process and determined that Vertica was the most reliable, scalable, and cost-effective analytics product for the party's needs. Vertica is essentially an analytics database housed on its own server. The DNC managed its voter file on a MySQL server and database they called "Golden." Vertica, by contrast, was where the analytics teams at Obama for America and the DNC did their modeling, and it pulled in data from Golden and various other databases the campaign used. Staffers at the party, for instance, loaded all the online, offline, fundraising, field, and modeling data into Vertica. The analytics platform enabled the Obama campaign, in addition to other state campaigns, to access this data.[19] Vertica also enabled the campaign to integrate the different data streams of platforms used by departments such as field and digital, which supported the development of tools such as Airwolf. The program enabled the campaign to send automated emails from local organizers with contact details and information about upcoming events to supporters who signed up for notifications from the campaign (the process was previously manual). As Matt Compton and Andrew Brown, the digital and technology directors of the DNC at the time of this writing, described:

> In 2012, when you signed up for information at BarackObama.com, a piece of technology code named Airwolf compared your voter profile against a data model to determine your support score, and then

automatically delivered a message from a local campaign organizer reminding you to cast a ballot, sign up to make calls, or volunteer to canvass your neighborhood. It made the connection between the online and offline worlds of the campaign nearly seamless and helped to make the best field program in the history of American politics a little bit more efficient, a little bit better.[20]

A number of staffers point to Vertica as the unsung hero of the Obama 2012 campaign and the most significant asset the party had in the years that followed it. Staffers built tools and applications designed to facilitate faster organizing in Vertica, in addition to it hosting all the algorithms and mathematics behind the campaign. Coordinating this work were three software developers at the DNC and 65 engineers at the campaign. One task of these developers at the party was to create tools for state parties and down-ballot candidates built from this data architecture. DNC staffers created the state party tool program, a precursor to Project Ivy (launched in early 2014 and designed to provide software and data to down-ballot campaigns), which resulted in a calling tool that any campaign could use, a polling place look-up tool that was used as part of Got to Register (a widget that the state parties and down-ballot candidates could put on their websites), and a voter registration tool (which the campaign customized for its own use from the DNC's code).[21] As Whitaker noted more broadly, "I mean half the stuff that got nominated for the RootsCamp most valuable technology in 2012 came out of [Vertica]."[22]

As detailed above, Vertica also supported the party's and the campaign's extensive analytics and voter modeling work, which was carried out by a cadre of skilled staffers. There were more people at the party and the Obama campaign organization in 2012 doing specialized work with data than in 2008, with the analytics team of the re-election bid alone swelling in size to encompass approximately 54 dedicated staff under the direction of former party staffer Dan Wagner. Meanwhile, the size of Roeder's data team grew considerably from 2008. A number of these data and analytics staffers worked with the party during the 2010 cycle. At the party, the director of data architecture in 2012 was Chris Wegrzyn, who worked on the 2008 campaign, was the lead targeting developer at the party in 2010, and would later cofound the technology and analytics firm BlueLabs. Wegrzyn managed the data environment for the modeling performed by staffers on the campaign such as Dan Wagner and battleground states analytics director Elan Kriegel, who as noted above served as a senior modeling analyst at the party during the 2010 cycle and later cofounded BlueLabs (and became the director of analytics for Hillary for America during the 2016 cycle).[23] More broadly, staffers argued that the people doing the work were more experienced, which reveals the infrastructural role of the party network in producing staffers with specialized expertise. As Roeder detailed, "We had people who had actually done this work before. In 2008 the people on our data team who had ever worked on a previous cycle doing political data was 3 out of 60 people and in 2012 it was still pretty low but it was more like 30 out of 100."[24]

This expertise underlay the campaign's extensive predictive modeling work. As detailed earlier, the old method for targeting voters was to generate static micro-targeting categories of voters based on polling, generally at a single moment in time. The insight that party staffers such as Dan Wagner had was that these larger conceptual demographic, psychographic, and behavioral groups do not really exist. Within every category of voter there is significant diversity. Wagner believed that modeling was more effective and accurate if it was premised on individuals, not groups. The analytics team on the campaign and within the party therefore worked to gather as much data as possible on individuals and continually analyzed millions of points of data on the electorate collected on an ongoing basis over many months—all of which was designed to score individuals in terms of their likely opinions and actions (such as turning out to vote) and test these models to help the campaign figure out the *exact* people to turn out and persuade (this was the goal, not necessarily the reality).

To do its predictive modeling, the campaign continually conducted polls asking individuals about their political preferences, matched respondents to identifiable individuals in the voter file, and then looked for patterns in the data about these individuals to create predictive models. These models probabilistically stated whether someone was likely to support Obama or not, likely to turn out to vote, likely to be persuadable, and likely to be responsive to specific appeals. Some basic categories of data were the most predictive, such as basic demographic, income, and party identification data, with additional categories of data adding marginal predictive utility. These models were then layered across the entire voter file, generating probabilistic scores of likely Obama support, turnout, and persuasion for every member of the electorate. Importantly, the campaign continually updated these models through both ongoing survey calls and data generated through voter contacts, such as on-the-ground canvasses.[25] Compared with static micro-targeting models, where information is generally collected at a single moment in time, the Obama campaign's modeling was ongoing and dynamic and offered a more fine-grained view of the electorate, including how individuals with particular characteristics were changing or not over time.

In the state of North Carolina alone, for instance, the campaign conducted upward of 23 polls over the course of the cycle, and was interviewing 2,000 people a week in the run-up to the election. This polling tracked the state of the race, revealed the movement of the electorate in terms of how subgroups and individuals were changing (or, more often, not) in the course of campaign events, and served as a test of external messaging. The campaign also tested and updated its voter models through millions of voter contacts made by volunteers and paid staffers. In addition, the analytics team ran more than 2,000 simulations of election outcomes. In terms of the advantages of predictive modeling, former Democratic Party staffers argued that individual polls conducted during the cycle suggested that there were much larger fluctuations in the race than the dynamic modeling of the Obama campaign. The predictive modeling revealed a stable electorate and found that campaign events during the race had very small effects on different subgroups. The campaign's modeling also suggested that on the order of 4%–6% of the electorate was actually undecided.

Voter modeling lay at the foundation of all the campaign's strategic communications (while the campaign often used qualitative data to craft messages themselves).[26] The campaign used the results of this modeling to allocate limited resources and make decisions such as where to buy advertising and which doors to knock on, whom to talk to, and what to say. Ultimately, the campaign aggregated individuals into groups for the purposes of targeting and tailoring strategic communications. The reason is that it would have been nearly impossible to create personalized messages for individual voters from a labor standpoint, even with the campaign's significant investment in creative talent to produce rich media content across platforms. And, even if the campaign could have somehow garnered the resources to produce this content, the cost of testing individual appeals to determine whether they were actually successful in order to justify the expense of creating them would have been astronomical. For example, in the context of television advertising, the campaign targeted particular groups of individuals based on their geographic region and the television programs and times of day they would likely be watching.

Importantly, the campaign's strategic appeals were continually tested. Former staffers stated that the campaign found that paid media worked best from summer through the conventions, while field contacts and earned media were the most effective from the debates through the election.[27] Staffers also cited that they found that messages around taxes, Medicare, and education were particularly effective for the groups they were targeting. The campaign also tested its targeting strategies, finding that women in particular used Facebook for political conversations and sharing content.

Testing also extended to the sorts of appeals the campaign was making. One of the significant innovations that former staffers pointed to was the campaign's testing of persuasive appeals and developing a model based on it. There were significant differences in how the campaign tested persuasive appeals in 2008 and 2012. The party and the 2008 campaign ran one-off tests of discrete pieces of strategic communication, such as a direct mail piece, and measured their effects through follow-up phone calls or interviews (and compared these treatment with control groups that did not receive any campaign communication at all). In 2012, the campaign conducted a randomized field experiment with 500,000 voters around the country to develop a persuasion model, a scale considerably beyond what the 2008 effort had the capacity to engage in.[28] This research consisted of developing a target universe, testing a persuasion message delivered at the doorsteps of voters by volunteers, and comparing the treatment and control groups to find which voters were persuadable and the characteristics they shared in order to identify others like them in the voter file.

Former staffers cited that through this experiment the campaign identified people who were actually changing their minds, learned the impact of real-world campaign activity, analyzed the work of its volunteers, and tested and updated its voter models. Two of the big lessons staffers learned were that many things they thought would actually persuade voters did not (and vice versa), and that different people were persuadable than they initially expected based on polling. Staffers also cited wanting to believe that people are persuaded by rational arguments, but this was often not the case. Instead, people were more responsive to social pressure and looked for authenticity as a key characteristic in candidates. The campaign also learned that narrowly targeting voters and crafting very specific appeals were not always the most effective strategy; often more general appeals were more persuasive.[29] The campaign then used the results of this test to create individualized scores around the likelihood of voters being persuadable and identified weak and strong targets, people to avoid (because sometimes more communication meant a reverse effect), and the types of appeals that might move voters.[30]

Despite an impressive amount of technological development on the campaign, which I now turn to, in many ways the starring parts of the Obama 2012 run were precisely those things that were part of the infrastructure of the Democratic Party and its extended network—the technologies that supported the field operations, the data architecture, and the analytics expertise honed across electoral cycles. As Whitaker added, "There were some minor tool victories that occurred but at the end of the day the work that got done, the real technology that impacted the election was Vertica, VoteBuilder, the Blue State emailer, the campaign technology payment processor where contribution processing happened, and the campaign's BarackObama.com."[31]

ORGANIZING TECHNOLOGICAL DEVELOPMENT ON THE 2012 CAMPAIGN

After being hired in January 2011, Michael Slaby immediately began drawing a number of different potential organizational charts for the campaign. This was, in part, informed by Slaby's experience in 2008, and he tried to rethink the data silos that existed during the earlier bid, as well as who reported to whom and how the departments of the campaign all fit together. In the end, the 2012 campaign made a number of significant organizational changes from the 2008 run that reveal the centrality of technology, data, analytics, and digital to the re-election bid. Reporting directly to Slaby were chief analytics officer Dan Wagner (a position that did not exist in 2008), director of data Ethan Roeder, chief information officer Rajeev Chopra, and chief technology officer Harper Reed. On the digital side, Joe Rospars, a veteran of the 2004 Dean campaign, cofounder of Blue State

Digital, and 2008 new media director for Obama, became the chief digital strategist to the campaign, which marked an even more expansive strategic role for digital than in 2008 and reflected how the campaign thought about digital being a part of all the campaign's operations.

During the early days of the 2012 bid, there were a number of organizational tensions. Staffers described an environment where the push for a new way of thinking about and organizing the campaign took place on top of inherited structures from Organizing for America, the Democratic Party, and the 2008 campaign. In addition, there was a mix of staffers on the campaign that created cognitive diversity, but it needed to be effectively managed. For example, in addition to the staffers who worked at Organizing for America and the party between elections, such as Wegrzyn and Wagner on the data and analytics side, a number of former staffers from the 2008 run came back to the campaign in 2012 after pursuing other ventures. They included digital director Teddy Goff (who worked as the WhileHouse.gov lead immediately after the campaign) and digital strategist Rospars, who both went back to Blue State Digital after the 2008 cycle.

As a result, staffers stated that department heads had to hash out questions about organizational roles and jurisdiction, and some tensions existed that never got resolved. Indeed, numerous staffers were candid in pointing to how difficult organizing and managing the campaign during early 2011 actually was. Former staffers argued that the re-election bid probably ended up with more people than it would have ideally had. Those people returning to the campaign, meanwhile, entirely understandably often did not want the same job they had in 2008 and desired something new, with more responsibility. To accommodate these people, whom the leadership wanted back given their talent, the campaign added additional layers of internal leadership, and expanded the top of the organizational hierarchy from what it had been in 2008. As a result, people had odd in-between titles and at times overlapping jurisdiction (Slaby himself cited that being the chief integration and innovation officer was "kind of a long way of saying nerdy deputy campaign manager").[32]

Added to this mix were the field crossers the campaign hired from industry to help coordinate and carry out technological development. With the time and money to devote to technological development, staffers drew on their experiences in 2008 and the subsequent knowledge and expertise they gained and deliberately assessed the technology needs of the campaign. As a result of the perceived limitations of vendors and the desire for accountability over technical development, campaign staffers sought to build new technologies in-house around a reconstituted data infrastructure. Slaby was responsible for conceptualizing and overseeing the technical development of the campaign, and had an unprecedented senior-level role and autonomy to direct the technology, data, and analytics operations. Slaby identified early on that he wanted to recruit and effectively use highly specialized talent from the technology industry: "We needed the capacity to sort of tackle some of these problems [with integration] on our own which meant a much more robust, a much different kind of technology team, a product-oriented technology team. In the Silicon Valley sense of 'product manager'; we had engineers on a much different level. Really world class technologists, not technologists for politics."[33]

Seeking to address the problems of the 2008 campaign and issues with integration in the vendor ecosystem, Slaby turned to the tech industry. He hired people such as the former chief technology officer of Threadless, Harper Reed, to become the campaign's CTO. In Slaby's assessment, Reed had "a perspective about start-ups, about engineering culture, and about product that we needed to go get."[34] At the same time, while these staffers had the highly specialized skills the campaign desired, there was a lot of work that went into managing, culturally and organizationally, these field crossers from other industries (as detailed in the first chapter in the areas of technology, digital, data, and analytics 2012 Obama campaign featured 48 staffers with primary employment backgrounds in the technology and data analytics industries, and 58 who had their primary professional work in the commercial sector). Slaby, who was tasked with hiring dozens of staffers, stated that a number of "cultural clashes" on the campaign resulted from the fact that in the technology sector, tech is the purpose of the organization, but on a campaign:

> that is not at all the purpose. Harper bought into that really fast; right, that we were a force multiplier for the rest of the campaign and novelty is not a meaningful outcome for us, we are not doing IPO [initial public offering], not patenting shit, like we just need to make the organization better. I think it was still culturally a little tough, right—engineers of Facebook and Google are rock stars, basically, and on the campaign they were just part of the machine. I think they are in a really different kind of organization than they have ever been in and the stakes are really different, the tolerance for mistakes is really different, and the focus of the organization is not on technology.[35]

As an example of these dynamics, in interviews with staffers across different departments of the campaign, it became clear that a number of people believed there were some outsized, and ultimately unrealistic, ambitions in terms of technical projects, especially during the initial stages of the campaign.[36] Former staffers stated that the tensions that arose from these ambitions were, in part, the result of the organizational and cultural challenges of integrating field crossers into the campaign, who often had different expectations for how technologies should work, different orientations toward politics and assessments of the utility of technology for electoral ends, and ultimately different professional knowledge, skills, and work practices from many of the political staffers on the campaign. These are frictions that come with the attempts of organizational units to create and manage cognitive diversity, which perhaps in this case was exacerbated by the particular culture of the technology industry.[37] One former staffer with extensive experience working in technology but not a member of that team recalled his early conversations with technology department staffers about the idea of replacing the core Democratic infrastructural technology of VoteBuilder: "I don't know if that was just a thought experiment because they were trying to get their heads around our legacy system or if they were really coming in with this full head of steam thinking, you know, 'we are just going to tear all this stuff down because it was made by political hacks and amateurs and we are going to build it right.'"[38] Meanwhile, for their part, more politically oriented staffers were often skeptical of the outsiders and saw them as arrogant, in addition to "not knowing politics."

Indeed, a number of former staffers suggested that at times there was skepticism regarding what the technology department was doing in terms of building new tools and questioned whether it was even a good idea given the resource demands. Staffers working in technology, meanwhile, stated that people in other departments expressed the desire for information technology to be invisible, without appreciating the work that has to go into making it so. Data integration alone was a resource-intensive undertaking that required the input of numerous stakeholders and ongoing efforts to create new data practices and build new systems, as well as repair and maintain extant ones. A lot of staffers were consumed with working on integration internally, and it took up a lot of the energy of the party and vendors. At the same time, there was not universal buy-in that integration's benefits in terms of analytics and efficiencies in voter contacts would be greater than the costs, especially at the beginning when it was really slow going and resource intensive. This is the back-end work of building and maintaining infrastructure that is often hidden from view, and only becomes a contestable object of concern when it is in development or breaks down.

In this context, Slaby played the role of a broker because he stood at the intersection of these two worlds as someone who worked on the 2008 bid and also had extensive industry experience. For example, as Slaby described, "Some of my job with Harper's team, it was being a shit umbrella for them, when people were frustrated that technology was taking too long."[39] While Slaby argued that much of this conflict was positive, such as different people questioning each other in meaningful ways given their different perspectives, he also said that at times tensions moved into the open and shaded into distrust. By all accounts, the speed and pressure of the campaign exacerbated these internal dynamics. Even with the comparatively long time horizon that came with an incumbent candidate, running a campaign is, in essence, similar to launching a start-up that has to ramp up and scale very quickly and is designed by its very nature to be a temporary organization.[40] While there was certainly carryover and continuity from the 2008 campaign and party work between elections, in a large organization that grew to approximately 650 staffers in Chicago at one point, only a small percentage of individuals had actually worked together before. In this climate, staffers stated that asking people to build products together and work across the multiple departments of the organization, often with distinct cultures, practices, and stores of knowledge, resulted in inevitable tensions.

A number of former staffers stated that, over time, many of the initial ambitions of the technology department were scaled back in favor of more modest and practical projects given the complexity of the Obama operation and the demands of electoral politics. That said, while the technology team pursued a number of small-scale projects that could be turned around relatively quickly, and that ultimately generated significant efficiencies and saved the campaign considerable amounts of money over the long run, there were some large development projects, such as Dashboard, that took many months to develop with a comparatively small team (six in this case).[41]

NARWHAL AND DASHBOARD: CREATING WHOLE AND RELATIONAL PEOPLE THROUGH DATA

Two of the ambitious projects that consumed much of the energy of the campaign in 2011 were Narwhal and Dashboard. Staffers intended Narwhal to accomplish data integration and Dashboard to be a field tool that could leverage it. Slaby and Reed sat down during their first meeting and drew out the schematics of the two systems that the former knew, based on past experience, the campaign needed. On the front-end, staffers wanted to provide people with an experience closer to their daily lives where they routinely used platforms such as Facebook to connect socially. In 2008, My.BarackObama.com (the BSD-provided online suite of campaign tools) was a discrete platform that was not integrated with social media. Creating a new campaign platform with people's use of the social web in mind required that data be integrated across the campaign's tools and voter file, as well as external, commercial social media platforms such as Facebook. If on the 2008 campaign voters were represented internally as discrete bits of information spread across many databases that rarely aggregated into a coherent whole, the ambition in 2012 was for identity resolution to create whole and relational people that, in turn, could be better modeled and leveraged by the campaign.[42]

Narwhal
Narwhal has received a lot of media attention, but these accounts have not fully appreciated the scope, or limitations, of the project. Carol Davidsen, the product manager for Narwhal who joined the campaign after a career in the commercial analytics industry, stated that it was a permanently unfinished project. Narwhal was designed to provide every individual with a unique personal identifier that was recognizable across the many different systems and databases used by the campaign. Staffers believed that identity resolution would improve the supporter experience in terms of the ways she or he interacted with the campaign and the ability of staffers to be responsive to individuals in the very contexts of their lives,

as well as provide the campaign with better data. As Slaby detailed, identity resolution was "just a way of seeing a person as a person. I put a sheet of values on everybody's desk when they started and one of the first ones was 'people are people.' Which is not the default setting in the other systems. People are an email address or people are a donor or people are a voter, which is just different."[43]

Davidsen's experience with Narwhal reveals how knowledge and skills from commercial contexts migrated to the campaign, and the organizational environment that field crossers encountered there. Further, Narwhal illustrates the challenges of technical development in political contexts that are often hidden to outside observers. Davidsen had years of experience working in the telecommunications and cable industry on billing and customer relations management systems, including with the databases that generated cable and phone bills. Davidsen went to work for a company called Navic Networks in 2006, which was a start-up at the time (in 2008 it was acquired by Microsoft). The firm figured out how to get basic diagnostic data from cable set-top boxes, so cable companies no longer had to send a technician to the houses of customers to fix their cable boxes. This then opened the door to the company figuring out how to start sending behavioral data about television viewing back to cable companies. These commercial experiences subsequently informed Davidsen's work on the campaign.

In July 2011, Davidsen received a targeted email from Dan Wagner. The database of the Obama campaign from the 2008 run was another significant advantage of incumbency, particularly given that campaigns are increasingly looking for technical and statistical expertise, often explicitly from outside the political field in the commercial and technology sectors. When Davidsen donated in 2008, she entered details on her profession, which she described along the lines of "technology, data, and analytics." Staffers in Chicago on the re-election bid searched for these skills when they were looking to hire, and Davidsen ended up in their email pool. Davidsen responded, and between July and October 2011 she was in communication with people on the campaign, joining on November 6 to work on analytics. At the time the campaign was having problems with testing and analytics integration and was also looking for someone to work in media analytics.

When Davidsen first arrived in Chicago, she worked on integrating the voter file with donation, email, event attendance, and volunteer activity data. She encountered a number of difficulties with reconciling the different systems of vendors to the campaign. Addressing this, Davidsen noted, took many conversations and much time and patience. The basic problem was that categories of data were often different across different systems. In BSD's database, a record was often just an email address and a zip code (a much cruder measure of geographic location than an address linked to a person or household). Meanwhile, people have multiple email addresses that may be in use across different campaign databases (for instance, in donor databases people may be represented by their work addresses and work emails); in addition, older Americans in particular often share email addresses. At the same time, emails are not in the public record that the party receives from secretaries of state, and therefore are less reliable and data is often incomplete. All of these factors made it difficult to figure out if a person in the BSD or a donation database was the same as another who had a full name and an address in VoteBuilder.

Even more, integration had to be ongoing because NGP VAN and BSD data were moving data sets. People were constantly changing their data such as their emails, and as detailed above updates to the voter file were ongoing during the course of the campaign. Updating the voter file was particularly important because core members of Obama's base, such as young people, urban dwellers, and people of color, are very mobile, which meant that it was less likely they had current addresses in VoteBuilder. And yet, people seldom update their public records through things such as submitting a national change of address form, and the campaign did not know if they moved unless they re-registered to vote.[44] Even more, staffers working on integration argued that during this time VoteBuilder was basically a collection of 51 different state databases (including Washington, D.C.), without a single master database for all of NGP VAN activity. This made it difficult to track individuals as they moved across states, or if volunteers engaged in cross-state actions.[45]

There were a number of other hurdles to integration relating to the fact that, as Davidsen stated, "people are really creative in storing data."[46] During the massive 2008 field effort, people stored data where they needed or found it convenient to, and it was often outside officially provided channels such as VoteBuilder or NGP VAN's volunteer database MyCampaign. Staffers argued that this was because during that cycle MyCampaign lacked inclusive data categories for the roles staffers and volunteers actually played in the field, such as "data captains" at the local level. To work around this, staffers and volunteers developed different ways of storing and working with data to meet their needs, even going so far as to create surveys to capture the data they needed on volunteers.[47] This presented a significant challenge for programmers working on integration in 2012, who were faced with needing to develop custom rules for every single place they received data from and what it looked like on the basis of that. In this context, programmers worked to try to find rules that somehow spanned multiple formats of data and strove to make different streams of data fit for a common database. The process involved a lot of manual labor given the lack of standardization.[48]

At the same time, attempts during the cycle by the campaign and vendors such as NGP VAN to design systems with the work practices of field staffers and volunteers in mind often failed to achieve data standardization. The challenge was that once people had a process in place, it was hard to get them to change it, even with redesigned systems that provided new functionalities that could potentially meet their needs. In addition, building new systems often meant that historical data got lost. So, for instance, even as the campaign developed new ways for data coming in to be reformatted and integrated, it often only applied to the data that came in after the release of the new version of the code, which meant that the people who needed the historical data were upset, and all of the old data needed to be converted into the new format.

Davidsen echoed the accounts of staffers detailed earlier in pointing out that there were often disconnects between the desires of staffers outside of analytics and technology and their understanding of the work that had to go into creating what they wanted and the limitations of the technology. Davidsen argued that as a product manager on Narwhal she needed to help staffers across the campaign's disparate departments understand what API integration was, and the issues and challenges it entailed.[49] As Davidsen described:

> Integration is a never-ending problem. There is always more data that you want to integrate into your system. And people did not totally understand technology, and engineers did not totally understand campaigns, so every request that the rest of the organization had for technology would early on be met with "oh yeah Narwhal can do that," more meaning that you could use integration to do that, but maybe that is a little bit too much at the beginning without comprehending how many engineers you are actually going to have and how much could all be done at once. For the first 6 months it was a little bit rocky. No one really understood what anyone was talking about.[50]

In the end, Narwhal worked on a limited basis for Obama staffers, and it was best characterized as an ongoing development project around integration given the constant data challenges.[51] Narwhal (however imperfectly) was a probabilistic matching engine that increased the match rates between the data sets in use by the four central departments of the campaign, field, digital, finance, and analytics, through their respective databases, VoteBuilder, BSD, NGP, and Vertica (in addition to those of a cluster of other vendors and entities that these teams used for data). As Roeder cited, once a record was tied together in a match, it was difficult to undo, making the system relatively stable. The data systems on the Obama campaign looked like a hub, with an array of outside actors and vendors clustered around it (see Figure 5.1). The model in Figure 5.1 makes it look more seamless than it actually was, but it was a working system premised on Slaby's idea detailed above that "a person is a person" in the campaign's systems. As one staffer put it, "integration was happening via Narwhal and Vertica. So even though NGP VAN and BSD weren't talking to each other technically, their data was being fed into Narwhal and Vertica and those systems were acting as hubs to feed data into the spokes."[52]

While the history of Narwhal (and indeed what this name actually referred to, given that it evolved over the course of the campaign) is complicated, it never provided what numerous staffers described as the "holy grail" of a persistent ID that could identify one individual across the numerous systems and data silos that the campaign had.[53] While from the outside the Obama campaign looked as if

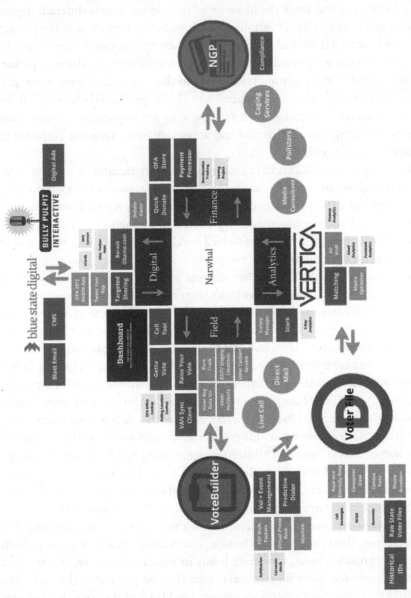

Figure 5.1 THE DATA ARCHITECTURE OF THE 2012 OBAMA CAMPAIGN. Screenshot from the NGP VAN Next Presentation, August 20, 2014, http://next.ngpvan.com/.

it had a seamless, integrated, and all-powerful data system and analytics around it, in actuality the campaign still had fractured views of people as they moved across their various systems and databases. After over a year of work on this project, every data point was not available at every data end point. Narwhal did enable staffers to observe and track the behavior of individuals across different digital platforms and the voter file at certain end points, but staffers close to the project noted that how well it worked depended on the department of the campaign. In some cases, the campaign could match two or three different databases together, but staffers cited that integration was limited to that in practice. Even more, getting data updated in real time was a persistent challenge. Not all data needs to be real time, but data from things such as canvassing are important to ensure that resources are being spent efficiently and voters are being targeted correctly in relation to electoral goals.[54]

One example of what this data integration project facilitated was the campaign's Optimizer, an algorithmic way of placing television ads based on real-time, set-top box data on how people were watching television. Davidsen, who became the head of a reconstituted five-person media analytics group within the analytics department, and her team started building the Optimizer at the end of March 2012 and finished roughly six weeks later in early May.

The Optimizer revealed the most efficient ways to target particular voters through television advertising. Davidsen's team received a list of targets and was tasked with delivering advertising to them on the basis of their television viewing habits. The targets were in two groups: persuadable voters, and low turnout, but likely, Obama supporters. Davidsen and her team matched these voters to set-top boxes using data from Rentrak and FourthWall (both television targeting firms) via the information services firm Experian. The team then received television consumption data back about these targeted groups and performed behavioral analyses (following commercial industry practices, all of this data was non-personally identifiable). Staffers looked at things such as if individuals in these targeted groups watched local news or children's programming and how their consumption patterns changed over time. The team then turned the initial two groups of persuadable and low turnout likely supporters into six groups of low/high local news, low/high children's programming, and low/high TV consumption.

Staffers then analyzed how individuals in these groups were watching TV, such as splitting their time between broadcast and cable, what their consumption had been in previous years, how their behavior switched between seasons, and how stable audiences were for particular time slots on particular channels. The Optimizer then evaluated how the campaign should buy ads to reach these groups given the rate modeling data provided by ad agencies. The later version of the Optimizer also permitted true frequency optimization, which enabled staffers to stipulate rules, such as only airing ads that were on the same channel in the same market once every 30 minutes to ensure against oversaturation. Senior staffers also looked at things such as competitive spending by the Republican Party network. The campaign also used the Optimizer to reserve its spots in advance for the last six weeks of the campaign, and cancel ads if rates were no longer cost-effective based on competition.

Optimizer buys started in the middle of May, and staffers completed running all optimizations though Election Day for the most part in mid- to late August. Davidsen cited that there was a widespread concern with oversaturation across the campaign, but at the same time the campaign was not prepared to reduce its overall budget on television. The media analytics team received budgets so big that staffers would pick the advertising buys they wanted using the Optimizer and they would still have budget left. Indeed, Davidsen argued that "[y]ou couldn't really go back to the campaign and say 'oh we saved you the difference, we saved you this amount of money we don't need to spend it, spend it somewhere else.' At least I was not going to have that fight, someone who kind of just didn't have any background in running campaigns before. So we would lift the frequency rule and then just continued to buy until we spent all of the money. It is really scary not to spend money on a campaign."[55]

While the Optimizer bought media efficiently, it is worth noting that this did not mean that staffers were able to "test" the effectiveness of content in a reliable way. The media analytics team could use FourthWall, which had unique anonymized household identifiers, to look at whether people were tuning in or out based on whether they fast forwarded through content or navigated away from the program. But, even then, the data was messy, delivered only in "pods" of five commercials. The first and last ads were the most interesting from an analyst's perspective, because that was when there was tune-in and tune-out behavioral data and practitioners could draw conclusions about the effectiveness of these ads. There was more consistent viewing data for the commercials in the middle, because audiences had already made decisions to tune-in or out, which said little about the ads themselves. As Davidsen described, similar to online advertising, all they could do is potentially test the "stickiness" of a piece of creative, there was no way to feed data from these ads and their consumption back into the voter file.[56]

Despite widespread scholarly concern over political privacy, campaign staffers have to follow the largely self-regulatory guidelines of commercial advertising industries in working only with non-personally identifiable data. In many respects, campaign staffers avoid having to have debates over privacy precisely because the governing standards of the industries they rely on are much narrower than what might be protected by the First Amendment.[57]

Dashboard: The New Geographic, Affiliation, and Social Graph Axes of Contemporary Campaigning

Dashboard was the campaign-developed volunteer platform, and it was premised on the data integration of Narwhal. The impetus behind Dashboard was to create a new platform for organizing that coupled the multiple ways people are socially embedded and the new technological contexts that shape the way they create and sustain their social lives with the electoral realities of needing to build tools in accordance with the geographically defined focus of the field operation.[58] It was also designed to be the instantiation of the idea that all aspects of supporter participation across the field and digital sides of the campaign could be boiled down into very simple terms—that, as Slaby put it, "it should just be organizing."[59]

Dashboard was built completely from scratch in a matter of months by Harper Reed's comparatively small team of approximately six men in collaboration with digital and field staffers in Chicago. This team explicitly sought to build a platform that overcame a number of the limitations former 2008 staffers perceived with the MyBO toolset, including the lack of data integration, the fact that it was not "aware" of "turf" (the standard geographic unit in VoteBuilder), and it was not designed to support key elements of the field program such as house parties. As a result, there was a general disconnect between the online organizing tools and the workings of the field campaign in 2008. Dashboard was designed to solve this problem by being connected to the field program and aware of turf, the staffing and volunteer hierarchy, and poll and office locations. At the same time, staffers also built Dashboard to extend beyond the universe of the field program (and geographic social ties) and encompass the broader "social graph" that citizens have across multiple social networking platforms. As digital director Teddy Goff described:

> So it was designed to be better connected to the field program, but then also, and this may sound like kind of a countervailing charge, we had to figure out how to make it not. We had to make it better connected to the social graph. You want the Dashboard reality to be more reflective of the field program and more suited to what the organizers actually want. You also want people to be able to connect with their Facebook friends, push content out to Facebook, and all that kind of stuff.[60]

For example, the campaign built Dashboard around the basic building block of the precinct, which was the basis for the entire field effort and the electoral system more generally (and yet few people even know what precinct they are in for voting purposes). Dashboard enabled people to organize into neighborhood groups within precincts. The data produced through organizing activities on Dashboard, such as supporter contacts with voters, in turn informed the analytics department's assessments of these efforts on the electoral map. Through their analysis of this data coming in online from the field, the analytics team directed voter contact operations to particular precincts and voters in line with electoral strategy.

At the same time, Dashboard was designed to overcome the fundamental tension between geography as the basis of political representation and the way contemporary social relations also encompass affiliations and distal ties.[61] In addition to the geographic "axis" of social life, which defines political representation, the second "axis" of social embeddedness that staffers discussed was the idea of group ties based on identity and affiliation. As Michael Slaby explained:

> We were going to have this underlying geographic hierarchy and we wanted to measure your work against that no matter how you wanted to measure your work, but we wanted you to be able to also do things like, "I don't care that much about my precinct but I wanted to organize with other women, I want to organize with other Latinos." It was also a good way to motivate people, a lot of people want to organize that way, they are more affiliated to some other affiliation than with their neighborhood. . . . [62]

The third "axis" of social embeddedness never quite came together on Dashboard. As Goff suggested, it entailed the ability of supporters to further the efforts of the campaign through their social graph. Platforms such as Facebook, Twitter, and Instagram render social ties both visible and actionable for supporters through providing channels for political expression. Social media provide campaigns with new ways to fashion supporters (and supporters with new ways to fashion themselves) into the conduits of strategic communication to their far-flung social ties, while providing relational data about them. For example, staffers saw the social graph as a key source of the motivation to participate in the campaign. Staffers believed that the visibility of supporters' participation on Dashboard across the various social network sites they used would help keep people motivated to volunteer and draw new people in to the campaign. Dashboard, for instance, enabled users to see who in their neighborhood teams, affinity groups, and broader social graph was doing the most work, and it enabled users to share their volunteer efforts on social media.

The social graph side of Dashboard never quite came together as many staffers hoped. As Slaby detailed, it is "computationally expensive" to connect users to their Facebook identities because "there are scale problems with doing this and the matching is hard; we just kind of honestly, we kind of ran out of time and so it wasn't as richly social as I wish it had been."[63] Numerous staffers involved in the effort stated that Dashboard was a struggle to put together, and that it took longer than many expected. One reason was the challenge of data integration, detailed extensively in the preceding text. Narwhal was developed concurrently with systems such as Dashboard, which posed significant technical hurdles given that they were often premised upon data integration. The campaign needed to match identities across many different data streams to merge these three axes of social embeddedness on Dashboard. Another challenge stemmed from the fact that staffers needed Dashboard to stay in sync with the turf cutting being continually performed by the field staffers in VoteBuilder. Dashboard had to continually adjust to the turf borders that field staffers were always redrawing based on canvass data, and computationally monitor who was going in and out of what turf and the teams that were matched to these turfs. Dashboard also needed to steer volunteers using the platform to the optimal team based on where they lived. Staffers stated that matching turf to volunteers to teams only came together comparatively late during the general election.

In addition to the data integration challenges, a number of staffers stated that there were management issues with respect to how the platform was designed and implemented. One staffer in Chicago suggested that Dashboard was "over-designed by committee" given the number of stakeholders the platform (rather unavoidably) had across departments of the campaign.[64] Others argued that there were disconnects between the staffers designing the platform, those tasked with administering it, and those actually using it for field organizing. Former campaign staffers argued that the people ultimately responsible for building Dashboard were members of the technology team, and yet the digital team was responsible for administering it. Others, especially field staffers at the state level, argued that it was pushed out to field and developed with too little input from them, even as it upended many of their established ways of working. As one former state staffer put it, echoing other senior and state-level staffers, "I think Dashboard might have been a little bit overly designed and conceptualized and talked about only in headquarters and then pushed out into the field, where it might have been better at the end of the day if it was a little bit more designed outward in—so there [were] more field engagements and involvement earlier on."[65]

In part to remedy these issues, campaign manager Jim Messina held an all-staff meeting in Chicago, and staffers at headquarters went on field trips to the states to do user experience testing. Staffers cited that over time people became more used to working with each other and the platform improved. Even still, as one former staffer related, "that underlying database technology, when it worked, was a magical thing that defined what digital could do for field—when it worked. But it didn't always work. And when it went wrong it went wrong in so many ways."[66]

Even with the technical advantage of incumbency that Obama enjoyed, developing technologies on a short-lived campaign was a challenge given the resource constraints and integration and scaling issues that are particularly vexing in politics. Technological development in politics is considerably different from commercial contexts. As Slaby described:

> It took them a really long time to build Facebook. We built Dashboard in a matter of months with a relatively small team. The Dashboard team was only like six guys. Twitter is a much simpler technology and they have 300 engineers just on the product side. We had six with a much more complicated product.[67]

Despite these issues, staffers argued that Dashboard did accomplish a number of things for the campaign. For the most committed volunteers, such as precinct captains, Dashboard helped them bridge the line of paid staff in some respects.[68] Dashboard also provided people with a way into the field program and broke down some of the distinctions between online and offline organizing. Narwhal ended up providing Dashboard with limited data integration, enabling the platform to have some real-time data flowing between systems that were disconnected in 2008, such as the online calling tool and VoteBuilder. This provided volunteers with new capacities to further the efforts of the campaign through making more high-priority voter contacts. For example, former staffers stated that a volunteer using Dashboard could update the voter file in close to real time, as well as the NGP VAN volunteer system, MyCampaign. Staffers also argued that Dashboard gave more credit to teams and enabled them to feel more engaged in the campaign. Dashboard enabled staffers in Chicago to better stay up to date on the progress of the state efforts and measure the work of really active people. Finally, Dashboard also facilitated the process of creating an identity and single sign-on system so that volunteers could log into Blue State Digital, VoteBuilder, the call tool, Dashboard, and the Election Day GOTV tools through one login ID.

DIGITAL ON THE CAMPAIGN

Former staffers argued that digital has taken on new importance in campaigning because social networking sites are part of people's lives in an infrastructural way.[69] Indeed, one example of how the world has changed, even in the four short years since the 2008 campaign, is that staffers on the 2012 bid realized they only had phone numbers for 50% of young voters (quite apart from how many could actually be reached at these numbers). Of the 50% the campaign did not have phone numbers for, staffers learned they could reach 85% of these individuals on Facebook through the social ties of supporters.[70] More generally, Ethan Roeder estimated that through the campaign's existing supporters and people who liked Barack Obama on Facebook, the campaign was able to contact approximately 90% of the Facebook population in the United States, a "number larger than the total number of people who cast ballots in the 2012 election."[71] As Roeder summarized: "Talking about how we contact people through social media is literally just a matter of reaching voters because if we weren't able, if we didn't have an aggressive online program, there just literally would not be any other way for us to get a hold of just a huge chunk of our voters."[72]

Reflecting this new reality, the digital department pursued a multifaceted digital and social media strategy. At the head of the digital team was Teddy Goff. In 2008, Goff served as the director of new media-battleground states, and then briefly worked on the transition as the WhiteHouse.gov lead before going back to New York to Blue State Digital. Like many of his colleagues, Goff cited that he had no intention of joining the re-election bid, and even actively decided that he did not want to do a second campaign. In January 2011, however, Jim Messina, at that point still the White House deputy chief of staff, asked Joe Rospars to a meeting at the White House. Rospars and Goff proactively put together a memo about what the re-election campaign ought to do. According to Goff, Messina basically said, "great, thank you. This is now the plan and you are now the team."[73] Goff and Rospars spent February and March 2011 planning for the launch of the re-election campaign, with Goff confident until the last few days before the campaign formally launched on Monday, April 4 that he would be handing the digital effort off to someone else. Things did not quite work out that way, with Goff staying on the campaign for the duration.

From the early stages of the re-election bid, staffers stated that there was an approach to valuing digital at the top of the campaign that carried over from the 2008 bid (which marked a significant difference from the role of digital on Romney's campaign). As Goff described, "one thing that Messina was pretty insistent on, you know, first of all philosophically he believed that you have got to go let the digital guys do what the digital guys want to do and not have the digital guys servicing a communications team who do not get digital and aren't going to get what is going to work."[74] This was consequential for staffers in terms of enabling them to have autonomy over digital strategy and content and to secure resources on the campaign.[75] This valuation of digital was written into the campaign's organizational structure. Goff became the digital director and worked in-house full-time on the campaign. As a senior staff member, Goff met with the other department heads such as communications and field at 9:00 a.m. Rospars served as a senior advisor to the campaign and was there quarter-time for approximately the first year, and then transitioned to half-time and finally full-time for the last month or so.

Digital and Social Media as Listening Technologies

Reflecting the emphasis on digital, the launch of the campaign was almost an entirely digital affair, featuring a website, digital video, an email, and some changes to the social media properties of the campaign. During this time, the digital team also launched a host of initiatives designed to enlist supporters from 2008 in the re-election effort. Staffers who worked on both bids stated that the re-election campaign acted in a very different political context in 2012, and staffers were cognizant of this fact very early on. Obama was no longer an outsider, transformative candidate. The former movement candidate was now a first-term president who had inevitably disappointed supporters in his constant battles with Republicans, pursuit of the compromises central to governance, and failure to advance some signature initiatives around closing the U.S. military prison at Guantanamo Bay and immigration reform (with health care being the big exception). Even more, staffers argued that sweeping losses during the 2010 midterm cycle left many former supporters dispirited.

Therefore, the first step among digital staffers was to re-enlist those who had worked so hard for the president in 2008 and were wary of Obama or just too exhausted to get involved this time out. The campaign launched a number of initiatives designed to reach out to and re-enlist these people. One was the "I'm In" button on the website, crafted as a soft initial ask for people to simply symbolically demonstrate support for the re-election bid. The digital team also came up with a "one-on-one" program that entailed attempting to reach out to every single person who donated to or volunteered on the 2008 campaign to invite them to a 10-minute phone call or in-person session with supporters who had recommitted to the campaign. The "ask" was then for the person who attended the session to go and talk to someone else. As Goff described, the project was designed to be "very much about listening more than talking, with the reality based view of how disappointed people were and how many people would really just want to unload before they were willing to do anything."[76] During the one-on-one meetings, volunteers took notes and the campaign ran them through software to inductively discover common themes in these conversations. Staffers then used these themes to inform their approach to the messaging for the campaign's digital properties in order to address supporter disenchantment (Jim Messina and field director Jeremy Bird also monitored the progress of these conversations.) Staffers stated that this effort netted approximately 20 million meetings and conversations with 2008 supporters.

During the spring and summer of 2011 the digital team also laid out its communications strategy and the core themes it would stress (broadly, issues as they connect with values, not specific legislation or policies). The campaign used its digital properties in a variety of ways. Ethan Roeder, for instance, noted how the campaign enabled people to share their stories—expressly conceptualizing digital and social media as listening technologies. For example, the campaign created a webpage called "share your healthcare stories" and developed a program called "Dream Catcher" that searched across different data sources for long-form comments that people provided the campaign. As Roeder explained regarding leveraging technologies of listening to analyze people's stories and incorporate them into the messaging of the campaign: "We did a better job of finding individual stories and making an individual kind of long-form perspective on the issues of our day a part of the fabric of our campaign and really putting that in front of our organizers and volunteers, making it a part of the conversation, highlighting it in our media."[77]

This use of digital media as listening devices for the campaign complemented what was taking place in the field. The 2012 campaign collected much more qualitative data than during Obama's first run. In 2008, canvass sheets and online applications that field volunteers used only collected limited amounts of data, such as who the contacted voter might be supporting and whether he or she planned to vote. In 2012, these sheets and the iPhone and iPad applications *invited* long-form notes from volunteers about what voters were telling them, such as what they were angry or frustrated about. This data then fed back into future conversations with these voters, as the campaign encouraged volunteers to reference earlier interactions recorded in that person's file during later visits. At the same time, the campaign updated its canvass techniques to emphasize a more dialogic approach to voter contacts. For one, staffers tested a number of scripts, and found that the most effective was none at all. What worked best was providing volunteers with some talking points and background information on basic issues, and then having them tell voters in their own words why they were supporting the president, what their "story" was, and what motivated them during the election.[78] The finely crafted script (long deployed in ground campaigns) was, staffers discovered, the antithesis of personal contact, and in practice seldom delivered to voters.[79]

Digital Constituency and State Teams

Aside from the campaign's own digital properties, staffers used social media in a variety of ways. A small core social media team of just four people in Chicago was responsible for the main Twitter, Facebook, Tumblr, Instagram, Google+, and Pinterest accounts. These four were the "keepers of the flame" and worked on all of the "inspirational stuff, the consumer-facing stuff."[80] Goff argued that the small size of the group in Chicago and their co-location explains how these staffers maintained a close, but loose, form of coordination over messaging activity. As Goff detailed the importance of the close working quarters, daily face-to-face interaction, and rapport, "We just had four people and they sat next to each other and they were in constant contact every day. If they needed to coordinate with states or constituencies or the communications team, you know we were all in one big office and people just talked all day every day. We really just had a very small team who we trusted completely and you know who were fantastic and very talented people."[81]

This team worked closely with a larger group of staffers that dealt with specific constituency and state campaign social media accounts. Former staffers in Chicago and the states referred to the campaign as having developed an "agency structure" that was run in-house, with specialized teams producing dedicated content for different constituencies. To staff these teams, Goff hired "creatives" to produce content, with more than 20 staffers coming to the campaign with primary work backgrounds in the commercial entertainment industry according to the biographical data on technology staffers, and sought to "insulate them from the politics" of the campaign organization and the banal happenings of the campaign trail.[82] The campaign was not only able to assemble a deeply talented pool of people with experience in the creative entertainment industry, it carved out specialized positions for them in terms of the content production and design for constituency and state groups so they could tell the story of these groups in the context of the election. Constituency accounts included Women for Obama and African Americans for Obama, among other groups, and a digital rapid response team of three to four staffers. In addition, the campaign hired dozens of state digital staffers to maintain state-specific accounts on social media platforms for every battleground state. This was an innovation in the way digital operations were organized on a campaign that arose from the idea that localized social media content that tracked state issues and concerns would have greater resonance with supporters, residents, and journalists living in these battleground states. State digital staffers also focused on raising money, recruiting volunteers, and telling the story of the state.

The state teams consisted of a digital director and at least one other staffer. Some battleground states, however, had larger staffs, including directors, deputies, videographers, and designers.[83] At the end of the campaign, some states even had their own digital analytics staffers (the analytics team in Chicago also provided the state digital teams with lists of people to target using social media, such as for early voting). The Chicago digital team had regional desks under the direction of digital organizing director Betsy Hoover. These desks were responsible for vetting the content produced by these state teams in their regions (Great Lakes/Mid-Atlantic, Midwest, Southern and Midwest, Western, and Northeast) and served as liasions with the field team (for some types of content, only the state digital director had to approve). Senior-level state staffers crafted state-specific emails (even as the email program was very centralized in Chicago and all emails had to go through headquarters to be approved). Former junior-level state digital staffers described being "basically journalists for the campaign," covering the election much as a partisan reporter would in terms of writing up campaign events (such as presidential and vice presidential visits), interviewing volunteers, and sharing the stories of people who had benefited from Obama's policies for an audience primarily of committed supporters.[84] As one former staffer who played a number of roles on digital state teams in 2012 related, "It was basically a content marketing program focused solely on the state. It was the belief that outside a centralized BarackObama.com there could be a state.barackobama.com with 4–6 staff or 2–6, depending on where it was, where they were running the show as much as they could because they were the ones who could tell the stories of the state better because it is hard for Chicago to know about really particular things."[85]

For example, staffers at the state level produced content around things such as the graphics designed in Chicago that went out on Facebook posts and tweets around events such as presidential visits. All of this was subject to the approval of the state digital director (who in essence had the autonomy to post on these social media platforms without Chicago's approval). Blog content had to be approved by state digital directors and the responsible regional desk staffer. All videos were sent to the state directors, the desk representative, Betsy Hoover, and the campaign's video team in Chicago. Reflecting staffers' desire for communication with "performative power," or influence over other actors' definitions of the situation and their consequent actions through well-timed, resonant, and rhetorically effective communicative action and interaction, there was no approval process for what staffers referred to as "live content."[86] As one state digital staffer related, "When it is live content there was no approval process. There was at the beginning but all the states quickly were like 'that is ridiculous. We are trying to cover events on the fly, we are not going to send you tweets as it is happening and expect you to approve this.'"[87]

While this was not without risk, another former staffer cited that she "internalized" the voice of the campaign.[88] Another pointed to the mutual respect that developed between Chicago and the states, and an abiding faith that they were all working toward the same goal of re-electing Obama: "There was kind of like an unspoken trust in the people, and among the people, who were tweeting for the states to not fuck up."[89] All that said, former staffers also noted that the campaign got stricter in the run-up to Election Day, with digital content needing to be pre-approved a week in advance.[90] However, while much content was supposed to be vetted by teams in headquarters during this period, a number of former state-level staffers cited many instances of what they called "going rogue." According to these staffers, it proved impossible for Chicago to vet everything coming in for approval. As a result, state-level staffers would just produce and distribute content for social media and even send emails, rather than going through the vetting process. That said, even when "going rogue," former staffers all stated that it was in the service of the campaign, and that their peers, higher-ups, and self-expectations all exerted tremendous normative pressure for staffers to self-regulate and put their best foot forward. As one former state-level staffer said, "You can imagine the immense pressure that we felt, and I would say that the campaign culture as a whole is very, very effective at making every single person from the lowest level to the highest feel like the fate of the campaign rests on their shoulders."[91]

The Digital Campaign on Facebook

In Chicago and in the states, staffers used social media in varying ways depending on their goals and understandings of the users of these platforms. As I have extensively documented, staffers used Twitter to shape the climate of opinion around the election and influence the agendas and frames of the professional press. Meanwhile, the digital team used Facebook in new ways during the 2012 electoral cycle.[92] The 2008 campaign mostly used Facebook as a way of convening and mobilizing targeted demographic and affinity groups. For example, new media organizers set up Obama Facebook groups for high schools and colleges, and then worked to organize the supporters who joined them and mobilize them to donate, volunteer, and turn out on Election Day.

In 2012, by contrast, the campaign used Facebook much more systematically to engage supporters, drive them to the campaign's other web properties, and spur them to volunteer and donate. Staffers tracked the reach of and engagement around their content in terms of likes, comments, and shares on the platform. The 2012 Obama campaign also used Facebook as a tool for targeted social communications.[93] The most prominent example was the campaign's "targeted sharing" program, a collaboration of the digital and analytics teams and, to a lesser extent, Blue State Digital. At the broadest level, the targeted sharing program identified and applied voter modeling to individuals in Obama supporters' social networks on Facebook. The campaign then asked supporters to become the conduits of strategic campaign communication to their social ties.

The motivation behind targeted sharing was, in the words of one staffer, "old fashioned."[94] The logic behind targeted sharing accords with sociologist Paul Lazarsfeld and his colleagues' findings in field studies during the 1940s and 1950s. These scholars first revealed the importance of "personal influence" in political attitude formation and the two-step flow of political communication from mass media to opinion leaders to broader publics, originally in the context of the 1940 presidential election and subsequently in studies of consumer preferences.[95] Campaign staffers knew from research and intuition that voters trust people who are close to them when it comes to political information. In an era of the widespread adoption of social media, it made perfect sense to staffers to attempt to leverage networked social ties for strategic purposes.

The targeted sharing tool coupled the social ties of supporters with the geographic concerns of the campaign. From the campaign's perspective, the challenge was to ensure that supporters were activating the right geographic ties. As Goff put it, "you would want people, to the extent they are going to be talking about the campaign online, you want them talking to the right people."[96] The "right people" meant "geographically relevant" in terms of electoral strategy. After the campaign identified the right people in supporters' social networks, the question was what supporters should say. Staffers recognized that many people are hesitant to talk about politics on social media, and thought that a targeted ask of a supporter to contact five friends with campaign-related content including appeals to register, volunteer, and turnout would be manageable.[97] The campaign asked supporters to post on their friends' Facebook timelines because they would be more likely to see it given the platform's algorithm.[98] For the campaign, staffers were getting access to five high-quality targets through a trusted medium. As Goff described, "It was obviously somewhat high tech but really all it was, in the exact same way that you would never send a volunteer out and say just go knock on every door. You would run a match to your persuadable list and say go knock on the 4th, 7th, and 21st doors. We were trying to do that on Facebook to the extent we could."[99]

Despite media reports that it was a successful program, targeted sharing was a highly fraught effort that in the end was not as extensive or useful as staffers originally had hoped.[100] The targeted sharing program was difficult to put together, and staffers spent almost the entire cycle working on it, beginning around April 2011 and finishing in August 2012. One of the challenges in building the targeted sharing program was that it, like Dashboard, was premised on the campaign being able to move data across a number of different platforms and databases. For targeted sharing, this meant staffers being able to have user data in Blue State, which the campaign used for emailing supporters, matched with the voter file and data from the social graph (i.e., Facebook). As is clear from the Narwhal discussion earlier, data integration was as much of an issue in 2012 as it was in 2008. Goff cites that the digital team expected to have complete integration of databases by November 2011 and never really got there, even by November 2012. That said, targeted sharing was both a new use of the platform and one likely to become conceptually adopted by campaigns using social media in the future, despite changes to Facebook's terms of service that no longer permit this type of marketing.[101]

Taking on the President: The Romney Campaign during the General Election

> I think people really unfairly judged the Romney campaign in comparison with us from 2012. What they should be doing is comparing the Romney campaign of 2012 to us in 2008, because they fought through a long protracted primary with no time to plan and uncertain resources. No big, deep, engineering team internally. Basically no party infrastructure. So they were in a very similar position to what we were in '08. And if you remember, they got all this attention because ORCA failed. We had the same system in '08 and it totally failed and nobody yelled at me because we won. But if you say the word Houdini to people from the '08 campaign they like throw up in their mouths a little bit. It is basically the same.
> —Michael Slaby[102]

In interviews, Obama's former staffers echoed Slaby in pointing to many of the structural constraints the Romney campaign faced, including the lack of time and resources and limited infrastructure inherited from the party. While the Obama campaign spent much of 2011 planning, hiring staff, working out organizational processes, and engaging in large-scale development projects, the Romney team went through a time- and resource-intensive primary. Many members of Obama's team had the benefit of learning what worked, and what did not, from the perspective of technology, digital, data, and analytics during the previous presidential cycle and spent the off years building on this experience at the party and affilated organizations. In addition, the extended Republican Party network lacked the data infrastructure, field tools, organizations, and expertise to support technology, digital, data, and analytics operations to match what the Democrats had been developing since 2005 since the 2004 cycle.

The Romney campaign also made a number of decisions with respect to its organizational structure and had a culture that compounded its comparative disadvantage of being the challenger. According to veterans of the effort, examples included the campaign's decision to allow its leadership and communications team to have significant vetting power over digital content, inconsistent use of data on the campaign, and failure to effectively organize technological projects among campaign departments. These failings were not simply the result of the whims of the campaign manager or the specific culture of the campaign; they were conditioned by the fact that the center of gravity within the Republican Party as a whole was oriented toward traditional (mass) communications, not technology, digital, or data, during the run-up to 2012.[103] In sum, the specific decisions that the Romney campaign made in terms of whom to empower, where to invest organizational authority and resources, how to divide up jurisdiction, and electoral strategy more broadly were conditioned by the general orientation of the Republican Party's extended network and the campaign's leadership that the candidate assembled from it.

ANALYTICS DURING THE GENERAL ELECTION

The campaign wanted to staff up in the areas of data and analytics after Romney became the presumptive nominee on April 25, 2012, and the RNC put resources behind the candidate. The campaign was significantly behind its rival in data and analytics at this point; as noted earlier, the Obama campaign had comparatively large departments in data and analytics in place throughout 2011 (and even earlier at the party during the run-up to the midterm cycle in 2010).[104] Russ Schriefer, senior strategist Stuart Stevens's business partner, reached out to Alex Lundry, who was then working at the Republican micro-targeting firm TargetPoint. Lundry took a leave from the firm soon after, and headed to Boston to become the campaign's director of data science at the end of May. Lundry was tasked, along with Brent McGoldrick (the former RNC Victory executive director of West Virginia during the 2004 cycle who subsequently worked for Grassroots Targeting and Edelman and had arrived on the campaign approximately two weeks prior to Lundry), with presenting their data at the daily, 10 a.m. morning meeting for the senior strategy team. At the meeting, Lundry and McGoldrick presented on the "state of the race: what has changed, what is new, what is on the air, what should we be putting on the air, what does this mean for other parts of the campaign and what did they want?"[105]

Lundry and McGoldrick joined the campaign's pollster Neil Newhouse, who ran the 10 a.m. meeting throughout the primaries as a daily poll briefing. The emphasis of these morning reports was on paid media and they were designed primarily to inform television ad buys, which Lundry said is what the campaign's strategists Stevens and Schriefer were interested in. A number of former staffers described how there was a consensus that the campaign needed to muster analytics, research, and data to inform advertising buys during the general election. The campaign did not have resources for "tonnage" vis-à-vis the Obama campaign in terms of bombarding voters with a disproportionate amount of advertising, a strategy that overpowered Romney's comparatively under-resourced opponents during the primaries.[106] The vision for data and analytics was that these staffers would fit between the polling and media teams and would primarily be tasked with making smarter advertising decisions, particularly given that it was where the vast amount of the campaign's money was being spent. This meant that, in contrast to the much larger Obama analytics team that had staffers dedicated to field, communications, digital, experiments, finance and operations, and modeling, Romney's core analytics team had both a comparatively narrow charge in terms of paid advertising and was only put together less than six months out from the general election.[107]

Briefings consisted of a poll (provided by Newhouse) coupled with semantic data from the web, occurrence data, competitive spending data, and data from canvass phone calls. Staffers put these disparate sources of data together to have some sense of the state of the race. In terms of voter contact, the campaign was doing tens of thousands of ID calls every night through an automated voice response system (the Obama campaign largely relied on volunteers and paid staffers for its thousands of live ID calls every night). The data from these calls were then incorporated into Lundry and his colleagues' report, along with the micro-targeting data of the campaign (handled by TargetPoint). Lundry also served as the liaison between the firm and campaign, and often was a self-described internal advocate for the firm inside the campaign (in contrast, the Obama campaign brought much of its analytics operations inside the organization and party).

Lundry and McGoldrick's goal was to influence the tactical decisions and strategy of the campaign and bring it into accord with the results of data analysis. The state of the race report was the driving force behind the 10 a.m. meeting, which was an important forum for senior staffers in often being the only time when they all would be together in person, and attendance was usually high.[108] And these meetings were important in the sense that a lot of key decisions were made there. As Lundry described, "that it was our information that was informing, that preceded and then informed the discussions and debates we had, I think it was taken very seriously. People reacted to what we saw and we had plenty of debates about what the data meant and what it meant we should do."[109]

That said, Lundry and other former staffers also argued that the buy-in to making data-based decisions was unevenly distributed across the campaign.

Sometimes, people made decisions in other places and forums on the campaign. At other times, people did not execute the decisions made in these planning sessions if they felt differently about the best course of action. Meanwhile, sometimes staffers would use data, quantitative or qualitative, to justify *preexisting* courses of action. All of these factors, former staffers argued, meant at best an uneven commitment to being data-driven from a broader electoral strategy perspective. One example comes in the context of the campaign's focus groups, which the polling team conducted every Sunday and Wednesday. Staffers cited that at times those in the campaign's hierarchy used data to justify decisions that people had already intuitively arrived at. As one former staffer argued, "I will tell you this— the advantages and disadvantages of focus groups were given different emphases depending upon the results that they produced. It wasn't the whole team. I think a lot of people on the team wanted to be more data-driven but you have to make a commitment very broadly to one side or the other and I think we had a tough time struggling with that."[110]

Lundry cited a different example than this staffer in arguing that data and analytics staffers lacked influence over television buys. Lundry argued that the campaign's data and analytics team was interested in optimizing paid media by merging the different data streams they were collecting with media consumption databases through a firm called CentraForce. In essence, this merged micro-targeting data with media consumption data (not set-top box data) and enabled the campaign to run customized ratings reports for persuasion and GOTV purposes. Lundry's team produced reports for the media buying team showing which shows were good and bad to advertise on in order to reach certain targeted groups of voters (in contrast to the Obama campaign, whose Optimizer revealed both shows and *time*). However, analytics staffers argued that they never had the sense that these reports were actually used by the media buying team. As Brent McGoldrick argued:

> There were deep philosophical differences within the campaign as to how targeted advertising could or should be, the levels at which you needed to run those things, and how you would measure it. While there were voices who were supportive of an analytical approach there was by no means a consensus. You are trying to convince people that this is the right way to think about it in addition to actually doing the analysis itself. So if I think about it I would not say there was an analytic and data-based culture within the campaign.[111]

Former staffers argued that a number of factors led to this organizational environment. One is that the campaign was generally wedded to an approach to communications that was well institutionalized across the Republican Party and lacked a rigorous focus on message development and testing (as well as failed to incorporate new commercial practices such as set-top box targeting). Another explanation that numerous staffers in different departments cited is that the campaign never needed to develop a culture around data, analytics, and message targeting during the primaries because the Romney campaign enjoyed a significant monetary advantage over its rivals. This meant that the campaign could weather the vicissitudes of the race by spending significantly to run a lot of non-message-discriminating and non-targeted ads in primary states.[112]

Still other staffers pointed to the fact that on the Romney campaign there was a more general lack of consensus over the messaging of the campaign and an unwillingness to use evidence to settle the debate. Senior staffers vacillated between a narrow focus on attacking Barack Obama and the state of the economy and stating what would be repealed in a Republican administration, versus emphasizing Romney's story, values, and priorities. Former staffers argued that this debate was ongoing, even though the latter approach was validated by data from surveys, focus groups, and social media. As one former staffer put it, internally the messaging strategy of the campaign was the focus of "constant debate," as staffers continually took up the questions of "when are we going to introduce Mitt, when are we going to talk about who he is and why he is running for president?"[113] As another former staffer described his questioning of the campaign's strategy, "Why do we keep going after Barack Obama? We were using the survey work, we were using the focus groups, the analytics, all of which pointed to—you need to tell people who this guy is. And there was a reluctance to it because there was a fear that talking about Mitt meant not talking about President Obama and there was a fear that if you, to use I think one of the phrases of our chief strategists, if you took 'the boot off of his throat' he would have a chance to recover."[114]

Other staffers echoed this sentiment in citing a widespread failure to provide voters with a viable alternative to Obama, with the campaign only seeking to make the election a referendum on the president. And, after the Obama campaign ran its barrage of early negative advertising against Romney, staffers on both sides of the aisle argued that the Republican could not recover his favorability ratings.[115] Presidential staffers, if not political scientists, credit this early advertising blitz with defining the Republican in a memorable, negative, and highly consequential way for voters, a similar strategy to what Bush did to Kerry in 2004.[116]

While political scientists provide a convincing argument that in the end the perceived failure to introduce Romney likely mattered very little with respect to the outcome of the race, these internal debates had significant consequences for the work of staffers on the campaign.[117] A number of staffers argued that the differences within the campaign over messaging hindered the work of the analytics team. Former staffers argued that Romney needed a first-order messaging strategy in order to have an analytics-based culture, and compared their campaign unfavorably in this regard to their rival. Romney staffers tracked advertising during the cycle via CMAG (Campaign Media Analysis Group), which included all political advertising (including party-affiliated and non-affiliated groups), although it lacks some key categories of data.[118] They did so in an attempt to reverse-engineer Obama's strategy. Romney staffers noticed that the Obama campaign had a very disciplined and methodical approach to messaging. Analytics staffers showed the senior staff on the Romney campaign how Obama's messages had a progressive arc that could be inferred through the sequencing of particular themes. Romney's analytics staffers argued that everything flowed from these decisions to emphasize and sequence particular themes, including the testing of the effectiveness of messaging through tracking movements in polls with regard to the themes featured in advertising.

In other words, there is a lot of conceptual work that goes into messaging, and it must be performed *prior* to any data and analytics approach that will ultimately be used to test and refine it. Campaigns need to know what their goals and targets for messaging are in order to operationalize the outcomes they desire. In contrast to Obama's efforts, former Romney staffers argued that their campaign created a fundamentally one-dimensional message about the economy and Obama's culpability in contributing to its poor state. Staffers argued that this message was the uniform theme across all of the campaign's advertising and communications across many different platforms. As a result, staffers argued that there was a pretty homogeneous approach to advertising and buying, where the campaign produced an ad and hit 1,000 points in each target market each week to send this message to a generally undifferentiated audience.

Former staffers argued that the campaign's hierarchy made these strategic choices regarding messaging during the primaries and generally pursued the same course of action through the general election, despite the leadership hiring Lundry and McGoldrick in their desire to be more data-driven as detailed earlier. A number of former staffers argued that the primaries not only drained the campaign of resources, they also led to the opposite of careful messaging and provided little incentive for the development of message architecture. The general pattern during the primaries was that the campaign went state to state, found a close race or Romney even down by a number of points in the final days before a vote to whomever the GOP newcomer was, and then dropped a massive amount of television advertising on the challenger. The challenger would not have the resources to respond, and Romney would eke out a narrow victory.[119] A campaign strategy premised on taking advantage of vast disparities in resources worked during the primaries, but did not work for the general election against an evenly matched opponent. As Zac Moffatt described:

> Everything we learned in the primary reinforced every bad tendency, which then when you got to the general couldn't be overcome, if you try and change it people are just like, you know, "no, no this is what worked before." And I sat in rooms where people said, "Obama is crazy.

They are doing 650 points but they are buying four different messages and if it comes to 2400 points we need to buy 2400 points and put it behind one message." And it was a mindset. We acknowledged at the time that one campaign would be correct and one campaign wouldn't be and unfortunately for us they were right and we weren't. They had found a messaging arc that made Mitt to some people unelectable, and we could never really get out of that.[120]

Outside the general state of the race report, Lundry stated that his team's role eventually evolved into becoming an "in-house data consultant" to the campaign that provided analytics services to other teams, such as media buying.[121] Lundry cited that there were approximately 30 people doing analytics on the campaign when everyone who was working in that capacity was considered (compared with the Obama campaign's 54 staffers in their own dedicated department).[122]

In the months leading up to the vote, the analytics team ran simulations and conducted polling, the results of which were not always made public for strategic reasons. While there was a seeming disconnect between the public statements of the Romney campaign and the actual state of the race (symbolically exemplified in Karl Rove's FOX News appearance on the evening of the election), the reality is more complicated. The role of polling on a campaign is multifaceted, a fact that is underappreciated in much journalism and political communication literature. Internally, polling helps campaigns make decisions about electoral strategy, targeting, and messaging, in large part by reducing uncertainty (as opposed to revealing the one correct course of action). Externally, polls are strategic communications tools. Campaigns deploy them to influence journalists and their coverage, in the process speaking to important stakeholders such as activists and donors. As Lundry described, polling is important for multiple audiences:

> The role of the pollster in a campaign also becomes one of an assurer. Somebody who essentially calms the nerves of donors and activists and tells them we are still in this, we still have a chance to win, right? And that has for better or for worse become a very important part of doing polling for a campaign, especially a presidential campaign. And related to that is also a desire to see a path to victory in the polls. Everybody wants to because you want to win and you want to imagine the circumstance or scenario in which you do win.[123]

In the months before the general election, former staffers argued that the Romney campaign was only publicly releasing its favorable polls in the attempt to keep its fundraising up and volunteers coming through the doors, as well as achieve a favorable press narrative about the state of the race. Internally, however, the story was more complicated. Staffers across departments stated that while the campaign's polling showed Romney winning independents and leading among those most enthusiastic about the race (which suggested to staffers that there was an opportunity for Romney to win), the top line polls still had the candidate losing. As Lundry described:

> There were some states that yes we were wrong on in terms of directionality, but they were typically within the margin of where it ended up. We ran simulations just like the Obama campaign did. The day of the election we ran our simulations of the most recent fresh polling. We were only winning 25%, or sorry, it wasn't even 25%, it was 18% of the simulations. Now, especially at that point, what do you do differently? It's Election Day, literally.[124]

Lundry subsequently went on to argue that while the Romney campaign was not that far off base in its projections of the race (a point that other staffers made as well), the Obama campaign was able to get closer to predicting the actual outcome. The Obama team's comparative success was premised on the greater amounts of data the campaign had coming in from sources such as its much more extensive field operation, which as described earlier was premised on infrastructural technologies half a decade in the making.[125] All that said, former staffers in different departments on Romney's bid, and at the party, questioned whether the state of the race revealed through simulations and polling made its way up to the candidate. I turn now to the technologies on the Romney campaign during the general election.

STAFFING AND DEVELOPMENT TIMELINES DURING THE GENERAL ELECTION

Around the end of March, Romney staffers cited that they began to have a good feeling they were going to win the primaries. In April, the campaign started staffing up for the general election. In six weeks over the course of May and June, staffers stated the digital team grew from approximately 22 to over 110 staffers and consultants (and ended with about 150 people in Boston and another 50 or so spread throughout the state).[126] These staffers included 55 developers working directly for both the campaign and consulting firms such as Targeted Victory on projects such as the main Mitt Romney web property as well as various microsites, splash pages, and mobile and Facebook applications. The bulk of this team was in place by the end of June, and this was the basic staffing structure that held through November.

This period of rapid growth was challenging, and reveals the structural advantages of the Obama campaign in terms of its large database of talent carried over from the 2008 bid, as well as the comparatively longer time it had to staff up and keep people employed, which staffers on both sides of the aisle argued was important with respect to recruiting people with specialized skills. Practitioners argued, for instance, that it is much easier for a developer to quit a job to go work on a campaign if the time frame is both known and substantial (i.e., the 18 months of campaign work that many of Obama's first hires had). On the Romney campaign, early on there were limited resources and the time horizon was unclear given the fundamental uncertainty of the primaries. All of this meant that it was hard to recruit people given that the campaign was asking them to leave stable, paid employment.

At the same time, a number of former Romney staffers, and practitioners in the extended party network, expressed that there was a talent gap between the two parties because Republican staffers want to be paid more for their work.[127] Whether Republican staffers demand higher salaries, or campaigns offer them, post-election analyses showed systematic differences between the two presidential campaigns, with seven Romney staffers making more money than any Obama staffer.[128] As one former Republican Party staffer characterized both the higher expectations for pay in the GOP and the time advantage that Obama had given the technical advantage of incumbency, "On the Republican side of the field you simply don't get developers or any individual who says 'this is a great cause I am going to work for 1/3 of my average salary.' It is my personal belief that there is plenty of talent on the Republican side, it just undermines all the values that they have, or many of the values that they have, because campaigns don't have money, at least initially."[129]

Other staffers argued that the campaign failed to reach out to technology industry networks for recruiting purposes and created constrained organizational roles for staffers with specialized skills. Aaron Ginn, the "growth hacker" who joined the campaign during the general election, rejected the suggestion, common in the media in the months after the 2012 election, that the Republican talent gap stemmed from a supposed lack of technologists who are members of the party or are aligned with its ideological aims. While it certainly may be true that Obama's base and the Democratic Party more generally has more potential staffers with specialized technology skills (in part given the party network's investments in producing these staffers since 2004), Ginn asked how many programmers the Republican Party actually needed.[130] Ginn argued that the Obama 2008 and 2012 campaigns were simply better at recruiting and making use of their technically skilled staffers given the relative autonomy of their technology, data, analytics, and digital media teams.[131] With considerably more time to plan and staff up, a cultural orientation of having buy-in at the highest levels of the campaign in terms of what to look for, invest in, and utilize with respect to talent, and a longer period of time and autonomy for staffers to ply their trade, Ginn argued that the Obama campaign created a more stable and ultimately compelling work environment for its engineers.

While former staffers cited different issues with respect to hiring, suffice it to say that it was a significant challenge to hire approximately 100 people in roughly six weeks (not to mention the need to coordinate mundane but time-consuming things such as securing laptops for everyone). In this general context, in May and June the Romney campaign spent much of its time getting people up to speed and figuring out how to manage workflow and leverage project management tools, in addition to beginning work on technical development projects. Former staffers on both campaigns cited that the differences in the starting lines of the two presidential bids were on full display in terms of the comparative hours each could devote to technical projects, with the Romney bid only talking about undertaking new projects after May 1. In a clear example of how competitive advantage in electoral politics is increasingly also the result of the longer technical development timelines that incumbents have, Moffatt echoes Michael Slaby, cited earlier, regarding the resource and timeline constraints the Romney team faced:

> I went back and did some basic calculations. The Obama campaign roughly had about 2.4 million hours available to its digital team and Romney had 680,000. So that is 78% to 22%. So we would have had to be four times better than them at everything that we did for it to be compared. Obama was not only "money ball," they were the Yankees running money ball. We are trying to be like the Oakland A's.[132]

To supplement its staff, as noted earlier, the campaign hired staffers through Targeted Victory and other firms, including field crossers from the technology and commercial sectors (many of whom do not show up in the FEC data reported earlier)—see note 126 to this chapter. The campaign also outsourced a number of its technical development projects to vendors instead of bringing them in-house (the strategy of the Obama campaign detailed earlier). Staffers stated, for instance, that the digital team went to specialized firms and literally rented project teams (of between four and 18 developers) for periods of time to work on discrete projects. The Romney campaign also relied on a number of commercial vendors, including Eventbrite, which provided the ticketing platform for the campaign's events.

Digital during the General Election
The digital team prioritized work around three key things for the general election. First, Romney would choose a vice presidential candidate, which would draw tremendous attention to the campaign and a lot of traffic across its web properties. Second, the Republican National Convention would generate a considerable amount of public interest and attention during the days of the event. Third, there would be three presidential debates and the vice presidential debate. These were the events around which the digital team oriented itself, in addition to the ongoing

fundraising and building out of the state digital political teams. In terms of the latter, the digital team put people in state organizations and had them report directly to Moffatt in Boston (if they were managed locally, Moffatt discovered they would quickly be reassigned to other tasks).

The work of the digital team during the general election reveals the degree to which the campaign lacked some key infrastructural resources from the Republican Party and was at a disadvantage with respect to the longer developmental timelines that the Obama campaign enjoyed. For example, in numerous independent accounts, staffers working for the Romney campaign and the party argued that despite proclamations of running a "convention without walls" (the name of the convention's Facebook app), the organizers at the RNC made few plans for digital media, and that what was planned was mismanaged. The party hired Campaign Solutions to develop the digital platform for the convention, but abruptly fired the firm at the end of May 2012 after its proprietor, Becki Donatelli, was listed as a participant in a potential plan to develop an advertising campaign highlighting Obama's relationship with Reverend Wright.[133] Practically speaking, this meant that three months out from the convention, Romney's digital team was asked to coordinate its digital presence, essentially from scratch, while also running the regular digital operations. This sequence of events lay behind staffers' decision to create a relatively static site for the convention and rely on a Facebook application and a livestream through a YouTube channel with a customized player. This approach also meant that the campaign did not have to pay for hosting, a decision that staffers argued was born out of limited budgets and the firing of Campaign Solutions. Even still, according to the campaign's figures, the convention generated more than 4 million tweets in four days and 5 million YouTube viewers for the convention.

While planning for the convention, the digital team also coordinated the rollout of the vice presidential pick, Paul Ryan. Former digital staffers cited facing a number of obstacles in the planning around this announcement, most important among them that they lacked the time frame for the announcement. The digital team decided to make the announcement via a mobile application that essentially served as a "Trojan Horse," an app people were enticed to download to learn Romney's choice of a running mate that would support new functionalities in the future, such as social media messaging or volunteer tools.[134] This did not quite go as planned. The professional press beat the push notification on the mobile application by a considerable margin, and the digital team went on to launch two other mobile applications over the course of the campaign. Even still, former staffers cited that 60% of the people who downloaded the application in anticipation of the vice presidential pick turned on push notifications, which provided a vehicle onto people's mobile devices.

In terms of events such as the debates, as I have previously documented, the Romney team engaged in considerable work to help shape and extend the narrative of Obama's failed performance during the first debate, in the process likely influencing the perceptions of political journalists during it and their questions afterward.[135] In subsequent debates, when the Obama campaign engaged in more planning in advance, the most significant organizational difference between the Romney and Obama digital teams lay in the significantly less autonomy the former had to produce and disseminate content. As detailed earlier, the digital staffers on the Romney campaign had an extensive vetting process for all of the content they produced.[136] This was important not only with respect to the campaign's ability to wield performative power, it also shaped the work of and content produced by the digital team.[137] For example, Moffatt argued that the digital team got pretty good at building standard things such as flash pages that the campaign could have up in 30 minutes because all the content, video, and graphics were already pre-approved. As Moffatt contrasted the two presidential bids with respect to digital, "In our model the comms team and the strategy department had to sign off on everything, in the Obama model their team, the digital team, seemed to have greater latitude about determining what it was going to be. So we had to write it and submit it and then get it back and then we could put it up."[138]

Former digital staffers argued that this vetting process ultimately meant less of the engaging and motivational content that could produce an inspired base of volunteers and small-dollar donors for the Republican candidate, precisely what they viewed as highly successful in the Obama effort. Indeed, former Romney staffers often pointed to content being the key difference between the two campaigns. They also cited that this vetting process hampered their ability to engage in the testing and analytics that was a staple of the Obama campaign. Moffatt argued, for instance, that the campaign was limited in its ability to A/B test because while digital staffers wanted to segment things such as email in 18 different ways, "they didn't want to write 18 pieces of copy and get them to approval."[139] More broadly, Aaron Ginn argued that the digital staffers were an "arm of the communications team."[140]

There were other differences in the digital media use on the two campaigns, particularly when it came to email. The Obama campaign did *manual* targeting, with an approximately 18-person email team creating lists, developing tailored content, and tracking outcomes. By contrast, the Romney campaign did automated targeting. When a known user visited a webpage, the platform automatically sent an email. For example, if a user visited an affinity group page, the campaign automatically sent an email encouraging them to join that group. If a user donated after a debate, the campaign sent a follow-up email a number of days later, encouraging her to contribute again. The difference with manual targeting is that the Obama campaign had more flexibility with respect to testing the structure, content, and timing of emails, while automated emails were tied to particular predetermined triggers. The different approaches of the two campaigns were, in part, an outgrowth of the comparative costs and benefits of each approach. Automation required fewer resources, both in terms of staff and technical capacity. And, this was also an approach that fit with the constraints imposed on the digital team with respect to the content approval process.

THE POLITICAL PROGRAM AND FIELD TOOLS

As noted earlier, the Romney primary campaign's strategy was about "island hopping," not "nation building," and as a result there was little durable political (i.e., field) infrastructure for the general election. In the end, there were significant differences in the investment in field campaigning made by the two bids, with the Obama campaign opening 786 field offices to Romney's 284. Romney political director Rich Beeson, and other staffers on the campaign, argued that this disparity was ultimately a question of resources. The Obama campaign had comparatively greater freedom to raise and spend money throughout the cycle as the Democratic Party's nominee, and did not have to contest any primaries. For its part, the Romney campaign went through a long and resource-intensive primary, and fundraising picked up only after the candidate became the de facto Republican nominee at the end of April 2012.[141]

At the same time, Romney's fundraising at this point primarily came through Romney Victory, a joint fundraising committee between the campaign, the RNC, and several state parties. Romney Victory faced a number of restrictions on how much could be spent on the campaign, compared with Obama's significant candidate-driven fundraising which netted approximately $690 million online, $504 million of which was driven by digital operations and often entailed small-dollar donations, all of which offered much greater flexibility in terms of campaign spending.[142] Indeed, as noted earlier, there were significant differences in the fundraising totals of the two campaigns and their extended networks more broadly, with comparatively more money raised by the Obama campaign itself and invested in field, while the Romney campaign outsourced much of its field operation to the party and was more reliant on outside groups that engaged mostly in broadcast advertising. These 527 organizations had to spend money without explicitly coordinating with the campaign or the party. Their dollars also did not go as far given that these organizations do not receive the same favorable advertising rates as campaigns and parties. From a field perspective, 527s are at a comparative disadvantage because they cannot access the strategic or historical data of parties. This helps explain the late advertising blitz that the Romney campaign had to rely on in the absence of a strong field program.[143]

For example, staffers on both sides of the aisle roundly argued that presidential campaigns and parties, with their comparatively greater mobilizing power, better-integrated data streams and resources, favorable advertising rates and access to state-provided voter rolls, more valuable data, and ability to advocate directly for the candidate and party, are better positioned to conduct electoral efforts than outside groups. A hallmark of the Obama 2008 and 2012 campaigns was how much they brought field operations and advertising in-house. Comparatively, in 2012 the Romney campaign relied, in no small part, on the outsourcing of core parts of its messaging to 527s given resource constraints. As one former Romney staffer put it, "When the Obama campaign had that money they could say exactly what they wanted to say and they could say 'vote for Barack Obama.' With those 527s it's two or three steps removed."[144] As Rich Beeson described the 527 canvass efforts in 2012, "Bottom line is, yes we knew there were other groups out there, we weren't sure who they were or what their scripts were, or targets were. The Obama campaign had an advantage that they were all singing from the exact same song script and you know we just weren't, we would have 10 or 12 different scripts going on out there."[145]

In this context, the Romney campaign identified three states that staffers knew they would have to win during the general election: Florida, Virginia, and Ohio. Outside this trio, the political department saw a number of potential paths to victory. One was what the campaign called the "Way West" strategy. Staffers cited having a good feeling about Colorado in looking at the absentee ballot numbers, as well as Nevada, where the campaign outdid Bush's numbers in rural counties. That said, in my interviews with former staffers, I emerged with a general sense of a campaign that simultaneously underestimated its rival (particularly the Obama campaign's ability to turn out many low-propensity voters) and overestimated its candidate's standing in the polls.[146] In terms of the Obama campaign's turnout efforts, for instance, Beeson cited that his campaign "hit the numbers that we thought we needed to hit to win but in every state we would find that, you know, it was 160,000 more African Americans that voted in Ohio in 2012 than voted in 2008. That is just not something that we were ever going to account for. The 18–24 vote in Colorado, the Hispanic vote in Florida. They just hit things that no reasonable person was going to think that they were going to hit."[147]

The fact that Alex Lundry argued that his polling numbers on the day of the election suggested Romney would win only in 18% of simulations suggests, at the very least, a disconnect between different departments on the campaign. That said, it is clear that the Obama 2012 campaign was able to turn out many of its historically low-propensity voters, such as African Americans in swing states.[148] Romney's political staffers, and others, attributed the Obama campaign's success to the fact that it had 2,700 field organizers on staff at the start of the election, and a number of innovative turnout efforts.[149] Indeed, there was a deep respect for what the Obama campaign achieved, particularly with respect to low-propensity voters, whom Romney staffers perceived Obama's staffers treated the same way as their high-propensity voters.

All of the Obama campaign's electoral efforts were premised on technology, digital, data, and analytics in some way—from the party's vast data infrastructure that underpinned extensive voter contact and registration operations and the tools that volunteers used in the field to the ways that digital efforts complemented this work and small-dollar online fundraising gave the campaign a monetary advantage. As Sasha Issenberg has written, the Obama campaign "began the election year confident it knew the name of every one of the 69,456,897 Americans whose votes had put him in the White House."[150]

Assessing the Electoral Impact of Technology, Digital, Data, and Analytics

In the end, the question is, what did the effective use of technology, digital, data, and analytics provide the Obama 2012 campaign in terms of a competitive advantage over its rival? As political scientists John Sides and Lynn Vavreck concluded in their own interview-based study of data and analytics on the campaign, "Being realistic also means acknowledging how hard it is to estimate the total impact of the campaign."[151] These scholars cited former analytics and field staffers not knowing the answer to the question of how much of Obama's four point margin of victory the campaign accounted for. Or, at most, staffers stated that the campaign was worth two points.[152] Echoing Sides and Vavreck, in my interviews former staffers similarly pointed to the ways that the impact of technology, digital, data, and analytics proved stubbornly difficult to quantify. Looking back at the Obama campaign, former staffers argued that what technology and analytics provided was efficiency in terms of identifying the right voters to contact and how to reach them, as well as what to say. For example, in response to a question about how these staffers won their arguments internally for the value of the resources the campaign spent on technology and analytics, Slaby argued that:

> [p]eople who say technology and analytics won the campaign I always argue with. I believe that candidates win campaigns. I believe that analytics is about efficiency in a lot of regards. We made 150 million voter contacts—which ones? That is the fundamental analytics question. The technology piece is like getting 150 million conversations, so they are about effectiveness and throughput and making volunteers more productive. Through these things efficiency and effectiveness work together. Together having the right 150 million conversations means that everywhere there is a close fight we won, which doesn't mean we won because of that, but it means the difference between 272 and 332. I think in a lot of ways the efficiency and effectiveness of the organization is the margin of victory, not the victory, which is a big distinction to me anyway.[153]

As is clear, to Slaby the value of technology, digital, data, and analytics lay in providing marginal advantages in terms of the efficiency and effectiveness of voter contacts. What unified the use of data and analytics across the campaign was the orientation toward using them to guide electoral strategy, improve the efficiency of voter contacts, and assess the comparative returns on investment of various communications strategies. For example, in terms of the field operation, the campaign used its extensive voter data primarily as a way to increase efficiency in terms of resource allocations to contest states and contact voters. Field staffers considered the electoral votes that each state had, priced out the cost of contesting them, and calculated the cost per electoral vote with an eye toward the likelihood that any particular state was the tipping point that would deliver the 270th electoral vote.[154] To construct this index of the tipping point state required an enormous amount of work and resources. The campaign relied on the extensive research it was conducting on a daily basis, interviewing approximately 10,000 people a night to look at changes in the electorate on the basis of campaign events, advertising, canvassing, and other forms of voter contact.[155]

Another aspect of the improved efficiency that technology, digital, data, and analytics afforded comes with respect to the old staple of email solicitations for money and volunteers, which was very much a data-driven practice in 2012, even more so than 2008. Former staffers said that the email team's motto was "don't trust your gut."[156] Testing resulted in the odd, and much lampooned, emails that had subject lines such as "Hey" and often featured a rough-hewn HTML look. Through experimental tests, staffers knew that this content and format outperformed other flashier or more polished content and design. Staffers estimated that testing and optimization of email netted the campaign an additional $100 million. This was particularly important given that it was this digital, small-dollar fundraising that kept the re-election campaign competitive with the Republican Party network in terms of monetary resources, and Obama's staffers had greater flexibility in terms of how they could be spent.

In the end, despite their relative youth within campaign organizations, technology, digital, data, and analytics mattered in some very old ways: fundraising and increased efficiencies and effectiveness in voter identification, contact, and resource allocations.

Conclusion

In concluding this chapter, I want to return to that symbol of the Republican candidate's failure: Project ORCA. Developing ORCA on the Romney campaign late in the cycle was necessary because the party and its extended network *failed* to build a tool with its functionality in the years between 2008 and 2012, even as its utility was clear. In the end, ORCA was a product of the failure of Republican Party infrastructure, the compressed time frame of the campaign, and the comparatively fewer resources it had, as well as a breakdown in organization.

ORCA originated not with digital, but in the political department of the campaign. Digital staffers argued that they did not know about the project until three weeks before it was rolled out, and they warned the political team about the challenges it would face.[157] Even more, these staffers argued that had ORCA been proposed in May or even August, it would not have been a priority for digital given the number of other projects that needed to be completed and the technical difficulty of pulling it off successfully. Indeed, a former political staffer on the campaign suggested that they did not approach the digital team about ORCA precisely because of this.

This points to the organizational issues the campaign had, especially with respect to a lack of prioritization of technological projects and collaboration between departments on the campaign. It also suggests more broadly the degree to which extended party network infrastructure, longer development timelines, resources available early in the cycle, the knowledge staffers gain across elections, and the field testing that occurs during off-presidential years are important with respect to building technologies. The Romney campaign developed tools, but mostly on an ad hoc basis and with short timelines, relied on a number of suboptimal out-of-the-box solutions, and organizationally distributed responsibility for them across many units, which led to limited integration. And, looking back, there was a general sentiment among staffers that technology is too sophisticated now to originate in non-technical departments (a sentiment echoed by Obama staffers). According to Abe Adams, the Romney campaign's deputy digital director, ORCA was just a very public example of a more general dynamic on the campaign:

> That is an extreme example where a couple of guys had a project. Logistically, it tied to a lot of other people, but the actual technology leveraged came from outside vendors contracted exclusively on that project. They worked on it completely on their own. This is common practice for non-incumbent campaigns. If you look at products other departments used out of the box, we didn't have the time and resources to build every tool from scratch or integrate every side project staff initiated.[158]

Beyond ORCA, the party's field tools also revealed the lack of infrastructure within the Republican Party network at this moment in time. According to the vast majority of accounts, and explored in greater detail in the next chapter, the primary field tool for accessing Republican Party data during the cycle, GOP Data Center (formerly Voter Vault), offered little in the way of the usability and functionality of the Democrats' VoteBuilder. Staffers across the Republican Party network cited that during the 2012 cycle the GOP Data Center had many different and often only loosely integrated components and had a number of functions that ceased to work, was designed with an unclear end user in mind, lacked integration with other forms of data, and failed to keep pace more generally with advances in technology. Former party staffers argued that the incumbent firms tasked with the maintenance of the GOP Data Center had few financial incentives to rebuild or make significant modifications to the platform. A number of. former party staffers argued that while Voter Vault was a pretty advanced product in 2004 and 2006, development from that point on was premised on bringing consultants in without planning for long-term developments, which was in part the consequence of the finances of the party during this period.

In other words, there was little infrastructure provided by the party or its extended network to compensate for the lack of resources and the electoral context faced by the campaign. This had consequences, namely in the need to develop technologies such as ORCA on the campaign in a comparatively short period of time. Furthermore, staffers argued that there were no vendors in the extended Republican Party network on the order of BSD or NGP VAN that had the financial incentives to build this infrastructure given the lack of investment in technology by the party and its extended network in the years between presidential elections. Given all this, after 2012 there were a number of challenges to the Republican Party's field tools and data, which I turn to in the next chapter.

6

Old Paths and New Beginnings

In the wake of Mitt Romney's loss, many Republicans, journalists, popular commentators, and members of the public found much to critique about the campaign and the party more generally. Many pointed to ORCA's extraordinarily public and well-documented unraveling as a sign that the candidate and his party were hopelessly behind their rivals in terms of technology.[1] Still others wondered where the Republican ground effort was, and marveled over the data-driven field operations of the Obama campaign, which mobilized many more volunteers and coordinated significantly more door knocks than its rival in the ultimately successful effort to get its low-propensity voters to the polls. Furthermore, to many, Karl Rove's seeming inability to grasp the math in Ohio on FOX News on the evening of the election seemed symptomatic of the larger polling and data failings of the Republican Party and its presidential campaign, especially given that staffers at both were publicly trumpeting the closeness of the race in the weeks before the election.[2]

These accounts were often incomplete and offered highly selective readings of the campaign.[3] They generally lacked much in the way of consideration of the structure of the 2012 race, such as the resource and time disadvantages that the Romney campaign faced compared to its rival. They paid little attention to the differences between the Republican and Democratic parties with respect to the digital and technological assets they provided to their nominees, their basic data infrastructures and tools for accessing them, or the staffers and organizations with specialized expertise available in their extended networks for candidates to draw on. And, even more, an extraordinary amount of technology and political journalism portrayed the Obama campaign's use of digital media, technology, data, and analytics in heroic terms, setting up an idealized and largely mythic account of an extraordinarily powerful and seamless operation—none of which reflected the reality of the campaign when viewed up close, or captured the fact that basic infrastructural technologies such as the party's Vertica, NGP VAN's VoteBuilder, and Blue State Digital's email platform were the behind the scenes stars of the campaign. Furthermore, many of these accounts implied that the Obama campaign's uptake of technology, digital, data, and analytics determined the result of the election, rather than provided for gains on the margin in terms of efficiency and effectiveness in voter contacts and enabled the Democrat to gain significant resource advantages over his rival.

Regardless of their factual grounding, these public narratives had significant consequences. Romney's loss served as a significant wake-up call to actors in the extended Republican Party network and prompted a serious evaluation of their infrastructure, investments, consulting ecosystem, electoral practices, staffer expertise, and campaign strategies. This moment of crisis unfolded in a similar manner to the aftermath of the 2004 cycle for Democrats when, perceiving that they lost a campaign they should have won, party network actors elected a new chairman to take the party into a technology, data, and organizing future, and they created opportunities for new ventures that transformed their organizational and technical infrastructure.

In their accounting, what Republican Party network actors found out after 2012 about the state of their party was not pretty. The Republican Party's internal Growth and Opportunity Project report used the 2012 cycle as a lens onto charting broader differences between the two parties. As the report stated with respect to data:

> To win campaigns, the GOP needs better data, better access to data, and better tools to make the most of that data.... Voter data and analytics are where Republicans most clearly trail Democrats according to our Internet survey of 227 GOP campaign managers, field staff, and other political professionals, consultants, and vendors. They compared the two parties' capabilities on +5 to −5 scale for 24 different campaign components and political activities. Democrats were seen as having the advantage in all but one.[4]

This chapter is, in part, about the Republican Party's efforts to pick up the pieces after a failed electoral cycle and head in a new direction toward the prototype that the 2012 Obama campaign had become with respect to its uptake of technology, digital media, data, and analytics. Regardless of the accounts of the election that many political scientists tell, which according to most was a foregone conclusion given the structural factors of incumbency and the state of the economy, the stories that practitioners tell about electoral success and failure matter because they shape how people perceive and act in the world. In the wake of the election, the symbolism of ORCA, public debates among party actors, and account of the Growth and Opportunity Project report led to a significant effort to improve the party's capacity and ability to compete with its rival in the context of technology, digital, data, and analytics.

For example, in the period between the 2012 presidential and the 2014 midterm cycles, incumbent vendors were delegitimized and challenged to an unprecedented extent in the party's recent history. Republican practitioners launched a number of new consultancies and ventures, including Deep Root Analytics, a media buying data and analytics firm cofounded by Romney analytics staffer Alex Lundry; Lincoln Labs, cofounded by former Romney staffer Aaron Ginn; and Red Oak Strategic, a data and analytics firm founded by former FLS Connect and party staffer Mark Stephenson. Meanwhile, after the cycle the data firm i360, founded after the McCain campaign by former staffer Mike Palmer, began developing software tools with new investments from the Koch brothers network, in part given the market opportunity provided by the discontent with what was on offer from the Republican Party. Meanwhile, the party launched new efforts to recruit and produce technically skilled staffers, including hiring a number of people with extensive experience in the technology industry and backgrounds in computer science, opening a Silicon Valley office, and launching an internal innovation effort called Para Bellum Labs.

This chapter also analyzes developments on the Democratic side of the aisle during the period from 2012–2014. Many of those victorious in re-electing the president walked away from the campaign and party after the election. Meanwhile, again revealing the ways the infrastructures of politics are fragile, many of the technologies that were the products of massive investments of resources and time, such as Dashboard and Narwhal, did not survive after the election. Their code bases were simply too expensive for the Democratic Party to maintain given the cost of keeping developers on staff. And the decision to build many of these tools in-house within the campaign and the party meant that there was not a clear way to provide for their maintenance and further development after the election, as the DNC lacks the business model of a software as a service company that would allow for the licensing and ongoing investment in its tools.

Despite all this, in keeping with the hybrid network ecosystem that the Democratic Party produced following the 2004 cycle and continued to expand after the 2008 cycle, a number of Obama 2012 veterans launched new firms after the cycle that institutionalized many of the innovations and much of the work of the campaign. These firms included the digital consultancy Precision Strategies, the analytics firms Civis Analytics and BlueLabs, and the field, digital, media, and analytics firm 270 Strategies. All are now prominent vendors in the Democratic Party's extended network. At the same time, firms such as NGP VAN, which hired former Democratic Party CTO Bryan Whitaker to be its chief operating officer in April 2013, set to work revamping their systems after the campaign, drawing on the many lessons learned during the cycle, particularly around the challenge of data integration. The result was a significantly revamped party network infrastructure, even coming off a presidential victory, heading into the 2014 midterm elections.

That the Democratic Party suffered a wave of electoral defeats during the midterm cycle in 2014 despite all of this work is telling. The 2014 midterm cycle featured an electoral context that was punishing to Democrats regardless of the data and analytic skills of its staffers and their sophisticated tools (much was the same in 2006 for the Republicans). That said, this basic truth belies a number of important differences between the two parties and their infrastructures in 2014 that will likely be consequential in the years ahead for the Democratic Party's continued competitive edge in technology, digital, data, and analytics. As this chapter shows through an analysis of various 2014 campaigns on both sides of the aisle, there is much broader and near universal buy-in to the basic data architecture of the Democratic Party and its field tools provided by NGP VAN, which means that data is much more seamlessly captured and shared across electoral cycles and organizations than in the more fractured Republican Party network. As a result of the two Obama campaigns and investments by a broad array of actors in the party network, the Democratic Party had a deeper bench of talent and technology in the areas of digital, data, and analytics. For example, even with the launch of new organizations such as Deep Root Analytics, the rates of firm founding on the Democratic side of the aisle among former presidential staffers was still higher than in the Republican Party. As detailed earlier, 24 Obama staffers founded 19 different firms and organizations after the campaign, compared with three Romney staffers founding three firms. And, according to the staffer data set, 22 technology, digital, data, and analytics staffers from the 2012 run went to the newly independent Organizing for Action and 18 joined state bids in 2014.

Nevertheless, as my analysis of the 2014 midterm cycle on the Democratic side of the aisle also reveals, there are many constraints on the flow of knowledge, practice, and technology from presidential campaigns to down-ballot races. This chapter shows how organizational structures, specifically the roles that former Obama staffers occupied on down-ballot campaigns, mattered for the work they were both called upon and able to do. The chapter shows how resource, time, and knowledge constraints, as well as relational ties, often lead down-ballot campaigns to utilize consulting services that practitioners (especially former Obama digital staffers) argued hampered effective digital organizing and data practices. As such, this chapter reveals how the diffusion of innovations across party networks is lumpy. Flows of staffers, practices, and technologies encounter organizational structures and local values and practices, as well as electoral contexts, that both enable and constrain the uptake of digital, data, and analytics.

Picking up the Pieces

In the months after the 2012 election, there was a top-to-bottom assessment of the Obama campaign by Republicans who saw it as a prototype of a new type of campaign and sought to learn from it amid their party's perceived failures during the cycle. Patrick Ruffini, a veteran of the Bush-Cheney 2004 bid and founder of the digital political consultancy Engage, produced a magisterial document analyzing the Cave, Obama's analytics department, that many of the re-election bid's own staffers pointed to as the best assessment of their work.[5] The Growth and

Opportunity Project report, a product of interviews and online surveys with hundreds of practitioners across all levels of the party network, meanwhile analyzed the Obama campaign and the Democratic Party and found that their opponents' edge was as much technological as cultural. As the report detailed:

> Another consistent theme that emerged from our conversations related to mechanics is the immediate need for the RNC and Republicans to foster what has been referred to as an "environment of intellectual curiosity" and a "culture of data and learning," and the RNC must lead this effort. We need to be much more purposeful and expansive in our use of research and more sophisticated in how we employ data across all campaign and Party functions. No longer can campaign activities be compartmentalized or "siloed" in a way that makes sharing resources and knowledge less efficient.[6]

The report then went on to detail gaps between the two parties with respect to data, measurement, testing, and turnout, and cited the need for Republicans to develop a "deeper talent pool that understands and can deploy data and technology/digital campaigning in decision-making processes and targeting efforts."[7]

To change the culture of the party, and recruit this talent, actors in the party turned to political veterans and newcomers with technological expertise and significant experience outside politics. To help revamp its operations, the party hired veteran digital media campaigner Chuck DeFeo, the former eCampaign manager for the Bush-Cheney bid in 2004, in September 2013 as its deputy chief of staff and chief digital officer, after his stint at the global public affairs firm Edelman. The Republican Party also made a very concerted effort to hire new talent into the party, including Azarias Reda, who left his enterprise software start-up Meritful to become the chief data officer of the Republican National Committee in 2013.

Reda had a background in both computational social science and the technology industry, experience that the party was looking for after 2012 to revamp its infrastructure and culture. Reda first worked in politics as a software developer for the political data firm Aristotle during the run-up to the 2008 elections. After a brief stint at the company, Reda went on to pursue a computer science PhD at the University of Michigan while also briefly working on projects for LinkedIn and Microsoft Research. After finishing his PhD, Reda launched a company called Meritful, which focused on matching college and high school students with companies as a way to create paths to careers and make the traditional recruiting process (such as campus visits) more efficient and valuable. After two years, Reda was looking for other opportunities. Reda's background in start-ups was a good fit for a Republican Party looking to head in a new direction, and after several conversations with DeFeo he was hired as chief data officer at the end of 2013 and was put in charge of data and metrics (he would later become the chief technology officer in January 2015 before leaving the RNC in October of that year).[8] The goal was to build out the data and analytics infrastructure of the party and make it accessible (through technical platforms and legal arrangements) to party organizations, campaigns, and actors across the party network.

After arriving, Reda assessed the organizational challenges of building technology at the party, as well as the state of its data and analytics infrastructure. Coming from the outside, Reda quickly learned that there were a number of challenges with respect to building technologies within parties, including variable resource flows, the demands of multiple stakeholders, turnover of staffers, and leadership changes that can bring new patterns of investment in politics. However, echoing Democratic Party staffers, Reda argued that parties are uniquely well positioned to take on the role of providing the core voter file for campaigns, in addition to making it accessible and actionable, given that parties have privileged access to public voter roles and can commission the development of things that exceed the capacity of any one campaign. In addition, parties can step in and develop technologies when there is not a financial incentive for a vendor to do so (such as polling place look up tools).

Reda argued that the Republican Party was struggling with its data and field tools when he started. The party was very good at collecting the public aspects of voter file data from state officials. However, Reda argued that the party's data infrastructure at the time lacked both accessibility and integration: "there wasn't pretty much any work around making this data accessible, around making it automated, around doing more analytics with it, around combining it with other sources of data, because voting just happens to be one of several activities that people do. In order to understand people you need to understand more than just voting history or the voting behavior."[9] Reda's assessment reveals the fact that there were a number of differences between the two parties' data architectures after the 2012 cycle. While they were comparable with respect to obtaining core public voter files, as the Growth and Opportunity Project report noted and Reda confirmed, the Democrats were ahead of their rivals in terms of making data on voters more accessible to campaigns and activists in the party network, their ability to capture and tie multiple sources of data together, and the possibilities they had for engaging in analytics around this data.

For example, there was no equivalent of VoteBuilder on the Republican side of the aisle in 2012 (and, as detailed later in this chapter, that was also the case in 2014). As Reda described the party's infrastructure that he inherited and its state in advance of the 2014 elections, the party was good at exporting data to candidates, but there was a lack of a "continuous back and forth" with campaigns.[10] Reda said that the party enriched state voter files multiple times a cycle with data from different sources, but if a campaign wanted to receive the updated files, it found it difficult to do so without overwriting the data it was producing on the ground, such as voter IDs and other records on voter contacts. The data that campaigns received from the party was primarily in one-time export files. This also meant that the data produced in the states by campaigns did not make it back to the party easily:

Even at the end of the campaign, being able to collect all that data and get it back to a place where the next Republican running there can take advantage of it is something that is very valuable, yet that we were not doing. And when the campaign is all over, people walk out with their laptops and with their clipboards and whatever they were using and data never really made it back. So data did not benefit the field, and the field did not benefit the data as much as it could. . . . [11]

What Reda described echoed exactly what Democratic field staffers said about their party's systems during the 2004 cycle.[12] The Democratic Party's work with VAN during Dean's chairmanship resulted in the VoteBuilder database and interface system that solved the twin issues of being able to systematically and in a nationally standardized way move data out to campaigns and capture data coming in from the field. VoteBuilder also provided a user-friendly and standard interface on which the party, campaigns, and organizations in the extended network trained staffers, field organizers, and volunteers. This resulted in VoteBuilder's near universal use by campaigns and state parties, which in turn facilitated data sharing across campaigns at all levels of office and electoral cycles, and ongoing improvements to the system over the course of a decade.

To address the lack of accessible and integrated data architecture and issues with capturing data from the field, Reda spent much of his initial time at the party recruiting talent, especially from outside the party network. In a candid assessment that was echoed by a number of former party staffers, Reda argued that the vendors in the party had varying levels of expertise, and many were better at selling rather than building things. Further, many former Republican staffers described how vendor services were not a "free market," with the party's hiring often being based on personal relationships and vetting occurring through social ties. To reach beyond the existing vendor pool and recruit staffers with specialized expertise, Reda framed political work as a *technical* challenge with significant practical applications in the hope that this would appeal to individuals not motivated by the same set of ideological or partisan concerns as party stalwarts.

The party also tried to create a start-up-like setting in the organization called Para Bellum Labs. Para Bellum was designed to be a space apart in the party that had a different culture and served as the incubator of new technologies. Similar to a start-up, the party sought to recruit technically skilled staffers through appeals that stated they would have a chance to develop and roll out products with significant import for democracy. For example, in the introductory recruiting video for Para Bellum Labs, a member of the data team stated, "You can go try to work on the West Coast and potentially make a cool app, or you can actually physically change history."[13] Through Para Bellum Labs, the party publicized its jobs list, and more broadly staffers argued that the branded stand-alone incubator enticed technology writers to publicize the seemingly new direction in which the party was heading (which further helped with recruiting). In addition, the party also restarted its campus recruiting program, focusing on top engineering schools such as at the University of Michigan, where staffers sought to find individuals who cared about Republican issues and causes, or were interested in engineering challenges with real-world applications. Reda began going to various universities to recruit talent for the party's D.C. and new Silicon Valley office, and specifically cited that the party's competition was firms such as Microsoft and Yahoo! The pitch was the opportunity to work on a platform that was going to be at the core of the 2016 presidential campaign.

These new hires worked on a number of major projects in the years after the 2012 election around the party's data and analytics platforms, data integration, APIs, predictive modeling, voter relations management technology, and field tools.[14] To analyze this work, I turn now to the 2014 midterm elections, and look at the cycle from the perspective of Republican state-level campaigns. As I detail, the lack of ability to move usable data out to campaigns and across election cycles and systematically capture what campaigns generated in the field were key differences between the two parties, at least through the 2014 election.

The 2014 Midterm Cycle and the Republican Party

Party staffers explicitly saw the 2014 midterm cycle as a test run for 2016 that would inform its work during the presidential cycle. The midterm election offered the party a chance to field test its work since the 2012 cycle on data architecture, digital tools, and analytic models, as well as perform field experiments in more than 20 states where there were competitive races. To analyze the Republican Party's work on its technology, digital, data, and analytics infrastructure after the 2012 presidential election, I take an in-depth look at Mitch McConnell's and Scott Walker's re-election campaigns during the 2014 midterm cycle (it was the latter's third election in four years, given a recall attempt in 2012).

The campaign for the senior Senate Republican, in particular, self-consciously adopted and invested in technology, digital, data, and analytics to quite explicitly *perform* the party's progress in these areas. Campaign staffers did so because they knew McConnell was going to have a Tea Party primary challenger and would face a well-funded general election opponent likely to attract national attention from Democrats. A victory, therefore, would be symbolic of the party establishment's progress at mobilizing grassroots energy through technology and closing the gap with Democrats.

The McConnell campaign hired the digital political consultancy Harris Media early in 2013, more than a year and a half before the election. Harris Media was a comparatively new firm, founded in 2008 by 20-year-old Vincent Harris after his stint as the Iowa online director and national blogger for Mike Huckabee's presidential campaign. The firm subsequently rocketed to national attention in 2012 through its digital work for Texas senator Ted Cruz.[15] Heavily outspent by over $10 million, Cruz defeated the Republican establishment candidate, Lieutenant Governor David Dewhurst.[16] In the popular and trade press, the digital operations of the candidate played a significant role in this victory.[17] It was precisely this digital mobilization and its symbolic value that McConnell's re-election bid sought to capture during the 2014 cycle, especially after Romney's loss and perceived technology, digital, data, and analytics failures in 2012. As Mike Duncan, who joined Harris Media in 2013 after working parallel to the firm for Freedom Works' Super PAC (which endorsed Cruz), described, "I think he really felt like it was up to him to kind of right the ship and use this race as a vehicle to really help move the party forward with regards to data and digital and a lot of aspects of the campaign."[18]

Duncan worked on a number of campaigns for the firm during 2014, which had teams of staffers dedicated to each account (this is one among many consultancy models that practitioners said had distinct strengths and disadvantages, as detailed later). For each campaign client, there were one or two account executives and then up to three people from creative or strategy at the firm working for the candidate, in addition to graphic designers and web developers. Duncan worked primarily for the McConnell campaign, but also helped with some other campaigns and non-profit and issue advocacy work, as well as continuing to do some work for Cruz (who maintained a large digital presence even when not on the ballot).

Duncan worked closely with the campaign manager and other members of McConnell's senior leadership which resulted in digital being incorporated across the campaign. In this, Duncan noted that his work for McConnell looked different from what he experienced with the firm's other campaign clients, where there was often disorganization and little coordination between departments. One reason is that it is often easier from a managerial perspective for departments to have their own independent slice of the budget to do what they want with, which enables the campaign manager (or general consultant) to simply play traffic cop. In contrast, Duncan argued that on McConnell's bid there was coordination across different units of the campaign both because the leadership had a clear idea of what it hoped to accomplish with digital media and the campaign used a centralized database.

The McConnell campaign went outside the party for its data infrastructure, turning to the nonprofit customer relationship management (CRM) platform and data firm NationBuilder, which was founded in 2009. Duncan and other Republican practitioners argued that the advantage of NationBuilder as a CRM for campaigns was that it better facilitated integration across different data streams than the party's GOP Data Center. As one staffer working with data on a different 2014 Republican campaign argued, there were a number of issues that remained with respect to the party's infrastructure. The voter file was not open through an API, which meant that the only way to update it was to manually import or export data.[19] Given staffers' perceptions of deficiencies with Republican systems during the cycle, according to sources not working for the campaign or the party during this time, McConnell's team negotiated with the party to pull data out of GOP Data Center and put it into NationBuilder. In essence, this meant that the campaign's voter file existed in NationBuilder and could be updated in real time. The campaign then built its website on top of this database and integrated things such as online volunteer sign-ups and canvass apps with it so it would contain new and continually updated information on supporters and voters.

Duncan argued that this enabled the McConnell campaign to make coordinated voter contacts across mediums. For example, the campaign could track whether someone donated online and the issues that he or she was concerned about, and then follow up via direct mail or phone calls to make further appeals. This was because, unlike GOP Data Center, which Duncan said was a static database, NationBuilder dynamically updated the data which also facilitated departments across the campaign being able to work off a common database:

> The ability to say someone donated online, right, they donated $20 and I want to hit them in direct mail or I want to do a phone call to see if we can get them to re-up before an important FEC deadline, what is the issue that they care about? Well I know that now because we are all using the same database. I don't have to go to a static database like [GOP Data Center] and export a whole list . . . and then call through them because, I tell you what, that person, whoever that person is, that vendor or whoever who does that export that data never comes back, it never gets back into the system so it never improves.[20]

Another example of how the campaign used NationBuilder to further its integrated communications concerns Facebook marketing, where there had been considerable developments since the 2008 and even the 2012 cycles. The original match rate for emails with Facebook identities was only 30%. During the 2014 cycle, Facebook opened up to third-party data firms such as DataLogix and Acxiom, which used data including name, address, and phone number, not just email, to match people to their Facebook accounts. As a result, practitioners stated that match rates increased to 65%–85%.[21] Facebook also invested heavily in finding people who were registered voters. The McConnell campaign created lists of targeted voters through its NationBuilder CRM, sent this data to warehouse firms such as DataLogix and Acxiom that matched these voters with Facebook identities, and then displayed advertisements to these people. This meant that the campaign could better coordinate messaging across channels, such as showing Facebook ads to people receiving direct mail. And the campaign extended its reach by using Facebook to find people with similar attributes to known McConnell supporters and Republicans.

As is clear, data is now enrolled into all aspects of campaigning, which makes integration and accessibility important in new ways. The first task for the digital team early in the campaign was to identify potential supporters on social media and their interests, especially for the purposes of raising money online. As Duncan described his work during this early period, echoing his counterparts on the other side of the aisle, "We are trying to bring people into a database. . . ."[22] This was particularly important early in the race given that practitioners argued that digital list building is comparatively cheaper early on, but expensive if compressed into a tight time frame. To identify and cultivate supporters, the campaign used daily graphics and posts on social media that were very image heavy, and produced content that staffers believed would mobilize people. The campaign also ran display ads contextually in news articles about the race and on platforms such as Facebook, where ads appeared alongside political content, to get reach and volume and saturate where people were on the Internet. As people interacted with ads and content, the campaign captured their names, emails, and social media identities.

Once the campaign brought people into a database (the campaign had a universe of about 1.2 million supporters, according to Duncan), it continually stayed with them throughout the race. The campaign matched this universe of supporters for the purposes of online advertising across platforms such as Twitter and Facebook.[23] Meanwhile, paid staff and volunteers knocked on the doors of individuals in this supporter universe, using a canvass application that moved data back into the NationBuilder database. Phone vendors called this universe and delivered specific messages tailored to these individuals (such as about the issues they cared about), while direct mail vendors sent issue-oriented mail that was coordinated with the creative content being produced for online targeting. Echoing a number of staffers on other bids, Duncan pointed to the fact that creative is now a significant challenge given that the ability to narrowly target across many different platforms has outstripped the ability of campaigns to generate content.

Again, Duncan argued that this work was possible because the NationBuilder CRM provided for the integration of and dynamic updates to the campaign's data. Even as data has grown in importance, other practitioners who worked on 2014 bids cited similar frustrating experiences with the Republican Party's data infrastructure. Matt Oczkowski, part of the eCampaign group at the party during the 2008 cycle who worked for a number of campaigns and firms before becoming the chief digital officer for Walker's 2014 gubernatorial re-election campaign and short-lived presidential bid, provided a detailed look at what launching a campaign on the Republican side of the aisle entailed from a data perspective: "Walking into the office on day one [for Walker's 2014 bid], I was given a state voter file from the party along with a host of disparate data sets from a variety of sources, including random excel files, volunteer spreadsheets, exports from a number of CRMs, and a mountain of donor data. Clearly, we needed to begin to exercise proper database management and warehousing practices."[24]

Similar to McConnell's bid, the Walker campaign made a number of independent decisions about its data architecture instead of relying on party-provided database and analytics tools. Oczkowski found that Salesforce enabled the campaign to integrate many different data streams, including data from the party and commercial data from firms such as Acxiom and Experian. Oczkowski also cited that Salesforce supported better analytics on top of this data than other platforms. The Walker campaign had a similar approach to individual predictive modeling as the Obama 2012 campaign, which Oczkowski argued was made possible by a dynamic data architecture. As detailed earlier, with older forms of micro-targeting, campaigns or their consultants go into the field in the months (especially summer) prior to the vote with a micro-targeting poll. Campaigns then use this poll to create segments for the purposes of GOTV and persuasion. The problem is that this permits no elasticity in the models to reflect movement in political attitudes between summer and Election Day. In contrast, as Oczkowski argued, "Our approach was centered around the idea of dynamic clustering through the consistent refreshing of data . . . . which would allow us to refresh our models on nearly a weekly basis leading up to the election. We had 10 scores in total, Walker score, turnout score, issue scores, etc. This allowed us to track electoral movement across various geos [geographic locations], demographics, and behaviors. . . ."[25]

Volunteer canvassing was an important source of the data that went into this modeling. Oczkowski stated that volunteers talked to over a million voters at their doorsteps and two million over the phone in the course of the governor's re-election bid. During these canvasses, volunteers asked the same questions as the official ballot. Field offices continually sampled voters and sent the results of these personalized conversations back to a live visualization platform so the campaign could see how certain groups of people were moving daily.

While going outside GOP Data Center was advantageous for these high-profile campaigns, from the Republican Party's perspective, numerous practitioners argued that it meant data was not captured as seamlessly in ways that future campaigns could benefit from. Indeed, after McConnell's successful re-election bid, Duncan argued that the *candidate* made decisions as to how much data the campaign would share back with the party (including voter IDs).[26] In contrast, the Democratic Party automatically captures the data from field and other contacts logged through VoteBuilder and makes it available to other campaigns for analytics and electoral purposes. Furthermore, the use of different systems on these Republican campaigns meant that it was comparatively more difficult to move data between entities. Duncan noted that after the election, NationBuilder set to work on a new system that would better facilitate the sharing of data between clients and other entities so that the data produced by campaigns could benefit other candidates and organizations down the road. This, in part, grew out of the firm's learning experience during the 2014 cycle, given that it was relatively new to working with political campaigns after getting its start and most of the adoption of its platform in relation to social causes.

Both Duncan and Oczkowski described a cycle where the RNC's core products in terms of its data and analytics infrastructure were not ready, and campaigns were better off relying on third-party firms or building their own tools. They also cited that the GOP did grow more responsive in the last three or four months before the vote, in part because there was a realization that campaigns were going to circumvent the party if it did not adapt to the market. That said, these staffers described their frustrations and wasted time with respect to working with various GOP and state party stakeholders around data, as well as other units on their own campaigns. As Duncan summarized the challenges he faced around getting buy-in to the campaign moving to the integrated and dynamic NationBuilder platform: "getting people to commit to something totally different than what they have done in their previous political experience was like pulling teeth, you know. . . . It is easier to not do this. It really is. And that is why no one really does it."[27]

In the end, across numerous interviews with Republican Party and 2014 staffers, practitioners argued that while they got better over the cycle, the GOP's field tools and data remained significant issues. As a result, even the party's highest profile Senate and gubernatorial campaigns went outside the party to meet their needs. The consequence, as Reda argued, is that data was not captured and did not flow as seamlessly through the Republican Party's ecosystem as on the Democratic side of the aisle, with near universal buy-in to VoteBuilder and the party's analytics platform Vertica. Indeed, internal Republican Party sources argued that the party's failures with respect to canvassing tools and making data integrated, live, and actionable in the years after the 2004 presidential cycle led to the data and software firm i360 (which as detailed earlier has considerable backing from the Koch brothers) rapidly expanding its market share and threatening the party's data ecosystem.[28] As one staffer working within the party's data ecosystem argued, in a statement in spring 2015 that echoed half a dozen others:

> All of a sudden, i360 comes along, selling to these different campaigns, and showing these guys what it is they could get for a very low price, and the RNC is like, "I don't know what you're paying them, you can get the data for free." Well, not really. Because I hate Data Center. . . . With the RNC, you get a dump of free data, you get a tool that nobody wants to use, and you have to pay for a third-party walk app. . . . And so i360 just gobbling up all these campaigns, and that's when you started hearing "oh my god." The problem with the RNC is that they tried to fix it last year [2014], to build this overhaul of all this stuff but it was just, just a disaster. Total disaster. . . . So this year [2015], as they know what they need to do, and are appropriately handling the situation,

they don't have any credibility. 'Cause people said, 'you were going to do this last year, so we're just going to sign with i360.' And that hurts everybody because what it's doing is taking data out of the system. It also gives a lot of leverage and control to an outside group.[29]

This was the state of the party through the 2014 cycle and the months following the midterm cycle. All of which looks very different on the Democratic side of the aisle, which as detailed earlier has near universal buy-in across its campaigns to NGP VAN's VoteBuilder, in place for nearly a decade in 2014, as well as a data architecture that by the midterm elections better supported data integration and analytics.

The Democratic Party Network, 2012–2014

> I stopped collecting the paycheck the Friday after the election.
> I am not just going to hang out. Like, I love the Democrats, I am a
> Democrat, I want all of this to happen, but you can't do it for free so
> you move on to your next thing and so does everyone else.
> —Carol Davidsen[30]

As detailed in previous chapters, parties face significant structural challenges with respect to technological development and, as a result, political infrastructures are fragile. As Davidsen suggested, after elections there is often little money available for parties to retain the staffers who worked on presidential campaigns, especially the field crossers coming from commercial and technology industries who cost a lot to employ. Given this dynamic, in cycles after 2004 the Democratic Party came to focus on what staffers perceived it did well (data aggregation, hygiene, and analytics), while making external investments in commercial firms such as NGP VAN to provide a uniform set of field tools to access and update data. Meanwhile, with high rates of organizational founding after the 2004, 2008, and 2012 cycles, there grew a robust hybrid network ecosystem of commercial firms and other organizations around the Democratic Party that built various applications and offered services around this data. These firms have the ability to develop more stable revenue sources than the party given their diversity of clients and software license and service business models. These organizations helped retain talent in the party network and carried technologies and skills honed at the presidential level across cycles and to down-ballot races.

In interviews, a number of campaign and party staffers stated that they regretted the decision to develop many of the Obama 2012 campaign tools in-house and within the party given that there were few resources or structures in place to maintain them after the election. Many former staffers argued that if the campaign invested in consultancies to develop tools instead, these organizations likely would have been able to maintain and further develop them through subsequent work for clients (much as VAN and BSD did after the 2008 election). Indeed, a number of former staffers argued that in the years after the 2012 election, the Democratic Party did little to institutionalize its advantages over its rival. As one senior staffer on the Obama re-election bid put it in an interview a year after the election, "There is basically no staff left to the DNC. There is no one to continue to work on the technology. . . . And so I think what you are seeing is us sitting on our ass thinking that we figured it out which is not at all true because no one is asking the right questions about what we should be doing next and we are going to get passed badly. I think, I think we are going to regress."[31]

TECHNOLOGY AND FIELD IN THE PARTY DURING THE RUN UP TO 2014

This is an overly pessimistic assessment rooted in frustration felt at a particular moment in time, especially given the work of the party's network of firms and organizations post-2012, but it captures the dynamics within the party after Election Day. Many people left because there were very few resources in place to retain them and maintain what they built. Coming off the president's re-election victory, the DNC had a lot of debt (on the order of $21 million), and stripped its staff bare to focus on paying it down (a similar dynamic to what happened in the Republican Party post-2010, when Priebus was elected chairman).[32] Maintaining technologies required financial and human resources that the party simply did not have and, as a result, as one former technology staffer put it, what happened was "the equivalent of [the campaign's technologies] sitting in a closet."[33] Signature efforts such as Narwhal and Dashboard that were the subject of enormous investments of time and resources during the campaign were summarily abandoned and, ultimately, no longer functional a year later. Vertica, the most important database on the 2012 campaign, remained, including all of the canvassing and contact data, as well as all the modeling data (which the party was able to provide to 2014 bids).[34]

That the party had to prioritize which technologies to continue to invest in again reveals how political infrastructures are fragile because they are in part the product of a network of actors (campaigns and parties) with variable resource flows, high degrees of staff turnover, and ultimately short windows of intense investment and development, followed by an abrupt end of attention. And, while political consultancies can make up for gaps in the infrastructures that parties provide, they face their own challenges in terms of variable resource flows and patterns of investment from parties and campaigns tied to election cycles.

The challenge with technologies such as Narwhal and Dashboard is that while matching data on the Obama re-election campaign occurred to an unprecedented extent, the various data files and ties between them needed to be continually maintained. While the DNC voter file data provided through NGP

VAN and the online data that came through BSD were matched during the campaign, these are moving data sets. People move, for instance, and there is constant churn in emails. Accordingly, data always grows and changes. Vendors such as VAN and BSD, meanwhile, change their systems and APIs as well. According to Slaby, maintaining the matching system that Narwhal provided required care and concern: "it's not the kind of thing that you can just turn on and turn off and turn back on and everything is going to be fine and all the connections and all those things are like totally reusable and totally stable . . . if you turn it back on it is going to need some kind of massaging."[35] The problem, as Carol Davidsen explained in an interview in 2013 looking ahead to the 2016 presidential cycle, is that it was unclear who was responsible for technological maintenance and development, "Is it Organizing For Action's job, is it Hillary's job to start mapping it now [2013]? So who is paying for it right now? You need to be doing that work right now. . . . So I think this is a fundamental problem, or reality, of campaign life. There is no consistent organization that can own this stuff."[36]

Compounding the party's lack of resources was the unsettled role of Organizing for Action after the 2012 election. As detailed earlier, the work around the 2010 midterm cycle by staffers at Organizing for America and the DNC was fully merged, resulting in innovations in field campaigning, technology, data, and analytics that greatly benefited the re-election effort. By contrast, Organizing for Action, the independent 501c(4) organization spun off from the re-election bid as a reorganized Organizing for America, was an entirely new nonpartisan entity both legally and culturally. Former staffers at Organizing for Action after the 2012 cycle stated that the organization inherited few resources from the re-election campaign. Staffers had to work out access to technology and data and rent the very expensive Obama email list, given that the new organization operated independently from the party. Former staffers also cited that Organizing for Action had fewer resources, both in terms of dollars and people, than Organizing for America, housed within the DNC from 2009 to 2012.

In part as the result of its legal organization, former staffers argued that in the years after 2012, Organizing for Action focused on digital engagement, as opposed to maintaining a field program. With respect to that digital engagement, according to former staffers the organization's independent 501c(4) status meant very carefully calibrated messaging that avoided criticism of the Republican Party (an approach advised by lawyers). All of Organizing for Action's content referred to "opponents" or "people in Congress"; if staffers criticized particular people, they had to make sure Democrats were included (however much of a stretch it may have been given the progressive issues the organization was promoting).[37] Even more, part of the challenge for Organizing for Action was that even though many perceived the organization as being linked to President Obama, it was difficult to activate people around a new entity, especially in a context where the objectives for supporter involvement and end goals were much less defined than in an election, given how complicated policymaking is.

The organization was also hamstrung by the fact that it could not coordinate its field efforts with the DNC, like its predecessor could from 2009 to 2012, and this ultimately meant fewer resources for a Democratic field program during the disastrous electoral cycle in 2014. Numerous staffers close to Organizing for Action, familiar with the field operations of the party in 2014, or active on campaigns during the cycle, argued that Organizing for America's state chapters pretty much disintegrated after the re-election bid, whereas the Obama campaign's field offices were maintained as part of the party from 2009 to 2012. Meanwhile, these same practitioners argued that the DNC struggled to invest in a field program between 2012 and 2014 because it did not have the resources. Former party staffers stated that rather than develop a national field program like in 2010, the party's leadership made the decision to let candidate campaigns and entities such as the Democratic Congressional Campaign Committee and Democratic Governors Association coordinate localized field programs. All of this meant a diminished party field infrastructure heading into 2014, according to multiple independent accounts of national- and state-level party and campaign staffers. As one former Obama 2012 and state 2014 campaign staffer with close knowledge of the party and Organizing for Action during this period described:

> So my understanding is that there was no field investment from the DNC because they would retire the debt after 2012, which makes sense. They made a very conscious decision not to hire field organizers, field directors in every state. The assumption was that OFA [Organizing for Action] would be doing that. So when I got to [state] in March [2014] the state party did not have a field director. They didn't have someone still talking to volunteers. We had an OFA person who the campaign then hired but there was no state party funded field program.[38]

To be clear, it is highly unlikely that Obama 2012 technologies such as Dashboard or a more robust field program would have helped Democrats weather the electoral headwinds of 2014. At best, they might have made a difference on the margins in some close races. But a look in greater depth at the structural conditions and organizational decisions that limited the work of the Democratic Party with respect to technology, digital, data, and analytics after 2012 reveals how political technologies are fundamentally fragile and need to be continually renewed cycle to cycle. Indeed, aside from the field program, staffers on 2014 campaigns also argued that the party's digital and technology operations were limited during the cycle. Numerous staffers working on various federal or state races in 2014 argued that after 2012 the digital operations at the party became much smaller. As one former Obama re-election campaign staffer with ties to

various Democratic campaigns after 2012 argued, describing his state-level perspective on the dynamics within the party leading up to the midterm cycle:

> They were barely doing email fundraising. They were left shorthanded.
> And part of that was the DNC was in debt . . . and the people that then
> came on kind of were focused on '16 instead of '14, 'we're building a
> long term program, we're building infrastructure for the next presi-
> dential candidate, we're focused on paying down our debt, and turning
> the organization back on the right in terms of budget' but they're not
> focused on winning [in 2014].[39]

The technological infrastructure of the Democratic Party looked leaky when
examined from a state-level staffer's perspective. The party's own post-2014
review cited lacking "the necessary resources to make significant investments in
paid communications in states, specialty media or digital communications" and
recommended "the development of digital communications strategies and tools
that will help reach voters that aren't accessible through traditional channels."[40]
This was the case despite the efforts of the party to offer more digital and technology support in the states after 2012. In early 2014, the party launched a branded
Project Ivy to move what remained of the technological innovations of the 2012
Obama campaign, such as Airwolf, down-ballot and provide software and data
to 2014 campaigns. And yet, a number of 2014 staffers argued that the DNC
offered little in the way of technology or digital support to state campaigns during the cycle. Echoing these accounts, writing in Epolitics.com, Dave Leichtman,
Democratic advisor for Microsoft campaign tech services and vice-chair for technology of the Democratic Party of Virginia, argued that:

> despite the Tech and Digital programs at the DNC doing the best with
> what they've got, the promise of down ballot tech has yet to materialize
> in a significant way. Why? As usual, the answer comes down to money
> and politics. After February's [2014] announcement [of Project Ivy],
> the DNC spent the rest of 2014 recovering from the monetary shock of
> absorbing the Obama campaign's debt, only to be walloped at the polls
> in November.[41]

That said, a number of other practitioners argued that the effort at making
tools and data available in the states was successful even in the face of a lack
of financial and staff resources for these efforts. These practitioners pointed to
the fact that there were a number of large assets that came out of the Obama
campaign and made their way down-ballot and to the states through Project
Ivy that would not necessarily have been visible to state-level staffers working
in digital. The Democratic Party received data on Obama volunteers after the

2012 campaign. There was a swap agreement between the DNC and the campaign, with the former making the national voter file, built in partnership with the state parties, available in exchange for the campaign sending back data on all of its volunteers after the election.[42] Meanwhile, the state parties did not initially receive the Obama email list relevant to their states because it was outside the voter file. However, Bryan Whitaker stated that emails went over to the states by summer 2013. Presumably this was so that staffers at the national level could use the email list to help get Obama for America and the DNC out of debt.

Even more the party had all of the canvass and modeling data from the 2012 bid, in addition to the integration work of the campaign and party which supported tying together various forms of voter file, polling, online advertising, digital, and media buying data, which former party staffers stated benefitted state campaigns during the 2014 cycle. As one former senior-level staffer in the party argued regarding Project Ivy:

> The thing that flowed best was the data—voter IDs, IDs for volunteers, turnout models, voter registration models and that sort of thing—because there is an infrastructure. It is because the VoteBuilder does exist, there is just 100% buy-in for its utility and value, it makes it easy to ensure that it does get passed down. The sort of anecdote that I use. . . . a staffer who is working their first real election. He is able to access the same voter file and core models around it that [a Senate campaign] was able to access. It is that level information he's able to access, for [a local] race. They were using a better model for targeting voter contact, they were able to use the voter file for modeling for digital ads. That is a level sophistication that is remarkable.[43]

THE DEMOCRATIC PARTY'S EXTENDED NETWORK AFTER 2012

Even as the party faced these resource and other constraints, there were a number of new firms launched in the wake of the 2012 cycle by former Obama staffers that served to maintain and extend parts of its fragile infrastructure. These firms worked to institutionalize many of the technology, digital, data, and analytics innovations of the Obama re-election bid and carry them to other sites in Democratic politics.[44] As detailed earlier, examples include Civis Analytics, which worked with the Democratic Senatorial Campaign Committee and other clients during the 2014 cycle, and BlueLabs, a data and analytics firm also founded by veterans of the 2012 Obama campaign.[45] A third is the digital marketing firm Precision Strategies, cofounded by Obama 2012 deputy campaign managers Stephanie Cutter and Jenn O'Malley Dillon and digital director Teddy Goff. Precision Strategies was active in a number of 2014 races and Goff served as a senior advisor to the Clinton 2016 campaign. The strength of the consultancy model lies in the ability of these organizations to take on a wide range of clients and therefore have diverse revenue streams.

It also means continual work for a range of different clients, which informs future political practice through the testing of ideas and learning that occurs in other contexts. Indeed, Goff stated that his client work during the months following the 2012 election was 75% corporate and 25% a mixture of "campaign, union, progressive organizations, nonprofits, and stuff like that."[46]

The work of NGP VAN in the years after the 2012 election illustrates the degree to which organizations in the extended party network took up the maintenance and rebuilding of fragile political infrastructures when the party could not. In the years after the 2012 election, there were a number of investments in technology, data, and analytics being made across the Democratic Party's extended network ecosystem, particularly at the premier firm for financial and voter data infrastructure, NGP VAN. The firm knew from the 2012 cycle that there were still issues regarding data integration across the many applications that Democratic campaigns (and their political organization allies) used, and attempted to solve this problem for its clients. While the issues with data integration were far from solved, it is worth considering the technological development that NGP VAN engaged in for the 2014 cycle (while the firm was also looking ahead to 2016) because it reveals the state of the party's systems, and this work will likely be at the foundation of Democratic campaigning in the years to come.

NGP VAN hired former Democratic Party chief technology officer Bryan Whitaker as its chief operating officer in April 2013, in large part to work on data integration. As a result of this work, the firm launched the NGP VAN Next "innovation platform" and API developer portal in a Silicon Valley–esque event during the summer of 2014. The platform and portal were designed to solve the basic problem of data silos, particularly for the party's organizational allies. As detailed earlier, on the 2012 Obama campaign Narwhal was in the middle of four different departments of the campaign: finance, analytics, field, and digital. Each of these different departments had an associated firm (or firms) providing technology, data, analytics, or web services for the campaign. For example, NGP provided financial reporting software and databases, the analytics team used HPs Vertica, the field campaign relied on VAN, and the digital team used a range of different databases for its web applications and online advertising, including those of Blue State Digital and Bully Pulpit Interactive. At the end of the day, while there was some data matching across the various databases and systems the campaign and these firms used, it was still limited in practice, which meant the Obama campaign was looking at fragmented, not whole people.

Changes in the party network after 2012 added new complications for data integration (which also reveals why it is always a moving target). After the election there were a number of new firms, such as BlueLabs and Precision Strategies, which political organizations in the Democratic Party network utilized. New firms mean new databases and increasing silos, a problem that data management needs to solve for. Meanwhile, for the party's extended network of political organizations, Catalist, which did not play a role in the presidential campaign in 2012, is an important source of data. Another data provider is the state Democratic parties' own for-profit National Voter File Co-Op, founded in 2011. The Co-Op makes the publicly available voter files that state parties acquire for elections more widely available to the extended network of allies (and the commercial firm TargetSmart appends other data to this voter file, such as predictive models, movement and death records, and commercial data). This redraws the data architecture diagram to look somewhat different (see Figure 6.1).

After 2012, NGP VAN took on the role of attempting to match people in databases across all the different service providers in the party's ecosystem. The fact that the firm stores DNC and Co-Op data, in addition to data from other sources such as Catalist, and makes it accessible, means that NGP VAN provides the basic data infrastructure for the entire extended-party network. The firm created a matching algorithm and database, called "PersonDB," that enabled staffers to have a composite picture of individuals assembled from different databases. In turn, an algorithm, called "relay" moved data across all the NGP VAN applications, as well as those accessing the firm's databases through APIs, so that staffers of different organizations could access data and make it actionable at the end-user application where they needed it—what the firm's chief technology officer referred to as "up-to-date and timely data, meaningful data."[47] For example, relay can move data from NGP to VAN and between firms such as BSD and Trilogy Interactive. To further facilitate the work of the Democratic Party's ecosystem around data in VoteBuilder, the firm also launched a developers' portal with the DNC at Developers.dnc.org. This enabled outside firms and modeling consultancies to work with the party's data as well as VAN's tools. For the progressive community, it was hosted at Developers.ngpvan.com.

The idea was that an NGP VAN client would be able to use multiple service providers and integrate data between them. This would strengthen the work of the ecosystem around the party by providing better access to the voter file (and other data stores) across the extended network, improving the coordination between organizations, and helping clients gain greater ability to leverage their different services. The firm stated that it created relay in advance of the midterm cycle but looking ahead to 2016, and that by Election Day in 2014 there were 68 API keys, with an additional 100 in preparation.[48] Indeed, it is clear that this integration was not fully in place during 2014. As one senior state-level staffer during the midterm cycle described:

> The data lives in two different places. You have NGP [VAN], which is great field software but their email is crappy so nobody wants to use it. BSD is really hard to integrate with, which is what most campaigns use, big campaigns use (in the end, small campaigns don't have the APIs built out to do it or the tech capacity for it). The data match itself is not great because usually online you are using email for your primary matching and if you have other information that is bonus, whereas in the field you are not usually getting email. You have to look and figure

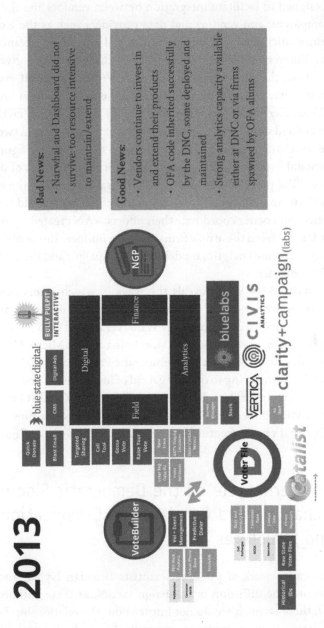

Figure 6.1 THE DATA ARCHITECTURE OF THE DEMOCRATIC PARTY AFTER THE 2012 ELECTION. Screenshot from the NGP VAN Next Presentation, August 20, 2014, http://next.ngpvan.com/.

out, maybe guess, in the voter file based on what people put on registration forms. But it is not perfect.[49]

Relay was designed to facilitate integration between vendors and the DNC's voter file for campaigns, and vendors and data providers such as the Co-Op or Catalist for Democratic-allied civil society and social movement organizations. While there are different stakeholders involved in these scenarios given rules around coordination, the near universal buy-in to VAN means that even with ongoing integration issues, the ecosystem around the party is larger and more seamlessly tied together than on the Republican side of the aisle. Practitioners argued that this created significant efficiencies in the extended party network. For example, one of the challenges post-2012 for the party network lay in figuring out which organizational entities would be responsible for what in terms of data and analytics services. The party helped convene conversations among the relevant players, such as Civis Analytics and BlueLabs, so that these firms could specialize in different services and better coordinate their efforts. VAN created a pipeline to move analytics data between these new firms and VoteBuilder. This enabled these firms to engage in real-time analytics modeling for campaigns and then bring this data back into VoteBuilder.

In the end, NGP VAN's work reveals the ways in which actors across the Democratic Party network worked collaboratively around data and analytics infrastructure and services. More broadly, as Whitaker argued with respect to the Democratic Party's data ecosystem post-2004, echoing a point Michael Beach and Zac Moffatt made in Chapter 4 about the Democratic Party's success, "We believe in public utilities. We were trying to quickly get rid of inefficiencies and then come to consensus around main utilities. For instance, we needed Catalist for the C3s and C4s, we built VoteBuilder for the DNC file, and of course we now have the Voter File Co-Op. So it's not as fractured and inefficient as it is on the Right."[50]

The 2014 Midterm Cycle on the Democratic Side of the Aisle: Enabling and Constraining Organizational Cultures and Structures

Despite the innovative work of political scientists Brendan Nyhan and Jacob Montgomery around the diffusion of campaign tactics, as these authors themselves point out, there is much we do not know about the relationship between political candidates, their campaigns, consultants, and electoral strategy. Campaign strategy often takes shape outside the view of researchers and is not easily discerned through visible data. We know little about why candidates make different decisions about the structure and staffing of their organizations, how they choose consultants from a range of potential firms, and how they decide when to turn to a vendor versus bring operations in-house. We know even less about how candidates, their campaigns, and parties (which train practitioners) understand the contemporary media environment and the impact these understandings have on electoral strategy.

In this section, I shed light on these things and expressly analyze the diffusion, or lack thereof, of the technological practices and values of Obama's digital staffers detailed in the previous chapter. I present data drawn from interviews with nine practitioners who worked in various aspects of digital during the 2014 midterm cycle. Four of these individuals were veterans of Obama's 2012 digital operations in Chicago or the states, two were party staffers who worked in digital and technology, two were the principals of consultancies that worked on multiple races around the country but whose firms had very different models and cost structures, and finally one was a digital staffer on a Democratic state-level bid who did not have previous campaign experience. The Obama 2012 veterans included here worked on closely fought Senate (2) and gubernatorial (2) races during the 2014 electoral cycle, at the level of digital director (3) or deputy digital director (1), although as detailed later these titles meant very different things in practice. Taken together, these interviews enabled me to look closely at these staffers' perceived experiences moving from the Obama campaign to down-ballot races.

I made the decision to depart here from the on-the-record historical nature of the book and provide these practitioners with anonymity. While I return to this decision in the Appendix, one important reason is that the staffers who worked on 2014 bids were comparatively younger and less well-established than many of the individuals who animated the presidential campaign and party history documented in this book. At the same time, in this section I am interested analytically in teasing out the enabling and constraining structures that shape the diffusion of campaign innovations in party networks, and shedding some empirical light on the dynamics of candidates, campaigns, consultants, and strategy.

THE DIFFUSION OF FORMER OBAMA STAFFERS

One recurring theme across all four of the interviews with Obama's digital veterans was the degree to which their placement at the state level in 2014 was the product of relationships forged on the campaign. Staffers, universally in their early to mid-twenties, cited reaching out to their former mentors, supervisors, and campaign contacts about their interest in working on a 2014 bid. These contacts then reached out to the campaign managers they knew across the country, spoke about the strengths of these digital staffers' work, and helped them secure interviews. As one former staffer on a 2014 campaign and Obama veteran described, in response to a question about how the hiring process worked, "Unfortunately it is absolutely true that in politics it is about who you know."[51]

These staffers, as well as those at the party, all argued that state-level Democratic campaign managers routinely came from worlds outside digital and as such had limited understanding of this area of campaign practice. Obama's digital veterans all said that it was incumbent upon them to ask questions and even educate campaign managers about digital's value and realistic online fundraising goals, as well as the resources needed to achieve them—even before they got hired. As this same staffer went on to describe:

> Most of the campaign managers in the country don't know jack shit about digital because they came in through traditional communications or the political shop.... So they don't know about digital and they don't ask questions about digital, you know? To be honest, the interview process is a lot of them talking.... The big thing that I made part of the interview was like, "what's the budget look like? What am I trying to raise online?"[52]

A number of informants for this book more generally cited this dynamic, and stated that it was the result, in part, of digital being a new area of practice on campaigns. Staffers on both sides of the aisle argued that there are few people who started their careers in digital who have made it to campaign management, and staffers and consultants in other more established areas of campaign practice often have more credibility and legitimacy on campaigns. Meanwhile, given the degree to which technologies rapidly change, campaign managers are often hard pressed to understand digital staffing and resource needs or even routine operations. As a result of all these things, former Obama digital staffers and those at the party all stated that digital is seldom the centerpiece of campaigns, particularly at the state level. While candidates and campaign managers understand the potential value of digital operations, practitioners pointed to a lack of depth of knowledge and stated that when campaigns embrace a digital first strategy, this tends to be based on who the candidate, campaign manager, and consultants are and what they have done in the past. Or, it even depends on who these people bring in the door to interview. As one senior staffer who worked for the party over the course of the last decade in various capacities including digital summarized:

> It all depends on who you hire, how persuasive they can be.... I was having a conversation with a friend last night who is a senior staffer ... and he was telling me the difference between [digital] and every other field is that you guys still have theories, whereas everybody else has concrete thoughts. The field director has a plan that has been done again and again and again, the direct-mail team has been doing the same thing over and over—but our stuff is changing so quickly and it is still so new it is in some way difficult to sit down with the candidate and

say "here is the way to do things." Because it doesn't exist. And even if it did, it's a moment in time, a new piece of technology introduced six months from now or a more sophisticated database that lets us do more, regression technology could change.[53]

All of these factors suggest that party networks change slowly and unevenly in terms of the cultural-cognitive understandings of campaign leadership and organizational valuations of digital media (and, by extension, other new areas of campaign practice such as technology, data, and analytics). While prototype campaigns are events that change valuations of new technologies and patterns of investment, provide the impetus for new positions (such as digital directors), and create new actors such as political consultancies as well as markets for them, the changes they set in motion may take years to diffuse across party networks, especially to more resource-constrained campaigns down-ballot. In other words, culture and practice change slowly, particularly when there are career and other incentives that reward following established ways of doing things, such as buying television advertising over investing in digital or hiring a consultancy over an in-house digital team. Even in the Democratic Party, which staffers on both sides of the aisle point to as having made comparatively greater investments in technology (at least through the 2012 cycle), there are networks of staffers with particular understandings of campaigning that privilege mass communications, not digital media, data and analytics, or new technologies. In the end, this means that technological diffusion is lumpy across party networks.

THE DIFFERENT ROLES OF DIGITAL DIRECTORS ON 2014 CAMPAIGNS

The statements in the preceding section reveal that hiring practices and organizational roles on campaigns are highly variable for digital staffers. As the staffers cited above argued, the uptake, organization, and role of digital on campaigns depended on the candidate (the experience he or she had and his or her understanding of best practices in digital), the team that he or she assembled (especially the campaign manager and consultants), who was responsible for hiring, and even the people campaigns decided to interview and how persuasive they were. In addition, staffers also argued that the resources available and the timing of initial conversations about digital mattered in terms of the role it played on campaigns.

In sum, while staffers generally landed their jobs through network connections, there were significant differences in the ways 2014 campaigns organized their digital operations and therefore the work their staffers were able to do. In interviews, 2014 staffers cited two primary organizational models for digital on campaigns. The first was a digital director in service to the consultants on the campaign. The second was a digital director who had comparative autonomy and hired and managed consultants. Staffers argued that the first model provided little leeway for Obama's veterans to enact digital operations in the ways they learned during the re-election bid. The second model, by contrast, enabled staffers to engage in digital practice in similar ways to what they learned on Obama's run.

For example, a "digital director" position meant many different things in 2014. The organizational title did not necessarily translate into a standardized role that a person played in a campaign, their responsibilities, or the authority they had to ply their trade. As one former Obama staffer active during 2014 stated, comparing his experiences as a digital director with those of his friends, "I was lucky, I would say. I was one of the digital directors who hired people, I made decisions in terms of what we did online, where we were spending our money, how we were spending our money, and who was helping us to do the work that we needed to do. Wherein I know some of my good friends, they did not have that in 2014."[54] On these campaigns, the driver of digital strategy was often a consulting firm, regardless of the experience of the staffer in the digital director role.

The dynamics this staffer described in terms of limited autonomy for the digital director often happened when a campaign hired a digital firm first. Consultants then often had a hand in hiring the digital director. A number of Obama's former digital staffers, and practitioners in digital more generally, argued that many campaigns bring firms on board first to provide a set of "off the shelf" tools or easily packaged services, such as building websites and getting email operations off the ground. In many cases, the reason is that these firms are present across electoral cycles and their principals often have strong relationships with campaign managers that enable them to get contracts for work. At the same time, practitioners stated that consultancies often have a high degree of legitimacy; no one is going to blame a campaign manager for making the decision to hire a reputable consultant to coordinate the campaign's digital operations (even if that consultant has not been successful in the past). For example, in some cases, former Obama staffers cited not even interviewing with the campaign manager of a 2014 bid. Instead, they only talked with the outside consultants handling the campaign's digital media. Revealing these hiring practices and their variability, one former Obama digital staffer cited going on three interviews with 2014 campaigns in battleground states. In the first, she spoke only with consultants; in the second, she spoke with consultants and the campaign manager; and in the third, there was an interview only with the campaign manager.

According to former Obama 2012 digital staffers, party staffers, and consultants, hiring a digital firm first has both advantages and disadvantages for campaigns. The digital consulting world is complex. Some shops are highly specialized and only do things such as create political websites, while others offer digital and social media marketing more broadly. Still others are general consulting firms that also offer digital services, providing everything from polling and general media strategy to online advertising and fundraising. In all these cases, practitioners argued that when candidates are preparing their bids, consulting firms can hit the ground running in terms of creating sites and social media accounts and engaging in list acquisition and email fundraising. Meanwhile, bringing general consultants on board early on can also simplify hiring and obviate the need for using many different firms. This is often also cost-effective for campaigns, at least in the short run (Obama's former digital staffers argued that good content takes a longer period of time to generate ROI, but in the end can result in higher returns).

And yet, despite these advantages, digital staffers and consultants also argued that there are a number of potential limitations to this model. One is that outsourcing operations to a consulting firm often means more packaged and less local digital and social media content. Many consulting firms used by down-ballot campaigns have multiple clients across the country, upward of 30 campaigns during an election cycle, and repackage digital marketing content for these races. The reason they do so is that profit margins in digital political consulting are narrow for the cheapest firms, and therefore they seek economies of scale. And yet, these firms, which charge a comparatively cheap rate of upward of $5,000 a month with a percentage of fundraising dollars, are often what congressional and gubernatorial campaigns can afford. One of the things that many state-level digital staffers noted was that the leading digital firms, such as Bully Pulpit Interactive in online advertising (founded by former Obama 2008 and 2012 veteran Andrew Bleeker), are too expensive for campaigns except for presidential runs and high-profile Senate and gubernatorial races. As a result, smaller campaigns use the same few firms that operate on a scale model, over and over again. As one senior-level staffer who has worked for both campaigns and the party argued with respect to the work of consulting firms, "You always see on down-ballot races a couple [of] big consulting firms . . . it's no surprise the programs are structured in similar ways, that they sound similar. If you're working for a consulting firm . . . you have to work to try to achieve some sort of economy of scale and that necessitates some shared language . . . across a whole slew of clients."[55]

The consequence, Obama's former digital staffers argued, is that firms sacrifice local voice by not producing labor-intensive digital content, and instead narrowly focus on transactional online fundraising that is lucrative for the consultancy. Former Obama staffers uniformly valued autonomy and control over content because they believed it would enable them to create "authenticity" in their campaign's digital communications (while generally leaving that term undefined).[56] Staffers discussed authenticity in various ways that encompassed writing from a "real person" such as the candidate (even though it was often a staffer producing an email or writing a tweet from a persona the campaign created), sounding as if it were a "real person," speaking "intelligently," not relying on "shame," "guilt," or fear appeals to drive fundraising, not making it hard for people to unsubscribe to email lists, not treating people like ATMs, and producing content that was interesting and engaging and spoke to local political issues of concern. Others spoke about authenticity in terms of crafting a narrative of the campaign that was hopeful and optimistic, and did not lead people to believe that if an opponent won the election it would be the end of the world.

On campaigns that had a firm driving the digital program, consultants often had decision-making authority over the digital staffers that precluded this approach to digital content. For example, two former Obama staffers working on campaigns that had preexisting relationships with consultants pointed to examples of times when they were frustrated or blocked with respect to being able to run the digital program they wanted to (and, in both cases, believed they were hired to run). Consultants, these staffers argued, often placed the emphasis of the entire digital program on building an email list and in a transactional fashion raising money from it by recycling content across races and often relying on fear appeals.[57] One former Obama staffer stated that when he tried to argue for another course, including building rapport with supporters, incorporating a range of potential asks such as volunteering, and fundraising at a slower pace to generate longer term returns, the consultants the campaign hired spoke directly to the campaign manager to foreclose any change in direction.

For example, former Obama 2012 staffers universally pointed to emails in particular as being one key area of difference between themselves and consultants. Former Obama staffers cited valuing what they referred to as an "authentic" narrative email style that told a story about the election, often through the voices of different characters on the campaign, all created by digital staffers.[58] Despite their constructed nature, Obama's digital veterans argued that narrative email practices are a way of treating supporters with respect and not simply as ATMs. As one former Obama campaign veteran described with respect to the two different schools of thought on digital:

> Folks that come from the OFA [Obama for America] school tend to build out in-house teams for their digital campaigns . . . you are able to create work that seems more unique to the campaign, that takes more creative leaps, they try new things. I think ultimately, in a lot of cases, this creates more successful programs. But it is more expensive. You have a lot of campaigns that just haven't made the choice to make that kind of investment. It is easier to go through the consultants, they will create consistent revenue for your email program and just hope for the best.[59]

As is clear from the preceding discussion, one challenge for firms is that they are responsible for writing emails for a number of different clients, which is a highly time-intensive practice, and they are not as close to the candidate or on the ground, which means these have to be done at a distance and often are blind to the nuance of local conditions. Compounding this are the economic incentives that digital firms have, which shape their communication in particular ways. For example, in addition to transactional email fundraising, consulting firms also have incentives to develop extensive online advertising programs. Practitioners described how most digital firms charged a flat rate and received a percentage of digital ad spending. This meant that these consultants often advocated for more digital ads. While they produce returns, one former digital state director described how campaigns often trusted consultants blindly without considering the goals, strategy, or standards for evaluating online advertisements, "they [consultants] are never going to be held accountable because the campaign manager does not know what good baseline numbers are for a return on digital ads: how many conversions, how many likes per dollar, are they targeting the right people? These are questions campaign managers do not ask, and you need to ask them if you are running digital ads."[60]

The two former digital directors who were in-service to consultants also cited the degree to which their work was vetted by consultants and staffers in the campaign's hierarchy, especially in one staffer's case given that the role of digital was subsumed under "communications" on the campaign. This former digital director during the 2014 cycle, for instance, stated that her approval chain for digital content included a television consultant, the campaign manager, two deputy campaign managers, two people from the communications team, and two people from the research team. While a long approval chain might have prevented staffers from producing well-timed, resonant, and rhetorically effective communication appropriate for social media, it also protected the campaign from gaffes and young staffers from the mistakes they might have made.[61] For example, one interviewee was a digital staffer who had little previous professional experience when she ran digital for a Senate campaign in a battleground state. This staffer cited being unsure of herself and her knowledge, and wanted people who had produced digital campaign content before to sign off on what she was doing.[62] On this campaign, a digital consultancy handled all of the content and design, with the exception of social media. Practitioners at the consultancy and staffers on the bid wanted social media to reflect the local context and campaign trail activities of the candidate as much as possible.

Even still, this digital staffer, who welcomed the check on all of her work, pointed to how the vetting process limited the content she was able to produce. Content around big events such as debates was largely prepared in advance to rebut the anticipated claims of the opposition or to amplify the known messages of the candidate. The campaign relied on vetted graphics in the hope that they would help the campaign "break through," a common desire among digital campaign staffers given how much content routinely gets ignored, even for a comparatively well-financed Senate campaign.[63] This staffer admitted that the prospect of breaking through was limited, however, because the content being produced for events such as the debates was predetermined. This staffer was not able to respond on the fly to the flow of communication around events, aside from the occasional retweet of content coming from other sources that were friendly to the candidate.

On two other campaigns, former Obama staffers described a situation in which campaign managers "understood," or came to understand, digital media (in the same way they did) and granted them autonomy. This is the organizational environment and digital director role to which former Obama 2012 staffers aspired.[64] Reflecting the high degree of variability in how campaigns made decisions to organize their digital operations, interviews revealed a few different paths to achieving this autonomous digital director position. One staffer stated that she successfully convinced the candidate and other relevant campaign stakeholders that digital mattered and that there were best practices for organizing and fundraising that required autonomy and control. She also had to educate these stakeholders about different platforms and their uses. Another staffer cited that his friend, also an Obama 2012 veteran and digital director during 2014, successfully argued for jurisdiction and resources during the interview process; he argued that his friend was successful in large part because the candidate and his campaign manager were comparatively new to politics and saw digital's value. Another former Obama 2012 digital staffer cited the fit between her skills and the campaign's needs as being responsible for the autonomy she was able to secure on the campaign, particularly in the context of being a good email fundraiser: "Most digital programs, email drives it. Social is second. Social is good, social matters, but email is what rationalizes the existence of the program. So you have to have someone who knows how to raise money."[65]

This independent and autonomous digital director generally had far-reaching jurisdiction over digital operations. These staffers cited that they were responsible for all of their campaign's social media, email marketing, online design, and technological development (which often consisted of campaign apps designed in-house to help people do things such as register to vote or look up their polling place). One former staffer cited being in a position to hire and fire digital consulting firms as the digital director. This staffer hired an outside firm to handle online advertising and also hired and managed an in-house digital department that ran the other digital operations, such as posting on the campaign's social media accounts and running the email program. As this staffer described his perspective on the value of local control over the email program, "I value having people on the ground writing those fundraising emails, versus having a consultant who is in Washington, D.C. writing fundraising emails for a bunch of different candidates. We know that the best emails are the most authentic emails."[66]

COMMONALITIES IN APPROACHES TO DIGITAL

Despite organizational differences in the roles of digital directors that shaped how they could approach their work, there were a number of similarities in their experiences on 2014 campaigns. For one, all of the staffers interviewed cited that they were expected to be a "jack of all trades" on state-level bids. In contrast to the Obama campaign in 2012, digital directors at the state level argued that their campaigns had few resources with which to specialize their staff roles.[67] As one former staffer compared her experience on Obama 2012 to her work for a comparatively smaller gubernatorial campaign:

> You think of the skill set you are asking for from a digital director. . . . You are asking for someone who is a writer, a creative, a content producer, a strategist, an analyst. Theoretically if they don't get a designer you want Photoshop skills. If they don't have a video team you want someone that could also make and edit video. . . . We didn't have 250 people in 2012 because we wanted to have a big team. It makes for a lot of problems, but those are really specialized skill sets and it is really hard to find someone that has them all because that doesn't exist. You can see the differences in the tools and vendors of state campaigns because it all connects to them trying to build out a complete program.[68]

As this staffer makes clear, digital operations on campaigns have the potential to be *specialized* to a degree unimaginable in 2004. In the absence of the resources of a presidential bid such as Obama's, the digital director position needs to be filled by a generalist who is fluent in many aspects of the work. These generalists also need to be highly aware of and adaptable to the changing contexts of technology and media use, especially given that the affordances of platforms can change, even during an election cycle, and the advent of new social media sites has placed new demands on campaigns to learn who their users are, their communicative norms, and craft goals for these platforms. Digital staffers detailed, for instance, how the Facebook algorithm is complicated to navigate. Staffers argued that too much content posted on the platform will select it out of the newsfeeds of supporters. In addition, in a story that was echoed by others on 2014 bids, a staffer on a Senate campaign related how when he started managing the Facebook account, the big thing was that graphics produced more engagement. However, during the cycle, Facebook made an unannounced (but observable to campaigns) algorithmic change that shifted how people were interacting with content to favor links. As a result, this staffer had to shift his media production practice. Others pointed to how, since 2014, Facebook has attempted to compete with YouTube in the context of digital video, and has favored content posted directly to platform over links to outside content.

These are a few of the examples of how platform changes present particularly complicated facts of life for campaigners. Facebook does not alert campaign staffers (or the public, for that matter) to these changes. Navigating social media means trying to discern how the algorithms behind platforms work and how they change. Staffers routinely cited that they had to keep up to date on the trade literature (in both marketing and politics) and cultivate networks of similarly positioned staffers on campaigns and in other organizations to explain the patterns they started seeing in their data, such as an increase in engagement around Facebook videos that were uploaded directly.[69] As another staffer put it, "you just have to constantly stay abreast of how the platforms are changing."[70] Changes in platforms during the 2014 cycle were not limited to Facebook. Digital staffers argued that Twitter changed the way it displayed photography, providing a tool that enabled users to upload three or four photos to a post instead of a single photo, which in turn changed the way digital staffers produced content for the site. Staffers across these 2014 bids cited numerous examples of changes such as these, in addition to the emergence of new technologies such as Instagram and the rise of mobile platforms that changed the ways content is displayed.

Staffers across these bids, regardless of the organizational roles they had, also stated that there was considerable pressure to continually demonstrate returns on investment from digital operations. Even when they enjoyed considerable autonomy, staffers cited that they needed to demonstrate fundraising success given the soaring expectations around the monetary potential of digital, which provided the standard for the evaluation of their work within these campaign organizations. For example, a number of digital practitioners noted how in the years after 2012 the expectation was that digital would raise 60% of a campaign's budget, given the bar set by the president. As one former Obama veteran and 2014 digital staffer described, speaking of a discussion at RootsCamp in 2014:

> Which means in 2014 the way that we rationalize ourselves, to say to the campaign manager, "you need to hire a digital director," is that they will raise 50% or 60% of your budget, which is not realistic for most candidates or campaigns. But that was the bar that was set and that is how we rationalized our existence. . . . Have we set expectations too high, and have we made money the only message that we sent—even to the point where if you can't raise money you are not doing a good job?[71]

In addition to this fundraising work, digital departments also complemented field operations. Staffers across these bids, and across the aisle as well, described markedly similar digital practices around list building and targeting individuals online in accordance with electoral strategy. As detailed earlier, campaigns often begin cycles with broad efforts aimed at list building for the purposes of fundraising and volunteerism and then engage in more specific attempts to target groups. With respect to list building (one digital director of a state-level campaign stated that his target was approximately 500,000 supporters), this entailed digital departments spending dollars on pre-roll advertising and doing things such as running online advertising directed at people Googling the candidate or liking particular issues on Facebook.[72]

To target voters of interest, digital staffers received lists from their data teams and outside firms, on the order of millions of targets, and then organized their operations around reaching these individuals with content that depended on the universe, the phase of the campaign, and electoral goals. In the context of persuasion, for instance, staffers across these bids sought to target people who fell in the middle in their candidate support scores, yet had high likely to vote scores. For GOTV, campaigns strove to serve ads to low-propensity voters that were modeled as supporting the candidate. These ads were often appeals around early voting and, in some states, vote by mail (with campaigns often designing web pages and applications to facilitate these things). Digital operations also constantly produced data, which staffers used to try to make sure they were not targeting people who had already voted (i.e., early or by mail), those who were already likely to vote and turn out, or those who were already being heavily targeted by field programs (in each case given that campaigns are only able to reach a limited number of individuals and they want to spend their resources efficiently). Campaigns had specific models that they used to serve digital ads to particular groups of voters of interest, such as Latino teens in a specific region, or they identified particular individuals of interest through the voter file and found them online. For example, to identify, find, and display advertising to targets online, campaigns variously used Facebook, IP address, and cookie matching through different vendors. These vendors matched names to online identities, and then uploaded campaigns' matched lists to ad servers. Given all this targeting, content was a massive issue. While in a dream world for practitioners everyone would receive content tailored to their interests, this is impractical. As one former Obama staffer and 2014 digital director explained:

> The reality is you will never have enough people, enough time, enough money to do [universal tailored content] so you pick and choose what your tracks are. So ideally you would have a track for women, a track for Hispanics, and a track for Hispanic women, a track for African American women, and so on . . . and then you would break it down to age groups, then break it down by interests, or realistically by behavior: are they sporadic voters, registered voters, donors, supporters, all those things? But you will never have enough content creators. There is just not enough content created. . . . Our ability to target has moved beyond our ability to create content.[73]

To show how this targeting and tailoring worked in the context of Facebook, the platform was roundly described across these campaigns as the central way to connect with more general audiences (given that it is the most widely used social network site) as well as engage in targeted communications to specialized groups. Digital staffers cited spending considerable resources to grow the audiences of their candidate pages on Facebook, and producing content in the hope of moving people to their campaign's other media properties. Campaigns grew their audiences through "push" media strategies that put Facebook ads and sponsored posts in front of targeted voters.[74] Facebook advertising and sponsored posts were essential to getting people to like these campaigns' Facebook pages and to visit the campaigns' sites, where they could take other actions such as registering to vote.

As detailed earlier, targeting on the platform took shape in a couple of different ways. Campaigns sent a list of voters of interest from the voter file to Acxiom, which then tried to match them to Facebook profiles. Campaigns also created custom audiences on Facebook, where they uploaded the email addresses or Facebook IDs of known individuals and displayed advertising to them if they were on the platform.[75] Campaigns also advertised or displayed sponsored posts to "lookalike" audiences. This involved campaigns uploading lists of individuals and then targeting others whom Facebook determined were similar to them based on their profiles, interests, or demographics. Campaigns used these matched and lookalike audiences to target voters and tailor content based on things such as geography (state or city), interests (such as people who liked particular candidates or sports teams), or demographics. For example, campaigns could post about candidates attending a sporting event and then display it only to those individuals who like a particular team or sport. Staffers cited that all of these things were workarounds for the loss of targeted social sharing that I documented in the previous chapter, which was no longer permitted under a change in Facebook's terms of service.

Conclusion

In detailing the work of the Democratic and Republican parties after the 2012 presidential election, this chapter again reveals how fragile political infrastructures are and how difficult it is to build and maintain them. The Democratic Party struggled to find the resources to keep developers on staff after Obama's re-election, given its massive debts from the cycle. Accordingly, some of the signature projects of the campaign, such as Narwhal and Dashboard, essentially disappeared, and campaign staffers cited having a lack of digital and technology support for their 2014 bids. That said, this chapter also revealed the incredible robustness and growth of the extended Democratic Party network that stepped in post-2012 to engage in infrastructure building and maintenance and to carry the innovations of the Obama campaign down-ballot. New organizations such as Civis Analytics, founded and populated by former Obama staffers, institutionalized much of the analytics work of the campaign and carried it to other sites in politics. Meanwhile, comparatively older organizations, such as NGP VAN, continued to learn from their experiences during presidential cycles and reworked their pieces of the party's infrastructure accordingly.

In the end, the chapter showed how the infrastructure of the party and work of the 2012 Obama bid were differentially carried forward on 2014 campaigns. There are a number of constraining and enabling factors that shape the ways that knowledge, skills, technologies, and practice diffuse through party networks, or fail to, including hiring processes that are often premised on network relationships, organizational cultures and structures, resources, and electoral contexts. The diffusion of former Obama staffers who shared a particular set of cognitive understandings, values, and skills honed on the re-election bid did not necessarily result in transformations in campaign practice or the spread of innovative technologies. These factors shaped what skills were valued on campaigns and the contexts within which staffers engaged in digital political communication work. In addition, the 2014 midterm cycle reveals how the Democrats' comparatively more sophisticated technology, digital, data, and analytics efforts meant little in the face of the larger electoral dynamics that handed the party sweeping and devastating losses.

On the Republican side of the aisle, this chapter documented the extraordinary efforts of the party to take stock of itself and make new investments in technology, digital, data, and analytics in advance of the 2014 midterm and 2016 presidential cycles. In the process, it showed how the party actively moved to recruit staffers with technical skills (which practitioners on both sides of the aisle argued were always in short supply) and set them to work rebuilding its data infrastructure. The chapter showed how this came to fruition in some respects on 2014 bids, but also revealed the considerable work the party had left to do, particularly with respect to moving data out to campaigns, standardizing it and making it actionable, and creating robust field tools that would enable campaigns to better access existing and capture new data. This has left a much more fragmented data ecosystem for Republican campaigns, and they face significant challenges around data integration and capture that will likely persist in the future.

7

The Dynamics of Technology-Intensive Campaigning

The 2016 presidential election took shape in a different world from 2012 and even 2014.[1] The Koch brothers, longtime Republican Party network actors, increased their commitment to influencing the primaries and the general election, pledging up to nearly a billion dollars to contest the election.[2] As this volume went to press, the Republican Party found itself increasingly challenged by the Koch-backed data and software firm i360, which reporting from the 2016 cycle argued had the potential to further pull data out of the party's ecosystem.[3] This is a direct consequence of the party's failure to keep pace with Democratic innovations in voter data and analytics, as well as database and interface technologies, over the past decade.[4] Meanwhile, Super PACs played new roles in the election in domains ranging from advertising to field campaigning, often through novel, though legal, attempts at coordination.[5] Jeb Bush's ultimately failed campaign, for instance, relied on a Super PAC in the primaries that spent significant money on data and analytics and was staffed by close allies who knew the candidate and attempted to anticipate the campaign's goals, strategies, and tactics.[6]

Rather than chase a moving target as this book goes to press during the extraordinary primary season in 2016, this chapter provides a broad overview of technology, digital, data, and analytics in political campaigning over the past two decades. I do so in the hope that taking a longer and wider view will not only provide insight into the 2016 election cycle, but also those in the years that follow. This chapter returns to the idea of technology-intensive campaigning and revisits the role that data plays in it, arguing both that parties are increasingly important as databases and that practitioners seek data integration so they can view and craft communications for "whole citizens," with the ultimate goal of influencing their attitudes, behaviors, and social relations. I conclude by arguing that contemporary campaigning can be conceptualized as a form of networked ward politics.

Technology-Intensive Campaigning

In their influential late 1990s article, political communication scholars Jay Blumler and Dennis Kavanagh argued that we have entered into a "third age of political communication."[7] In their account, which complements much of Pippa Norris's argument outlined in the first chapter, a first age of stable political institutions and beliefs and a second professionalized age of mass media have given way to an emerging third age that has characteristics including communication abundance, intensified professionalization, increased competition for attention among political actors, a new anti-elitism and populism amid media change, and a diversification of the forms, genres, and mediums of political communication. This work has proved prescient in many ways as a conceptual piece, with these scholars ending with a call for more "observational research . . . to ascertain how political communicators and media organizations are navigating change, redefining their purposes, and resolving their conflicts. . . ."[8]

In the years since, a number of scholars have heeded this call for close empirical research to understand how political actors adapt to changing media and social contexts. For example, political communication scholars Travis Ridout and Michael Franz show how campaigns adapted to the proliferation of broadcast and cable outlets by "microcasting" advertising to targeted segments of the electorate.[9] Communication scholar Phil Howard revealed how campaigns take up political databases to find and appeal to voters, given an electorate with increasingly fragmented attention.[10] Rasmus Nielsen demonstrated how media fragmentation, advertising saturation, and mounting evidence that in-person contacts are effective led to the resurgence in data and technology-driven field campaigning over the past two decades in ways that fundamentally transformed political practitioners' reliance on "air wars."[11] Jessica Baldwin-Philippi's work shows how the values of practitioners as they intersect with electoral exigencies shape their uptake of digital campaign tools and mediated practices of citizenship.[12]

These works, along with this book, reveal the ways in which electoral politics has become increasingly technology-intensive, at the level of campaigns and the parties and organizations that provide core infrastructures for them. This book has identified how this shift toward technology-intensive campaigning has had a number of often surprising consequences. Campaign staffs are far more unevenly professionalized, including by design, than scholars have previously assumed, and there is significant variation in the ways campaigns use consultants and the occasions when they choose to do so. In a world where people working in politics for the first time rise to relatively senior positions on campaigns, twenty-year-olds right out of college run social media accounts for presidential and Senate candidates, and young digital staffers have managerial authority over consultancies, scholars need to revisit their assumptions about what constitutes professionalized politics. Field crossers and new entrants to the field, meanwhile, are an important

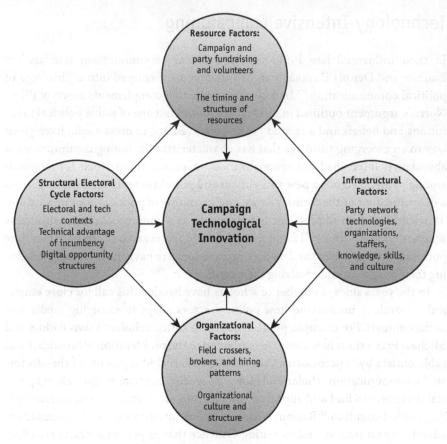

Figure 7.1 THE FOUR FACTORS OF CAMPAIGN TECHNOLOGICAL INNOVATION.

part of the story of technological adoption and innovation, as are the ways that parties and campaigns organizationally manage their technology operations and have cultures that support them, or fail to.

The history and analysis in this book suggests that there are outlines four main factors behind technological innovation in electoral politics that, taken together, reveal the constraints and opportunities in electoral and technological contexts and network structures, the conditioning of history, the importance of infrastructures and resources, and the agency of campaigns (see Figure 7.1).

Structural electoral cycle factors are features of the environment that constitute the hands that candidates are dealt and shape the possibilities for technological innovation in campaigns. These factors include the broader electoral context, such as the state of the economy and the party in power, and the technological context, or the general state of media and technology. Structural factors also include the technical advantage of incumbency, which grants some candidates more time to plan and develop technologies as well as coordinate with their political parties, and digital opportunity structures, those features of the political environment and candidates' relational positions in it such as the field of candidates, the candidate's charisma, and the strength of factions within parties and their media practices that shape the possibilities for digital mobilization—if staffers themselves perceive and can take advantage of these opportunities (which is in part the product of the historical workings of party networks). These structural factors also shape, but do not determine, the possibilities for gaining resources and hiring.

Organizational factors include the hiring done by campaigns and their cultures and structures. With respect to innovation, what is important is the desire, effort, and ability of campaigns to hire staffers from outside the political field, such as in the technology and commercial sectors, who can bring new knowledge, skills, and technologies to politics. Importantly, the conflicts that may arise from cognitive diversity on campaigns (given that it is important to have groups of staffers with political field-specific knowledge) have to be managed through the overlapping ties among staffers from different fields and brokers who can speak multiple languages and negotiate issues. Organizational factors also include culture, conceptualized broadly in terms of what campaigns value with respect to electoral strategy and how they adjudicate conflicts over jurisdiction and resources, and structure, which shapes the resources and autonomy technology, digital, data, and analytics staffers have to ply their trade.

Resource factors include the money that campaigns and parties have to devote to technological development, and the volunteers that are essential to recruiting supporters, making voter contacts, and even developing new technologies. Resources are shaped by the electoral context, the features of the candidate, and infrastructure (such as donor and volunteer databases and staffer expertise). Resources also matter with respect to their timing (the beginning of a campaign provides more time for investment) and the entities raising them (if fundraising is split with organizations such as Super PACs, candidates and parties have less money to devote to technological work). The monetary resources expended by campaigns during presidential cycles also have long-term consequences, such as investments in party infrastructure that in turn benefit later campaigns.

Finally, infrastructural factors form the background contexts that campaigns take shape within. These factors include the historically constituted sets of resources that candidates assemble when creating their campaigns, such as party network technologies ranging from field tools to voter files, and can innovate around. They also include the organizations, such as consultancies, that campaigns can turn to for technologies and expertise, as well as the staffers available to them with specialized skills in technology, digital, data, and analytics. Parties and campaigns can also create infrastructural digital media resources over time, such as building up a small-dollar donor culture and email lists to make it actionable, creating opportunities for the future. This means that digital opportunity structures are, in part, historically and institutionally created by the work of parties, campaigns, and their staffers. These infrastructural factors shape, but do not determine, resources and organizational factors such as how campaigns value technology with respect to electoral strategy.

As is clear, as technology has become increasingly entwined with politics, this has meant that infrastructure building and system design, long familiar to science and technology studies scholars, are now essential to contemporary political communication. And infrastructure building is fundamentally oriented around changing the very media and information environments that political practitioners will encounter in the future. Daniel Galvin, writing in the context of political party building, noted this very nicely in his critique of rational choice theories for being overly presentist and narrowly focused on structural constraints, rather than on how actors work to change the future contexts in which they will ultimately have to act.[13]

Indeed, another surprising finding about technology-intensive campaigning, at least from the perspective of rational choice theories, are the persistent differences between the two parties when it comes to technology, digital, data, and analytics. This book argues against the idea of uniform adaptation to digital media environments by rational actors. It reveals how the historical workings of institutions and networks shape technological development and condition perceptions of the electoral efficacy of technology among campaign and party actors. In the history detailed in this book, Democrats have enjoyed some key advantages accrued over the course of election cycles, not least of which is an appreciation of the value of technology, digital, data, and analytics, and the development of a hybrid network ecosystem, organizational structures, and staffing patterns that reflect and continue to cultivate this. Over time, technologies, data, and digital and analytics expertise became differentially available in the two parties' extended networks (and always in short supply). And, these differences not only persisted over the course of two presidential cycles, the parties are adopting fundamentally different data ecosystems that will impact their electoral competitiveness in the future. What this book makes clear is that political actors do not all perceive the world in the same ways, nor do they simply act according to a purely rational analysis of media environments. Institutional contexts, network relationships, and historical processes condition what acting rationally means.[14]

Finally, the idea of political prototypes reveals that there is nothing inevitable about specific features of technology-intensive campaigning. In the broader arc of history, there is no inherent, technologically or environmentally determined reason why it was the Dean campaign that suddenly became open to large infusions of outsiders during the 2004 cycle. It was the campaign's narration as a prototype of technologically enabled politics that attracted these new entrants to the field. And, after the election, it was not inevitable that the Democratic Party network would embrace Dean and his former staffers, especially given how spectacularly the campaign failed. It was only after party actors collectively discussed their failings and future that they embraced the campaign as a prototype, and worked to diffuse its emphasis on digital media throughout the party through investments in technology and talent. There were other options. The party could have ignored Dean's digital innovations and spurned the failed candidate's attempt to become party chair. Even more, the party could have rejected (and indeed, almost did) Dean's efforts to create a truly national voter file and its database and interface system VoteBuilder, choosing instead to direct its resources to vendors outside of the party or stick with a state party-driven system.

This also means that the paths of technological development that party networks go down are not inevitable either. These paths are responsive to, but not wholly driven by, the constraints of exogenous media and social structures or actors striving for greater efficiencies in contacting voters. Systems have their own internal dynamics, and technological development and infrastructure building in politics involve the interaction of many different actors and entail heterogeneous feats of engineering that have legal, political, technological, infrastructural, and cultural dimensions as they play out in contingent, historical processes.[15] As Thomas Hughes concluded in his monumental historical study of the electric power system and the ways that it was both a cause and effect of social change, "Power systems reflect and influence the context, but they also develop an internal dynamic. Therefore, the history of evolving power systems requires attention not only to the forces at work within a given context, but to the internal dynamics of a developing technological system as well."[16]

All of which means that scholars looking to understand technology-intensive campaigning need to analyze not only features of the technological and social environment but also the existing paths of systems and the relations they are embedded in that shape future development and condition the future contexts practitioners act within.

Parties as Databases and the Search for the "Whole Citizen"

Much of the backstage infrastructural work of politics is oriented around the data architectures of the two parties. As detailed throughout this book, both US political parties have massive voter databases encompassing hundreds of data points on every member of the electorate. Campaigns at all levels of office, as well as party network organizations, increasingly value parties for their capacity to serve as databases. This is not to say that they do not perform other crucial functions, such as creating the rules under which primaries are contested, providing education and training to candidates and campaign managers, raising and spending monies to promote candidates, and connecting campaigns with vendors. It is simply to say that in a technology-intensive campaign era, parties are increasingly defined by and valued for their role in providing the data infrastructure for their entire party network ecosystem.

Parties provide databases with public, historical, and commercial records on voters to campaigns directly, while entities such as the RNC's Data Trust and Democratic state parties' National Voter File Co-Op serve extended party network organizations, who use the public non-strategic data they provide for things such as voter identification, registration, turnout, and strategy more broadly.[17] This has come to be among parties' most important roles given the shifts in social and media structures detailed earlier, the institutionalization of this work in parties, their unique positioning as nonprofit organizations at the center of the political process, and the business models of vendors who craft tools and services around this data.

At the same time, as this book has extensively detailed, there are differences between the two parties and their respective data ecosystems. The Democratic Party's voter file provides a common object around which distributed actors collaborate. A number of organizations draw on the party's data for their campaign and other clients through APIs and interfaces, from analytics consultancies such as Civis Analytics to digital firms such as Blue State Digital. The Democratic Party's voter file is a mediator that helps gather the party network and coordinate the work of many different political actors, which is why integration has been such a crucial (and elusive) goal.

In late 2015, the Democratic Party's model of party-provided voter data made accessible to campaigns through NGP VAN's VoteBuilder became the subject of fierce controversy. While it is impossible to conduct original research around the Bernie Sanders campaign's breach of the Hillary Clinton campaign's data in VoteBuilder given the timeline of the book, I wanted to offer some broad thoughts here. The basic facts behind the Sanders data breach seem clear enough. Exploiting vulnerability in the NGP VAN system, staffers on the Bernie Sanders presidential campaign pulled multiple lists of voters from the Clinton campaign's voter data in NGP VAN. According to published journalistic reports, this included data on things such as strong Clinton supporters in Iowa and New Hampshire, 24 lists in all.[18] The DNC responded by temporarily suspending the Sanders campaign's access to VoteBuilder, in effect preventing staffers from using their voter data less than two months out from the Iowa caucuses.

There are legal questions here relating to the actual contracts that users of VoteBuilder and the DNC's data sign that, without direct knowledge of the matter at hand, I am not going to opine on.[19] The consensus among practitioners is that Sanders's staffers knew what they were doing and it was a clear ethical violation of the use of the NGP VAN system (indeed, the campaign's national data director was summarily fired and the candidate apologized).[20] What I want to focus on here is the call among some practitioners and firms with a stake in the outcome, such as NationBuilder, to open up the DNC's voter data so campaigns, and not the party, own what they use and produce. Part of this response stems from fears over monopoly power. It is an undisputed fact that the Democratic Party has built the most powerful political database in the world, and serves as the "obligatory passage point" through which all of its political campaigns must go to gain access to it.[71] Presidential campaigns essentially rent the DNC's voter file, which is in essence a collection of 51 different state voter files (including Washington D.C.) that states share with the national party and are all hosted in the same system, VoteBuilder. As campaigns use VoteBuilder, they enrich the voter file through all of their canvassing and voter contacts. The voter contact and identification data generated by campaigns are firewalled from each other during elections. However, after elections, this voter contact and identification data created by campaign volunteers and paid staffers goes back to the DNC and the state parties, and is ultimately made available to subsequent Democratic candidates. Campaigns do not own these voter files that they helped to enrich.

This was the basic architecture put in place by Chairman Howard Dean, with VAN gaining the contract in 2007 to put together VoteBuilder as the interface and database system for the party's voter files.[22] The national party provides access to VoteBuilder for its presidential candidates, while state parties determine access for state-level campaigns.[23] This architecture grew out of the party's experiences during the 2004 cycle, when John Kerry's data infrastructure that was cobbled together from multiple state voter files, housed in many vendor systems responsible for providing access to them, crashed in important states. The data was unstandardized across states, vendors had uneven track records, there was little in the way of field tools for accessing voter files, much historical data on voter contact was simply lost, and candidates even had trouble accessing state voter files. During the 2004 cycle, the Democratic Party was significantly behind its rival in the basic data and systems for contesting elections. The work of Dean and his staff turned the Democratic Party's data architecture from a mess of often vendor-controlled state voter files into the nationalized system it is today.

A core argument of this book is that the near universal buy-in across the Democratic Party network to the party's voter file and database and interface system provided by NGP VAN has resulted in a powerful and robust piece of infrastructure that the party's technology ecosystem convenes around. The DNC's voter file has proved to be an asset for the party because of its very centralization. As a result of the fact that there is broad buy-in to VoteBuilder, the party's data is standardized and accrues across election cycles and moves up and down-ballot. There is one system for accessing the voter file, so volunteers without much in the way of technical skills or training in states such as Iowa can use it easily from cycle to cycle. Even more, as detailed in the last chapter, modeling can flow downward from comparatively well-resourced presidential campaigns to state and even local races. At the same time, the fact that campaigns have to provide the data they generate through canvasses and contacts back to the party (excluding proprietary data on donors), means that data is a shared asset across the party as a whole and the voter file is run as a partisan club good controlled by the party. And, as importantly, the near universal buy-in to the party's data has meant that the expansive, hybrid network ecosystem of firms and organizations that former presidential campaign staffers and others have launched after cycles all work from the same basic data infrastructure. These organizations adopt and use the party's voter file and tools for accessing it—which facilitates the complementarity of services and collaboration.

Even still, there are a number of potential concerns with the party's data architecture. Dean's team created a set of agreements between the national and state parties, where the former works to ensure that state parties are fair arbiters of their voter files and the latter can hold the national party to account for what it does with the data. That said, disputes between candidates and state parties do occur. The policies of state parties with respect to challengers to incumbents in primaries vary, with states such as Missouri only providing access to VAN for incumbent office holders as the "winner of the last primary." What this in effect means is that, in some states, challengers to incumbents cannot access the party's extensive voter file and the competitive advantages it offers. This policy was recently called into question by an African American state senator active in the protests over the police shooting of Michael Brown after she sought access to VAN to contest a congressional incumbent.[24] However, the rationale of the state party is that there needs to be an incentive for incumbents to continue to use the party's voter data and share their voter contacts back with other candidates, or they will view their electoral work across cycles simply as being used against them. At the same time, another fear is that with monopoly comes the possibility for suboptimal technologies and stasis. However, the fact that the Democratic Party has been well ahead of its rival with a more fragmented ecosystem for a decade suggests that this fear is overblown. Finally, some practitioners worry that the party might behave arbitrarily, such as in the case of the Sanders breach when it appeared its own policies regarding the consequences of breaches were unclear. However, there are a host of normative pressures and regulative agreements and policies against this.[25] Indeed, the Sanders situation was ultimately resolved in 24-hours with the campaign again gaining access to its voter data after the DNC stated it fulfilled its requests for more information and the campaign filed a federal lawsuit.

While there is a romantic notion that candidates should be free of parties and just make their own direct appeals to voters, especially among a number of entities that stand to profit from the decentralization and fragmentation of the party's data, the Democratic Party's voter file is an acknowledgment of the fact that American political life is, for worse but mostly for better, organized through parties.[26] The DNC's voter file is ultimately a distinctly *partisan* resource, designed to strengthen its candidates' ability to contest elections by providing them with far more data than they could ever muster on their own in discrete electoral runs, or even through data swaps with allies. There is nothing precluding candidates that do not want to opt-into this system from relying on third party data firms such as Aristotle, Catalist, and NationBuilder, and taking advantage of any of the commercial customer relationship management platforms available to manage it. And, there is nothing preventing them from purchasing data, generating their own contacts, and then building their own independent operations. But it will never be as powerful as the DNC's communal and partisan resource, and they will find that even if they gain office, they will diminish the resources available for their partisan and ideological allies to do so as well—in the end, this hurts their ability to enact legislative change. In essence, the Democratic Party has created a powerful and robust tool that facilitates its efforts to secure political power. And, I believe, in keeping with the normative role of parties in democratic societies, the party should have the ability to control access to it according to their own policies designed to further their governance interests. As a matter of course, these policies and remedies should be transparent and ultimately contestable (which appeared to be part of the issue in the Sanders and Missouri cases), but in the end I believe it is a good thing that as a multi-issue coalition of heterogeneous actors the Democratic Party sets its own policies and procedures for its use as a database.

On the Republican side of the aisle, there are both more data providers and more tools for storing and accessing this data, as the previous chapter detailed. While the Republican Party still remains at the center of the right's data ecosystem, it remains to be seen if this will change based on the party's failure to develop a more robust voter database and interface system over the past decade, which practitioners argued opened the door to competition from third-party firms such as i360.[27] Either way, the Republican Party's network is more diffuse and disaggregated with respect to data than the Democrats' network.[28] And, numerous practitioners pointed to a lack of integration across the Republican Party's data ecosystem, and comparatively few research organizations on the order of the Analyst Institute and Civis Analytics to make it actionable for campaigns as being important differences between the two parties. It also remains to be seen whether the emergence of rivals to the party's data means that establishment candidates will be more susceptible to challenges from activists in the extended Republican Party network. Indeed, the Tea Party activists that helped defeat Eric Cantor used the rVotes database and interface system (developed by a cofounder of VAN and based on the same original codebase) to put together various data files of allied organizations.[29] Access to comparatively cheaper and better data and tools, including those controlled by organizations within the Koch brothers network, may provide already well-organized activist groups with greater ability to influence Republican Party primaries by extending the reach of their electoral organizing capacity.[30] And we should not expect this to dissipate in the future. As political scientists Matt Grossmann and David Hopkins argued, "A party primarily united by ideology will always remain particularly vulnerable to charges from within its ranks that elected leaders, faced with the constraints of a separation-of-powers system and the need to maintain popular appeal beyond the party base, have strayed from principle and must be forced back into line."[31]

As is clear throughout this book, in the words of Romney's digital director Zac Moffatt, the voter file (through the modeling derived from it) serves as the "north star" for campaigns, orienting their activities and especially their attempts to communicate with the electorate. To facilitate these efforts, over the past two decades practitioners have continually strived to create data that reveals whole citizens. Practitioners attempt to reveal, through data, not only the psychological attitudes and beliefs, political dispositions, media use, cultural practices, and behavior of citizens, but also their geographic, affiliational, and social embeddedness. Revealing whole citizens requires assembling a comprehensive view of individuals, including their social identities and connections, and this effort has not been fully realized, at least not when this book went to press. On the Obama campaign in 2012, for instance revealing and appealing to whole citizens was more aspirational than actual. That said, this is the quest that political staffers on both sides of the aisle have been and will continue to be on, and it is the goal that drives much of the infrastructural work behind contemporary campaigning, particularly around data integration (and more data always means more integration).

In many respects, the effort to know and appeal to whole citizens resembles an earlier pre-mass media era during the decades before and after the turn of the nineteenth century. The primary political style of this era entailed a politics of organization, personalization, and social attachment.[32] The Tammany leader and former New York State Senator George Washington Plunkitt understood and articulated the importance of blending machine politics with a deep knowledge of his constituents. Plunkitt described how:

> Tammany Hall is a great big machine, with every part adjusted delicate to do its own particular work.... Take me, for instance. My district, the Fifteenth, is made up of all sorts of people, and a cosmopolitan is needed to run it successful. I'm a cosmopolitan. When I get into the silk-stockin' part of the district, I can talk grammar and all that with the best of them.... As for the common people of the district, I am at home with them at all times.... So you see, I've got to be several sorts of a man in a single day, a lightnin' change artist, so to speak. But I am one sort of man always in one respect: I stick to my friends high and low, do them a good turn whenever I get a chance, and hunt up all the jobs going for my constituents.[33]

Plunkitt's views were the object of much scorn among the reformers of his era.[34] That said, as the historian Terry Golway's sweeping history of Tammany Hall reveals, during the first decades of the 1900s Tammany provided essential social services, jobs, training in political activism, and ultimately political power for the destitute, primarily immigrants, of New York City.[35] While these may have been the latent functions of machine politics, the historical evidence suggests that it was a deeply social and personalized form of political representation, premised on deep knowledge of constituents. Speaking of the party services that Tammany provided, Plunkitt noted, "the Tammany district leader reaches out into the homes of his district, keeps watch not only on the men, but also on the women and children; knows their needs, their likes and dislikes, their troubles and their hopes, and places himself in a position to use his knowledge for the benefit of his organization and himself."[36]

While explicit patronage is (largely) a thing of the past, at least in the United States, the idea of striving to know whole citizens, their needs, likes, dislikes, troubles, and hopes, and strategically leveraging that knowledge for electoral gain, is resonant in our own time. Contemporary campaigning is not so much an embodied or organization-based practice on the order of Tammany, as an attempt to use digital observational technologies and databases developed over the past two decades to reveal and leverage the psychological dispositions and social lives of citizens for electoral purposes. To leverage these tools, however, requires combining and integrating data across the many different applications and data stores that offer only partial, fragmented views of individuals.

This attempt of the political field to create whole citizens in data is nicely captured in the NGP VAN Next presentation from August 2014, the Silicon Valley-esque rollout of the firm's new platform and APIs detailed in the previous chapter. NGP VAN developed APIs so that multiple vendors could access their clients' data, and developed its "relay" algorithm so that data could be moved across systems to create a "unified view" of people, in essence putting the fragmented data pieces of individuals together (see Figure 7.2). In the words of John Lee, the chief

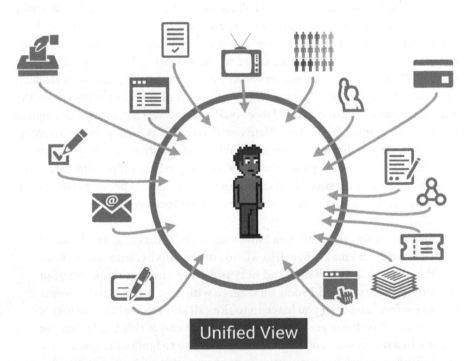

Figure 7.2 THE UNIFIED VIEW. Screenshot from the NGP VAN Next Presentation, August 20, 2014, http://next.ngpvan.com/.

technology officer, the firm sought to reveal "a person in their whole, in all their glory," for its progressive political clients.[37]

The idea behind this is twofold. First, fragmented data, or data from a single source, tells practitioners little about who people actually are and how they live their lives. As Michael Slaby concisely put it, all of the identity resolution work on the Obama campaign in 2012 was "just a way of seeing a person as a person."[38] Second, creating a unified view of individuals across the many applications, platforms, and databases used by campaigns would enable practitioners to leverage this information to a much greater extent and to create truly relational forms of strategic political communication. Some of the examples listed in the NGP VAN Next presentation included sending direct mail and running online advertisements to individuals who did not answer their door during a canvass; showing television ads to people who tweeted about particular issues; personalizing and customizing websites based on offline engagement; and, finally, emailing supporters who tweeted about a candidate to enlist them in doing rapid response around political events.

These multiple sources of data do not reveal the world as it really is, and the picture they create is much cruder than the deep contextual, embodied knowing of Plunkitt. The data that campaigns use renders certain aspects of the world visible, perform the world in particular ways, and provide a baseline for action within the broader context of a goal-driven focus on electoral victory.[39] Campaign staffers are well aware of the shortcomings of all methods of collecting data, which is why they use different sources for different purposes. The Obama campaign in 2012, for instance, triangulated between national and state polling, online panels, and data produced through field calls. According to the Obama 2012 director of opinion research David Simas, the campaign not only conducted more quantitative research than any other in history—which received the bulk of attention in the media and among scholars—it also generated more qualitative research than any campaign in history.[40] The campaign used qualitative research such as focus groups to develop the very messaging that would later be the subject of quantitative testing. In general, campaigns have a deeply pragmatic set of working relationships with data given their need to make it actionable in rapidly unfolding contexts before all the empirical returns come in. For example, as Lundry argued, focus groups:

> help humanize the data. You know one of the things that I make all of our staff do, is I make them listen in to survey calls because you get back this data set and it is nice and neat and clean and you think "oh yeah sure this person said I somewhat agree with legislation X and it seems so perfect" and then you listen in to the call and you realize how messy it is and how there are human beings on the end of this. . . . So like we are in a messy data collection business and so to ignore the qualitative I think is foolish because even the quantitative is pretty qualitative.[41]

Networked Ward Politics

This discussion of the search for the whole citizen in the data that campaigns gather brings me to what I call "networked ward politics," a data-driven, personalized, and socially embedded form of campaigning that parties and campaigns, especially the Democrats, developed through prototypes as they contested elections and responded to changes in American culture, social structure, and communication technologies.[42] In essence, what I refer to as networked ward politics is the high tech form of the personalized and socially embedded campaigning that Plunkitt practiced in his district. Campaigning is newly "personalized" in a three-fold sense: first, in terms of campaigns leveraging "people as media" in the course of field canvassing and social media appeals; second, in terms of campaigns meeting citizen expectations to determine their own levels of often highly temporal political engagement; and third, in terms of campaigns increasingly appealing to citizens as individuals and not as representatives of demographic groups.[43]

While networked ward politics is unevenly realized across the political field, the concept ties together the various strains of mediated electoral practice revealed in this book. The first aspect of personalization relates to how campaigns seek to leverage citizens and their social relationships as the strategic implements of campaign communications. The broader shift toward what Rasmus Nielsen has called "personalized political communication" involves not only field canvassing but also the 2012 Obama campaign's work to transform supporters into the conduits of strategic communication to their social networks. This form of personalization often entails extensive data and analytics work at the back end. In the field, data is about maximizing the efficiency of voter contacts and probabilistically increasing the likelihood that people will be persuaded by appeals from fellow citizens (whom campaigns often try to pair with voters that share the same geographic ties, affiliations, or demographic characteristics).[44] On social media platforms, campaigns use data and analytics to identify their supporters, determine their influence, and track their engagement. Campaigns urge their supporters to share political content and make personal appeals to their friends on these platforms. As Bryan Whitaker described the rationale behind the workings of NGP VAN's social organizing tool, which the firm launched in July 2012, "Organizing is valuable when you have a trusted validator talking to another person in their family or friend group, what we call a social graph, because they are able to relate to that individual based on history and context."[45]

In other words, campaigns yoke data to networked sociality to engage in strategic, targeted, and tailored communications for persuasion and mobilization purposes, which is especially important in a world of geographic mobility and where people have dispersed and increasingly voluntaristic social ties made visible and often communicatively held together through platforms such as Facebook. Data has grown more important in electoral politics because it is more difficult for campaigns to break through the noise and distractions and find and gain the attention of voters, engage them in politics, and make them care.[46]

The second sense of personalization refers to the ways that campaigns have been responsive to citizens having new expectations to set their own terms of political engagement. As political scientists Bruce Bimber, Andrew Flanagan, and Cynthia Stohl argued, citizens not only have more options to participate, they increasingly expect personalized opportunities to volunteer on their own time and according to their own expressive needs.[47] Campaigns need massive amounts of volunteer labor to make voter contacts across platforms.[48] The expectations of citizens and the needs of campaigns have given rise to the new ways in which staffers work to become responsive to supporters, including using what political scientist Dave Karpf has called "passive democratic feedback," which broadly means listening and learning through digital data.[49] Staffers use passive democratic feedback to learn about the thoughts and desires of supporters, which is important in an era of highly voluntaristic engagement.[50] The Obama campaign's use of social media metrics, user behavioral data, and technologies of listening, detailed in Chapter 5, should be read on these terms.

The third sense of personalization lies in the ways that campaigns strive to represent and appeal to whole citizens. David Simas echoed Plunkitt's words when he described the re-election effort as engaging in "retail politics at a distance"; Obama's staffers "ran their national campaign like a ward fight, [the campaign] can have personalized and relevant conversations" with citizens across its media platforms and in its ground operations.[51] Simas described how the campaign used data and digital technologies to have more personalized communications with individual members of the electorate, including through targeted online advertising and outreach through social media. While this is an overstatement given how challenging the campaign's data integration problems were, the impossibility of creating such finely grained content and measuring its effectiveness, and the fact that the social graph aspect of Dashboard never quite came together, Simas's statements should be understood in aspirational terms. Campaigns leverage data and analytics in the attempt to identify and make personalized and social appeals to voters in the new mediated contexts within which they live out their social lives.

Digital campaign communications are an important and comparatively new part of electoral campaigning, and are premised on technology, data, analytics, and media. Unlike retail politics of the past, it is a technology-intensive, not labor-intensive, practice, and there is no enduring social, on-the-ground knowledge that comes through physical presence. Campaigns use technologies such as online advertising and cable set-top box targeting to find and speak to voters distributed geographically. Meanwhile, as communication scholar Jessica Baldwin-Philippi has extensively documented, campaigns use social media as a form of "digital retail politics," or "the online reproduction of the campaign standby of face-to-face retail politics marked by campaign stops in diners, kissing babies or signing autographs on a rope line. . . ."[52] Digital retail politics and behind the scenes mediated looks at campaigns are means of extending the performances of candidates outward across the vast physical, ideological, and cultural distances that define American society, even as they provide opportunities for candidates to adopt the "home styles" that foster communion with citizens.[53]

Meanwhile, campaigns use technology to try to fashion their supporters into the stewards of their own networked wards that they themselves cultivate. These wards are networked because they are constituted through technology. While the "wards" of the past were defined geographically and at times as legal units of political representation, today they are expansive spaces of mediated social relations that encompass the geographic communities, families, professional and identity affiliations, and acquaintances of supporters.[54] The sociologist Anthony Giddens argued that it was a condition of modernity that individuals create and cultivate their social lives, affiliations, and identities themselves, rather than rely on the received identities of religious and other institutions.[55] Meanwhile, media theorist José van Dijck has argued that social connectivity is increasingly constructed through media practice and socio-technically shaped, in the sense that the affordances of different social media platforms shape the forms of sociality and communication that take shape within them.[56]

Campaigns want supporters to fashion their mediated social ties into networked wards and cultivate them for electoral purposes. Campaigns increasingly see citizens as implicitly and explicitly cultivating their social lives on social media in ways that have deep political implications, even if citizens do not always intend them. Citizens cultivate their social relationships, sharing the details of their lives and engaging in all sorts of discourse with people important or simply technically present to them. For the majority of citizens, very little of their social lives are expressly oriented toward institutional politics, as a number of scholars have pointed out.[57] Even more, "context collapse" on social media may lead to self-censorship with regard to the posting of political content.[58] That said, everyday discourse on social media is often explicitly *political*, just not in ways that people ordinarily think of. These quasi-public spaces are constituted through the casual relations of everyday life and shaped through the affordances of social media platforms.

Campaigns want to influence the discourse in these quasi-public spaces because they are often the way to reach those citizens who are less attentive to politics. Our highly complex, hybrid media environment is increasingly integrated through social media. Social sharing is becoming the primary means of receiving political information and supports the "inadvertent exposure" to politics that political scientist Marcus Prior argued we lost with the proliferation of cable channels in the 1970s.[59] Parties and campaigns take strategic symbolic and social action on social media platforms, seeking to influence their supporters so they can indirectly connect with citizens in these mediated and networked spaces through a trusted validator. Electoral politics provides the ritualized occasions, and parties and campaigns provide the symbols for their supporters to share in their social networks that signal their political affiliations, identities, and values. Campaigns seek to leverage context collapse by generating symbols and content that supporters can convene around and share in their own networked wards of social attachment, which include things such as logos, infographics, and images. Campaigns believe that supporters share this content because they find it compelling, want to help a candidate or cause, or want to signal their identity. Campaigns also create social systems such as Dashboard to help supporters signal publicly what they are doing for a cause. Unlike the returns of the old ward politics, which were transactional and included things such as patronage jobs, the returns of networked ward politics come in less tangible forms of identity and expression, and ultimately of helping to elect a candidate and party to govern (which is no small thing in an age of significant philosophical, value, and policy differences between the two parties).[60]

Communication scholar Zizi Papacharissi has argued that these new personalized and identity-based forms of political engagement are now a primary mode of democratic life.[61] As such, campaigns look for metrics of engagement on social media platforms (likes, shares, retweets) to assess their work, even if it is difficult to map them directly onto electoral outcomes. Campaigns seek their strategic political communication to radiate outward through the mediated social networks of their supporters, and they are guided in doing so by the data and analytics that shape their understanding of the citizens they should target, what they should say, and how they should reach them. Networked ward politics entails campaigns strategically, and on the basis of data, asking supporters to be visible and carry the torch, to make the message part of their identity, and to weave the candidate's symbols and the election's meaning into the fabric of their mediated social lives.

Studying Technology and Politics

This book lies in the tradition of cultural history and historical sociology, but takes as its object of analysis institutional politics as it intersects with shifts in technology, media, and society over the past two decades. I have sought to tell a story that blends individual, institutional, and technological histories to explain why parties and campaigns adopt technologies in different ways. I hope that one of the main contributions of this book will be to locate too often easily abstracted and generalized processes of political campaign communication in time and, further, to show how they are the outcomes of historical patterns of sociotechnical relations. I conclude this book by arguing why a historical and relational study of the evolution of technology, digital media, data, and analytics in contemporary campaigning is necessary to understand the differential uptake of technology by campaigns and parties.

Politics and Time

In "Politics as Cultural Practice," Michael Schudson's methodological statement on his masterful historical study *The Good Citizen*, the historian stated that one of his central precepts is to locate things in time. Schudson suggested that students of social life should ask themselves this question: "Is the conclusion I am coming to about this phenomenon true generally, or is it caused by something peculiar to this time and place?"[1]

Schudson's point is that we always need to locate political, cultural, social, and technological practices in time for both comparative and analytical purposes. This is especially important when the basic contours of what we take to be social structures are contingent upon global networks of information flows, changes in technology, and evolving cultural practices.[2] One familiar example is the ways that networked communications technologies have undergone rapid changes over the past two decades, which in turn have seemingly shaped the relationships and connections that people create with other people, organizations, and institutions, and how they sustain and maintain these connections. Locating these practices in time enables us to find comparison points to help us understand the nature of these changes and what has not changed, or what might be the product of a much longer historical process than simply the advent of digital media.

Analytically, the broader point made by many scholars, including those working under the rubric of science and technology studies, is that what we experience is the outcome of a set of historical and evolutionary processes that brought us a particular configuration of the world at our contemporary moment.[3] Many studies of technological innovation and infrastructure take historical approaches to analyzing the development, stabilization, and unraveling of technical systems. Thomas Hughes's classic *Networks of Power*, for instance, reveals the long process of building the electrical infrastructure that provides the basis for much of contemporary social life. To understand the world, this work demonstrates, scholars must describe historical processes that are also highly contingent and, as such, broadly unpredictable in advance. Closer to home in political science, Matt Grossmann's novel work draws on historical case studies to reveal that abstract theorizing of the media's role in policymaking fails to explain the historically situated networks of relationships and unfolding of events that produce political outcomes.[4]

John Padgett and Woody Powell draw on biological theory and place an analytical emphasis on temporality to explain the emergence of innovations and new organizations and forms. In their work, explaining historical processes requires a rich, *descriptive* accounting of relations and context, in order to develop theoretical categories that might enable us to predict a narrower range of possible future outcomes.[5] Padgett and Powell argue that:

> Organizational genesis does not mean virgin birth. All new organizational forms, no matter how radically new, are combinations and permutations of what was there before. Transformations are what make them novel. Evolution, therefore, is not teleological progress toward some ahistorical (and often egocentric) ideal. It is a thick and tangled bush of branchings, recombinations, transformations, and sequential path-dependent trajectories, just as Darwin said it was. Invention "in the wild" cannot be understood through abstracting away from concrete social context, because inventions are permutations of that context. Historical path dependency does not imply that there are no transformational principles at the base of endless open-ended generation. Scientific prediction in open-ended, creative systems such as life is not the specification of a fixed-point equilibrium. It is the description of processual mechanisms of genesis and selection in sufficient detail to be capable, in the rich interactive context

of the study system, of specifying a limited number of possible histories. This is the biology, not the physics, view of science.[6]

This book attempts to apply this biological view of science to the analysis of contemporary technology-intensive political campaigning. Despite works such as Michael Schudson's *The Good Citizen*, historical and relational thinking is generally absent from much political communication research.[7] The center of the field is still resolutely concerned with uncovering universal laws (although few may espouse that specific language) relating to psychological political communication processes, rather than considering how particular practices, organizations, technologies, and media forms emerge from specific contexts at particular moments in time, and help produce future contexts. Indeed, it is apparent from the hybrids that have increasingly bedeviled the study and conceptualization of political campaigns, social movements, civil society and political organizations, journalism, media, and collective action more broadly that the physics view of political communication has run up against its limits.

We cannot understand contemporary political communication, and the infrastructures, technologies, and practices that underlie it, without accounting for the work of political actors over time.[8] Methodologically, the book argues that we need to look closely at sequences and events. In doing so, I am guided not only by the literature cited earlier on political communication and technological innovation and invention, but also Thomas Sewell's eloquent work about the need to bring historical thinking to bear on the theories and methods of social science, and vice versa. In *Logics of History: Social Theory and Social Transformation*, a brilliant book that compiles essays crafted over 20 years, Sewell compellingly argues that while social scientists have a rigorous understanding of social theory and an impressive array of methods for empirical inquiry, their explanations of social life often fail to account for the importance of temporality in the shaping of social processes. As a result, while the social scientist is at her best at explaining order and structure, accounting for change is often more difficult. Historians, by contrast, see heterogeneous time, where certain events are highly consequential in shaping the course of what comes after. Sequences matter; the order of events and the processes that constitute those events shape social outcomes.[9] It is this sensibility of the historian that provides purchase over understanding the dynamics of social change. Furthermore, as the political scientist Paul Pierson summarized his arguments regarding the time horizons of causes and outcomes in the remarkable *Politics in Time*: "As in the case of the physical sciences, not all processes of interest to social scientists are likely to fit comfortably in [the domain of short causes and short outcomes.] Many causes and outcomes have long time horizons."[10]

Pierson discussed a number of temporal mechanisms that shape social outcomes, among them path dependence, events, sequences, timing, and unintended consequences. While Pierson noted that within political science there have been a number of "historical turns" with variable success at changing the field, there has been little discussion of temporality specifically within political communication research. To this end, it is worth considering how Sewell's work has a number of implications for political communication research, particularly in terms of enabling scholars to construct richer objects of analysis. Sewell distinguished between three conceptions of time in historical work—"teleological," "experimental," and "eventful" temporality—and argues in favor of the latter. "Teleological" temporality "is the attribution of the cause of a historical happening neither to the actions and reactions that constitute the happening nor to concrete and specifiable conditions that shape and constrain the actions and reactions but rather to abstract transhistorical processes leading to some future historical state."[11] In general, according to a teleological view of temporality, sociological and psychological laws "are essentially assumed as ever-present and ever-rising forces, a kind of eternal yeast" that will lead inexorably to some future state that in turn explains the presence of the past.[12] On the other hand, an "experimental temporality" is a comparative method that freezes history "by cutting up the congealed block of historical time into artificially interchangeable units."[13] Experimental temporality offers a way of clarifying analytical arguments, but lacks explanatory power by abstracting from the sequences of events that produce social outcomes.

An "eventful history," by contrast, "recognizes the power of events in history"; it "is one that takes into account the transformation of structures by events."[14] Sewell argues that, for historians, events are significant happenings that transform structures. There are three aspects of eventful histories in Sewell's account: path dependence, causal heterogeneity, and contingency. While I discussed this in the opening chapter, path dependence means, generally, that earlier happenings affect later occurrences and social outcomes. Causal heterogeneity means that causal mechanisms are not uniform and can be altered by events, in addition to the fact that "the consequences of a given act are not intrinsic in the act but rather will depend on the nature of the social world within which it takes place."[15] In political communication, for instance, Michael Schudson has pointed out that whether a message has an effect depends not only on what the psychological characteristics of the recipient are, but also the time when a person encounters that message, in what sequence with other messages, the context in which it is received, and the capacities the person has to act at a given moment.[16] Another way of saying this is that the causes are not inherent in the agent (or, indeed, the message) itself. One has only to look at Michael Steele's investment in the Republican Party's technological infrastructure and data architecture detailed in Chapter 4 as one example of causal heterogeneity. Investment, so conducive to the Democratic Party's success in the years 2005–2008 under Dean's chairmanship, proved much less consequential on the other side of the aisle with a different chairman in a vastly different cultural and political context. Finally, contingency means that outcomes cannot be deduced from general laws. Social outcomes are contingent upon sequences of happenings or events, including those that are unexpected, and therefore the future is inherently unpredictable (as Padgett and Powell imply, at best we can predict a limited range of future possibilities.) Given there is always the possibility for the unexpected and unpredictable event to transform durable structures, everything has the potential to change.

Methodologically, this means that each "case" that we might take as our object of analysis is, fundamentally, one that proceeds through a temporal sequence. If we are to compare between cases in political communication research, we must adopt a method that accounts for temporality, or sequence and events. The goal of political communication research, under this analytical approach to temporality, is not to develop causal laws. It is to historically explain cases and develop categories that may be applied to the analysis of other, temporally unfolding cases. As Sewell argued, comparison of temporally bound cases can "generate propositions whose potential generality is tested by their ability to illuminate the conjunctural unfolding of analogous causal processes" in other cases.[17] It is worth noting that all of these perspectives on social science research are premised on the idea that historical inquiry can, and does, make causal and explanatory claims (a foreign notion in much of the political communication literature on method).[18] As Jack Katz has argued in "From How to Why: On Luminous Description and Causal Inference in Ethnography," regarding how ethnographic work can make causal claims: "Causal explanation does not require positivism in the form of assertions that one can predict, on the basis of knowing realities at time 1, what will occur at time 2. At a minimum, 'explanation' as I use it here requires 'retrodiction,' claims that, if we observe a given phenomenon at time 2, we can state what will have happened earlier, perhaps in a particular sequence of stages that led to the outcome."[19]

I hope the preceding chapters in this book have provided an example of what an eventful history of political communication can look like. I turn now to the sources of evidence I gathered for this study.

Empirical Approach

There are various sources of data for this book, but it is animated by interviews with 55 individuals active in politics from the 2000 presidential cycle through the 2014 midterm elections (31 Democrats and 24 Republicans). In addition, I also drew on approximately a dozen interviews that I conducted for *Taking Our Country Back*. While that book only went up through the 2008 presidential cycle, I conducted the majority of those interviews in 2009–2011, and spoke with former Democratic campaign staffers about their post-campaign work in the White House, or for political consultancies, federal agencies, Organizing for America, and subsequent campaigns. I ended up drawing on a number of these interviews in the course of writing this book. In addition, I also spoke with dozens of individuals both on and off the record at various conferences and political events over the past four years on topics directly related to this book.

I purposively selected interviewees based on staffers' organizational roles in campaigns, political organizations, and political parties, focusing on individuals working in technology, digital media, data, and analytics, in addition to conducting considerable snowball sampling. Information on the organizational roles of staffers often came from the indispensable resource Democracy in Action (DIA), which cobbles together data on campaign and party staffers from a host of sources, including Federal Election Commission (FEC) filings, press reports, and communications with staffers themselves. DIA has data going back to 1998, and it was the starting point for many of my attempts to identify potential interviewees. Once identified, tracking individuals down was often a significant challenge. To this end, I did whatever I could to find contact information on these practitioners, including conducting general Google searches, scouring LinkedIn profiles, and often just engaging in considerable guesswork at the structure of email addresses at a current employer. When I concluded an interview, I always asked whom else I should contact and often requested virtual introductions.

Interviews are, of course, challenged by the inherent tension that sociologist Howie Becker noted long ago: there are likely differences between what people do, and what they *say* they do.[20] In the attempt to confirm the interview data presented here, I solicited multiple individuals to speak on the same issues or about the same organizations. I also thought very deliberately about the sequence of interviews, attempting to use their order to elicit richer and more forthcoming responses from participants. For example, before conducting interviews, I always considered the work and social locations of interviewees, especially the interests they had, reputational or otherwise, in how they would be portrayed in the book. This included considering the motives of my interviewees, their positions in organizations of interest, and the work they pursued after the campaign or political organization I was interested in (including employment at the time of the interview). I also sought to get perspectives from many different staffers in the same and different departments on the matters I was raising. As a general (but not uniform) approach, I often started interviewing at the lower end of the organizational hierarchy within campaigns, parties, or political organizations. In part, this was about access; asking people to refer me horizontally to their colleagues and vertically to those to whom they reported was one way I was able to move across and up campaign and political organization hierarchies. Often I found that people served as validators of the research project, unlocking doors to others who trusted them. This helped me get into the upper echelons of campaigns and parties a number of times, both by the implicit and explicit trust these former staffers conveyed to their higher-ups and, more mundanely but often no less importantly, by providing an email address to an account people routinely checked.[21]

That said, even when I had access up the chain of command at a party or campaign, in many cases I held back on the interview until I had the opportunity to talk with lower-level staffers. I did so strategically. For one, I was better prepared and able to ask much more concrete questions more efficiently after conversations with comparatively junior-level staffers, which was particularly important given that some of my interviewees regularly charged hundreds of dollars an hour for their time with clients, which I received for free. For another, I found that the quality of the interview was much higher if the person I was interviewing knew that I did my legwork in advance. Part of this stemmed from my questions, which could be more finely grained and pointed about the things I sought to discover if I had background context and was clear about what I needed to know or had clarified as much as possible in advance. At the same time, I repeatedly found that making individuals aware that I had interviewed others about matters relevant to what I was asking them about led to less generality, more specifics, and more honesty in people's responses. And when people were not necessarily forthcoming immediately (for example, about when things technologically did not come together in ways that were often reported in the press), I could refer to other people's perspectives and play interviewees off against one another. Where I could not find multiple corroborating accounts for interview data, preferably among differently situated individuals, I sought other sources, such as internal campaign documents, journalism and trade reports, and public data. Inevitably, given the small numbers of staffers who worked in the contexts detailed in this book, I had to include a number of single-sourced claims. In these cases, I attributed them to a single individual.

In terms of background context and triangulation, I cannot stress enough how much my experiences as a precinct captain in San Francisco and other volunteer work during the cycle in 2008 for the Obama campaign informed not only *Taking Our Country Back* but also this volume, often in non-directly reported ways. In addition, the limited fieldwork I did during the 2012 and 2014 cycles, including my field observations at the Democratic National Convention in 2012, canvass observation with Working America, and trips to the offices of consultancies and parties during the 2014 midterm cycle, provided essential background research for the interviews conducted here.[22] For example, to see the current version of NGP VAN tools in the field, during the 2014 cycle I spent six hours observing a canvass with an organizer from Working America (an AFL-CIO affiliate organization working in support of former North Carolina senator Kay Hagan). I also traveled to the offices of the Democratic Party, Targeted Victory, NGP VAN, and Catalist, where I had the opportunity to see firsthand many aspects of the work documented in this book and to have a wider range of conversations with practitioners than what was simply captured in the formal interviews.

I have consistently found that these experiences enabled me to ask much better questions of the staffers I was interviewing. From my volunteer experiences in 2008 I got to see what worked and what did not work with respect to the Obama field operations, as well as experience what it was like to use the tools the campaign offered (and develop workarounds when they failed). I learned that these tools were good for some things (such as organizing a visibility event at the Kaiser Permanente Marathon in San Francisco in 2007), but awful for others, so much so that my fellow precinct captains and I used GoogleGroups for planning neighborhood events and Excel files for voter data when calls needed to get done quickly and no one in the field much cared about the data (such as when I was a virtual precinct captain for Laredo in advance of the Texas "two-step" primaries and caucuses). These experiences not only informed the writing of *Taking Our Country Back*, they gave me a firsthand view of much of what the re-election bid sought to correct in 2012. These experiences also taught me the important lesson to be skeptical of much of the journalism produced during and even after campaigns. I experienced firsthand the messiness of systems that were often portrayed as seamless, all encompassing, and always working in popular accounts. These experiences also enabled me to challenge interviewees who claimed that this was the case (although when I told people I was a former precinct captain in interviews for both the previous book and this work, it seemed there was less tendency to provide an overly rosy narrative).

At times throughout this book, inconsistencies arose in staffers' accounts, in part because memory is faulty and the speed and stress of political campaigns, especially presidential bids, do not help with recall. Even more, organizational dynamics change over time, and interviews after the fact are less precise than field observations when very specific moments in time are at issue. To convey uncertainty, I reported discrepancies in practitioner accounts. I reported these discrepancies. One example is the statement of Caitlin Checkett that 22 people had to approve the content produced by the digital team on the Romney campaign. Attentive readers will have noted that I paired that quote with Zac Moffatt's statement that the campaign had the best tweets that 17 people would approve. In this case, the specific number of people was less important (although headline grabbing) than the fact that there was an extensive vetting process of digital content by the organizational hierarchy in the Romney campaign.[23] I had confidence that this vetting process existed and that it was extensive given multiple, independent confirmations from staffers on the campaign. After the article that first presented this research was published in *New Media & Society* and became national and even international news, two individuals contacted me to deny these statements. Stuart Stevens, the campaign's senior strategist, stated publicly on Twitter that it was simply not true. However, I was unable to schedule an on-the-record interview with Stevens, despite numerous attempts in the month after the article was published online. The other individual reached out to me via email stating that he was on the rapid response vetting team, and disputed these staffers' accounts as well. This individual declined to be interviewed, however, citing possible future political work. In this context, I weighted the multiple, independent, and on-the-record accounts that confirmed one another over assertions to the contrary.

Nevertheless, this episode reveals the challenges of doing this type of research. As an outsider, I often had to interpret the work processes that practitioners were describing. It was in follow-up conversations with Checkett and Moffatt after the story of the Romney vetting process went viral that they clarified that while not all of these individuals signed off on all content every single time, they had the opportunity, and the fact that this approval chain existed led to much internal self-regulation and cautiousness among digital staffers. That the existence of the vetting process shaped staffers' beliefs about what they could produce and, as a result, the content itself, is a clarification in interpretation that I report here.

As a general approach, I structured my interview questions to proceed chronologically, aiming to elicit narrative biographical details regarding individuals' political and other work since the start of their careers. I did so to let political practitioners reflect upon changes in their work over time and discuss changes in technology, digital, data, and analytics across cycles (through my ability to ask staffers to compare campaigns), and based on a theoretical interest in how individuals cross domains of activity, given that scholars postulate this as a mechanism for innovation and organizational invention. In prepping for interviews, I scoured the Internet for biographical and professional details and went through all previous interview data that touched upon the work of the staffer I would be interviewing. In all, I estimate that I spent at least three hours preparing for every interview I conducted (and sometimes considerably longer, depending on the practitioner's career). This often included drawing on the thousands of documents of campaign journalism and trade publication coverage of digital media and politics, as well as firsthand accounts of practitioner experiences published on the Internet, that I have collected since I began my dissertation work in 2007. The review of these documents often constituted research for the book in its own right. To prep for interviews, and providing primary source material for the book itself, I also drew on an approximately 400-page internal postmortem on the 2008 Obama campaign, published party (the GOP Growth and Opportunity Project report) and campaign (the 2012 Obama Campaign Legacy Report) reports on the 2012 election, and internal campaign documents from both 2012 bids, in addition to consultancies that worked with them, that I was provided access to.

As is clear, I tailored every interview specifically for the staffer I was interviewing and what I was hoping to learn as to the operations of campaigns or parties in the context of the broader history I was seeking to tell. I had no general set of questions that I carried across interviews. With respect to employment outside the political field, as specifically as possible I asked participants about their work, the skills they had or acquired, how these things informed (or did not) their work in politics, and why and how they entered the political field. In the context of their political work, I generally asked how and when they joined the campaign(s), organization(s), and the party they worked for, the work they performed, to whom they reported, the technologies they used and developed, how the goals and the strategies of the campaign(s) and the party took shape, and how all these things changed (or did not) over time. I also used these interviews to test hypotheses and develop new ones, confirm factual details, and gain multiple perspectives on the same events. In this approach to questioning, I drew on Robert Weiss's guidelines for qualitative in-depth interviewing that is tailored to individuals based on their unique experiences and dialogic yet guided by the researcher.[24]

All interviews were "on the record" using participants' real names, except in cases detailed later in this Appendix, although participants could declare any statement "off the record," "not for attribution," or "on background" at their discretion. Throughout the book, if one practitioner stated something under the terms of "not for attribution," I used the singular identifier of a "former staffer" (or a similar phrase such as "practitioner"). If more than one practitioner identified a common issue or expressed a similar sentiment, I used the plural of "former staffers" or "practitioners."

Regarding these terms, the vast majority of participants agreed to conduct their interviews on the record (while declaring specific statements not for attribution or off the record). I also stated that these interviews were part of an academic study, with a comparatively long timeline, and as such if interviewees said anything they later reconsidered I would be happy to revisit it with them. Others requested (but did not demand) that they have the opportunity to review anything directly quoted in advance of publication. Given the fact that many of these staffers continued to pursue professional work in politics, and their statements could potentially complicate working relationships, I granted this request. In a few cases, staffers stated that they would only explicitly speak on off the record terms and that I must seek approval before directly publishing anything from their interviews ($n = 7$). While not ideal, I judged that this was unavoidable at times given people's desire to speak honestly about the things described in this book, while also not jeopardizing their future professional careers. At other times, individuals explicitly stated that they were subject to organizational rules at their current place of employment that required them to approve the use of direct, identifiable quotes. I accepted these conditions for access. In no case was anything I sought to use denied. In my reaching out to potential people to interview, only two explicitly declined to participate. I was ultimately unable to actually schedule interviews with an additional four individuals, even though practitioners agreed to it in theory. A much greater number of individuals, although I did not keep count, simply did not respond to multiple email requests to be interviewed. In terms of the presentation of the interview data itself, while I recognize that there are considerable debates over "cleaning" quotes, I edited them slightly to improve readability (taking out things such as "like" to better conform to the norms of written text).[25] I did so, in part, given my undoubtedly unfortunate penchant for presenting long interview quotes.

Constructing a history of the recent past is a fraught enterprise, since the primary sources are still living and working and there are potential stakes in terms of professional reputations. I have no doubt that some of these interviews were colored by people being concerned with their reputations or proud of their work, and the teams they were a part of, and not wanting to speak ill of them. In a small handful of cases, I suspect people were deliberately misleading with an eye to their role in history. Given these challenges, I have approached this book as a social scientist, seeking to craft a narrative that both documents and explains changes in political technology over the last decade and the differences between the two parties in a way that is as fair, rigorous, and comprehensive as possible. Throughout, I have been guided by a basic presupposition to conduct as much of this work in public as possible. By "in public," I mean both eschewing the traditional social science tool of pseudonyms in the attempt to tie the interview data here to actual people as much as possible and making my work available in stages to both the sources I interviewed and the wider public. These things made, and make, this work considerably open to scrutiny. In the end, I believe these decisions made for better research. It has certainly made me more accountable to my sources and a broader community of readers than would have been the case with using pseudonyms (although that was also a near impossibility given my aim of historical explanation here) and producing only a finished product for public consumption.

Of course, writing without pseudonyms makes for a challenging task, and it is not possible (or desirable) in all research projects. Interviews conducted on the record might make people less forthright or forthcoming. I also fully recognize that for some electoral field studies there is no practical way to conduct research without a guarantee of anonymity, particularly studies that involve comparatively lower level staffers where candidly talking about their experiences might mean not working in politics again.[26] I agree with Rasmus Nielsen that sometimes research is impossible without pseudonyms given the nature of the field site.[27] At the same time, I also suspect that social scientists too often default to using pseudonyms, even when it may be possible to use real names. I agree with Mitch Duneier and Arlene Stein that pseudonyms often protect the researcher, not necessarily the subjects of research, and using real names can hold scholars to higher evidentiary standards and increase accountability.[28] The point is that the researcher needs to think these issues through in advance and weigh the strengths and disadvantages of each approach.

In my own case, there is no doubt that at times I have couched my language here when referring to specific individuals and always had the particular person speaking in mind when quoting them, so as not to jeopardize their careers or unduly embarrass anyone. While undoubtedly people have their own idiosyncrasies and make mistakes, they also act within contexts that are not of their own making and under conditions of institutional constraints and possibilities. In general, as a strategy of reporting interview data about situations or decisions that might prove controversial, I favored the accounts of comparatively senior, high-profile members of campaigns, parties, and organizations, especially given they could shoulder responsibility for failure given their prominence. People who feature prominently in this book include Michael Slaby, Zac Moffatt, Ethan Roeder, and Bryan Whitaker.

When the accounts of these staffers were disputed, or contradicted other things I heard, I noted this. I also drew on the accounts of these more senior practitioners because they not only had authority in these organizations, they are simply less vulnerable should their accounts be disputed or others seek to retaliate. At the same time, while many other practitioners whom I interviewed spoke to the matters that the individuals featured prominently in this text do, and I could have presented a considerably wider range of sources, for the consistency of the narrative and to relate the history told here through the focused lens of some staffers' experiences, I tried to be as consistent with the perspective as possible.

Furthermore, in Chapter 6, I took the step of proactively making a number of statements not for attribution both because I wanted to show, analytically, the barriers to the diffusion of technological practice, and because I believed that the young staffers behind these accounts could face career repercussions in the future given the close-knit world of staffers and vendors. I have the power of representation, and there is a responsibility that comes with that. While I have a number of commitments in this study, to both the participants and the public, a large part of that responsibility here as a researcher is to protect the future interests of the former, particularly when there is not a clear public good at stake.[29]

Finally, I also made the unorthodox decision to both circulate a draft of this manuscript to 30 of my sources and make the underlying staffer data set publicly available in order to provide people with an opportunity to respond to my work. In July and August 2015, I circulated the full version of a draft of this text and solicited comments, criticism, and factual and interpretative corrections. Of this group, 12 practitioners responded with substantive feedback (outside of minor suggestions to clean quotes or correct misspellings). In terms of the staffer data set, in July 2015 I posted the full spreadsheet of the 629 staffers and their careers on my website and invited others to point out if anything was missing, add to it given the difficultly of working with LinkedIn and FEC data, or use it in the course of additional research projects.

The question that perhaps comes most frequently from peer reviewers of journal articles is "how did you analyze your interview data?" This proceeds from the assumption that there is a formal and systematic process for analyzing qualitative data. In my own experience, this assumption does not fit my actual practices relating to data analysis. The closest published description I have found that captures my own way of working comes from the sociologist Kristin Luker's brilliant conceptualization of the research and analysis process. The goal of social science, for Luker, is to develop new theoretical categories that help researchers understand and explain social life. Luker advises researchers to continually and simultaneously move between theory, data collection, and analysis, and makes a compelling argument for research that proceeds through a "logic of discovery," not a "logic of verification."[30] Luker's approach requires both the inductive analysis of data and the placing of emergent conceptual categories in relation to the extant theoretical approaches in academic literatures. As such, Luker advises that scholars should always be reading (and very widely, anything that can possibly bear on the matter at hand) and analyzing while collecting data.

Following pragmatist thought, I think of theoretical concepts as tools to think with that are more or less useful in the course of empirical inquiry.[31] The inductive development of concepts through immersion in the field, analysis of data, and breadth of academic reading is a way of disclosing new aspects of the world that, in turn, can potentially shape how we understand and think about and act in it. My own way of working involves what I think of as "living with my data." In the course of researching and writing this book, I listened to, read, and re-read interview transcripts (especially in preparation for other interviews), I highlighted things, and I rewrote what participants said in my own words. At times, I analyzed my data through what Langley has called a "narrative strategy of sensemaking," in which I prepared narrative, chronological accounts of organizational processes on the two 2012 campaigns based on the interview and other forms of data such as journalistic accounts and organizational records.[32] I then moved back and forth between my inductive analysis of these accounts and the theoretical tools of various literatures to develop the narrative and categories detailed here. In my earlier drafts, I often relied on very long block quotes from participants interspersed by my analysis and the threads of narrative history. Through these writing practices, which are also a method of data analysis, concepts began to emerge which connected to the "banked" literature that I carry around in my head, the materials I was reading while researching and writing the book, and other scholarly works that I found and explored through targeted literature reviews. The entire time that I collected data, analyzed it, and wrote this book I was also always reading and attempting to fit what I was seeing to what other scholars have argued (and used that to open up new avenues of inquiry in my data), all while marking my potential contributions.

To help me be as accurate as possible in my reporting of data from interviews, my research assistants Christopher Jasinski and Kylah Hedding cleaned the transcripts and went over the entire manuscript to assess every direct quote for accuracy, both literal and contextual.

I also supplemented this interview data by looking systematically, with my graduate students, at the career backgrounds of technology, digital, data, and analytics staffers active in presidential politics from 2004 through 2012.[33] Using data from the nonprofit and nonpartisan website DIA, which gathers organizational and staffer information directly from campaigns and public accounts of elections while also drawing on FEC data, in addition to FEC reports on campaign disbursements, we compiled a list of all staffers who either worked in campaign divisions dedicated to technology, digital, data, or analytics or who had these or related words in their organizational titles on primary and general election bids from the 2004, 2008, and 2012 presidential cycles. The staffer data has data on employment through summer 2014, when we began data analysis.

We chose to start with the 2004 cycle, the first time that campaigns routinely began developing stand-alone "Internet" divisions. The campaigns in this analysis are Howard Dean (2004), John Kerry (2004), Dennis Kucinich (2004), Wesley Clark (2004), John Edwards (2004), Joseph Lieberman (2004), George W. Bush (2004), John Edwards (2008), Bill Richardson (2008), Dennis Kucinich (2008), Chris Dodd (2008), Joe Biden (2008), Hillary Clinton (2008), Barack Obama (2008), Mitt Romney (2008), Rudolph Guiliani (2008), John McCain (2008), Ron Paul (2008), Mike Huckabee (2008), Fred Thompson (2008), Barack Obama (2012), Mitt Romney (2012), Newt Gingrich (2012), Ron Paul (2012), Rick Santorum (2012), John Huntsman (2012), Michelle Bachman (2012), Gary Johnson (2012), Rick Perry (2012), Herman Cain (2012), and Fred Karger (2012).

Our work netted a total of 629 staffers, 507 Democratic, and 123 Republican (one staffer worked on both sides of the aisle). The total number of staffers hired by presidential campaigns in these domains is higher given that some of these staffers worked on multiple presidential bids. We then searched for and manually entered details on staffers' professional careers using the professional social networking site LinkedIn. When data was missing, we attempted to find personal, work, or other websites that contained biographies or resumes. This allowed us to find at least limited employment histories for *every staffer* in our data set, with comprehensive data being the norm, which is revealing of the nature of contemporary social network use for professional purposes.[34] Given our theoretical interest in identifying staffers who crossed between industries and fields of activity, Christopher Jasinski coded their professional work manually based on self-reported, manifest descriptions of their employers on LinkedIn and their websites and used the following general, mutually exclusive *organizational* categories: *previous campaign, campaign, political, journalism, entertainment media, technology, education, data/analytics, commercial industry firm, legal services, government*, and *DNC/RNC*. To check the reliability of these organizational category codes, a second graduate student coded a random subset of the data (the agreement was 91.2%). Importantly, we categorized previous professional work based on the type of organization that employed the staffer, not her role in that organization. We did so based on our analytical interest in staffers crossing between professional fields and for clarity in categorizing previous professional work given the difficulties of parsing job responsibilities with the lack of standardization of titles.

We coded as "campaign" work on a political campaign at any level of office. We also noted the number of staffers who had campaign work in their background at any level of office (reported as "total staffers with previous campaign work"). We coded as "political" if the position entailed work for political consulting firms, nonprofit, movement, and advocacy organizations, or state and local party organizations. "Journalism" refers to work for blogs or more traditional outlets such as CNN. "Entertainment media" refers to work in organizations like MTV Networks, production companies, and other creative media firms. "Technology" designates organizations whose primary business relates to computing, digital media, or mobile technologies. "Education" denotes organizations such as Pearson, universities, or similar institutions. "Data/analytics" denotes companies whose primary business is gathering, storing, or analyzing data. "Commercial industry firm" refers to firms that are not technology, data and analytics, political consulting firms, or any of the other categories listed here. "Legal services" refers to law firms or legal aid organizations. "Government" refers to public sector work at the local, state, or national level. "DNC/RNC" denotes employment by an official national party organization (the Democratic National Committee and Republican National Committee, respectively). We coded as "N/A" when the campaign appeared to be a staffer's first job while in college or following graduation, or the staffer's employment history prior to the campaign was unclear.

Given our interest in field crossing, after categorizing the sectors they worked in we coded each staffer for their *primary* field of employment prior to each presidential campaign. This is the code that occurred most frequently. We coded a staffer's background as "mixed" when a category did not occur most frequently (both the "N/A" and "mixed" categories speak to the question of professionalization). Staffers who worked multiple cycles were counted and coded anew for each campaign. For example, Uday Sreekanth worked on Hillary Clinton's 2008 campaign and the 2008 Obama general election campaign and is coded for each. Broadly, this gave staffers the possibility of having different primary fields for each presidential campaign. We believe that coding staffers for every presidential campaign they worked on, and their primary field prior to *each* campaign, enabled us to accurately trace rates of field crossing.

To analyze rates of organizational founding, we coded whether a staffer founded a firm or organization following a presidential campaign and tracked the total rates of founding for each party and campaign. In the interest of being as inclusive as possible, we coded as organizational founders staffers who indicated their titles in LinkedIn profiles, or we found them on other organizational websites listed as, "founder," "founding partner," "partner," "principal," or "CEO" (at the time of the founding). The idea is that these legal and commercial distinctions are less important than being on the ground floor of a new venture after a presidential campaign. We opted to include all organizations founded after a founder's presidential campaign work regardless of the timing or subsequent non-presidential work. And we chose to classify these individuals as presidential campaign founders given they likely had shared experience, knowledge, and skills with others who were employed on the presidential bid. For example, Zac Moffatt was coded as having founded a firm following the Bush 2004 campaign although Targeted Victory was founded in 2009 after his stint working at the Republican Party. Meanwhile, we also accounted for some staffers founding multiple firms or groups of individuals cofounding firms by calculating the number of unique organizations founded as well as the number of founders following a presidential campaign.

This data set is not perfect. Notably, disbursements to consultancies that handled technology, digital, data, and analytics operations for campaigns are not reflected in this data.[35] Further analyses that look into the role of and services provided by technology, digital, data, and analytics consultants on presidential campaigns is necessary - especially furthering the work of Adam Sheingate in his *Building a Business of Politics*, which unfortunately was published too late to fully build upon here. And, future analyses can examine the work of the new organizations charted here across election cycles and down-ballot races. And, the data set is likely not exhaustive (there is no perfect source given the difficulties of working with FEC data). The data set is limited to paid staff and those directly paid by campaigns (and does not include volunteers who can also contribute to network folding or staffers hired through consultancies). In addition, the data only includes organizations founded by presidential campaign staffers, not the entire field of new ventures. Republicans who were not presidential staffers, for instance, could have founded a number of new firms from 2004–2012 to partially compensate for the difference between the two parties (although the interview data clearly suggests this was not the case). That said, we believe we compiled the most comprehensive data set in existence on technology, digital, data, and analytics staffers on presidential campaigns going back to 2004.[36]

In addition to the interviews and this data set, a number of other research projects published previously have informed this work. First, I conducted interviews with practitioners and performed a qualitative content analysis on archived versions of the two 2012 general election campaigns' Twitter feeds from 2012, which I published in *New Media & Society*.[37] Second, with two graduate research assistants, I conducted a mixed methods field study and content analysis of media production at the 2012 Democratic National Convention, published in *Journalism*.[38]

Notes

Chapter 1

1. In addition, the campaign ran ORCA out of Boston's TD Garden arena, but did not test its systems in advance. The Garden's systems rejected data coming in from ORCA as a security concern and the Wi-fi crashed under the traffic. See Mooney, "How a Canceled Boston Bruins Game Led to a Mitt Romney Campaign Meltdown." For perspectives on why ORCA failed, see Farber, "Why Romney's Orca Killer App Beached"; Gallagher, "Inside Team Romney's Whale of a Meltdown"; Gallagher, "Which Consultants Built Romney's 'Project Orca'?"; see also Stromer-Galley, *Presidential Campaigning in the Internet Age*, 167–169.

2. For its promotion, see Terkel, "Project Orca: Mitt Romney Campaign Plans Massive, State-of-the-Art Poll Monitoring Effort."

3. Thomas and Peoples, "GOP Moves to Plug Technology Gap." For interesting reporting on Obama's comparative strength among workers in the technology industry, see Silver, "Technology Gap Threatens G.O.P. Campaigns." As Wilner at the *Cook Political Report* noted, the "fallout [post-2012] also has inspired several new consultancies as well as some serious reconfiguring among the party's data set." For a list of firms, see Wilner, "Political Report 'Big Data at-a-Glance.'"

4. For a discussion of the issues surrounding Project Houdini on the 2008 campaign, see Kreiss, *Taking Our Country Back*, 182. For a discussion of the 2010 midterm cycle, see Issenberg, *The Victory Lab*. For details on Pollwatcher, Obama's mobile application that enabled volunteers at polling locations to update turnout records, which was a collaboration between the campaign, party, and NGP VAN (a Democratic-allied firm), see Trevelyan, "Democratic/Progressive Voter Contacts"; Fitzpatrick, "Obama Campaign Launches Poll-Watching App."

5. Throughout this book, I use the phrase "technology, digital, data, and analytics" to refer to these generally discrete areas of campaign practice. The terms practitioners use have changed over the past two decades. "Technology" is increasingly its own area of campaign practice, and refers broadly to the building of or working with information technology infrastructure. "Digital" (or "digital media") was only recently used widely during the 2012 cycle, although it captures what in previous cycles practitioners referred to as "new media," "Internet," and "eCampaign" operations. "Analytics" is a comparatively recent term as well, but broadly captures the use of data analysis for the purposes of what is variously grouped under the labels of "micro-targeting" and "modeling." The term is also applied in the context of new practices such as algorithmic media buying and web optimization. These nomenclature changes reflect an ongoing process of specialization in these areas. See Lilleker and Negrine, "Professionalization of What?"

6. Michael Slaby, personal communication, September 4, 2013.

7. For a discussion of the application layer of the Internet, see Zittrain, *Future of the Internet*.

8. Karpf, "Social Science Methods in Internet Time", 640; emphasis in the original.

9. These shifts at the application layer of the Internet are joined by other changes in media and communications technologies, social structures, and cultural practices over the past four decades. With respect to media, see Prior, *Post-Broadcast Democracy*; Williams and Delli Carpini, *After Broadcast News*; Stroud, *Niche News*; Chadwick, *The Hybrid Media System*. These changes in media and communications technologies have contributed to, and are shaped by, broader changes in social structures and cultural practice. W. Lance Bennett and Jarol Manheim argued that there have been shifts away from "group-based society" and the mass polity and toward "new emotional and identity processes around self-expression and lifestyle" that give rise to new social structures; "The One-Step Flow of Communication," 218, 221. Scholars argue that digital, networked technologies facilitate the individualized production and consumption of culture and the crafting of new social relationships outside, and sometimes in lieu, of organizational, institutional, and geographic ties; see Rainie et al., *Networked*. As Bennett and Segerberg nicely summarize their recent exploration of the idea of "communication as organization," more "individuated citizens" pursue "personalized brands of politics organized around individual lifestyles and social networks"; *The Logic of Connective Action*, 6. A number of scholars have pointed to the consequences of these changes in media and social structures for citizenship and civic participation. Communication scholars W. Lance Bennett, Deen Freelon, and Chris Wells argued that the contemporary era is marked by new forms of "actualizing citizenship," where civic participation is shaped by identity, emotion, expression, interest, and peer networks, not formal institutional relationships or the "dutiful" obligations to be informed and responsible citizens; "Changing Citizen Identity," 397–398. Meanwhile, formal civil society organizations try to adapt to these dynamics and the changing "collective action space"; Bimber, Flanagin, and Stohl, *Collective Action in Organizations*. See also Wells, *The Civic Organization and the Digital Citizen*.

10. Throughout this book, I use the term "technology" to refer to material or digital artifacts as well as the knowledge, skills, and practices that produce and exist around them. There is an enormous literature in this area. See John Durham Peters on the lineage of the definition of "technology" conjoining the ideas of making and knowing; *The Marvelous Clouds*, especially 87–91.

11. See Norris, *Politics and the Press* and *A Virtuous Circle*, Chapter 8. For an adaptation of this framework in the context of a study of political parties, see Negrine, *The Transformation of Political Communication*. Negrine argues that since the 1970s we are in a "capital-intensive" era of "politics as profession"; 64–66.

12. Norris, "The Evolution of Election Campaigns," 7.

13. Chadwick, *The Hybrid Media System*.

14. For work on campaign consultants, see Sheingate, *Building a Business of Politics*.

15. See, Star, "Ethnography of Infrastructure," for this expansive definition of 'infrastructure'. Over the past two decades, scholars have produced an extensive set of writings on infrastructures and "infrastructuring." Paul Edwards argues that "infrastructure" is defined by "[n]ot only hardware but organizations, socially communicated background knowledge, general acceptance and reliance, and near-ubiquitous accessibility"; "Infrastructure and Modernity," 188. Infrastructures are both background, and invisible, until they fail. See also Edwards et al., "Agenda for Infrastructure Studies." See Nielsen, *Ground Wars*, on how campaigns need to assemble their component parts in a work that builds explicitly from DeLanda's assemblage theory.

16. Nielsen, *Ground Wars*.

17. See Issenberg, *The Victory Lab*; Alter, *The Center Holds*; Engage, *Inside the Cave*; Sides and Vavreck, *The Gamble*.

18. GOP, *Growth and Opportunity Project report*, 24.

19. Bartels, "The Impact of Electioneering," 267.

20. See Bimber, "Digital Media in the Obama campaigns of 2008 and 2012." Bimber argues that the commodification of digital tools, greater recognition of their utility, and a seemingly uniform understanding of the contemporary media environment will ultimately mean that we will gradually see less variation between campaigns.

21. There is now significant evidence that adoption of digital media by state parties and campaigns is increasingly pervasive. For a review, see Baldwin-Philippi, *Using Technology, Building Democracy*. That said, it is also clear that there is differential adoption. Hatch found that Democratic state parties hire more technology-oriented staffers for the purposes of database management, analytics, and voter outreach than their counterparts; "Party Organizational Strength and Technological Capacity."

22. Galvin, *Presidential Party Building*.

23. Nyhan and Montgomery, "Connecting the Candidates," 293.

24. Padgett and Powell, *Emergence of Organizations and Markets*, 1, 5; emphasis in the original.

25. Ibid., 6–7.

26. Ibid., 11.

27. Kreiss, *Taking Our Country Back*.

28. de Vaan, Stark, and Vedres, "Game Changer: The Topology of Creativity."

29. Ibid., 1186.

30. Gibson, "Messina Touts Grassroots Strength." Ironically enough, the examples Messina provided all featured political veterans: Ethan Roeder headed the data team and he was a veteran of the 2008 bid, and "targeted sharing" was the result of a collaboration between digital and analytics staffers, among whom there were a number of 2008 campaign alumni.

31. Ibid.

32. For an extended discussion of the methodology, see Kreiss and Jasinski, "The Tech Industry Meets Presidential Politics."

33. Seventy-nine staffers (65 Democrats and 14 Republicans) founded firms and organizations. In keeping with theoretical expectations, of these staffers, 46 (58%) had primary work backgrounds in domains outside of campaigns and politics, such as commercial industry, technology, data/analytics, and journalism, or new or mixed work experiences.

34. We estimate that approximately 87.8% of these entities were for-profit firms, and 12.2% were nonprofit organizations. Of these firms and organizations, we estimate that approximately 71.9% pursue at least some expressly political work promoting or furthering the ends of candidates or causes (although with considerable variation among them; for example, most of the for-profit consultancies work for a range of commercial and political clients, although generally along party lines).

35. Google's executive chairman Eric Schmidt was an investor in Civis Analytics and played a role in the 2012 campaign. See Green, "Google's Eric Schmidt Invests in Obama's Big Data Brains." After the election, Schmidt also invested in a start-up called Timshel, where Michael Slaby was the managing partner. Timshel was the parent company of an entity called The Groundwork that helped build the infrastructure for Clinton's 2016 run; see Pasick and Fernholz, "The Stealthy, Eric Schmidt Backed Start-Up."

36. Bryan Whitaker, personal communication, January 30, 2015. Whitaker became the chief innovation officer at TargetSmart in the summer of 2015. On December 31, 2010, NGP, the Democratic Party's premier provider of fundraising and compliance tools, and VAN, its leading voter contact and volunteer management software firm, merged. Throughout this book I generally refer to VAN and NGP separately during the periods of time prior to their merger.

37. Padgett and Powell, *Emergence of Organizations and Markets*, 3.

38. Masket et al., "Networking the Parties." See also Cohen et al., *The Party Decides*.

39. For a review, see Gillespie, Boczkowski, and Foot, *Media Technologies*.

40. See Karpf, "Open Source Political Community Development."
41. Sydow, Schreyögg, and Koch, "Organizational Path Dependence," 696. See also, Pierson, *Politics in Time*; Schreyögg, Sydown, and Holtmann, "How History Matters in Organisations."
42. Sydow, Schreyögg, and Koch, "Organizational Path Dependence," 693.
43. See Reed, *Interpretation and Social Knowledge.*
44. Suchman, Trigg, and Blomberg of Xerox Palo Alto Research Center argue that prototypes have a "performative" dimension and align "multiple, discontinuous social worlds" around the possibilities of new technologies; "Working Artefacts," 177. For other works on prototypes, see Turner, *From Counterculture to Cyberculture.*
45. *Oxford English Dictionary*, "prototype," noun.
46. Turner, *Digital Keywords*, 328. While most of the literature on prototypes focuses on small-scale artifacts in research labs, there is no theoretical reason that prototypes do not also exist at the field level in terms of creating new alignments among the stakeholders of political campaigns, opening the door to people from other fields, and creating new models for technological campaign practice. What is of consequence in making prototypes is the creation of new alignments between people, material and digital things, and organizational forms through cultural and technological processes, and then narrating and demonstrating these new alignments as models for future practice. Culturally, prototypes are part of a broader "theater of use" that science and technology studies scholar Wally Smith has documented in the context of demonstrations within the technology industry; Smith, "Theatre of Use," 449.
47. See Streeter and Teachout, *Mousepads, Shoe Leather, and Hope.* Dean's progressive policy stances and statement that he represented "the Democratic wing of the Democratic Party" also likely inspired many individuals to join the campaign, similar to Bernie Sanders's primary campaign in 2016.
48. As this book went through press in early 2016, it appeared the Bernie Sanders campaign attracted a bevy of grassroots volunteers to work on technical projects through a similar technologically-enabled vision of electoral politics. See, for instance, Corasaniti, "Legion of Tech Volunteers Lead a Charge for Bernie Sanders"; and, the volunteer development of the "Field the Bern" field app, Lapowsky, "Sanders' New Canvassing App On-boards Volunteers in Seconds." Field staffers on the 2012 Obama campaign created a software platform called NationalField for field organizing and, after the election, launched a firm by the same name (which was subsequently acquired by NGP VAN). The Clinton 2016 campaign, meanwhile, engaged in deliberate recruiting from the technology industry for its candidate's run; Krueger, "How the Hillary Clinton Campaign Built a Staff as Diverse as America."
49. Chris Hughes, personal communication, July 20, 2010.
50. There are a couple of different perspectives on this dynamic in the literature. Rasmus Nielsen argues for the power of the presidency to focus party efforts on solidifying advantage; *Ground Wars.* Dave Karpf argues for "out party innovation incentives," where the party no longer in power has the incentive to seek out new models for doing things; *The MoveOn Effect.* Other scholars taking the incentive approach include Klinkner, *The Losing Parties*; Shefter, *Political Parties and the State.* In *Presidential Party Building*, Galvin argues that it is party actors' *perception* of an erosion of competitive standing that matters, not necessarily a downturn in a party's numerical strength. The cost of party building (including investments in infrastructure and staffers) is particularly high, and therefore requires this perception to spur institutional action. Meanwhile, Galvin traces the roots of institutional change through piecemeal efforts over the course of many election cycles. Because of this dynamic, securing majorities has the potential to bring about organizational stasis. In this book, I take a complementary approach and argue that when a party loses a race that *party network actors* expected to win, such as the Democratic Party in 2004 and the Republican Party in 2012, they search for new models of campaign practice and make new investments. With respect to Galvin's work, I wholeheartedly embrace

the importance of perception and cultural orientation within parties (which provided the cultural context that made Dean's 50-state solution imaginable and urgent for party actors, for instance). I extend the idea of perception here to the level of party network actors (not just presidents), and expand it beyond competitive standing to include perceptions of what is efficacious in electoral terms. Events, including losing a campaign party network actors believed they should have won, engender critical breaks in established patterns of cultural orientation, such as changing what actors perceive to provide competitive electoral advantage. As this book argues, the cultural understandings of the actors involved and their perceptions as to the state of the two parties, their electoral competitiveness, and *what that very competitiveness was premised on,* as well as the ways all these things favored certain actors in party networks, including vendors and technologies, were consequential with respect to technological development.

51. For borrowing, see Stromer-Galley, *Presidential Campaigning in the Internet Age*. More broadly, we can see this in terms of "mimetic isomorphism"; see Powell and DiMaggio, *The New Institutionalism in Organizational Analysis*.

52. For an interesting piece on values and technological adoption in the context of movements, see Agarwal et al., "Grassroots Organizing in the Digital Age."

53. For an extensive discussion, see Nielsen, *Ground Wars*.

54. For a discussion of micro-targeting at the time and its evolution in the context of the 2004 Bush campaign, see Sosnik, Fournier, and Dowd, *Applebee's America*.

55. Even to the extent that it became a model for Obama's run in 2008, see Plouffe, *The Audacity to Win*.

56. Nielsen, *Ground Wars*; Stromer-Galley, *Presidential Campaigning in the Internet Age*.

57. For historical evidence and details on the contracts and technical arrangements that underlie the DNC's data architecture, see chapters 3 and 4 in Kreiss, *Taking Our Country Back*. It was this model of party voter data coupled with a database and field tools provided by the firm NGP VAN that was the subject of fierce controversy during the 2016 election cycle, as detailed in the conclusion.

58. See Stromer-Galley, *Presidential Campaigning in the Internet Age*.

59. In 2015, there were widely reported management issues and financial travails at the New Organizing Institute, and the organization became part of Wellstone Action: http://www.wellstone.org/noi.

60. See Kreiss, *Taking Our Country Back*, 87.

61. Alex Lundry, personal communication, June 25, 2013. Lundry's title from the Romney campaign comes from his LinkedIn page, but he is not in FEC filings, suggesting that he was paid through TargetPoint (where he reports being the chief data scientist at the time). Lundry is included in the 629-staffer data set, however, given the interview data. The Analyst Institute brings social science methods to Democratic campaigning, and Catalist is a Democratic Party–aligned data firm; for an extensive discussion of both, see Hersh, *Hacking the Electorate*.

62. Patrick Ruffini, personal communication, January 15, 2013.

63. See Sides and Vavreck, "Obama's Not So Big Data," for an argument about the new forms of expertise required for the technological basis of campaigning.

64. Former Republican Party staffer, personal communication, not for attribution.

65. Azarias Reda, personal communication, August 21, 2014. Reda announced he was leaving the RNC in 2015. For the RNC's hiring post-2012, see Lapowsky, "GOP Hires Silicon Valley Vet."

66. Katie Harbath, personal communication, August 27, 2013.

67. Chuck DeFeo, personal communication, January 18, 2013.

68. Targeted Victory is coded as a Bush-Cheney 2004 firm given that Moffatt's presidential campaign work preceding the founding was that bid. See Kreiss and Jasinski, "The Tech Industry Meets Presidential Politics," for a detailed statement of our approach to analyzing the staffer data set.

69. They include Andrew Bleeker's Bully Pulpit Interactive (now the premier Democratic digital advertising firm), Scott Goodstein's Revolution Messaging (the firm behind digital for Bernie Sanders's run in 2016), and Dan Siroker's non-partisan Optimizely.

70. For a discussion of the Democratic Party's work around the 2010 midterm cycle with respect to voter data and analytics, see Issenberg, *The Victory Lab.*

71. See Issenberg, *The Victory Lab*, 253–301; Hersh, *Hacking the Electorate.*

72. Ward, "GOP's Biggest Tech Challenge." The party-aligned nonprofit organization ActBlue, founded during the 2004 cycle, also played an infrastructural role with respect to facilitating small-dollar online donations for Democrats, and continued to play this important role in 2016. See Lichtblau and Corasaniti, "Small Donors Are Clicking More with Democrats."

73. Some former party staffers also argued that these investments were not made wisely or strategically.

74. See Hatch, "Party Organizational Strength and Technological Capacity."

75. DiMaggio, "Culture and Cognition."

76. Former Republican Party staffer, personal communication, not for attribution.

77. Alex Lundry, personal communication, June 25, 2013.

78. See also Issenberg, "How Obama Used Big Data to Rally Voters," on the value of Wagner to the 2012 campaign. For Wagner's work in 2008, see Issenberg, *The Victory Lab*, 277.

79. It is worth noting that the Democrats were in a similar situation until the aftermath of the 2004 cycle.

80. Former Obama 2012 campaign staffer, personal communication, not for attribution.

81. The practice of computational management was first honed on the Obama 2008 campaign; Kreiss, *Taking Our Country Back.* As I showed in that book, however, and Sides and Vavreck also argue, not everything was tested; Sides and Vavreck, "Obama's Not So Big Data." Practitioners saw many aspects of digital design and aesthetics, for instance, as laying beyond the ability to test them.

82. Former Romney 2012 campaign staffer, personal communication, not for attribution.

83. This is according to staffers' accounts; I cannot independently verify this in the FEC data.

84. Caitlin Checkett, personal communication, December 16, 2013.

85. Zac Moffatt, personal communication, January 31, 2014.

86. There is literature on permanent campaigns that focuses on campaign communications and the ways elected officials are seemingly always campaigning (see, for instance, Elmer, Langlois, and McKelvey, *The Permanent Campaign*). This work points to the ways that there are shorter gaps between campaign cycles in terms of positioning for the next race, but it does not apply to technological development. Rasmus Nielsen has also showed how there is little in the way of a permanent campaign when it comes to field infrastructure and organization in *Ground Wars*; see 58–62.

87. As Sides and Vavreck note in *The Gamble*, however, narrower appeals might not be the most effective. For digital social influence, see Kreiss, *Taking Our Country Back.*

88. For the dynamics of the race, see Sides and Vavreck, *The Gamble.*

89. Aaron Ginn, personal communication, December 8, 2012. Romney's in-house social network was called MyMitt. See Sifry, "Meet Mitt Romney's New Social Network."

90. Lincoln Labs also launched the "Reboot" conferences in 2014, which are designed to convene practitioners and the new digital intermediaries in the political space such as Rentrak, Google, and Facebook. Lincoln Labs, "Reboot Conference." Lincoln Labs became "Lincoln Network" and "Lincoln Initiative" in 2016.

91. For a discussion of the differences in the strategies of the two campaigns, with Obama investing more in field and Romney in late advertising during the general election, see Sides and Vavreck, *The Gamble.*

92. Issenberg, *The Victory Lab.*

93. Former Republican Party staffer, personal communication, not for attribution.

94. There have been a number of critiques of FLS Connect, a firm that has long been at the center of the Republican Party's vendor ecosystem. See Erickson, "Incestuous Bleeding of

the Republican Party"; and "66 Canal Center Plaza." See also Edsall on FLS's connection with Karl Rove and the firm's history with the Republican Party and Romney campaign; "In Data We Trust." Jonathan Alter wrote about FLS Connect in *The Center Holds*; see 225.

95. See, for instance, this write-up of the GOP Data Center during the 2012 campaign; Judd, "Republican Party's Technology Revival Hopes Hinge on Data and Data Analysis."

96. Although this is a complicated archival source, see Ankerson, "Writing Web Histories."

Chapter 2

1. McCain, "New Hampshire Primary Victory Speech."

2. For more about Fose's role on the campaign, see Johnson, *Routledge Handbook of Political Management*; Kaid, *The Millennium Election*; Sobieraj, *Soundbitten*; Bimber, *Information and American Democracy*.

3. See van Natta, Jr., "McCain Gets Big Payoff"; Klotz, *Politics of Internet Communication*; Chadwick and Howard, *Routledge Handbook of Internet Politics*; Mintz, "McCain Camp Enjoys Net Advantage."

4. Chadwick, *The Hybrid Media System*.

5. Chadwick argued that media systems across historical eras have always been hybrid, but hybridity looks different in different eras. The layering of newer forms of interactive digital media on top of comparatively older forms of mass media characterizes the contemporary era.

6. For the evolution of web campaigning, see Foot and Schneider, *Web Campaigning*; Stromer-Galley, *Presidential Campaigning in the Internet Age*.

7. Nielsen, *Ground Wars*.

8. Ibid.; Hersh, *Hacking the Electorate*.

9. See Kreiss, *Taking Our Country Back*, for the history of the Democratic Party's data efforts during the cycle.

10. For Dean's election to party chair, see Kreiss, *Taking Our Country Back*, 92.

11. For a discussion, see also Nielsen, *Ground Wars*, 166–167.

12. Chuck DeFeo, personal communication, January 18, 2013.

13. Weisberg, "McCain's Web Explosion"; Reichart-Smith and Smith, "What a Difference a Download Makes."

14. Fose also recalls looking closely at the Bill Bradley campaign early during the cycle, namely the work that Internet manager Lynn Reed was doing. See also Bimber, *Information and American Democracy*, 182.

15. Max Fose, personal communication, February 22, 2013.

16. Ibid.

17. This accords with Rob Kling's social interactionist approach to organizational technologies. See Kling, "What is Social Informatics?"

18. Stark, *The Sense of Dissonance*, 4.

19. Indeed, scholars argue that much of the political use of the Internet during this time came in the form of "brochureware." See Foot and Schneider, *Web Campaigning*.

20. See Cornfield, *Politics Moves Online*.

21. For Dean, see Kreiss, *Taking Our Country Back*.

22. It is worth noting just how similar this system was to the one that the 2008 Obama campaign used, where comparatively lower priority contacts were steered into the online calling program.

23. Bimber, Flanagin, and Stohl, *Collective Action in Organizations*.

24. For a similar point, see Baldwin-Philippi, *Using Technology, Building Democracy*.

25. Max Fose, personal communication, February 22, 2013.

26. The McCain campaign also built in organizational and technical checks on its volunteer base to protect against malfeasance.

27. Even before Internet-driven volunteerism and fundraising could occur, a number of legal questions needed to be resolved or negotiated, which McCain, Bush, and Dean's staffers all cited.

28. This is a common sentiment, particularly in progressive circles. Historically, the existence of the McCain 2000 and Bush 2004 bids suggests that digital innovations in campaigning and emphases on participatory politics are not limited to Democrats.

29. See, for instance, Lempert and Silverstein, *Creatures of Politics*.

30. Although with the important caution that, as political scientist Bruce Bimber argued, it is unclear how much of this is new money that would not have been given otherwise through traditional means such as phone calls or direct mail; Bimber, *Information and American Democracy*.

31. Max Fose, personal communication, February 22, 2013.

32. The literature on campaign effects is too vast to summarize, but for the electoral dimension, see Hillygus, "Campaign Effects and the Dynamics."

33. For the history here, see Nielsen, *Ground Wars*.

34. Michael Turk, personal communication, January 22, 2013.

35. See Hersh, *Hacking the Electorate*, 152: "In a confidential memo that I obtained that assessed dozens of commercial models like these, it was reported that the following variables contain nearly all of the predictive power in all targeting models: vote history, party registration, gender, age, geography, race, marital status, presence of children, Census measures (like percent urban, percent black), and precinct data."

36. The Democrats' system was implemented nationwide for the 2006 cycle.

37. Rich Beeson, personal communication, October 24, 2012.

38. Nielsen, *Ground Wars*, 45–46.

39. Ibid., 49–51.

40. See ibid.; Gerber and Green, "The Effects of Canvassing, Telephone Calls, and Direct Mail on Voter Turnout."

41. Brent McGoldrick, personal communication, January 23, 2014.

42. DeFeo, "LinkedIn Profile." https://www.linkedin.com/in/chuckdefeo.

43. DeFeo subsequently worked in a number of conservative media positions before becoming president and CEO of the merged Campaign Solutions and Connell Donatelli in June 2009, and the Republican National Committee deputy chief of staff and chief digital officer in September 2013, where he joined Andy Barkett, the chief technology officer (formerly of Facebook), to revamp the party's digital operations and data infrastructure.

44. Chuck DeFeo, personal communication, January 18, 2013.

45. See Kreiss, *Taking Our Country Back*.

46. Chuck DeFeo, personal communication, January 18, 2013.

47. Patrick Ruffini, personal communication, January 15, 2013.

48. See Edward Walker, *Grassroots for Hire*.

49. Rich Beeson, personal communication, October 24, 2013.

50. Michael Turk, personal communication, January 22, 2013. For details on the predictive modeling of the time, see Nielsen, *Ground Wars*, 140–142, and Issenberg, *The Victory Lab*.

51. Chuck DeFeo, personal communication, January 18, 2013.

52. Bimber, Flanagin, and Stohl have identified this in the context of the contemporary responses of civil society organizations to changes in media structure in *Collective Action in Organizations*.

53. Michael Turk, personal communication, January 22, 2013.

54. See Pearlman, *Margin of Victory*, 156. DeFeo argued that on the Republican side of the aisle it was unique for a campaign to run its own political effort instead of the party.

55. This is common in organizing circles across the movement, civil society, and nonprofit sectors as well. See Han, *How Organizations Develop Activists*.

56. See Anderson and Kreiss, "Black Boxes as Capacities."

57. For details on all of these things, see Kreiss, *Taking Our Country Back*.

58. For an account of the Obama campaign, see McKenna and Han, *Groundbreakers*. For a defense of this on normative grounds of an ethics of partisanship, see Rosenblum, *On the*

Side of Angels. For a lovely reading on the normative value of electoral politics, see Hart, *Campaign Talk.*

59. Chuck DeFeo, personal communication, January 18, 2013.
60. For an expansive discussion of ACT, see Nielsen, *Ground Wars.*
61. Ibid.
62. Michael Beach, personal communication, January 23, 2014.

Chapter 3

1. See Geraghty, "Who's Left on Team McCain"; Jacoby, "Firms Tied to Campaign Manager"; Calmes, "McCain Manager Roils Campaign."
2. Martin, "McCain's Comeback Plan."
3. See Calmes, "McCain Manager Roils Campaign."
4. Ibid.
5. Jacoby, "Firms Tied to Campaign Manager."
6. For the history of the Democratic Party and Blue State Digital, see Kreiss, *Taking Our Country Back.* One of the advantages of the Obama campaign during the cycle vis-à-vis Hillary Clinton's primary bid was a technical infrastructure that was in place to capture the extraordinary energy and enthusiasm around the candidate and translate it into electoral resources: money and volunteers. The Clinton campaign in 2008 did not make comparable investments early in the race. For a broader argument that the enthusiasm for candidates drives online mobilization, see Vaccari, "Technology Is a Commodity."
7. See Denis and Pontille, "Material Ordering and the Care of Things"; Jackson, "Rethinking Repair"; Mol, Moser, and Pols, *Care in Practice.*
8. A particularly nice illustration of the cultural diversity within the Democratic Party comes in the context of a recent body of work on party asymmetry. See Grossmann and Hopkins, "Ideological Republicans and Group Interest Democrats."
9. Michael Turk, personal communication, January 22, 2013.
10. http://www.p2012.org/candidates/romneyorg. See also Alter, *The Center Holds.*
11. Michael Turk, personal communication, January 22, 2013.
12. In contrast with the Democratic Party under Dean, who made large-scale investments in both digital and field.
13. Michael Turk, personal communication, January 22, 2013.
14. Matt Lira, personal communication, February 13, 2014.
15. Ibid.
16. On the distinction between "push" and "pull" media, see Nielsen, *Ground Wars*; Vaccari, *Digital Politics in Western Democracies.* On the realization that supporters were most likely to be visiting campaigns' web properties and engaged online, see Bimber, *Information and American Democracy*; Bimber and Davis, *Campaigning Online.*
17. http://mittromneyroadtothewhitehouse.blogspot.com/2007/08/create-your-own-romney-ad-contest.html.
18. Cyrus Krohn, personal communication, February 8, 2013.
19. Ibid.
20. Steiner passed away in 2013. Livingston, "Republicans Mourn Operatives."
21. Cyrus Krohn, personal communication, February 8, 2013.
22. Proffitt, "What APIs Are and Why They're Important."
23. As my previous work demonstrated, few people used BSD's PartyBuilder developed for the DNC either—it took the massive mobilization around *candidate* Obama to drive use of the My.BarackObama.com platform.
24. Cyrus Krohn, personal communication, February 8, 2013.
25. See Issenberg, "Behavioral Science Remaking Politics"; and Medvetz's work on think tanks at the edges of fields; Medvetz, *Think Tanks in America.*
26. In many ways, the fact that the Democratic Party was able to put together an extensive hybrid network ecosystem recalls Jo Freeman's classic argument that the Democratic

Party is made up of constituencies that organize their members with power flowing upward into the party, while the Republican Party is primarily made up of ideological factions and power flows downward; "The Political Culture of the Democratic and Republican Parties." See also Grossmann and Hopkins, "Ideological Republicans and Group Interest Democrats."

27. For collective invention, see Powell and Giannella, "Collective Invention and Inventor Networks." For the composition of the Democratic Party, see Grossmann and Hopkins, "Ideological Republicans and Group Interest Democrats"; Harris and Bailey, *Democratic Party: Documents Decoded.*

28. Chuck DeFeo, personal communication, January 18, 2013.

29. Patrick Ruffini, personal communication, January 15, 2013.

30. Mindy Finn went on to found two ventures in 2014 and 2015, too late to be included in the data set: Misschief Media and Empowered Women. Patrick Ruffini founded Echelon Insights with Republican pollster Kristen Soltis Anderson in 2014, a firm dedicated to providing better opinion data—also too late to be included in the data set here (the firm data is current through May 2014).

31. Brent McGoldrick, personal communication, January 23, 2014.

32. There are some discrepancies about the year of this merger being in 2004 or 2005. I am using 2005 based on when Donatelli lists becoming president on her LinkedIn profile page. https://www.linkedin.com/pub/rebecca-becki-black-donatelli/4/125/209.

33. The Wikipedia entry for Connell compiles a list of resources about his death and work during the 2004 election cycle. https://en.wikipedia.org/wiki/Michael_Connell.

34. Chuck DeFeo, personal communication, January 18, 2013.

35. Karpf, "Moments Reconsidered."

36. Indeed, even heading into the 2016 campaign cycle, on the Democratic side of the aisle there was concern about the number of staffers with specialized expertise that presidential and Senate campaigns would have access to. See Delany, "A Dearth of Digital Staff in 2016?" For concerns on the right about staffers, see Schultheis, "Democrats' Secret Staffing Advantage."

37. http://www.democraticunderground.com/discuss/duboard.php?az=view_all&address=132x2797786.

38. Max Fose, personal communication, February 22, 2013.

39. Former Republican Party staffer, personal communication, not for attribution.

40. Ibid.

41. See Kreiss, *Taking Our Country Back.*

42. For details on this arrangement, see Kreiss, *Taking Our Country Back,* 129.

43. See Bradley, "Final Fundraising Figure."

44. Cyrus Krohn, personal communication, February 8, 2013.

45. See, for instance, Willis, "Why Democrats Still Lead Republicans."

46. Contemporary data on social media users who are politically engaged looks less skewed. For data on social media at the time this book went to press, see Duggan et al., "Demographics of Key Social Networking Platforms." For uses of Facebook in 2008, see Vitak et al., "It's Complicated." Bruce Bimber provides a useful run-down of how the demographics (age and race) and media use of Obama supporters in 2012 favored the candidate taking up digital media for mobilizational purposes, and suggests a "generational bias" in terms of digital media uptake by campaigns; "Digital Media in the Obama Campaigns." That said, this view does not take into account the differences between audiences across different platforms (such as Twitter being a site where candidates seek primarily to influence journalists). Neither does it take into account the previous campaign experiences of candidates that shape the way they structure, staff, and run their campaigns; see Popkin, *The Candidate.* And, the idea that demographics of supporters is destiny in terms of the uptake of digital media also fails to account for how campaign strategies are crafted by practitioners. The data set clearly reveals broad differences between candidates on the same and

different sides of the aisle in terms of their uptake of technology and digital media, even when they are competing over voters with similar demographics. As the following chapters reveal, the candidate's position in the field, and staffers' perceptions of it as well as what is electorally efficacious, in addition to the media context, also need to be considered. These perceptions are conditioned by the historical workings of party networks, as are the available staffers and resources that campaigns have to draw on for their digital operations. "Ron Paul's 2008 run is interesting because the campaign was highly innovative and the origin of the Internet "money bomb," yet according to the data set only one firm, Justine B. Lam Consulting, was directly founded by a staffer after the bid (and it specialized in commercial services). There are a number of potential explanations for why there were not more firms coming out of the Paul campaign and why it did not become a prototype for the party. First, that because there was little urgency in the Republican Party network after 2008 Paul's run never became a prototype for the party network and there were few new market opportunities for digital. Second, that ideologically Paul was libertarian and appealed to these members of the electorate and therefore Republican party network actors saw his digital mobilization as being candidate-specific and did not see the campaign as a potential model that could be adapted to different races. Alternatively, perhaps these staffers did not seek out other Republican campaigns; of the four technology staffers on the Paul campaign, only one went to work for another presidential bid, the libertarian Gary Johnson in 2012 (and this staffer, Tyler Whitney, founded Amagi Strategies after that campaign). And, oddly, the Paul 2012 campaign appears to have had no digital or Internet department, despite raising an estimated $38 million.

47. Alexander, *Performance and Power.*
48. Former Republican campaign staffer, personal communication, not for attribution.
49. See, Kreiss, *Taking Our Country Back.*
50. McKenna and Han, *Groundbreakers.*
51. This occurred in 2012 as well, according to a confidential internal memo from the Romney campaign.
52. Ryan Meerstein, personal communication, February 10, 2014.
53. Former Republican campaign staffer, personal communication, not for attribution.
54. Former Republican Party staffer, personal communication, not for attribution.
55. For a discussion, see Issenberg, *The Victory Lab*, Chapter 9.
56. Former Republican data consultant, personal communication, not for attribution.
57. McCain, "Concession Speech."
58. Alexander, *Performance and Power.*
59. Chuck DeFeo, personal communication, January 18, 2013.

Chapter 4

1. Although political scientists know little about the workings of the invisible primaries that determine general election nominees, other than that they exist.
2. Karpf, "Social Science Research Methods."
3. Doug McAdam has made the basic point that actors need to perceive that structural opportunities exist; McAdam, *Political Process.*
4. Samuelsohn, "Hillary's Nerd Squad."
5. See Perrin et al., "Cultures of the Tea Party."
6. As detailed in Kreiss and Jasinski, "The Tech Industry Meets Presidential Politics," there is no reliable data on "pass through" money, where campaigns bring in outside firms to handle technology, digital media, data, and analytics, and indirectly hire staffers who work for these consultancies (given that general FEC disbursement data says little about what that money is spent on except in terms of broad categories of services). There are advantages to bringing operations in-house, namely transparency and usability, as Issenberg notes in *The Victory Lab.*

7. For the ways that the past actions of presidents shape the future capacities of parties to act, see Galvin, *Presidential Party Building*.

8. For the literature on 2012, see Sides and Vavreck, *The Gamble*.

9. On the field side, see McKenna and Han, *Groundbreakers*. In terms of digital, see Chapter 5 of this volume.

10. For a broad overview of the campaign from a media perspective, see Kenski, Hardy, and Jamieson, *The Obama Victory*.

11. Patrick Ruffini, personal communication, January 15, 2013.

12. See Farrar-Myers and Vaughn, *Controlling the Message*; Hendricks and Schill, *Presidential Campaigning and Social Media*; Fox and Ramos, *iPolitics*; Lawrence et al., "Tweeting Conventions."

13. See Kreiss, *Taking Our Country Back*, 23.

14. For an extensive critique of the concept of fragmentation and argument that the idea of overlapping audiences better captures the new dynamics of attention, see Webster, *The Marketplace of Attention*.

15. Ironically, the appreciation of Obama's data-driven innovations with respect to computational management went largely unnoticed until the 2012 cycle by public intellectuals and the media, which focused on social media and the supposedly "grassroots" campaign (itself a hybrid form of coordination and control; see Kreiss, *Taking Our Country Back* and McKenna and Han, *Groundbreakers*).

16. Chuck DeFeo, personal communication, January 18, 2013.

17. Ibid.

18. For the history of VAN, see Kreiss, *Taking Our Country Back*.

19. See Allen and Vogel, "Inside the Koch Data Mine."

20. Rebuild the Party, http://www.rebuildtheparty.com/.

21. Todd Herman, personal communication, April 2, 2013.

22. Ibid.

23. The messaging appears to have originated with a petition launched by the National Republican Congressional Committee in October 2009; see Herman, "How a Search Engine Fired Nancy Pelosi."

24. Todd Herman, personal communication, April 2, 2013.

25. Ibid. It was noted in the press as well; see Herman, "How a Search Engine Fired Nancy Pelosi," and Fiano, "RNC's Amazing Success with the Fire Pelosi Website."

26. Kuang, "The New GOP.com Socks It to Commies"; https://gop.com/.

27. Judd, "GOP.com to Roll Out Points API."

28. Todd Herman, personal communication, April 2, 2013.

29. In actuality, the power went out at a single polling place: "Voting Oddities, Irregularities across the Nation."

30. Todd Herman, personal communication, April 2, 2013.

31. Ibid.

32. See Issenberg, *The Victory Lab*.

33. Writing in Mashable in September 2010, Geoff Livingston provided a detailed look at the social media and web properties of the two parties, and argued that they had different emphases, with the GOP focus on listening and empowering local people to become "brand advocates" versus the Democratic emphasis on canvassing tools and peer-to-peer organizing. One of the things the article clearly notes at this stage is the Democratic advantage in mobile tools for canvassing; Livingston, "Social Media: The New Battleground for Politics."

34. This was widely reported. For these figures, see Cummings, "Steele's Spending Spree Angers Donors"; Elliott, "RNC Debt at $23 Million." The GOP Growth and Opportunity Project report also details the party's anemic fundraising during this time; GOP, *Growth and Opportunity Project Report*.

35. Former Republican Party staffer, personal communication, not for attribution.

36. Chuck DeFeo, personal communication, January 18, 2013. This is just a sampling of coverage about Steele, see Charen, "Go Quietly, Michael Steele."

37. Former Republican Party staffer, personal communication, not for attribution.

38. Katie Harbath, personal communication, August 27, 2013.

39. Ibid.

40. Michael Beach, personal communication, January 23, 2014.

41. For a discussion of what economists call "club goods"—a good that many can enjoy but that can be excludable—and Blue State Digital's partisan model of managing their platform in a way that Democratic-allied organizations make investments in it that benefit all members of the "club," see Kreiss, *Taking Our Country Back*, 207.

42. Kreiss, *Taking Our Country Back*.

43. This approach was also apparent in Targeted Victory's roll-out of their self-service advertising platform "Targeted Engagement" post-2012. While they have received comparatively little attention in the political communication literature, there are economic constraints on consulting firms that shape the work they do. For a look at the political economy of consulting, see Edward Walker, *Grassroots for Hire*.

44. Both VAN and BSD had early institutional investors, including the Democratic Party, that made large-scale investments in the capacities of their platforms, see Kreiss, *Taking Our Country Back*.

45. Zac Moffatt, personal communication, January 23, 2014.

46. Michael Beach, personal communication, January 23, 2014.

47. Zac Moffatt, personal communication, January 23, 2014.

48. Vega, "Campaigns Choose Email over Fancy Technology."

49. Rich Beeson, personal communication, October 24, 2012.

50. See Darr and Levendusky. "Relying on the Ground Game."

51. See Sides and Vavreck, *The Gamble*, 217–218, 221: "Overall, we estimate that Obama gained roughly an additional 248,000 votes from his field operations." Indeed, Sides and Vavreck "found some effects of field offices, but only Obama field offices," perhaps given the difference between Obama's candidate-centric organization as opposed to Romney's party-centered one. Other scholars have reached different conclusions. See Enos and Fowler, "The Surprising Parity of the 2012 Ground Game."

52. See McKenna and Han, *Groundbreakers*.

53. For a detailed breakdown, see http://elections.nytimes.com/2012/campaign-finance.

54. Source: FEC quarterly reports.

55. See, for instance, Briffault, "Super PACS."

56. This was one reason that the party enforced discipline on the states regarding their primary calendars in advance of the 2016 presidential cycle. Ironically, the party's rules (adopted in 2014), which were designed to shorten the active 2016 primary season, likely helped Donald J. Trump. This demonstrates the contingency of social outcomes, as elaborated in the conclusion.

57. Rich Beeson, personal communication, October 24, 2012.

58. For a timeline, Wikipedia offers the most comprehensive resource: https://en.wikipedia.org/wiki/Republican_Party_presidential_primaries,_2012.

59. See, for instance, Jacobs, "More Date Debate."

60. Rich Beeson, personal communication, October 24, 2012.

61. McKenna and Han, *Groundbreakers*. Some of this is likely unique to Obama as a candidate.

62. Alex Lundry, personal communication, June 25, 2013.

63. See Alter's account in *The Center Holds*, 224–225.

64. Alex Lundry, personal communication, June 25, 2013.

65. See Kreiss, "Seizing the Moment."

66. See Kreiss, *Taking Our Country Back*.

67. See Kreiss, "Seizing the Moment."

68. Caitlin Checkett, personal communication, December 16, 2013.
69. Zac Moffatt, personal communication, January 31, 2014.
70. The campaign ended up raising $183 million online in conjunction with the RNC from May through November; Willis, "Why Democrats Still Lead." By comparison, Obama raised $690 million digitally in 2012.
71. Beach, "Voters Going off the Grid."
72. See Franklin, "The Future of Journalism."
73. Zac Moffatt, personal communication, January 31, 2014.
74. Ibid. Indeed, as Sides and Vavreck suggested in *The Gamble*, sometimes broad appeals are more effective.
75. See Kreiss, "Seizing the Moment."
76. Rebecca Heisler, personal communication, February 17, 2014.
77. The choice of Drupal is interesting in light of the fact that the Dean campaign was the origin point for the US diffusion of the open source content management system. Staffers attributed great symbolism to the Dean campaign adopting open source tools (see Kreiss, *Taking Our Country Back*).
78. Caitlin Checkett, personal communication, December 16, 2013.
79. Ibid.
80. Ibid.
81. Targeted Victory was essentially the digital marketing arm of the Romney campaign, not the technical infrastructure or the in-house development team. After 2012, staffers argued that the firm grew into a technology company engaging in product development.
82. Zac Moffatt, personal communication, January 31, 2014.
83. Caitlin Checkett, personal communication, December 16, 2013.
84. For a comparison between the two, see Politi, "Did Romney Campaign Copy Obama Website?"; Miller, "Romney Campaign Appears to Copy Text from Obama Website"; https://donate.barackobama.com/page/content/quick-donate.
85. Zac Moffatt, personal communication, January 31, 2014. That said, it was clear that the Romney campaign attracted more high-dollar donor support. See Magleby, *Financing the 2012 Election.*
86. Tarrow, *Power in Movement*, 85. This is a sprawling literature. See also further refinements in McAdam, *Political Process and the Development of Black Insurgency*, and Jasper, *The Art of Moral Protest*. Scholars have generally used the idea of political opportunity structures to detail the environmental features that shape the capacities movements have to mobilize. They entail things such as the ability of actors to access the state, stability of institutional arrangements, possibilities to gain allies, and inter-elite conflict. In general, the concept describes the structural features that shape the opportunities for the mobilization of movements independent of strategic action. For a review, see Kriesi, "The Political Opportunity Structure of New Social Movements." For a recent adaptation to media, see Cammaerts, "Protest Logics and the Mediation Opportunity Structure." This idea of digital opportunity structures can also be extended to encompass the opportunities that movements and other organizations have specifically with respect to mobilizing digital action.
87. See McAdam, *Political Process and the Development of Black Insurgency,* Introduction to the 2nd edition.
88. See, for instance, Parmelee and Bichard, *Politics and the Twitter Revolution.*
89. A number of scholars have argued that there are "discursive opportunity structures," which add a cultural dimension to collective action that is implied in the discussion here. For an overview, see Kriesi, "Political Context and Opportunity." Knorr-Cetina argues that "charisma is in fact not a quality of an individual person at all but an attribution by the followers, on which it is entirely dependent"; "What is a Pipe?," 131. This makes charisma a feature of the environment given that it is premised on people's capacities to believe, but to realize it requires the successful playing of "many instruments" to reach out and touch a candidate's followers; Ibid., 135.

90. Sides and Vavreck, *The Gamble.*

91. A full breakdown of fundraising by quarter, based on FEC reports, is available here: https://en.wikipedia.org/wiki/Fundraising_for_the_2012_United_States_presidential_election.

92. Zac Moffatt, personal communication, January 31, 2014.

93. Abe Adams, personal communication, February 10, 2014.

94. Ibid.

95. Moffatt cites that the Romney campaign directed 65% of its budget to lead generation and acquisition and 35% to persuasion and mobilization. Zac Moffatt, personal communication, January 31, 2014.

96. For a narrative of the race in far more detailed terms, see Sides and Vavreck, *The Gamble.*

97. For perspectives on the invisible primary, see Aldrich, "The Invisible Primary and Its Effects on Democratic Choice."

98. Magleby, *Financing the 2012 Election.*

99. Gallagher, "How Team Obama's Tech Efficiency Left Romney IT in Dust" and "Romney Campaign Got Its IT from Best Buy, Staples, and Friends."

Chapter 5

1. See Rainie and Wellman, *Networked*; Ellison and boyd, "Sociality Through Social Network Sites"; Loader, Vromen, and Xenos, "The Networked Young Citizen"; van Dijck, *The Culture of Connectivity.*

2. See, for instance, Braun regarding contemporary news distribution, *This Program Is Brought to You By*; Webster, *The Marketplace of Attention.*

3. Scholars argue that broad changes in social structure, political culture, and political institutions eroded formal parties' control over the nomination process and the capacities of local chapters to organize, even as they made media and activists more central to the electoral process. For aspects of this story, see Wilson, *The Amateur Democrat*; Nielsen, *Ground Wars*; Schudson, *The Good Citizen*; Polsby, *Consequences of Party Reform*; Cohen et al., *The Party Decides*; Masket, *No Middle Ground.*

4. See Nielsen, *Ground Wars.*

5. Former Republican Party and campaign staffer, personal communication, not for attribution.

6. These things also help campaigns figure out how to target people. See Issenberg, *The Victory Lab*, 274–275.

7. Part of the data for this book is based on that postmortem. It is also a data source in Hersh's *Hacking the Electorate.*

8. Ethan Roeder, personal communication, January 31, 2013.

9. A common sentiment among many staffers formerly connected with the Democratic Party, its campaigns, and Organizing for America itself in both its post-2008 and post-2012 incarnations is that the organization struggled to make the transition from electoral politics to policymaking. Between 2009 and 2010 Organizing for America had a highly legislative focus in terms of advancing the president's agenda, and governing is not like campaigning. Instead of having clearly defined goals (such as electing the first black president) and clear metrics for success tied to them (such as registering and contacting voters and raising money), Organizing for America faced a much more complicated governance landscape. The perception among many former staffers was that people were not inspired or engaged by legislative-oriented tasks, and generally did not believe that they would have any actual impact on the process.

10. See Issenberg, *The Victory Lab.*

11. Michael Slaby, personal communication, September 4, 2013.

12. Ethan Roeder, personal communication, January 31, 2013.

13. Ibid. It is easy to critique the party purely from a technological standpoint, but part of the problem more generally is that the needs of infrastructure building from an information technology and data perspective are not always aligned with the political demands on parties and their chairs, or their timelines, goals, and strategies. Decisions about things such as resource investments have to be made with many competing factors in mind.

14. Slaby could not hire Whitaker because he was not actually at the DNC. It was Patrick Gaspard, then executive director of the DNC, who extended the offer.

15. Bryan Whitaker, personal communication, January 30, 2015.

16. Hersh, *Hacking the Electorate*.

17. Ibid.

18. Staffers argue that the utility of phones is changing, however, given significant drop-off in answering mobile versus landline phones (survey researchers face the same challenge).

19. For more information on Vertica, see Alexandre, "Democratic National Committee Leverages Big Data"; Cselland@vertica.com, "Disruptive Power of Big Data"; Lampitt, "The Real Story of How Big Data Analytics Helped Obama Win." In terms of Vertica after the election, BlueLabs, founded by former Obama 2012 staffers, and the Corey Booker campaign in 2013 used it for the purposes of voter modeling; Thibodeau, "Obama and Romney Big Data Experts Continue the Battle as Businesses."

20. Compton and Brown, "What's Really Happening With the Technology and Data that Helped President Obama Win."

21. For details about Project Ivy, see http://ivy.democrats.org/; Democratic Party, "Project Ivy"; Miller, "Project Ivy."

22. Bryan Whitaker, personal communication, January 30, 2015. For a discussion of Airwolf, see Issenberg, "How President Obama's Campaign Used Big Data to Rally Individual Voters." At the time this book went to press, Vertica still existed at the DNC and is the place where all the analytics modeling for the party happened. The DNC paid for Vertica to be installed on its servers. Former party staffers also stated that Vertica is where all of the Obama data is stored, as well as all the IDs from past Democratic campaigns that have gone through VoteBuilder, as well as appended data (such as commercial data). Whitaker argued that "Vertica is the most important asset at the DNC."

23. Samuelsohn, "Hillary's Nerd Squad."

24. Ethan Roeder, personal communication, January 31, 2013.

25. Campaigns typically put long-form surveys into the field that ask a range of questions about attitudes toward the candidates, likelihood to turnout, issue priorities and preferences, and happenings on the campaign trail. Campaigns also contact people who had already been contacted so as to be able to track movement in the race.

26. The campaign supplemented this quantitative data with qualitative data. The campaign ran online panels involving 150 undecided voters that refreshed every four weeks. Staffers showed news clips and other media to these panels and gauged their real-time reactions both quantitatively and qualitatively. The campaign also used focus groups to develop messaging designed to appeal to particular groups, such as women and African Americans (staffers cited the "I've got his back" advertising campaign designed for the latter group). The campaign also used focus groups to inform their communications efforts more generally, in addition to findings from their analysis of the 2008 campaign after the race, where staffers learned that people do not talk about policy and remembered images of Obama and his girls from that campaign. The 2012 campaign even conducted interviews with people while they were in their living rooms watching television.

27. This contradicts what political scientists Sides and Vavreck found, see *The Gamble*.

28. See Issenberg, "How Obama Used Big Data to Rally Voters."

29. See Sides and Vavreck, *The Gamble*, and "Obama's Not-So-Big Data." As these authors note, along with Eitan Hersh in *Hacking the Electorate*, there are also risks in targeting given that campaigns and parties often have to probabilistically guess key categories of information such as race and religion.

30. As Hersh notes, these things may have limited utility outside the context of the Obama campaign given limitations in how widely things such as 500,000-person field trials can be taken up by comparatively less resourced campaigns and uncertainty over whether findings will be applicable in the future. See *Hacking the Electorate*, 151–152.

31. Bryan Whitaker, personal communication, January 30, 2015.

32. The campaign had three formal deputy campaign managers in addition to Slaby (who served de facto in this role) reporting directly to Messina.

33. Michael Slaby, personal communication, September 4, 2013. The idea of "product managers" seemingly appeared for the first time during this campaign cycle.

34. Ibid.

35. Michael Slaby, personal communication, September 4, 2013.

36. See Lee Vinsel, "How to Give Up the I-Word Parts 1 and 2."

37. See de Vaan, Stark, and Vedres, "Game Changer," on cognitive diversity. For the culture of engineers in the technology sector more broadly, see Neff, *Venture Labor*; Turner, "Burning Man at Google."

38. Former Obama 2012 campaign staffer, personal communication, not for attribution.

39. Ibid.

40. Irwin, Neil. "Why a Presidential Campaign Is the Ultimate Start-Up."

41. For what this "in-sourcing" strategy of the Obama campaign was able to accomplish, see Gallagher, "How Team Obama's Tech Efficiency Left Romney IT in Dust." Gallagher also discusses the open source tools the campaign used, the licenses it purchased, and the use of Amazon's cloud services for the applications it built in-house.

42. Ibid.

43. Michael Slaby, personal communication, September 4, 2013.

44. The campaign developed tricks just to identify where people were currently living, such as sign-ups for free bumper stickers. Indeed, the campaign routinely used bumper stickers and yard signs, long of questionable value in terms of persuasion or electoral outcomes more generally, primarily as a way to enrich the database. These giveaways also furthered the match rate across different databases by generating current information.

45. As Whitaker noted, "this is why Vertica was so important. It took updates from NGP VAN, from both MyVoters and MyCampaign, and created the national database on the back end." Bryan Whitaker, personal communication, January 30, 2015.

46. Carol Davidsen, personal communication, June 12, 2013.

47. I witnessed this firsthand as a precinct captain in 2008.

48. Davidsen argued that this is an issue as common in the cable industry as in politics. Carol Davidsen, personal communication, June 12, 2013.

49. Davidsen stated that the team working on Narwhal consisted of five engineers in November 2011 (two working on the API, two on integration, and one person on the people matching algorithm). The Narwhal integration team never grew to more than three people, and the whole team was never more than eight people (which included people working on single sign-on identity and payment processing).

50. Carol Davidsen, personal communication, June 12, 2013.

51. Staffers argued that "Narwhal" actually underwent a few different conceptualizations, and the campaign ultimately abandoned the name altogether to solve problems of cross-departmental coordination and data integration.

52. Former Obama 2012 campaign staffer, personal communication, not for attribution.

53. Firms have long had unique IDs for their platforms. Whitaker cited that NGP and VAN had unique IDs, with VANID being around since the beginning of VAN. In 2013, NGP and VAN, after their merger, created a common ActionID across their two systems. Bryan Whitaker, personal communication, January 30, 2015.

54. For the data collected through canvassing, see Whitaker, "Obamamania."

55. Carol Davidsen, personal communication, June 12, 2013.

56. Ibid. Another former Obama 2012 staffer also noted that almost all of the people who came up with messaging were white men: "part of the reason we need so much message effectiveness testing is because we do not have a diverse group of people coming up with the messaging, despite the messaging being diverse." Former Obama 2012 campaign staffer, personal communication, not for attribution.

57. For a discussion of First Amendment issues in the context of campaign data and political privacy, see Rubinstein, "Voter Privacy in the Age of Big Data."

58. See Bimber, Flanagin, and Stohl, *Collective Action in Organizations*.

59. Michael Slaby, personal communication, May 16, 2013.

60. Teddy Goff, personal communication, September 17, 2013.

61. See Rainie and Wellman, *Networked*.

62. Michael Slaby, personal communication, September 4, 2013.

63. Ibid.

64. Former Obama 2012 campaign staffer, personal communication, not for attribution.

65. Former Obama 2012 state campaign staffer, personal communication, not for attribution.

66. Former Obama 2012 campaign staffer, personal contribution, not for attribution.

67. Michael Slaby, personal communication, September 4, 2013.

68. As a product, Dashboard was designed with super-volunteers in mind, not the broader pool of less engaged supporters. Indeed, staffers involved in the project stated that they regretted not designing Dashboard more explicitly to facilitate moving less engaged supporters up what practitioners call the "ladder of engagement" in organizing circles, spurring them into being more active rather than just designing for the people who were already fully committed the really active people.

69. See this very point in Bimber, Flanagin, and Stohl, *Collective Action in Organizations*. For precisely this environmental view of media as context or infrastructure, see Peters, *The Marvelous Clouds*.

70. See Judd, "Obama's Targeted GOTV." There was a similar phenomenon in 2008. See Issenberg, *The Victory Lab*, 283.

71. Ethan Roeder, personal communication, January 31, 2013.

72. Ibid.

73. Teddy Goff, personal communication, September 17, 2013.

74. Ibid.

75. As I have argued previously, it is likely that a number of factors influenced these organizational decisions; Kreiss, "Seizing the Moment." For one, Messina clearly made a choice to value an autonomous and independent digital department (which there appears to be a greater valuation of on the Democratic side of the aisle). For another, given that Goff worked on the 2008 bid and was coming to the campaign from one of the most prominent firms in the business, there was likely a significant degree of trust in his work among the leadership. Goff argued that with autonomy comes the responsibility to know what is "on" or "off" message. Teddy Goff, personal communication, September 17, 2013.

76. Ibid.

77. Ethan Roeder, personal communication, January 31, 2013. For Roeder's op-ed, see "I Am Not Big Brother."

78. For discussions of this "personal" story, see Alexander, *The Performance of Politics*; McKenna and Han, *Groundbreakers*.

79. See Nielsen, *Ground Wars*, on exactly this point.

80. Teddy Goff, personal communication, September 17, 2013.

81. Ibid.

82. Ibid.

83. The campaign had "digital field updates" at the beginning of the cycle, a program that was particularly important early on before state-level staffers were in place. The team in Chicago provided prewritten Twitter and Facebook as well as other content for all of the state social network accounts, including videos, graphics, and microsites, as well as

content from the White House. Interns and volunteers in the states copied and pasted this content to the state social media accounts. Numerous former state-level staffers argued that this content helped educate these state-level volunteers as to what good content looks like (and these volunteers and interns often became state digital staffers later in the campaign).

84. Former Obama 2012 state digital staffer, personal communication, not for attribution.

85. Ibid.

86. See Reed, "Performative Power"; Kreiss, "Seizing the Moment."

87. Former Obama 2012 state digital staffer, personal communication, not for attribution.

88. Ibid.

89. Ibid.

90. Former staffers cited that there were a number of legal concerns around electioneering in the weeks before Election Day that required a more extensive level of vetting by the legal team.

91. Former Obama 2012 state digital staffer, personal communication, not for attribution.

92. See Kreiss, "Seizing the Moment."

93. In late November 2014, Facebook changed its terms of service, which effectively precluded the possibility for targeted social sharing; Ward, "Facebook Shutting Down a Key Path."

94. Teddy Goff, personal communication, September 17, 2013.

95. Katz, "The Two-Step Flow of Communication."

96. Teddy Goff, personal communication, September 17, 2013.

97. See Judd, "How Obama for America Made its Facebook Friends into Effective Advocates."

98. Ibid.

99. Ibid.

100. See, for instance, Scherer, "Friended."

101. See Ward, "Facebook Shutting Down a Key Path."

102. Michael Slaby, personal communication, September 4, 2013.

103. Both Stuart Stevens, a senior advisor to the campaign, and Matt Rhoades, the campaign manager, came to the campaign with backgrounds in communications. For the campaign's expenditures on media and digital, see Eggen and Hamburger, "Private Consultants See Huge Election Profits."

104. Although it is also clear that the Romney campaign paid its staffers comparatively more. See Eggen and Hamburger, "Private Consultants See Huge Election Profits"; and Sullivan, "The 2012 Election—By Pay."

105. Brent McGoldrick, personal communication, January 23, 2014.

106. See Sides and Vavreck, The Gamble.

107. For the Obama campaign organization, see http://www.p2012.org/candidates/obamaorg.html.

108. Over time, this evolved into Lundry and McGoldrick working closely with Newhouse and his team given how important the polling data was. In addition to the routine production of these reports, this group also used TargetPoint's "National Dialogue Monitor," a form of cross-platform content analysis designed to measure the effectiveness of campaign frames and messages, which also included some field experiments that measured the effects of various interventions (such as a new advertising campaign). For a description, see Issenberg, "How the Obama Team Used Big Data to Rally Voters."

109. Alex Lundry, personal communication, June 25, 2013.

110. Former Romney 2012 campaign staffer, personal communication, not for attribution.

111. Brent McGoldrick, personal communication, January 23, 2014.

112. See Sides and Vavreck, The Gamble, for the dynamics of the race.

113. Former Romney 2012 campaign staffer, personal communication, not for attribution.

114. Ibid.

115. John Sides and Lynn Vavreck present extensive data that suggest this was not the case; *The Gamble*. These sentences present the perceptions of practitioners.

116. Political scientists are exceedingly skeptical about the effectiveness of this—in addition to events such as Romney's 47% comments having a significant effect on the election given the structural factors in place that largely predicted the outcome. See also Obama staffers' statements on the fundamental stability of the race; Sides and Vavreck, *The Gamble*, 175.

117. For a review, see Sides and Vavreck, *The Gamble*.

118. As a former Obama staffer noted, the CMAG data is incomplete in lacking information about local cable spot insertions. Former staffers cited that the Obama campaign moved a significant amount of its advertising spend to local cable, so the Romney campaign would not have seen that if they were just looking at CMAG data. Former Obama 2012 campaign staffer, personal communication, not for attribution.

119. Indeed, Sides and Vavreck note this general pattern in their exegesis of the 2012 Republican primaries, but do not consider the *internal* organizational consequences of this dynamic. For one, it left the campaign with little in the way of resources or time to put together things such as an extensive field campaign. See Sides and Vavreck's analysis of the Obama field operation on pp. 216–222 in *The Gamble*. They also argue that it was Romney's large ad blitz in the days before the election that likely was more effective than the early advertising of the Obama campaign.

120. Zac Moffatt, personal communication, January 31, 2014.

121. Ibid.

122. I have not been able to independently confirm this number. Indeed, Lundry and McGoldrick themselves do not appear in FEC reports, and the word "analytics" does not appear in the Democracy in Action dataset for the Romney campaign.

123. Zac Moffatt, personal communication, January 31, 2014.

124. Ibid.

125. Field programs generate massive amounts of data.

126. There are fewer digital staffers actually listed on payroll in the FEC data. Using FEC data, we found 87 total staffers in technology, digital, data, and analytics on the campaign. I report the campaign's more expansive numbers here given they are likely to be estimates of people working on the campaign who were paid through consultancies and who do not appear in the FEC data.

127. A common explanation for the differences between the two parties is the fact that more Silicon Valley workers are Democrats. While this may be true (although we lack solid data), it is also clear that there are plenty of conservatives (and libertarians) in the technology industry. Given the comparatively small number of people who work in technology in politics compared to the far larger technology industry, and the fact that there are a number of examples of technology-forward Republican campaigns, it is likely there are other explanations for the differences between the two parties (such as their histories, different recruiting patterns, and different valuations of organizational autonomy for technology staffers).

128. See Roeder, "Who Are the Campaigners in America?"; Sullivan, "The 2012 Election—By Pay."

129. Former Republican Party staffer, personal communication, not for attribution. See Gallagher, "How Team Obama's Tech Efficiency Left Romney IT in Dust." Gallagher's analysis revealed that the Obama campaign's highest-paid staff member was Slaby, at an annualized salary of $130,000. Romney's staffers were paid considerably more, with Moffatt making approximately $175,000.

130. Staffers on both sides of the aisle, however, argued that there is never enough talent with respect to specialized programming, data, and analytics skills.

131. Aaron Ginn, personal communication, December 8, 2012.

132. Zac Moffatt, personal communication, January 31, 2014.

133. Rutenberg and Zeleny, "Republican Officials End Relationship with Adviser Tied to Ad Proposal"; Strategic Perception, Inc., *The Defeat of Barack Hussein Obama*.

134. Zac Moffatt, personal communication, January 31, 2014. Moffatt cited that 200,000 people downloaded the app in the first 48 hours.

135. Kreiss, "Seizing the Moment."

136. Ibid.

137. Ibid.

138. Zac Moffatt, personal communication, January 31, 2014.

139. Ibid.

140. Aaron Ginn, personal communication, December 8, 2012.

141. Fundraising picked up considerably, $140 million from April through July, after Romney became the presumptive nominee. This fundraising was through Romney Victory (a joint fundraising committee between the campaign, the RNC, and several state parties). See Vogel, "Romney Victory Fund Pulls in $140M."

142. For an overview of the campaign funding dynamics at this point, see Cline, "Obama Outraises, Outmaneuvers Romney."

143. Sides and Vavreck, *The Gamble*.

144. At the same time, practitioners argued that 527 ads can damage candidates, even if the campaign had nothing to do with them. Practitioners cite the Jeremiah Wright advertising proposal detailed earlier as one example.

145. Rich Beeson, personal communication, October 24, 2012.

146. The Romney team did make significantly more voter contacts than the 2008 McCain campaign. According to internal Romney campaign documents, the Republican field effort in 2012 outstripped that of 2008 and experienced some gains over Democrats with respect to the absentee and early vote numbers.

147. Rich Beeson, personal communication, October 24, 2012.

148. See Bump, "A State-By-State Look at the Record Black Turnout in 2012."

149. Obama's more expansive field campaign made a difference boosting turnout. Sides and Vavreck cited that it likely held Florida for Obama; *The Gamble*, 221.

150. Issenberg, "How the Obama Team Used Big Data to Rally Voters."

151. Sides and Vavreck, "Obama's Not-So-Big Data."

152. Ibid.

153. Michael Slaby, personal communication, September 4, 2013.

154. See Denton, *The 2012 Presidential Campaign*.

155. David Simas, personal communication, September 22, 2012.

156. Former Obama 2012 campaign staffer, personal communication, not for attribution.

157. This is striking given that former staffers argued that the political team met with their digital colleagues every day to talk about how they could coordinate efforts on things such as absentee ballots, early votes, GOTV, and voter identification. The campaign had a strategy call every morning with everyone on it, and then a senior staff meeting with participants from all the departments. Beeson and Moffatt cited that they would regularly meet after, although their offices were also right next to each other, so they would see each other multiple times a day.

158. Abe Adams, personal communication, February 10, 2014.

Chapter 6

1. Pollak, "Inside ORCA."

2. Poniewozik, "Election Watch."

3. In the digital age, often the collective debate about a candidate or party's failures unfolds across social media, digital publishing outlets, and legacy media.

4. GOP, *Growth and Opportunity Project Report*, 26–28.

5. For local detail and color regarding the work of the cave, see Alter, *The Center Holds*, 98–110.
6. GOP, *Growth and Opportunity Project Report*, 24.
7. Ibid.
8. In January 2015, Reda founded Republic Computer Science, a Republican firm specializing in software engineering. The firm developed Republic VX, a campaign field CRM; see Crichton, "Republic Launches New Platform to Send GOP to the White House."
9. Azarias Reda, personal communication, August 21, 2014.
10. Ibid.
11. Ibid.
12. See Kreiss, *Taking Our Country Back*, 107.
13. Weinstein, "The GOP Just Named."
14. Practitioners argued that the 2013–2014 team at the RNC built an API that applications such as Targeted Victory's Targeted GOTV are built on.
15. While Harris had also worked as a blogger for the Huckabee campaign during the 2008 cycle, and served as the digital director for Perry and Gingrich during 2012, it was the Cruz campaign that made his reputation.
16. Sullivan, "The Biggest Upset of 2012."
17. Friess, "The Man Who Invented the Republican Internet."
18. Mike Duncan, personal communication, November 13, 2014.
19. Former Republican 2014 campaign staffer, personal communication, not for attribution.
20. Mike Duncan, personal communication, November 13, 2014.
21. Other sources cite similar ranges; see Delany, "Facebook Advertising for Politics & Advocacy."
22. Mike Duncan, personal communication, November 13, 2014.
23. For an overview of voter file matching, see Delany, "Voter File Digital Ad Targeting."
24. Matt Oczkowski, personal communication, January 22, 2015.
25. Ibid.
26. It is standard, however, for the party to require that campaigns sign a list exchange agreement and provide voter IDs and database enhancements (including hygiene and matches) back to the party.
27. Ibid.
28. See, for instance, Gold, "Koch Network Strikes New Deal," about a data-sharing partnership, involving non-strategic data, between Data Trust and i360, and the development of a new RNC app in response to the threat from i360; Issenberg, "The RNC Hopes This App Will Keep Campaigners from Going All in with the Koch Brothers."
29. Former Republican Party staffer, personal communication, not for attribution.
30. Carol Davidsen, personal communication, June 12, 2013.
31. Former Obama 2012 campaign staffer, personal communication, not for attribution.
32. This debt was on the order of $21 million for the party (with $4.3 million cash on hand) at the start of 2013. The campaign was $5.8 million in debt (with the party having $3.3 million cash on hand). See Blumenthal, "DNC Debt Totals $21 Million."
33. Former Obama 2012 campaign staffer, personal communication, not for attribution.
34. See NGP VAN Next at http://next.ngpvan.com/.
35. Michael Slaby, personal communication, May 16, 2013.
36. Carol Davidsen, personal communication, June 12, 2013.
37. The trade-off was that Organizing for America, housed within the DNC, could not criticize Democrats.
38. Former Obama 2012 and Democratic 2014 campaign staffer, personal communication, not for attribution.
39. Ibid.
40. See the Democratic Victory Task Force: http://thehill.com/sites/default/files/democratic_victory_task_force_preliminary_findings.pdf.

41. Leichtman, "What Happened to Project Ivy?"
42. State parties inherited all the data at the state level on Obama volunteers after the 2008 and 2012 cycles. Meanwhile, after 2012 Obama was not going to be on the ballot again, so Obama for America's MyCampaign data hosted in VAN became an asset for the party. This did not extend to donor data or the full email list, but it did feature volunteers' emails.
43. Former Democratic Party staffer, personal communication, not for attribution.
44. While we do not have the empirical data yet, I suspect that technology, digital, data, and analytics will remain at best unevenly professionalized given the need for up-to-date skills and expertise in the face of ongoing changes in technology and media. I anticipate that these areas will continue to become increasingly specialized domains of political practice, and be continually refreshed by people from industry contexts given technological change.
45. For more about Civis Analytics's work during the cycle, and how that intersected with the party's Bannock Street Project, a data and analytics-based voter registration and mobilization effort, see Parker, "Democrats Aim for a 2014 More like 2012 and 2008."
46. Teddy Goff, personal communication, September 17, 2013.
47. Bryan Whitaker, personal communication, January 30, 2015.
48. Applications for API keys are online at developers.ngpvan.com.
49. Former Democratic 2014 campaign staffer, personal communication, not for attribution.
50. Bryan Whitaker, personal communication, January 30, 2015.
51. Former Obama 2012 campaign and Democratic 2014 campaign staffer, personal communication, not for attribution.
52. Ibid.
53. Former Democratic Party staffer, personal communication, not for attribution.
54. Former Obama 2012 campaign and Democratic 2014 campaign staffer, personal communication, not for attribution.
55. Ibid.
56. For a discussion of authenticity in performative terms in the context of politics, see Alexander, *The Performance of Politics.*
57. Former Obama staffers also characterized emails by organizations such as the Democratic Congressional Campaign Committee in this way, which often drew their ire during interviews.
58. For the origins of this practice on the Dean and then its migration to the Obama campaigns through the work of Joe Rospars, see Kreiss, *Taking Our Country Back.*
59. Former Obama 2012 campaign and Democratic 2014 campaign staffer, personal communication, not for attribution.
60. Ibid.
61. Kreiss, "Seizing the Moment."
62. Former Democratic 2014 campaign staffer, personal communication, not for attribution.
63. See Webster, *The Marketplace of Attention.*
64. This was also part of the discourse at RootsCamp after the 2012 election among digital staffers, suggesting both that a lack of autonomy is a broad phenomenon and that it is a widespread aspiration.
65. Former Obama 2012 campaign and Democratic 2014 campaign staffer, personal communication, not for attribution.
66. Ibid.
67. For an argument about specialization, see Negrine and Lilleker, "Professionalization of What?"
68. Former Obama 2012 campaign and Democratic 2014 campaign staffer, personal communication, not for attribution.
69. This is also where Democrats have an advantage in possessing infrastructural resources such as M+R Consulting's Progressive Exchange listserv, where progressive digital staffers gather to share resources, best practices, seek help, and discuss things they are observing.

70. Former Democratic 2014 campaign staffer, personal communication, not for attribution.
71. Former Obama 2012 campaign and Democratic 2014 campaign staffer, personal communication, not for attribution.
72. To do all of this, digital advertising requires a constant stream of content, which staffers cite as an ongoing challenge. That said, producing this content is partly a question of resource allocation. Staffers across all of these campaigns discussed how the majority of budgets were dedicated to television advertising, throughout much of the campaign, and then they received windfalls in the final days before the election, when campaigns could not buy any more television and had money left over for digital.
73. Former Obama 2012 campaign and Democratic 2014 campaign staffer, personal communication, not for attribution.
74. For push versus pull media, see Nielsen and Vaccari, "Do People 'Like' Politicians on Facebook?"; Webster, *The Marketplace of Attention.*
75. For a description, see https://www.facebook.com/help/341425252616329. Campaigns can also create custom audiences based on visitors to their websites. https://www.facebook.com/help/449542958510885.

Chapter 7

1. See, for instance, reporting about Super PACs during the early stages of the 2016 presidential election: Willis, "Super PACs Are Gobbling Up Even More Power" and Rutenberg, "Then Next Era of Campaign-Finance Craziness Is Already Underway." For Ready for Hillary's efforts in the run-up to the cycle around data, see Mattingly, "Inside the First Super-PAC Dedicated to Collecting Data All about You."
2. Confessore, "Koch Brother's Budget of $889 Million for 2016 Is on Par with Both Parties' Spending."
3. See Stan, "How the Presidential Primary Is a Proxy War" and Ward, "The Koch Brothers and the Republican Party Go to War."
4. Ibid.
5. Gabriel, "'Super PACs' Take on New Role, Organizing Voters"; Gold, "It's Bold, But Legal."
6. Kaye, "Jeb Bush's Super PAC Has Spent over Half a Million on Data."
7. Blumler and Kavanagh, "The Third Age of Political Communication."
8. Ibid., 225.
9. Ridout and Franz, *The Persuasive Power of Campaign Advertising.*
10. Howard, *New Media Campaigns and the Managed Citizen.*
11. Nielsen, *Ground Wars.*
12. Baldwin-Philippi, *Using Technology, Building Democracy.*
13. Galvin, "Presidential Party Building."
14. DiMaggio, "Culture and Cognition."
15. See Law, "Technology and Heterogeneous Engineering."
16. Hughes, *Networks of Power,* 2.
17. See, for instance, http://www.smartvandata.com/about. For an overview, see Issenberg, "For Sale: Detailed Voter Profiles." An important point is that data generated by these organizations in the extended party network in the course of their voter contacts does not flow back into the national or state party databases in real time, which practitioners in both parties said their lawyers stated would be illegal in violating FEC rules around coordination. The parties and the 501(c)4s can engage in swaps, however. Swapping involves providing a static picture of voter contacts that have been conducted, a bulk file that reveals only that an entity talked to a group of people at a point in time (but does not reveal the real-time voter contact actions of these organizations).
18. Atkins, "An Explanation of What Bernie Sanders Staffers Actually Did."

19. See Lessig, "The Sanders Complaint."
20. Bender, Epstein, and Harris, "Sanders Wins Back DNC Data Access."
21. On obligatory passage points, see Callon, "Elements of a Sociology of Translation."
22. California does not use the national party system, using instead a voter file technology provided by Political Data Inc. called MOE (Mobilize, Organize, Elect). See California Democratic Party, "Introduction to MOE."
23. For more details, see Kreiss *Taking Our Country Back*, Chapter 4.
24. Temple, "MDP Voter File Access Questions." See also Kreiss, "Back Into the Breach". The national Democratic Party determines access to VoteBuilder for presidential candidates, while state parties do so for state-level candidates (and the Democratic Senatorial Campaign Committee and the Democratic Congressional Campaign Committee manages access for Senate and House campaigns, respectively). For example, the Pennsylvania Democratic Party states: "Campaign access to Pennsylvania VoteBuilder (and the registered voters per specific district) is regulated by the Pennsylvania Democratic Party. To be a permitted user, a political committee or candidate must: Be for the benefit of the Democratic Party and/ or Democratic political committees (endorsement rules may apply for certain counties for local/county races); Be authorized to use VoteBuilder by the Pennsylvania Democratic Party and/or Democratic County Committees; Sign a VoteBuilder usage agreement; Pay the required fees." Pennsylvania Democratic Party, "What Can VoteBuilder do for You."
25. Hendler, "Why the Bernie Breach isn't About Technology."
26. See Rosenblum, *On the Side of Angels*; Cohen et al., *The Party Decides*. Roller, "The Democrats' Database Fight."
27. Although, journalistic reports suggest that there was more collaboration in the latter half of 2015, and the RNC's data reportedly was made accessible through i360's platform and the entities developed list-swap agreements. That said, practitioners suggested that a reliance on swaps means less dynamic modeling. See Kaye, "Democrats' Data Breach"; Gold, "Koch Network Strikes New Deal"; Halper, "Republicans Lag Behind on Voter Information."
28. Indeed, this threat suggests another motivation for the RNC to invest heavily in back-end data infrastructure. For an overview of where the party was in 2015, see Fidelman, "Republicans Launch Game Changing Data Center."
29. Adler, "How a Tiny GOP Data Firm Helped David Brat Win."
30. In essence, through offering cheap alternatives to the party's database and interface system. There seem to be fewer activist challenges on the ideological left (in part, perhaps, because of the ways that left movements are wary of institutional politics); see Kreiss and Tufecki, "Occupying the Political." One 2016 Republican presidential campaign staffer put this in a normatively desirable light, arguing that "a fragmented, movement party keeps Washington Republicans honest and tied to the base of the party, even though in the short term there are large transaction costs"; Republican 2016 presidential campaign staffer, not for attribution. A number of practitioners on both sides of the aisle pointed to the Bipartisan Campaign Reform Act of 2002 ("McCain-Feingold") limiting the amount of money that parties could raise as providing a space for outside groups such as the Koch network to step in.
31. Grossmann and Hopkins, "Ideological Republicans and Group Interest Democrats."
32. McGerr, *The Decline of Popular Politics*.
33. Riordan, *Plunkitt of Tammany Hall*.
34. The historian Michael Schudson argues that many democratic theorists inherited their normative ideals of the "information-based citizen." Schudson, *The Good Citizen*.
35. Ibid.
36. Riordan, *Plunkitt of Tammany Hall*.
37. Presentation is archived here: http://next.ngpvan.com/.
38. Michael Slaby, personal communication, September 4, 2013.
39. Law, "Seeing like a Survey."
40. David Simas, personal communication, September 22, 2012.
41. Alex Lundry, personal communication, June 25, 2013.

42. Jonathan Alter argues that staffers on the Obama 2012 campaign sought to create a "new kind of political machine" that combined voter contacts with technology. See *The Center Holds*, 84.

43. See Nielsen, *Ground Wars*, for this argument about "people as media" in the context of field campaigning. See Bimber, Flanagin, and Stohl, *Collective Action in Organizations*, about "collective action space."

44. For a discussion, see Nielsen, *Ground Wars*.

45. Bryan Whitaker, personal communication, January 30, 2015.

46. Karpf, *The MoveOn Effect*; Bimber, Flanagin, and Stohl, *Collective Action in Organizations*. Webster argues that instead of fragmentation, we see the overlapping of audiences. Webster, *The Marketplace of Attention*. See Giddens, *The Consequences of Modernity*, on the voluntary nature of contemporary social ties.

47. Bimber, Flanagin, and Stohl, *Collective Action in Organizations*.

48. See Nielsen, *Ground Wars*.

49. Karpf, "The Technological Basis of Organizational Membership."

50. Karpf, *The MoveOn Effect*.

51. David Simas, personal communication, September 22, 2012.

52. Baldwin-Philippi, *Using Technology, Building Democracy*, 110.

53. Ibid., 117–118. For digital performance, see Alexander, *The Performance of Politics*.

54. The *Oxford English Dictionary* lists various iterations of the idea of "wards" dating back to the 1300s, with uses entailing "guardianship," "keeping control," "charge," and "duty." In politics, a "ward" entails an "administrative division of a borough or city" with various means of formal (alderman) or informal (party or civil society) representation. This geographic definition sits alongside the use of "wards" symbolically to refer to people who are within districts.

55. As Giddens points out, a basic condition of modernity is living with disembedness, where people make their own space of social relations; Giddens, *The Consequences of Modernity*.

56. van Dijck, *The Culture of Connectivity*.

57. One of Schudson's key points in *The Good Citizen* was that representative democracy enables people to be free from having to be care about politics. For social media and context navigation, see Quinn and Papacharissi, "Social Media and Sociality."

58. See, for instance, recent studies of Facebook, including Das and Kramer, "Self-Censorship on Facebook"; Kwon, Moon, and Stefanone, "Unspeaking on Facebook?" While she did not use these terms, an older form of context collapse was documented by Nina Eliasoph in *Avoiding Politics*.

59. While social relations being a primary means of exposure to political information has probably always been a feature of social life, it is the ways that social media platforms become the distribution mechanism for mass media that are qualitatively new, as are the ways in which the affordances of these platforms shape sociality and information flows; for this argument, see van Dijck, *The Culture of Connectivity*; Mossberger and Tolbert, *How Politics Online Is Changing Electoral Participation*; Brundidge, "Encountering 'Difference' in the Contemporary Public Sphere"; Lee et al., "Social Media, Network Heterogeneity, and Opinion Polarization."

60. See Masket, *No Middle Ground*.

61. Papacharissi, *Affective Publics*.

Methodological Appendix

1. Schudson, "Politics as Cultural Practice."

2. See Castells, *The Rise of the Network Society*; van Dijck, *The Culture of Connectivity*.

3. This is at the core of the assumptions behind actor-network theory. See Asdal, "Context in Action."

4. Grossmann, *Artists of the Possible*.

5. See also, Gerring, "Mere Description."

6. Padgett and Powell, *The Emergence of Organizations and Markets*, 2.

7. Schudson, *The Good Citizen*.

8. Joseph Turow has argued that studying "the texts that viewers and readers receive in the first place" is at the core of production studies; Turow, "Audience Construction and Culture Production." I focus on campaigns in this work and draw on a long line of work in production studies. Broadly, this book concerns campaigns' and parties' engagement in the "networked construction of audiences" through mediated practices that have evolved and changed over time. For other works on politics that adopt a similar production-level view, see Michael Serazio, "The New Media Designs of Political Consultants," "Managing the Digital News Cyclone"; Schradie, "Bringing Organization Back In."

9. See also Kathleen Blee's work on how groups form; Blee, *Democracy in the Making*.

10. Pierson, *Politics in Time*, 92.

11. Sewell, *Logics of History*, 84.

12. Sewell, *Logics of History*, 91. There is, perhaps, an analogy here to communication research paradigms that posit a-historical social processes persisting in the same form despite vast media, social, and technological changes; see Bennett and Iyengar, "A New Era of Minimal Effects?" For a methodological reason why these paradigms continue on, see Karpf et al., "A New Era of Field Research in Political Communication?"

13. Sewell, *Logics of History*, 95.

14. Ibid., 100.

15. Ibid., 10.

16. Schudson, "How Culture Works."

17. Sewell, *Logics of History*, 99.

18. Hewitson, *History and Causality*.

19. Katz, "From How to Why."

20. See Becker, "The Epistemology of Qualitative Research." For a great overview of the issues involved with interview-based studies in politics, see Lilleker, "Interviewing the Political Elite."

21. One other thing that helped me secure interviews for my first book: a book contract that seemed to magically transform the dissertation into something that would have real presence in the world.

22. For the methods behind the DNC study, see Kreiss, Meadows, and Remensperger, "Political Performance, Boundary Spaces, and Active Spectatorship."

23. I reported this in a similar way in Kreiss, "Seizing the Moment."

24. See Weiss, *Learning from Strangers*.

25. For a review of issues with cleaning quotes, and a call for reflexivity, see Bischoping, "Quote, Unquote."

26. See, for instance, Nielsen, *Ground Wars*; Baldwin-Philippi, *Using Technology, Building Democracy*.

27. Nielsen, *Ground Wars*.

28. Duneier, *Sidewalk*; Stein, "Sex, Truths, and Audiotape."

29. See Spicker, "Ethical Covert Research."

30. Luker, *Salsa Dancing into the Social Sciences*.

31. See Bacon's discussion of John Dewey's thought; Bacon, *Pragmatism: An Introduction*.

32. Langley, "Strategies for Theorizing from Process Data," 695.

33. The following is adapted from Kreiss and Jasinski, "The Tech Industry Meets Presidential Politics."

34. In some cases that did not involve first jobs out of college, staffers only had one or two previous listings for their work before a presidential bid.

35. The FEC data on disbursements from campaigns to consultancies is notoriously complicated; it is not clear what services are actually being rendered given the lack of

standardization in reporting. In addition, campaigns will at times fund consultancies to directly hire staffers, which is also not reflected in FEC data. Given that this is the case, the interview data presented in Chapter 5 provides narrative context with regard to how the Romney campaign relied on a bevy of outside firms for technology, digital, data, and analytics services.

36. For Democracy in Action's disclaimer about the data, see http://www.p2016.org/parties/disclaimer10.html.

37. Kreiss, "Seizing the Moment."

38. Kreiss, Meadows, and Remensperger, "Political Performance, Boundary Spaces, and Active Spectatorship."

Bibliography

"66 Canal Center Plaza, Suite 555." *New York Times*, February 25, 2012. Accessed September 26, 2015. http://www.nytimes.com/interactive/2012/02/26/us/politics/66-canal-center-plaza-suite-555.html?_r=0.

Adler, Steve. "How a Tiny GOP Data Firm Helped David Brat Win." *Campaigns & Elections*, June 24, 2014. Accessed October 14, 2015. http://www.campaignsandelections.com/magazine/1699/how-a-tiny-gop-data-firm-helped-david-brat-win.

Agarwal, Sheetal D., Michael L. Barthel, Caterina Rost, Alan Borning, W. Lance Bennett, and Courtney N. Johnson. "Grassroots Organizing in the Digital Age: Considering Values and Technology in Tea Party and Occupy Wall Street." *Information, Communication & Society* 17, no. 3 (2014): 326–341.

Aldrich, John. "The Invisible Primary and Its Effects on Democratic Choice." *PS: Political Science & Politics* 42, no. 1 (2009): 33–38.

Alexander, Jeffrey C. *Performance and Power.* Cambridge, UK: Polity, 2011.

Alexander, Jeffrey C. *The Performance of Politics: Obama's Victory and the Democratic Struggle for Power.* New York: Oxford University Press, 2010.

Alexandre, Jean. "Democratic National Committee Leverages Big Data to Turn Politics into Political Science." *Vertica (blog)*, October 28, 2013. Accessed September 28, 2105. https://www.vertica.com/2013/10/28/democratic-national-committee-leverages-big-data-to-turn-politics-into-political-science/.

Allen, Mike, and Kenneth P. Vogel. "Inside the Koch Data Mine." *Politico*, December 8, 2014. Accessed September 25, 2016. http://www.politico.com/story/2014/12/koch-brothers-rnc-113359.

Alter, Jonathan. *The Center Holds: Obama and His Enemies.* New York: Simon & Schuster, 2013.

Anderson, C. W., and Daniel Kreiss. "Black Boxes as Capacities for and Constraints on Action: Electoral Politics, Journalism, and Devices of Representation." *Qualitative Sociology* 36, no. 4 (2013): 365–382.

Ankerson, Megan Sapnar. "Writing Web Histories with an Eye on the Analog Past." *New Media & Society* 14, no. 3 (2012): 384–400.

Asdal, Kristin. "Contexts in Action—And the Future of the Past in STS." *Science, Technology & Human Values* 37, no. 4 (2012): 379–403.

Atkins, David. "An Explanation of What Bernie Sanders Staffers Actually Did and Why It Matters." *Washington Monthly*, December 19, 2015. Accessed January 27, 2016. http://www.washingtonmonthly.com/political-animal-a/2015_12/an_explanation_of_what_bernie059035.php.

Bacon, Michael. *Pragmatism: An Introduction.* Cambridge, UK: Polity, 2012.

Baldwin-Philippi, Jessica. *Using Technology, Building Democracy: Digital Campaigning and the Construction of Citizenship.* New York: Oxford University Press, 2015.

Bartels, Larry M. "The Impact of Electioneering in the United States." In *Electioneering: A Comparative Study of Continuity and Change,* edited by David Butler and Austin Ranney, 244–277. Oxford: Clarendon Press, 1992.

Beach, Michael. "Voters Going off the Grid." *Targeted Victory,* September 14, 2011. Accessed September 27, 2015. https://www.targetedvictory.com/2011/09/14/off-the-grid/.

Becker, Howard S. "The Epistemology of Qualitative Research." In *Contemporary Field Research: Perspectives and Formulations,* 2nd edition, edited by Robert M. Emerson, 317–330. Long Grove, IL: Waveland Press, 2001.

Bender, Michael C., Jennifer Epstein, and Andrew M. Harris. "Sanders Wins Back DNC Data Access after Day of Clashes." *Bloomberg Politics,* December 18, 2015. Accessed January 27, 2016. http://www.bloomberg.com/politics/articles/2015-12-18/sanders-campaign-fires-data-director-after-breach-of-clinton-files.

Bennett, W. Lance, Deen Freelon, and Chris Wells. "Changing Citizen Identity and the Rise of a Participatory Media Culture." In *Handbook of Research on Civic Engagement in Youth,* edited by Lonnie R. Sherrod, Judith Torney-Purta, and Constance A. Flanagan, 393–423. Hoboken, NJ: John Wiley & Sons, 2010.

Bennett, W. Lance, and Jarol B. Manheim. "The One-Step Flow of Communication." *The Annals of the American Academy of Political and Social Science* 608, no. 1 (2006): 213–232.

Bennett, W. Lance, and Alexandra Segerberg. *The Logic of Connective Action: Digital Media and the Personalization of Contentious Politics.* New York: Cambridge University Press, 2013.

Bimber, Bruce. "Digital Media in the Obama Campaigns of 2008 and 2012: Adaptation to the Personalized Political Communication Environment." *Journal of Information Technology & Politics* 11, no. 2 (2014): 130–150.

Bimber, Bruce. *Information and American Democracy: Technology in the Evolution of Political Power.* New York: Cambridge University Press, 2003.

Bimber, Bruce, Andrew Flanagin, and Cynthia Stohl. *Collective Action in Organizations: Interaction and Engagement in an Era of Technological Change.* New York: Cambridge University Press, 2012.

Bimber, Bruce, and Richard Davis. *Campaigning Online: The Internet in US Elections.* New York: Oxford University Press, 2003.

Bischoping, Katherine. "Quote, Unquote: From Transcript to Text." In *Doing Ethnography: Studying Everyday Life,* edited by Charlene Elizabeth Miall, Dorothy Pawluch, and William Shaffir, 141–154. Toronto: Canadian Scholars' Press, 2005.

Blee, Kathleen M. *Democracy in the Making: How Activist Groups Form.* New York: Oxford University Press, 2012.

Blumenthal, Paul. "DNC Debt Totals $21 Million at Start of 2013; Obama Campaign Owes Too." *The Huffington Post,* January 31, 2013. Accessed September 30, 2015. http://www.huffingtonpost.com/2013/01/31/dnc-debt-01-2013_n_2594282.html.

Blumler, Jay G., and Dennis Kavanagh. "The Third Age of Political Communication: Influences and Features." *Political Communication* 16, no. 3 (1999): 209–230.

Bradley, Tahman. "Final Fundraising Figure: Obama's $750M." *ABC News,* December 5, 2008. Accessed October 21, 2015. http://abcnews.go.com/Politics/Vote2008/story?id=6397572&page=1.

Braun, Joshua A. *This Program Is Brought to You By . . .* New Haven, CT: Yale University Press, 2015.

Briffault, Richard, "Super PACS." *Columbia Public Law Research Paper* No. WP 12–298, April 16, 2012. Accessed October 21, 2015. Available at SSRN: http://ssrn.com/abstract=2040941.

Brundidge, Jennifer. "Encountering 'Difference' in the Contemporary Public Sphere: The Contribution of the Internet to the Heterogeneity of Political Discussion Networks." *Journal of Communication* 60, no. 4 (2010): 680–700.

Bump, Philip. "A State-by-State Look at the Record Black Turnout in 2012." *The Wire*, May 9, 2013. Accessed September 28, 2015. http://www.thewire.com/politics/2013/05/black-turnout-2012-state-by-state-maps/65053/.

California Democratic Party. Introduction to MOE (Mobilize, Organize, Elect). Accessed January 27, 2016. http://inyopro.com/MOEchure_final.pdf.

Calmes, Jackie. "McCain Manager Roils Campaign: Davis Returns after Ouster Amid Questions on Spending, Ties." *Wall Street Journal*, July 23, 2007. Accessed September 26, 2015. http://www.wsj.com/articles/SB118515181783374359.

Callon, Michel. "Some Elements of a Sociology of Translation: Domestication of the Scallops and the Fishermen of St. Brieuc Bay." In *Power, Action, and Belief: A New Sociology of Knowledge*, edited by John Law, 196–223. London: Routledge, 1986.

Cammaerts, Bart. "Protest Logics and the Mediation Opportunity Structure." *European Journal of Communication* 27, no. 2 (2012): 117–134.

Castells, Manuel. *The Rise of the Network Society: The Information Age: Economy, Society, and Culture*. Vol. 1. John Wiley & Sons, 2011.

Cetina, Karin Knorr. "What is a Pipe? Obama and the Sociological Imagination." *Theory, Culture & Society* 26, no. 5 (2009): 129–140.

Chadwick, Andrew. *The Hybrid Media System: Politics and Power*. New York: Oxford University Press, 2013.

Chadwick, Andrew, and Philip N. Howard. *Routledge Handbook of Internet Politics*. New York: Taylor & Francis, 2010.

Charen, Mona. "Go Quietly, Michael Steele." *National Review*, April 6, 2010. Accessed September 26, 2015. http://www.nationalreview.com/article/229481/go-quietly-michael-steele-mona-charen.

Cline, Seth. "Obama Outraises, Outmaneuvers Romney in Money Battle." *U.S. News & World Report*, September 12, 2012. Accessed September 30, 2015. http://www.usnews.com/news/articles/2012/09/21/obama-outraises-outmaneuvers-romney-in-money-battle.

Cselland@vertica.com. "The Disruptive Power of Big Data." *Vertica (blog)*, March 19, 2013. Accessed September 29, 2015. https://www.vertica.com/2013/03/19/the-disruptive-power-of-big-data/.

Cohen, Martin, David Karol, Hans Noel, and John Zaller. *The Party Decides: Presidential Nominations before and after Reform*. Chicago: University of Chicago Press, 2009.

Compton, Matt, and Andrew Brown. "Project Ivy: What's Really Happening with the Technology and Data That Helped President Obama Win." *Medium*, February 25, 2014. Accessed January 27, 2016. https://medium.com/soapbox-dc/whats-really-happening-with-the-technology-and-data-that-helped-president-obama-win-706865a211b8#.tlp008v69.

Confessore, Nicholas. "Koch Brothers' Budget of $889 Million for 2016 Is on Par with Both Parties' Spending." *New York Times*, January 26, 2015. Accessed October 20, 2015. http://www.nytimes.com/2015/01/27/us/politics/kochs-plan-to-spend-900-million-on-2016-campaign.html?_r=0.

Corasaniti, Nick. "Legion of Tech Volunteers Lead a Charge for Bernie Sanders." *New York Times*, September 3, 2015. Accessed January 27, 2016. http://www.nytimes.com/2015/09/04/us/politics/bernie-sanders-presidential-campaign-tech-supporters.html?_r=2.

Cornfield, Michael. *Politics Moves Online: Campaigning and the Internet*. New York: Century Foundation Press, 2004.

Crichton, Danny. "Republic Launches New Platform to Send GOP to White House." *TechCrunch*, August 4, 2015. Accessed January 27, 2016. http://techcrunch.com/2015/08/04/republic-launches-new-platform-to-send-gop-to-white-house/#.9yoeo9o:8dDg.

Cummings, Jeanne. "Steele's Spending Spree Angers Donors." *Politico*, February 23, 2010. Accessed October 21, 2015. http://www.politico.com/story/2010/02/steeles-spending-spree-angers-donors-033324.

Darr, Joshua P., and Matthew S. Levendusky. "Relying on the Ground Game: The Placement and Effect of Campaign Field Offices." *American Politics Research* 42, no. 3 (2014): 529–548.

Das, Sauvik, and Adam Kramer. "Self-Censorship on Facebook." In *Proceedings of the Seventh International AAAI Conference on Weblogs and Social Media*, 2013. Accessed October 20, 2015. http://www.aaai.org/ocs/index.php/ICWSM/ICWSM13/paper/viewFile/6093/6350%C2%A0.

Delany, Colin. "A Dearth of Digital Staff in 2016?" *Epolitics.com*, January 15, 2015. Accessed October 21, 2015. http://www.epolitics.com/2015/01/15/a-dearth-of-digital-staff-in-2016/.

Delany, Colin. "Facebook Advertising for Politics & Advocacy." *Epolitics.com*, May 14, 2014. Accessed September 30, 2015. http://www.epolitics.com/2014/05/14/facebook-advertising-for-politics-advocacy-ebook-excerpt/.

Delany, Colin. "Voter File Digital Ad Targeting: Reality vs. Hype." *Campaigns and Elections*, July 17, 2012. Accessed September 30, 2015. http://www.campaignsandelections.com/magazine/1804/voter-file-digital-ad-targeting-reality-vs-hype.

Democratic Party. "Project Ivy." YouTube video, 2:59. Posted March 1, 2014. Accessed October 22, 2015. https://www.youtube.com/watch?v=5B3f4zRCenU.

Denis, Jérôme, and David Pontille. "Material Ordering and the Care of Things." *Science, Technology & Human Values* 40, no. 3 (2015): 338–367.

de Vaan, Mathijs, David Stark, and Balázs Vedres. "Game Changer: The Topology of Creativity." *American Journal of Sociology* 120, no. 4 (2015): 1144–1194.

DiMaggio, Paul. "Culture and Cognition." *Annual Review of Sociology* 23 (1997): 263–287.

Duneier, Mitchell, and Ovie Carter. *Sidewalk.* New York: Macmillan, 1999.

Duggan, Maeve, Nicole B. Ellison, Cliff Lampe, Amanda Lenhart, and Mary Madden. "Demographics of Key Social Networking Platforms." *Pew Research Center*, January 9, 2015. Accessed October 21, 2015. http://www.pewinternet.org/2015/01/09/demographics-of-key-social-networking-platforms-2/.

Edsall, Thomas B. "In Data We Trust." *New York Times*, May 8, 2013. Accessed October 20, 2015. http://opinionator.blogs.nytimes.com/2013/05/08/in-data-we-trust/?_r=0.

Edwards, Paul N. "Infrastructure and Modernity: Force, Time, and Social Organization in the History of Sociotechnical Systems." In *Modernity and Technology*, edited by Thomas J. Misa, Philip Brey, and Andrew Feenberg, 185–225. Cambridge, MA: MIT Press, 2003.

Edwards, Paul N., Geoffrey C. Bowker, Steven J. Jackson, and Robin Williams. "Introduction: An Agenda for Infrastructure Studies." *Journal of the Association for Information Systems* 10, no. 5 (2009): 6.

Eggen, Dan, and Tom Hamburger. "Private Consultants See Huge Election Profits." *Washington Post*, November 20, 2012. Accessed September 28, 2015. http://www.washingtonpost.com/politics/decision2012/private-consultants-see-huge-election-profits/2012/11/10/edaab580-29d8-11e2-96b6-8e6a7524553f_story.html.

Eliasoph, Nina. *Avoiding Politics: How Americans Produce Apathy in Everyday Life.* New York: Cambridge University Press, 1998.

Elliott, Philip. "RNC Debt at $23 Million As it Gears Up for 2012." *Associated Press, The Huffington Post*, January 31, 2011. Accessed September 30, 2015. http://www.huffingtonpost.com/2011/01/31/rnc-debt-at-23-million-as_n_816633.html.

Ellison, Nicole B. and Danah Boyd. "Sociality Through Social Network Sites." In *The Oxford Handbook of Internet Studies*, edited by William Dutton, 151–172. New York: Oxford University Press, 2013.

Elmer, Greg, Ganaele Langlois, and Fenwick McKelvey. *The Permanent Campaign: New Media, New Politics.* New York: Peter Lang, 2013.

Engage. *Inside the Cave: The Definitive Report On the Keys to Obama's 2012 Success.* Accessed January 27, 2016. http://enga.ge/projects/inside-the-cave/.

Enos, Ryan D. and Anthony Fowler. "The Surprising Parity of the 2012 Ground Game." *The Washington Post*, February 27, 2014. https://www.washingtonpost.com/news/monkey-cage/wp/2014/02/27/the-surprising-parity-of-the-2012-ground-game/.

Erickson, Erick. "The Incestuous Bleeding of the Republic Party." *Red State*, November 28, 2012. Accessed September 24, 2015. http://www.redstate.com/2012/11/28/the-incestuous-bleeding-of-the-republican-party/.

Farber, Dan. "Why Romney's Orca Killer App Beached on Election Day." *CNET*, November 9, 2012. Accessed September 24, 2015. http://www.cnet.com/news/why-romneys-Orca-killer-app-beached-on-election-day/.

Farrar-Myers, Victoria A., and Justin S. Vaughn, eds. *Controlling the Message: New Media in American Political Campaigns*. New York: New York University Press, 2015.

Fiano, Cassey. "RNC's Amazing Success with the Fire Pelosi Website." *Hot Air*, March 23, 2010. Accessed October 21, 2015. http://hotair.com/greenroom/archives/2010/03/23/rncs-amazing-success-with-the-fire-pelosi-website/.

Fidelman, Mark. "Republicans Launch Game-Changing Data Center That Will Forever Change Politics." *Forbes*, August 3, 2015. Accessed October 14, 2015. http://www.forbes.com/sites/markfidelman/2015/08/03/exclusive-republicans-launch-game-changing-data-center-that-will-forever-change-politics/.

Fitzpatrick, Alex. "Obama Campaign Launches Poll-Watching App." *Mashable*, November 5, 2012. Accessed September 24, 2015. http://mashable.com/2012/11/05/obama-election-app/#znYDDeNEsmqE.

Foot, Kirsten A., and Steven M. Schneider. *Web Campaigning*. Cambridge, MA: MIT Press, 2006.

Fox, Richard L., and Jennifer M. Ramos, eds. *iPolitics: Citizens, Elections, and Governing in the New Media Era*. New York: Cambridge University Press, 2011.

Franklin, Bob. "The Future of Journalism: In an Age of Digital Media and Economic Uncertainty." *Journalism Practice* 8, no. 5 (2014): 469–487.

Freeman, Jo. "The Political Culture of the Democratic and Republican Parties." *Political Science Quarterly* 101, no. 3 (1986): 327–356.

Friess, Steve. "The Man Who Invented the Republican Internet." *Bloomberg Politics*, October 22, 2014. Accessed September 30, 2015. http://www.bloomberg.com/politics/features/2014-10-22/the-man-who-invented-the-republican-internet.

Frizell, Sam. "Sanders Campaign's Breach of Clinton Data More Serious Than Disclosed." *Time*, December 18, 2015. Accessed January 27, 2016. http://time.com/4155185/bernie-sanders-hillary-clinton-data/.

Gabriel, Trip. "'Super PACs' Take On New Role, Organizing Voters." *New York Times*, July 7, 2015. Accessed October 20, 2015. http://www.nytimes.com/2015/07/08/us/politics/super-pacs-take-on-new-role-organizing-voters.html.

Gallagher, Sean. "How Team Obama's Tech Efficiency Left Romney IT in Dust." *Ars Technica*, November 20, 2012. Accessed October 25, 2015. http://arstechnica.com/information-technology/2012/11/how-team-obamas-tech-efficiency-left-romney-it-in-dust/.

Gallagher, Sean. "Inside Team Romney's Whale of a Meltdown." *Ars Technica*, November 9, 2012. Accessed September 24, 2015. http://arstechnica.com/information-technology/2012/11/inside-team-romneys-whale-of-an-it-meltdown/.

Gallagher, Sean. "Romney Campaign Got Its IT from Best Buy, Staples, and Friends." *Ars Technica*, November 18, 2012. Accessed October 25, 2015. http://arstechnica.com/information-technology/2012/11/romney-campaign-got-its-it-from-best-buy-staples-and-friends/.

Gallagher, Sean. "Which Consultants Built Romney's 'Project Orca?' None of Them." *Ars Technica*, November 15, 2012. Accessed September 24, 2015. http://arstechnica.com/information-technology/2012/11/which-consultants-built-romneys-project-Orca-none-of-them/.

Galvin, Daniel. *Presidential Party Building: Dwight D. Eisenhower to George W. Bush*. Princeton, NJ: Princeton University Press, 2010.

Geraghty, Jim. "Who's Left on Team McCain? Five Departures Today." *The Campaign Spot (blog)*, *NationalReview*,July10,2007.AccessedSeptember24,2015.http://www.nationalreview.com/campaign-spot/12303/whos-left-team-mccain-five-departures-today-updated-jim-geraghty.

Gerber, Alan S., and Donald P. Green. "The Effects of Canvassing, Telephone Calls, and Direct Mail on Voter Turnout: A Field Experiment." *American Political Science Review* 94, no. 3 (2000): 653–663.

Gerring, John. "Mere Description." *British Journal of Political Science* 42, no. 4 (2012): 721–746.

Gibson, Ginger. "Messina Touts Grassroots Strength." *Politico*, November 20, 2012. Accessed October 20, 2015. http://www.politico.com/story/2012/11/messina-obama-built-biggest-grassroots-campaign-084080#ixzz3p2k9BOnr.

Giddens, Anthony. *The Consequences of Modernity*. Hoboken, NJ: John Wiley & Sons, 2013.

Gillespie, Tarleton, Pablo J. Boczkowski, and Kirsten A. Foot. *Media Technologies : Essays on Communication, Materiality, and Society*. Cambridge, MA: MIT Press, 2014.

Gold, Matea. "It's Bold, but Legal: How Campaigns and Their Super PAC Backers Work Together." *Washington Post*, July 6, 2015. Accessed October 20, 2015. https://www.washingtonpost.com/politics/here-are-the-secret-ways-super-pacs-and-campaigns-can-work-together/2015/07/06/bda78210-1539-11e5-89f3-61410da94eb1_story.html.

Gold, Matea. "Koch Network Strikes New Deal to Share Voter Data with RNC-Aligned Firm." Post Politics, *Washington Post*, July 29, 2015. Accessed September 30, 2015. http://www.washingtonpost.com/news/post-politics/wp/2015/07/29/koch-network-strikes-new-deal-to-share-voter-data-with-rnc-aligned-firm/.

Golway, Terry. *Machine Made: Tammany Hall and the Creation of Modern American Politics*. New York: W. W. Norton, 2014.

GOP. *Growth and Opportunity Project Report*, 2013. Accessed October 20, 2015. http://goproject.gop.com/rnc_growth_opportunity_book_2013.pdf.

Green, Joshua. "Google's Eric Schmidt Invests in Obama's Big Data Brains." *Bloomberg Business*, May 30, 2013. Accessed January 27, 2016. http://www.bloomberg.com/bw/articles/2013-05-30/googles-eric-schmidt-invests-in-obamas-big-data-brains.

Grossmann, Matt. *Artists of the Possible: Governing Networks and American Policy Change since 1945*. Oxford: Oxford University Press, 2014.

Grossmann, Matt, and David A. Hopkins. "Ideological Republicans and Group Interest Democrats: The Asymmetry of American Party Politics." *Perspectives on Politics* 13, no. 1 (2015): 119–139.

Halper, Evan. "Republicans Lag Behind on Voter Information." *Los Angeles Times*. June 19, 2015. Accessed January 29, 2015. http://www.latimes.com/nation/la-na-republicans-voter-data-20150618-story.html.

Han, Hahrie. *How Organizations Develop Activists: Civic Associations and Leadership in the 21st Century*. Oxford: Oxford University Press, 2014.

Harris, Douglas B., and Lonce H. Bailey. *The Democratic Party: Documents Decoded*. Santa Barbara, CA: ABC-CLIO, 2014.

Hart, Roderick P. *Campaign Talk: Why Elections Are Good for Us*. Princeton, NJ: Princeton University Press, 2009.

Hatch, Rebecca S. "Party Organizational Strength and Technological Capacity: The Adaptation of the State-Level Party Organizations in the United States to Voter Outreach and Data Analytics in the Internet Age." *Party Politics* (2015). Published electronically September 28, 2015. doi: 10.1177/1354068815605673.

Hendler, Josh. "Why the Bernie Breach Wasn't About Technology, and What's At Stake." *Medium*, December 19, 2015. Accessed January 28, 2015. https://medium.com/@joshhendler/why-the-bernie-breach-isn-t-about-technology-and-what-s-at-stake-c383ee7b840a#.1qepsw5gk.

Hendricks, John Allen, and Dan Schill, eds. *Presidential Campaigning and Social Media: An Analysis of the 2012 Campaign*. New York: Oxford University Press, 2014.

Herman, Todd. "How a Search Engine Fired Nancy Pelosi." *Daily Caller*, December 14, 2010. Accessed October 21, 2015. http://dailycaller.com/2010/12/14/how-a-search-engine-fired-nancy-pelosi/4/.

Hersh, Eitan. *Hacking the Electorate: How Campaigns Perceive Voters*. New York: Cambridge University Press, 2015.

Hewitson, Mark. *History and Causality*. London: Palgrave Macmillan, 2014.

Hillygus, D. Sunshine. "Campaign Effects and the Dynamics of Turnout Intention in Election 2000." *Journal of Politics* 67, no. 1 (2005): 50–68.

Howard, Philip N. *New Media Campaigns and the Managed Citizen*. New York: Cambridge University Press, 2006.

Hughes, Thomas Parke. *Networks of Power: Electrification in Western Society, 1880–1930*. Baltimore: Johns Hopkins University Press, 1993.

Irwin, Neil. "Why a Presidential Campaign Is the Ultimate Start-Up." *The Upshot (blog)*, *New York Times*, June 4, 2105. Accessed September 28, 2015. http://www.nytimes.com/2015/06/07/upshot/why-a-presidential-campaign-is-the-ultimate-start-up.html?hpw&rref=business&action=click&pgtype=Homepage&module=well-region&region=bottom-well&WT.nav=bottom-well&abt=0002&abg=0&_r=0.

Issenberg, Sasha. "For Sale: Detailed Voter Profiles." *Slate*, January 30, 2012. Accessed September 25, 2015. http://www.slate.com/articles/news_and_politics/victory_lab/2012/01/the_co_op_and_the_data_trust_the_dnc_and_rnc_get_into_the_data_mining_business_.html?wpisrc=newsletter_slatest.

Issenberg, Sasha. "How Behavioral Science Is Remaking Politics." *New York Times*, October 29, 2010. Accessed September 25, 2015. http://www.nytimes.com/2010/10/31/magazine/31politics-t.html?_r=0.

Issenberg, Sasha. "How Obama Used Big Data to Rally Voters." *MIT Technology Review*, December 19, 2012. Accessed September 25, 2015. http://www.technologyreview.com/featuredstory/509026/how-obamas-team-used-big-data-to-rally-voters/.

Issenberg, Sasha. "The RNC Hopes This App Will Keep Campaigners from Going All in with the Koch Brothers." *Bloomberg Politics*, August 4, 2015. Accessed September 30, 2015. http://www.bloomberg.com/politics/articles/2015-08-04/the-rnc-hopes-this-app-will-keep-campaigns-from-going-all-in-with-the-koch-brothers.

Issenberg, Sasha. *The Victory Lab: The Secret Science of Winning Campaigns*. New York: Broadway Books, 2012.

Jacobs, Jennifer. "More Date Debate: New Hampshire Official Floats December Primary Date." *2012 Iowa Caucuses (blog)*, *Des Moines Register*, October 12, 2011. Accessed September 26, 2015. http://caucuses.desmoinesregister.com/2011/10/12/more-date-debate-new-hampshire-official-floats-december-primary-date/.

Jackson, Steven J. "Rethinking Repair." In *Media Technologies: Essays on Communication, Materiality, and Society*, edited by Tarleton Gillespie, Pablo J. Boczkowski, and Kirsten A. Foot, 221–239. Cambridge, MA: MIT Press, 2014.

Jacoby, Mary. "Firms Tied to Campaign Manager Received 10% of McCain's Budget." *Wall Street Journal*, July 17, 2007. Accessed September 24, 2015. http://trugop.org/JSM/Firms_Tied_to_Campaign_Manager.htm.

Jasper, James M. *The Art of Moral Protest: Culture, Biography, and Creativity in Social Movements*. Chicago: University of Chicago Press, 2008.

Johnson, Dennis W. *Routledge Handbook of Political Management*. New York: Routledge, 2009.

Judd, Nick. "GOP.com to Roll Out Points API." *Tech President*, May 20, 2010. Accessed September 26, 2015. http://techpresident.com/blog-entry/gopcom-roll-out-points-api.

Judd, Nick. "How Obama for America Made Its Facebook Friends Into Effective Advocates." *Tech President*, November 19, 2012. Accessed January 27, 2016. http://techpresident.com/news/23159/how-obama-america-made-its-facebook-friends-effective-advocates.

Judd, Nick. "Obama's Targeted GOTV on Facebook Reached 5 Million Voters, Goff Says." *Tech President*, November 30, 2012. Accessed September 29, 2015. http://techpresident.com/news/23202/obamas-targeted-gotv-facebook-reached-5-million-voters-goff-says.

Judd, Nick. "Republican Party's Technology Revival Hopes Hinge on Data and Data Analysis." *Tech President*, February 7, 2013. Accessed October 20, 2015. http://techpresident.com/news/23479/republican-partys-technology-revival-hopes-hinge-more-just-skype.

Kaid, Lynda Lee. *The Millennium Election: Communication in the 2000 Campaign*. Lanham, MD: Rowman & Littlefield, 2003.

Karpf, D., Kreiss, D., Nielsen, R. K., and Powers, M. "The Role of Qualitative Methods in Political Communication Research: Past, Present, and Future." *International Journal of Communication* 9 (2015): 1888–1906.

Karpf, David. "Macaca Moments Reconsidered: Electoral Panopticon or Netroots Mobilization?" *Journal of Information Technology & Politics* 7, no. 2–3 (2010): 143–162.

Karpf, David. "Open Source Political Community Development: A Five-Stage Adoption Process." *Journal of Information Technology & Politics* 8, no. 3 (2011): 323–345.

Karpf, David. "Social Science Research Methods in Internet Time." *Information, Communication & Society* 15, no. 5 (2012): 639–661.

Karpf, David. *The MoveOn Effect: The Unexpected Transformation of American Political Advocacy*. New York: Oxford University Press, 2012.

Karpf, David. "The Technological Basis of Organizational Membership: Representation of Interests in the New Media Age." *Representation: Elections and Beyond* (2013): 215.

Karpf, David, Daniel Kreiss, Rasmus Kleis Nielsen, and Matthew Powers, eds. "Qualitative Political Communication Research: New Methodological Approaches in a Time of Technological and Institutional Change." Special Section, *International Journal of Communication* 9 (2015): 1888–2091.

Katz, Elihu. "The Two-Step Flow of Communication: An Up-to-Date Report on an Hypothesis." *Public Opinion Quarterly* 21, no. 1 (1957): 61–78.

Katz, Jack. "From How to Why: On Luminous Description and Causal Inference in Ethnography (Part 1)." *Ethnography* 2, no. 4 (2001): 443–473.

Kaye, Kate. "Jeb Bush's Super PAC Has Spent over Half a Million on Data." *Advertising Age*, September 2, 2015. Accessed October 20, 2015. http://adage.com/article/campaign-trail/jeb-s-super-pac-spends-big-data/300176/.

Kaye, Kate. "Democrats' Data Breach Exposes Risks of Political Data Beast." *Advertising Age*, December 20, 2015. Accessed January 28, 2016. http://adage.com/article/campaign-trail/sanders-data-dive-exposed-underbelly-political-data/301893/.

Kenski, Kate, Bruce W. Hardy, and Kathleen Hall Jamieson. *The Obama Victory: How Media, Money, and Message Shaped the 2008 Election*. New York: Oxford University Press, 2010.

Kling, Rob. "What Is Social Informatics and Why Does it Matter?" *The Information Society* 23, no. 4 (2007): 205–220.

Klinkner, Philip A. *The Losing Parties: Out-party National Committees, 1956–1993*. New Haven, CT: Yale University Press, 1994.

Klotz, Robert J. *The Politics of Internet Communication*. Lanham, MD: Rowman & Littlefield, 2004.

Kreiss, Daniel. "Back to the Breach: Sanders, Clinton, and the Democratic Party's Data. *Cyborgology*, February 29, 2016. Accessed March 14, 2016. https://thesocietypages.org/cyborgology/2016/02/29/back-into-the-breach-sanders-clinton-and-the-democratic-partys-data/.

Kreiss, Daniel. "Seizing the Moment: The Presidential Campaigns' Use of Twitter during the 2012 Electoral Cycle." *New Media & Society*. Published electronically December 5, 2014. doi: 10.1177/1461444814562445.

Kreiss, Daniel. *Taking Our Country Back: The Crafting of Networked Politics from Howard Dean to Barack Obama*. New York: Oxford University Press, 2012.

Kreiss, Daniel, and Chris Jasinski. "The Tech Industry Meets Presidential Politics: Explaining the Democratic Party's Technological Advantage in Electoral Campaigning, 2004–2012."

Political Communication. Published electronically January 13, 2016. doi: 10.1080/10584609.2015.1121941.

Kreiss, Daniel, Laura Meadows, and John Remensperger. "Political Performance, Boundary Spaces, and Active Spectatorship: Media Production at the 2012 Democratic National Convention." *Journalism* 16, no. 5 (2015): 577–595.

Kriesi, Hanspeter. "The Political Opportunity Structure of New Social Movements: Its Impact on Their Mobilization." In *The Politics of Social Protest: Comparative Perspectives on States and Social Movements,* edited by J. Craig Jenkins, 167–198. Minneapolis: University of Minnesota Press, 1995.

Krueger, Alyson. "How the Hillary Clinton Campaign Built a Staff as Diverse as America." *Fast Company,*January6,2016.AccessedJanuary27,2016.https://www.fastcompany.com/3055032/most-creative-people/how-the-hillary-clinton-campaign-built-a-staff-as-diverse-as-america.

Kuang, Cliff. "The New GOP.com Socks It to the Commies." *Fast Company,* October 13, 2009. Accessed September 26, 2015. http://www.fastcompany.com/1403155/new-gopcom-socks-it-commies.

Kwon, K. Hazel, Shin-Il Moon, and Michael A. Stefanone. "Unspeaking on Facebook? Testing Network Effects on Self-Censorship of Political Expressions in Social Network Sites." *Quality & Quantity* 49, no. 4 (2015): 1417–1435.

Lampitt, Andrew. "The Real Story of How Big Data Analytics Helped Obama Win." *Think Big Data (blog), InfoWorld,* February 14, 2013. Accessed September 28, 2015. http://www.infoworld.com/article/2613587/big-data/the-real-story-of-how-big-data-analytics-helped-obama-win.html.

Langley, Ann. "Strategies for Theorizing from Process Data." *Academy of Management Review* 24, no. 4 (1999): 691–710.

Lapowsky, Issie. "GOP Hires Silicon Valley Vet to up the Party's Tech Game." *Wired,* November 2, 2015. Accessed January 27, 2016. http://www.wired.com/2015/11/gop-hires-silicon-valley-vet-to-up-the-partys-tech-game/?mbid=social_twitter.

Lapowsky, Issie. "Sanders' New Canvassing App On-Boards Volunteers in Seconds." *Wired,* January 5, 2016. Accessed January 27, 2016. http://www.wired.com/2016/01/sanders-new-canvassing-app-on-boards-volunteers-in-seconds/.

Law, John. "Seeing like a Survey." *Cultural Sociology* 3, no. 2 (2009): 239–256.

Law, John. "Technology and Heterogeneous Engineering: The Case of Portuguese Expansion." In *The Social Construction of Technological Systems: New Directions in the Sociology and History of Technology,* edited by Wiebe Bijker, Thomas P. Hughes, and Trevor Pinch, 111–134. Cambridge, MA: MIT Press, 1987.

Lawrence, Regina G., Logan Molyneux, Mark Coddington, and Avery Holton. "Tweeting Conventions: Political Journalists' Use of Twitter to Cover the 2012 Presidential Campaign." *Journalism Studies* 15, no. 6 (2014): 789–806.

Lee, Jae Kook, Jihyang Choi, Cheonsoo Kim, and Yonghwan Kim. "Social Media, Network Heterogeneity, and Opinion Polarization." *Journal of Communication* 64, no. 4 (2014): 702–722.

Leichtman, Dave. "What Happened to Project Ivy?" Epolitics.com, September 23, 2015. Accessed October 20, 2015. http://www.epolitics.com/2015/09/23/what-happened-to-project-ivy/.

Lempert, Michael, and Michael Silverstein. *Creatures of Politics: Media, Message, and the American Presidency.* Bloomington: Indiana University Press, 2012.

Lessig, Larry. "The Sanders Complaint." *LESSIG Blog, v2,* December 2015. Accessed January 27, 2016. http://lessig.tumblr.com/post/135477537937/the-sanders-complaint.

Lichtblau, Eric, and Nick Corasaniti. "Small Donors Are Clicking More with Democrats Than Republicans." *New York Times,* November 3, 2015. Accessed January 27, 2016. http://www.nytimes.com/2015/11/04/us/politics/small-donors-are-clicking-more-with-democrats-than-republicans.html?_r=0.

Lilleker, Darren G. "Interviewing the Political Elite: Navigating a Potential Minefield." *Politics* 23, no. 3 (2003): 207–214.

Lilleker, Darren G., and Ralph Negrine. "Professionalization of What? Since When? By Whom?" *The Harvard International Journal of Press/Politics* 7, no. 4 (2002): 98–103.

Lincoln Labs. "Reboot Conference: Conference Focus." Accessed September 25, 2015. http://lincolnlabs.com/events/2015/reboot-sf.

Livingston, Abby. "Republicans Mourn Operatives Bill Steiner, Dan Morgan." *Roll Call*, September 9, 2013. Accessed September 25, 2015. http://www.rollcall.com/news/republicans_mourn_operatives_bill_steiner_dan_morgan-227471-1.html.

Livingston, Geoff. "Social Media: The New Battleground for Politics." *Mashable*, September 23, 2010. Accessed September 26, 2015. http://mashable.com/2010/09/23/congress-battle-social-media/#cojIIvM5dmqy.

Loader, Brian D., Ariadne Vromen, and Michael A. Xenos. "The Networked Young Citizen: Social Media, Political Participation and Civic Engagement." *Information, Communication & Society* 17, no. 2 (2014): 143–150.

Luker, Kristin. *Salsa Dancing into the Social Sciences: Research in an Age of Info-Glut.* Cambridge, MA: Harvard University Press, 2008.

McAdam, Doug. *Political Process and the Development of Black Insurgency, 1930–1970.* Chicago: University of Chicago Press, 2010.

McCain, John. "McCain's Concession Speech Transcript." *New York Times*, November 5, 2008. Accessed September 25, 2015. http://www.nytimes.com/2008/11/04/us/politics/04text-mccain.html?_r=0.

McCain, John. "New Hampshire Primary Victory Speech." *Project Vote Smart*, February 1, 2000. Accessed September 26, 2015. http://votesmart.org/public-statement/716/new-hampshire-primary-victory-speech#.Vgcf-vS-ZGZ.

McGerr, Michael E. *The Decline of Popular Politics: The American North, 1865–1928.* New York: Oxford University Press, 1986.

McKenna, Elizabeth, and Hahrie Han. *Groundbreakers: How Obama's 2.2 Million Volunteers Transformed Campaigning in America.* New York: Oxford University Press, 2014.

Magleby, David B., ed. *Financing the 2012 Election.* Washington, DC: Brookings Institution Press, 2014.

Martin, Jonathan. "McCain's Comeback Plan." *Politico*, July 17, 2007. Accessed September 26, 2015. http://www.politico.com/blogs/jonathanmartin/0707/McCains_comeback_plan.html.

Masket, Seth. "Are Bushes Actually Better?" *Mischiefs of Faction*, June 10, 2015. Accessed September 24, 2015. http://www.mischiefsoffaction.com/2015/06/are-bushes-actually-better.html.

Masket, Seth. *No Middle Ground: How Informal Party Organizations Control Nominations and Polarize Legislatures.* Ann Arbor: University of Michigan Press, 2009.

Masket, Seth E., Michael T. Heaney, Joanne M. Miller, and Dara Z. Strolovitch. "Networking the Parties: A Comparative Study of Democratic and Republican National Convention Delegates in 2008." Paper presented at the annual meeting of the American Political Science Association, Toronto, Ontario, Canada, 2009.

Mattingly, Phil. "Inside the First Super-PAC Dedicated to Collecting Data All about You." *Bloomberg Politics*, April 15, 2015. Accessed October 14, 2015. http://www.bloomberg.com/politics/features/2015-04-15/the-care-and-feeding-of-the-ready-for-hillary-list.

Medvetz, Thomas. *Think Tanks in America.* Chicago: University of Chicago Press, 2012.

Miller, Zeke. "Project Ivy: Democrats Taking Obama Technology Down Ballot." *Time*, February 24, 2014. Accessed October 20, 2015. http://swampland.time.com/2014/02/24/project-ivy-democrats-taking-obama-technology-down-ballot/.

Miller, Zeke. "Romney Campaign Appears to Copy Text from Obama Website." *BuzzFeed*, September 10, 2012. Accessed September 26, 2015. http://www.buzzfeed.com/zeke-jmiller/romney-campaign-appears-to-copy-text-from-obama-we.

Mintz, John. "McCain Camp Enjoys a Big Net Advantage." *Washington Post*, February 9, 2000. Accessed September 25, 2015. http://www.washingtonpost.com/wp-srv/WPcap/2000-02/09/090r-020900-idx.html.

Mol, Annemarie, Ingunn Moser, and Jeannette Pols, eds. *Care in Practice: On Tinkering in Clinics, Homes and Farms.* Vol. 8. Bielefeld: Transcript Verlag, 2015.

Mooney, Harrison. "How a Canceled Boston Bruins Game Led to a Mitt Romney Campaign Election Day Meltdown." *Yahoo! Sports,* November 14, 2012. Accessed October 20, 2015. http://sports.yahoo.com/blogs/nhl-puck-daddy/cancelled-boston-bruins-game-led-mitt-romney-campaign-151621331--nhl.html.

Mossberger, Karen, and C. J. Tolbert. *How Politics Online Is Changing Electoral Participation.* New York: Oxford University Press, 2010.

Neff, Gina. *Venture Labor: Work and the Burden of Risk in Innovative Industries.* Cambridge, MA: MIT Press, 2012.

Negrine, Ralph. *The Transformation of Political Communication: Continuities and Changes in Media and Politics.* London: Palgrave Macmillan, 2008.

Nielsen, Rasmus Kleis. *Ground Wars: Personalized Communication in Political Campaigns.* Princeton, NJ: Princeton University Press, 2012.

Nielsen, Rasmus Kleis, and Cristian Vaccari. "Do People "Like" Politicians on Facebook? Not Really. Large-Scale Direct Candidate-to-Voter Online Communication as an Outlier Phenomenon." *International Journal of Communication* 7 (2013): 24.

Norris, Pippa. *A Virtuous Circle: Political Communications in Postindustrial Societies.* New York: Cambridge University Press, 2000.

Norris, Pippa. *Politics and the Press: The News Media and Their Influences.* Boulder, CO: Lynne Rienner, 1997.

Nyhan, Brendan, and Jacob M. Montgomery. "Connecting the Candidates: Consultant Networks and the Diffusion of Campaign Strategy in American Congressional Elections." *American Journal of Political Science* 59, no. 2 (2015): 292–308.

Padgett, John F., and Walter W. Powell. *The Emergence of Organizations and Markets.* Princeton, NJ: Princeton University Press, 2012.

Papacharissi, Zizi. *Affective Publics: Sentiment, Technology, and Politics.* Oxford, UK: Oxford University Press, 2014.

Papacharissi, Zizi. *A Private Sphere: Democracy in a Digital Age.* Cambridge, UK: Polity, 2010.

Parker, Ashley. "Democrats Aim for a 2014 More like 2012 and 2008." *New York Times,* February 6, 2014. Accessed October 20, 2015. http://www.nytimes.com/2014/02/07/us/politics/democrats-aim-to-make-2014-more-like-2012-and-2008.html?_r=0.

Parmelee, John H., and Shannon L. Bichard. *Politics and the Twitter Revolution.* Lanham, MD: Lexington, 2012.

Pasick, Adam, and Tim Fernholz. "The Stealthy, Eric Schmidt-backed Startup That's Working to put Hillary Clinton in the White House." *Quartz,* October 9, 2015. Accessed January 27, 2016. http://qz.com/520652/groundwork-eric-schmidt-startup-working-for-hillary-clinton-campaign/.

Pearlman, Nathaniel G., ed. *Margin of Victory: How Technologists Help Politicians Win Elections.* Santa Barbara, CA: ABC-CLIO, 2012.

Pennsylvania Democratic Party. "What Can VoteBuilder do for You?" Accessed January 28, 2016. http://www.padems.com/content/what-can-votebuilder-do-you.

Perrin, Andrew J., Steven J. Tepper, Neal Caren, and Sally Morris. "Cultures of the Tea Party." *Contexts* 10, no. 2 (2011): 74–75.

Peters, John Durham. *The Marvelous Clouds: Toward a Philosophy of Elemental Media.* Chicago: University of Chicago Press, 2015.

Pierson, Paul. *Politics in Time: History, Institutions, and Social Analysis.* Princeton, NJ: Princeton University Press, 2004. http://www.politico.com/story/2013/05/karl-rove-company-gop-data-deal-090834.

Plouffe, David. *The Audacity to Win: The Inside Story and Lessons of Barack Obama's Historic Victory.* New York: Viking, 2009.

Pollak, Joel B. "Inside ORCA: How the Romney Campaign Suppressed Its Own Vote." *Breitbart.com,* November 8, 2012. Accessed September 30, 2015. http://www.breitbart.com/big-government/2012/11/08/Orca-how-the-romney-campaign-suppressed-its-own-vote/.

Polsby, Nelson W. *Consequences of Party Reform*. New York: Oxford University Press, 1983.

Poniewozik, James. "Election Watch: Karl Rove vs. the Arithmetic." *Tuned In (blog), Time*, November 7, 2012. Accessed September 30, 2015. http://entertainment.time.com/2012/11/07/election-watch-karl-rove-vs-the-arithmetic/.

Popkin, Samuel L. *The Candidate: What It Takes to Win—and Hold—the White House*. New York: Oxford University Press, 2012.

Powell, Walter W., and Paul J. DiMaggio, eds. *The New Institutionalism in Organizational Analysis*. Chicago: University of Chicago Press, 2012.

Powell, Walter W., and Eric Giannella. "Collective Invention and Inventor Networks." *Handbook of the Economics of Innovation* 1 (2010): 575–605.

Prior, Markus. *Post-broadcast Democracy: How Media Choice Increases Inequality in Political Involvement and Polarizes Elections*. Cambridge, UK: Cambridge University Press, 2007.

Proffitt, Brian. "What APIs Are and Why They're Important." *Readwrite*, September 19, 2013. Accessed October 21, 2015. http://readwrite.com/2013/09/19/api-defined.

Quinn, Kelly, and Zizi Papacharissi. "The Place Where Our Networks Reside: Social Media and Sociality." In *Media and Social Life*, edited by Mary Beth Oliver and Arthur A. Raney, 189–208. New York: Routledge, 2014.

Rainie, Harrison, and Barry Wellman. *Networked: The New Social Operating System*. Cambridge, MA: MIT Press, 2012.

Reed, Isaac Ariail. *Interpretation and Social Knowledge: On the Use of Theory in the Human Sciences*. Chicago: University of Chicago Press, 2011.

Reed, Isaac Ariail. "Power Relational, Discursive, and Performative Dimensions." *Sociological Theory* 31, no. 3 (2013): 193–218.

Reichart-Smith, Lauren, and Kenny D. Smith. "What a Difference a Download Makes." In *Handbook of Research on Digital Media and Advertising: User Generated Content Consumption*, edited by Matthew S. Eastin, Terry Daughtery, and Neal M. Burns, 577–603. Hershey, PA: Information Science Reference, 2011.

Ridout, Travis N., and Michael M. Franz. *The Persuasive Power of Campaign Advertising*. Philadelphia: Temple University Press, 2011.

Riordan, William L. *Plunkitt of Tammany Hall: A Series of Very Plain Talks on Very Practical Politics*. New York: Penguin, 1995.

Roeder, Ethan. "I Am Not Big Brother." *New York Times*, December 5, 2012. Accessed September 28, 2015. http://www.nytimes.com/2012/12/06/opinion/i-am-not-big-brother.html?_r=0.

Roeder, Ethan. "Who Are the Campaigners in America?" *Journal of News Organizing Blog*, December 13, 2013. Accessed September 28, 2015. http://archive.neworganizing.com/content/blog/who-are-the-campaigners-in-america.

Roller, Emma. "The Democrats' Database Fight." *The New York Times*, December 22, 2015. Accessed January 28, 2016. http://www.nytimes.com/2015/12/22/opinion/campaign-stops/the-democrats-database-fight.html?_r=2.

Rosenblum, Nancy L. *On the Side of the Angels: An Appreciation of Parties and Partisanship*. Princeton, NJ: Princeton University Press, 2010.

Rubinstein, Ira S. "Voter Privacy in the Age of Big Data." *Wisconsin Law Review* 2014, no. 5 (2014): 861–936.

Rutenberg, Jim. "The Next Era of Campaign-Finance Craziness Is Already Underway." *New York Times Magazine*, April 21, 2015. Accessed October 14, 2015. http://www.nytimes.com/2015/04/21/magazine/the-next-era-of-campaign-finance-craziness-is-already-underway.html?hp&action=click&pgtype=Homepage&module=second-column-region&region=top-news&WT.nav=top-news&_r=0.

Rutenberg, Jim, and Jeff Zeleny. "Republican Officials End Relationship with Adviser Tied to Ad Proposal." *The Caucus (blog), New York Times*, May 21, 2012. Accessed September 28, 2015. http://thecaucus.blogs.nytimes.com/2012/05/21/republican-officials-end-relationship-with-adviser-tied-to-ad-proposal/?_r=0.

Samuelsohn, Darren. "Hillary's Nerd Squad." *Politico*, March 25, 2015. Accessed September 25, 2015. http://www.politico.com/story/2015/03/hillarys-nerd-squad-116402.

Scherer, Michael. "Friended: How the Obama Campaign Connected with Young Voters." *Time*, November 20, 2012. Accessed January 27, 2016. http://swampland.time.com/2012/11/20/friended-how-the-obama-campaign-connected-with-young-voters/.

Schradie, Jen. "Bringing the Organization Back In: Social Media and Social Movements." *Berkeley Journal of Sociology*. Published electronically November 3, 2014. Accessed January 27, 2016. http://berkeleyjournal.org/2014/11/bringing-the-organization-back-in-social-media-and-social-movements/.

Schreyögg, Georg, Jörg Sydow, and Philip Holtmann. "How History Matters in Organisations: The Case of Path Dependence." *Management & Organizational History* 6, no. 1 (2011): 81–100.

Schudson, Michael. "How Culture Works." *Theory and Society* 18, no. 2 (1989): 153–180.

Schudson, Michael. "Politics as Cultural Practice." *Political Communication* 18, no. 4 (2001): 421–431.

Schudson, Michael. *The Good Citizen: A History of American Civic Life*. New York: Free Press, 1998.

Schultheis, Emily. "The Democrats' Secret Staffing Advantage in 2016." *National Journal*, February 9, 2015. Accessed September 26, 2015. http://www.nationaljournal.com/twentysixteen/2015/02/09/Democrats-Secret-Staffing-Advantage-2016?ref=t.co&mrefid=walkingheader.

Serazio, Michael. "Qualitative Political Communication | Managing the Digital News Cyclone: Power, Participation, and Political Production Strategies." *International Journal of Communication* 9 (2015): 19.

Serazio, Michael. "The New Media Designs of Political Consultants: Campaign Production in a Fragmented Era." *Journal of Communication* 64, no. 4 (2014): 743–763.

Sewell, William H., Jr. *Logics of History: Social Theory and Social Transformation*. Chicago: University of Chicago Press, 2005.

Shefter, Martin. *Political Parties and the State: The American Historical Experience*. Princeton, NJ: Princeton University Press, 1994.

Sheingate, Adam. *Building a Business of Politics: The Rise of Political Consulting and the Transformation of American Democracy*. Oxford: Oxford University Press, 2016.

Sides, John, and Lynn Vavreck. "Obama's Not-So-Big Data." *PS Mag*, January 21, 2014. Accessed September 24, 2015. http://www.psmag.com/books-and-culture/obamas-big-data-inconclusive-results-political-campaigns-72687.

Sides, John, and Lynn Vavreck. *The Gamble: Choice and Chance in the 2012 Presidential Election*. Princeton, NJ: Princeton University Press, 2014.

Sifry, Micah. "Meet Mitt Romney's New Social Network." *CNN*, October 26, 2011. Accessed September 26, 2015. http://www.cnn.com/2011/10/25/tech/web/mitt-romney-social-network/index.html.

Silver, Nate. "In Silicon Valley, Technology Talent Gap Threatens G.O.P. Campaigns." *FiveThirtyEight (blog)*, *New York Times*, November 28, 2012. Accessed September 24, 2015. http://fivethirtyeight.blogs.nytimes.com/2012/11/28/in-silicon-valley-technology-talent-gap-threatens-g-o-p-campaigns/?_r=2.

Smith, Craig Allen. "Strategic Keys to Challenging the Incumbent in 2012." In *The 2012 Presidential Campaign: A Communication Perspective*, edited by Robert E. Denton, Jr., 57–76. Lanham, MD: Rowman & Littlefield, 2014.

Smith, Wally. "Theatre of Use: A Frame Analysis of Information Technology Demonstrations." *Social Studies of Science* 39, no. 3 (2009): 449–480.

Sobieraj, Sarah. *Soundbitten: The Perils of Media-Centered Political Activism*. New York: New York University Press, 2011.

Sosnik, Douglas B., Ron Fournier, and Matthew J. Dowd. *Applebee's America: Successful Political, Business, and Religious Leaders Connect with the New American Community*. New York: Simon & Schuster, 2007.

Spicker, Paul. "Ethical Covert Research." *Sociology* 45, no. 1 (2011): 118–133.

Stan, Adele M. "How the Presidential Primary Is a Proxy War Between the Kochs and the Republican Establishment." *American Prospect*, June 17, 2015. Accessed October 14, 2015. http://prospect.org/article/how-presidential-primary-proxy-war-between-kochs-and-republican-establishment.

Star, Susan Leigh. "The Ethnography of Infrastructure." *American Behavioral Scientist* 43, no. 3 (1999): 377–391.

Stark, David. *The Sense of Dissonance: Accounts of Worth in Economic Life*. Princeton, NJ: Princeton University Press, 2011.

Stein, Arlene. "Sex, Truths, and Audiotape: Anonymity and the Ethics of Exposure in Public Ethnography." *Journal of Contemporary Ethnography* (2010).

Strategic Perception, Inc. *The Defeat of Barack Hussein Obama: The Rickets Plan to End His Spending for Good*, May 10, 2012. Accessed October 20, 2015. http://www.nytimes.com/interactive/2012/05/17/us/politics/17donate-document.html?ref=politics.

Streeter, Thomas, and Zephyr Teachout. *Mousepads, Shoe Leather, and Hope: Lessons from the Howard Dean Campaign for the Future of Internet Politics*. Boulder, CO: Paradigm, 2007.

Stromer-Galley, Jennifer. *Presidential Campaigning in the Internet Age*. New York: Oxford University Press, 2014.

Stroud, Natalie Jomini. *Niche News: The Politics of News Choice*. New York: Oxford University Press, 2011.

Suchman, Lucy, Randall Trigg, and Jeanette Blomberg. "Working Artefacts: Ethnomethods of the Prototype." *The British Journal of Sociology* 53, no. 2 (2002): 163–179.

Sullivan, Sean. "The Biggest Upset of 2012." *The Fix (blog), Washington Post*, November 28, 2012. Accessed September 30, 2015. http://www.washingtonpost.com/news/the-fix/wp/2012/11/28/the-biggest-upset-of-2012/.

Sydow, Jörg, Georg Schreyögg, and Jochen Koch. "Organizational Path Dependence: Opening the Black Box." *Academy of Management Review* 34, no. 4 (2009): 689–709.

Tarrow, Sidney, and J. Tollefson. *Power in Movement: Social Movements, Collective Action and Politics*. Cambridge, UK: Cambridge University Press, 1994.

Temple, Roy. "MDP Voter File Access Questions." *Medium*, February 2, 2016. Accessed March 14, 2016. https://medium.com/@roytemple/mdp-voter-file-access-questions-e8dc18ec374d#.whfpqz71e.

Terkel, Amanda. "Project Orca: Mitt Romney Campaign Plans Massive, State-of-the-Art Poll Monitoring Effort." *The Huffington Post*, November 1, 2012. Accessed September 24, 2015. http://www.huffingtonpost.com/2012/11/01/project-Orca-mitt-romney_n_2052861.html?utm_hp_ref=elections-2012.

Thibodeau, Patrick. "Obama and Romney Big Data Experts Continue the Battle as Businesses." *Computerworld*, August 15, 2013. Accessed September 28, 2015. http://www.computer-world.com/article/2483731/big-data/obama-and-romney-big-data-experts-continue-the-battle-as-businesses.html.

Thomas, Ken, and Steve Peoples. "GOP Moves to Plug the Technology Gap with Democrats." *Associated Press*, March 29, 2013. Accessed September 24, 2015. http://bigstory.ap.org/article/gop-moves-catch-democrats-technology.

Trevelyan, Stu. "Democratic/Progressive Voter Contacts: 387 Million." *Ngpvan (blog)*, November 3, 2014. Accessed September 24, 2015. http://blog.ngpvan.com/democraticprogressive-voter-contacts-387-million.

Turner, Fred. "Burning Man at Google: A Cultural Infrastructure for New Media Production." *New Media & Society* 11, no. 1–2 (2009): 73–94.

Turner, Fred. *From Counterculture to Cyberculture: Stewart Brand, the Whole Earth Network, and the Rise of Digital Utopianism*. Chicago: University Of Chicago Press, 2010.

Turner, Fred. "Prototype." In *Digital Keywords: A Vocabulary of Information Society and Culture*, edited by Benjamin Peters, Princeton, NJ: Princeton University Press, forthcoming.

Turow, Joseph. "Audience Construction and Culture Production: Marketing Surveillance in the Digital Age." *The Annals of the American Academy of Political and Social Science* 597, no. 1 (2005): 103–121.

Vaccari, Cristian. "Technology Is a Commodity: The Internet in the 2008 United States Presidential Election." *Journal of Information Technology & Politics* 7, no. 4 (2010): 318–339.

Vaccari, Cristian, and Rasmus Kleis Nielsen. "What Drives Politicians' Online Popularity? An Analysis of the 2010 US Midterm Elections." *Journal of Information Technology & Politics* 10, no. 2 (2013): 208–222.

van Dijck, José. *The Culture of Connectivity: A Critical History of Social Media.* New York: Oxford University Press, 2013.

Van Natta, Don, Jr. "McCain Gets Big Payoff on Web Site." *New York Times,* February 4, 2000. Accessed September 25, 2015. http://www.nytimes.com/2000/02/04/us/the-2000-campaign-the-money-game-mccain-gets-big-payoff-on-web-site.html.

Vega, Tanzina. "Campaigns Choose Email over Fancy Technology." *CNN Politics,* July 31, 2015. Accessed September 26, 2015. http://www.cnn.com/2015/07/09/politics/2016-campaigns-email/.

Vinsel, Lee. "How to Give up the I-Word, Parts 1 and 2." *Culture Digitally,* September 22–23, 2015. Accessed October 20, 2015. http://culturedigitally.org/author/lee-vinsel/.

Vitak, Jessica, Paul Zube, Andrew Smock, Caleb T. Carr, Nicole Ellison, and Cliff Lampe. "It's Complicated: Facebook Users' Political Participation in the 2008 Election." *CyberPsychology, Behavior, and Social Networking* 14, no. 3 (2011): 107–114.

Vogel, Kenneth P. "Romney Victory Fund Pulls in $140M." *Politico,* July 16, 2012. Accessed September 28, 2015. http://www.politico.com/story/2012/07/romney-victory-fund-pulls-in-140m-078537.

"Voting Oddities, Irregularities across the Nation." *Decision 2010,* NBC News, November 3, 2010. Accessed October 21, 2015. http://www.nbcnews.com/id/39975809/ns/politics-decision_2010/t/voting-oddities-irregularities-across-nation/#.Vid20Guu2nJ.

Walker, Edward T. *Grassroots for Hire: Public Affairs Consultants in American Democracy.* New York: Cambridge University Press, 2014.

Ward, Jon. "Facebook Shutting Down a Key Path Obama Used to Reach Voters." *Yahoo Tech,* November 17, 2014. Accessed September 28, 2015. https://www.yahoo.com/tech/s/facebook-slams-the-door-on-political-campaigns-212248365.html.

Ward, Jon. "The Behind the Scenes Story of the RNC Data Supremacy." *Huffington Post,* April 21, 2014. Accessed September 30, 2015. http://www.huffingtonpost.com/2014/04/18/rnc-data_n_5153927.html.

Ward, Jon. "The GOP's Biggest Tech Challenge for 2016 Is Closing the Small-Donor Gap." *Yahoo News,* January 16, 2015. Accessed September 26, 2015. http://news.yahoo.com/the-gop-s-biggest-tech-challenge-for-2016-is-closing-the-small-donor-gap-225855092.html.

Ward, Jon. "The Koch Brothers and the Republican Party Go to War—With Each Other." *Yahoo Politics,* June 11, 2105. Accessed October 14, 2015. https://www.yahoo.com/politics/the-koch-brothers-and-the-republican-party-go-to-121193159491.html.

Webster, James G. *The Marketplace of Attention: How Audiences Take Shape in a Digital Age.* Cambridge, MA: MIT Press, 2014.

Weinstein, Adam. "The GOP Just Named Its Hot New Innovation Lab after a Nazi Pistol." *Gawker,* February 4, 2014. Accessed September 30, 2015. http://gawker.com/the-gop-just-named-its-hot-new-innovation-lab-after-a-n-1515675052.

Weisberg, Jacob. "McCain's Web Explosion." *Slate,* February 11, 2000. Accessed September 25, 2014. http://www.slate.com/articles/news_and_politics/net_election/2000/02/mccains_web_explosion.html.

Weiss, Robert S. *Learning from Strangers: The Art and Method of Qualitative Interview Studies.* New York: Simon & Schuster, 1995.

Wells, Chris. *The Civic Organization and the Digital Citizen: Communicating Engagement in a Networked Age.* New York: Oxford University Press, 2015.

Whitaker, Bryan. "Obamamania: How the Democrats Campaign Machine Works." *Policy Network*, March 27, 2013. Accessed October 20, 2015. http://www.policy-network.net/pno_detail. aspx?ID=4359&title=Obamamania-How-the-Democrats-campaign-machine-works.

Williams, Bruce A., and Michael X. Delli Carpini. *After Broadcast News: Media Regimes, Democracy, and the New Information Environment*. New York: Cambridge University Press, 2011.

Willis, Derek. "Super PACs Are Gobbling Up Even More Power, Jeb Bush Edition." *The Upshot (blog), New York Times*, April 21, 2015. Accessed October 13, 2015. http://www.nytimes. com/2015/04/22/upshot/super-pacs-gobbling-up-even-more-power-jeb-bush-edition. html?abt=0002&abg=0.

Willis, Derek. "Why Democrats Still Lead Republicans in Online Fund-Raising." *The Upshot (blog), New York Times*, January 22, 2015. Accessed September 26, 2015. http://www. nytimes.com/2015/01/23/upshot/why-democrats-still-lead-republicans-in-online-fund-raising.html?_r=0.

Wilner, Elizabeth. "The Cook Political Report 'Big Data At-A-Glance.'" *The Cook Political Report*, August 22, 2013, Updated May 2, 2014. Accessed September 24, 2015. http://cookpolitical.com/story/5804.

Wilson, James Q. *The Amateur Democrat: Club Politics in Three Cities*. Chicago: University of Chicago Press, 1962.

Zittrain, Jonathan. *The Future of the Internet—and How to Stop It*. New Haven, CT: Yale University Press, 2008.

Index